Culture and Biblical Hermeneutics

Culture and Biblical Hermeneutics

Interpreting and Applying the Authoritative Word
in a Relativistic Age

William J. Larkin, Jr.

Wipf and Stock Publishers
EUGENE, OREGON

Wipf and Stock Publishers
199 West 8th Avenue, Suite 3
Eugene, Oregon 97401

Culture and Biblical Hermeneutics
Interpreting and Applying the Authoritative Word in a Relativistic Age
By Larkin, William J.
Copyright©1988 by Larkin, William J.
ISBN: 1-59244-306-0
Publication date 8/5/2003
Previously published by Baker Book House, 1988

Contents

Illustrations

Preface

This volume began as a joint venture with Robertson McQuilkin, president of Columbia Bible College and Seminary. I agreed to provide historical background chapters which would set in context several articles McQuilkin had written in the 1970s concerning the crisis in biblical authority created by the control the behavioral sciences were exercising over the process of interpretation and application. My contribution soon became disproportionate to the original design of the work, and my collaborator released me to pursue the study on my own. This volume, however, reflects the same concerns and basic conclusions as the original project did. Thus a great debt is owed to Robertson McQuilkin for his formative influence, though I take full responsibility for the content of the work in its present form.

The reception by the American public of Allan Bloom's *Closing of the American Mind* indicates that ongoing—indeed, intensified—concern exists over the impact of relativism on authority. When the authority at issue is the Bible, which claims to communicate God's message concerning salvation, truth, and conduct, the matter is of paramount importance. In an age of relativism can a way be found to understand and apply the authoritative Word of God so that its saving message can still be heard and obeyed? This book intends to contribute to answering this question by returning to the Scriptures to see how the Bible addresses the questions and constructs of the contemporary hermeneutical discussion. In this way I hope to find a place to stand beyond the horizons of both the ancient text and the modern

9

interpreter and from there perform the transhistorical and transcultural hermeneutical task.

All manuscripts are team efforts. I wish to thank the administration of Columbia Bible College and Seminary for providing a sabbatical leave and word-processing services. Diane Crutchfield, Katie Wilson, and Lillie Burgess must be mentioned for their secretarial expertise in seeing the project through to completion. The work's content was greatly enhanced by interaction with colleagues on the faculty of Columbia Biblical Seminary and Graduate School of Missions. Over fifty evangelical scholars responded to inquiries about my handling of their views and in the process helped me grow in my understanding. Christine Benagh greatly improved the style.

My wife Edna and my children, Thomas and Priscilla, deserve special mention for their prayers, support, and sacrifice. My extended family, especially my parents, Dr. and Mrs. William J. Larkin, Sr., and my father-in-law, John R. Dennis, has continued to provide encouragement. For the grace of God exhibited in the lives of all, I praise our Lord Jesus Christ.

Abbreviations

Bauer	Walter Bauer, *A Greek-English Lexicon of the New Testament and Other Early Christian Literature,* 2d ed., rev. and aug. Frederick W. Danker and F. Wilbur Gingrich (Chicago: University of Chicago Press, 1979)
BS	*Bibliotheca Sacra*
CBQ	*Catholic Biblical Quarterly*
CT	*Christianity Today*
EBC	*Expositor's Bible Commentary,* ed. Frank E. Gaebelein, 12 vols. (Grand Rapids: Zondervan, 1976–)
ERT	*Evangelical Review of Theology*
GTJ	*Grace Theological Journal*
IDBSup	*Interpreter's Dictionary of the Bible, Supplementary Volume,* ed. Keith R. Crim (Nashville: Abingdon, 1976)
JBL	*Journal of Biblical Literature*
JETS	*Journal of the Evangelical Theological Society*
KJV	King James Version
LXX	Septuagint
NASB	New American Standard Bible
NIDNTT	*New International Dictionary of New Testament Theology,* ed. Colin Brown, 3 vols. (Grand Rapids: Zondervan, 1978)
NIV	New International Version

SJT	*Scottish Journal of Theology*
TDNT	*Theological Dictionary of the New Testament*, ed. Gerhard Kittel and Gerhard Friedrich, trans. Geoffrey W. Bromiley, 10 vols. (Grand Rapids: Eerdmans, 1964–1976)
TEV	Today's English Version
TT	*Theology Today*
TWOT	*Theological Wordbook of the Old Testament*, ed. R. Laird Harris, 2 vols. (Chicago: Moody, 1980)
USQR	*Union Seminary Quarterly Review*
WBC	*Word Biblical Commentary*, ed. David A. Hubbard and Glenn W. Barker, 52 vols. (Waco, Tex.: Word, 1982–)
WTJ	*Westminster Theological Journal*

Part 1

Historical Background

1

Biblical Authority in an Age of Relativism

The Crisis

Biblical study and interpretation sprang into new life at the Reformation. Turning away from the many-layered literal, moral, spiritual, and anagogical interpretation prescribed during the patristic and medieval periods, the eager Reformation scholars embraced the literal sense alone as the surest location of the meaning of a text. In literal interpretation the historical factor looms large: here at this place and in this time these people were doing and saying these eternally significant things. It comes as something of a surprise to discover that over the last few centuries these very freshets have swelled and converged to form the murky sea of the current hermeneutical crisis.

Contemporary interpreters, especially those concerned with the mission of the church across cultures, are also aware of a gap that yawns between the culture in which the Bible was written and to which it was originally addressed, and the contemporary cultures to which the Word must now be addressed and in which it must be understood and applied.

"How can the helpful and legitimate tool of assessing the cultural context be used for understanding Scripture without violating its authority?" Certainly there are historical elements that do not apply to the contemporary context. Are there transitory cultural elements as well? If so, on what basis does one distinguish between the authoritative and enduring message of the original author and the temporary historical or cultural context?[1]

These questions are more than academic because the answers of some scholars have intensified the crisis of biblical authority to such an extent that what rampaged among nonevangelicals in the sixties now confronts evangelicals.[2] In the discipline of missiology, these questions and answers are particularly sensitive, and as Harvie Conn has noted, some recent answers have generated perilous currents: the overextended application of anthropological models to missiology, and also syncretism.[3]

These questions concerning historical distance and cultural difference between ancient text and modern interpreter must be asked. The challenge resides in many of the answers proposed in the intellectual climate dominated by relativism, "a stream in the philosophy of the past two hundred years that began as a trickle, [and] has swelled in recent times into a roaring torrent."[4] How can the Bible continue its functional control of the beliefs and conduct of contemporary human beings who increasingly are convinced that no beliefs or values are universally and eternally valid, that nothing can have binding authority over them? To understand the impact of such a climate on the approach to biblical authority in Western Christianity, we first must define relativism.

Relativism

Broadly speaking, relativism is the "view that beliefs and principles, particularly evaluative ones, have no universal or timeless validity but are valid only for the age in which, or the social group or individual person by

---

1. J. Robertson McQuilkin, "Limits of Cultural Interpretation," *JETS* 23 (1980): 117.

2. Brevard S. Childs, "The Search for Biblical Authority Today," *Andover Newton Quarterly* 16 (1976): 199–206. For purposes of this study, I distinguish between evangelicals and nonevangelicals in terms of one's view of Scripture. The evangelical affirms that God's verbal propositional revelation comes to us as inspired, inerrant, authoritative Scripture (see "The Chicago Statement on Biblical Inerrancy," in *Inerrancy*, ed. Norman L. Geisler [Grand Rapids: Zondervan, 1979], 493–502). The nonevangelical does not have this view of Scripture. Note that I count as evangelicals those who label themselves as such and affirm the inspiration and authority of Scripture but who may deny inerrancy—e.g., James D. G. Dunn ("The Authority of Scripture According to Scripture," *Churchman* 96 [1982]: 99–122, 201–25) and I. H. Marshall ("Culture and the New Testament," in *Gospel and Culture*, ed. John Stott and Robert T. Coote [Pasadena, Calif.: William Carey Library, 1979], 21–46).

3. Harvie M. Conn, *Eternal Word and Changing Worlds: Theology, Anthropology, and Mission in Trialogue* (Grand Rapids: Zondervan, 1984), chap. 5.

4. Richard J. Bernstein, *Beyond Objectivism and Relativism: Science, Hermeneutics, and Praxis* (Philadelphia: University of Pennsylvania Press, 1983), 13; see also Steven W. Stall, "Sociology of Knowledge, Relativism, and Theology," in *Religion and the Sociology of Knowledge: Modernization and Pluralism in Christian Thought and Structure*, ed. Barbara Hargrove (New York: Mellen, 1984), 61–78.

which, they are held."[5] As it normally manifests itself, relativism "is less a systematic philosophy than a series of loosely knit arguments woven into a somewhat rough but identifiable garment of belief."[6] Arguments are applied with varying consistency from scholar to scholar and sometimes within the work of a single scholar.

Two types of relativism, however, can be distinguished.[7] *Hard perspectivism*, or *radical relativism*, is thoroughgoing in that it denies that a person can have true or valid knowledge of anything outside his or her own historical or cultural context. It denies that moral content can be universal, since there is no way to judge between the competing truth and ethical claims of different contexts. The individual is faced with an irreducible plurality of equally valid historical and cultural contexts.

Soft perspectivism, that is, *qualified* or *moderate relativism*, holds in tension two assertions: (1) there is a foundational framework of reality and rationality, and so rational assessment of historical and cultural contexts or perspectives is possible; (2) one can advance in the "project of truth" only by drawing conclusions based on many different historical and cultural contexts or perspectives. The contributions of various cultural environments may be different without being logically incompatible. Moderate relativists insist that this multiperspectival approach is necessary because all knowledge is conditioned by the historical or cultural context in which it is generated, and it is further conditioned by the historical or cultural context of the interpreter.

Relativism in historical matters, or *historical relativism*, affirms that a "work or text composed in an ancient time and an ancient culture has its meaning in that time and culture, and in our time and culture may have a different meaning, or indeed may have no meaning at all."[8] Hard perspectivism in historical matters contends that the meaning *will* be different because all meaning is the result of interpretation, and the historian's perception is conditioned by personal beliefs and presuppositions.[9] For a relativist,

---

5. *The Harper Dictionary of Modern Thought*, s.v. "Relativism." In its strongest form it might represent "the basic conviction that when we turn to the examination of those concepts that philosophers have taken to be the most fundamental—whether it is the concept of rationality, truth, reality, right, the good or norms—we are forced to recognize that in the final analysis all such concepts must be understood relative to a specific conceptual scheme, theoretical framework, paradigm, form of life, society or culture. . . . These concepts can[not] have a determinate and univocal significance. . . . There is no substantive overarching framework or single metalanguage by which we can rationally adjudicate or univocally evaluate competing claims of alternative paradigms" (Bernstein, *Beyond Objectivism*, 8).

6. Van A. Harvey, *The Historian and the Believer: The Morality of Historical Knowledge and Christian Belief* (Philadelphia: Westminster, 1966), 205. Note that he is speaking of historical relativism only.

7. Stall, "Sociology of Knowledge," 66.

8. James Barr, *The Bible in the Modern World* (New York: Harper & Row, 1973), 39.

9. Harvey, *Historian*, 206.

whether hard or soft, radical or moderate, it is not possible to conclude that the Bible can or necessarily will communicate the same message in the contemporary context that it did in its ancient one. It meant one thing in terms of the ancient context; it will mean something else for those who interpret it in the only way they can—in terms of the modern context.

In the continuing discussion on interpreting and applying the U.S. Constitution, Supreme Court Justice William J. Brennan exemplifies the relativistic approach. He contends that after two hundred years we cannot possibly know what the original framers of the Constitution intended to say. All present-day judges can do is "read the constitutional text 'as 20th century Americans,' asking what its words mean 'in our time.'"[10]

Clearly such views disclaim any binding authority for the original message of a historical text in the modern context. Dennis Nineham takes this view toward the Bible, asserting that it would be most disconcerting "if we supposed that to be a Christian meant making one's own the beliefs and attitudes of the New Testament in the precise form in which the believers of that time held them." Admittedly some forms of Protestantism have been encouraged to do so, but "the impossibility of it has been recognized for a long while now."[11]

Cultural relativism appears in several forms. It may involve what anthropologists sometimes refer to as the ethnographic method. The observer following this approach transcends his or her own cultural conditioning and values and assumes the attitudes of those in the culture being studied. The researcher then seeks to describe the culture objectively on its own terms, and the cultural phenomena are evaluated in terms of their significance in that particular setting.

As a theory or philosophy of knowledge, cultural relativism emphasizes the way in which experience is understood. Persons interpret all experience as it is mediated through the recognized conventions of a given cultural group. The cultural context gives meaning by providing the thought-structures for organizing experiences in a meaningful way. Indeed, in this view, the only reality one can know is cultural reality.[12] The sociology-of-knowledge approach to meaning contends the same thing: "Social circumstances, by shaping the subject of knowing, also determine the objects which come to be known."[13]

The Akamba of East Africa have a two-dimensional concept of time which "lays emphasis on a dynamic present and an ever-increasing past—

10. Walter Berns, "The Words According to Brennan," *Wall Street Journal*, 23 October 1985, 32.

11. Dennis Nineham, "The Strangeness of the New Testament, I and II," *Theology* 85 (1982): 253.

12. *International Encyclopedia of the Social Sciences*, s.v. "Culture: II. Cultural relativism."

13. *Encyclopedia of Philosophy*, s.v. "Sociology of knowledge"; see also Peter L. Berger and Thomas Luckmann, *The Social Construction of Reality: A Treatise in the Sociology of Knowledge* (Garden City, N.Y.: Doubleday, 1967).

giving History a backward momentum."[14] From the point of view of cultural relativism, the Akamba cannot express any concept of eschatology that is future-oriented. There can be, for example, no idea that the world will come to an end, for all discussion of time must be conducted in terms of the Akamba orientation to the past.

Cultural relativism is also applied as an approach to the appraisal and validation of values.[15] It asserts that "values and morals are relative to their socio-cultural context and that one way of life (culture) cannot be judged to be superior to another."[16] Reasoning from the principle that all human experience is culturally mediated, the cultural relativist concludes that all value judgments, which are an aspect of human experience, are culturally conditioned. They are a function of, and relative to, a given cultural system. If value judgments are thus limited in their origin, meaning, and significance, then their validity is also limited to their original social and cultural contexts. They may not be treated as valid for other cultures; hence there can be no transcultural or universal ethic, and all value systems must be regarded as equally valid. The consequences of such a view for the authority of the Scripture, its commands and precepts, are obvious: its authority is limited to its own cultural environment.

As an approach to ethics, cultural relativism looks at the diversity of ethical beliefs around the world and concludes that no one set of values is universally valid. How can one choose, for example, between one culture in which there is a strong standard of truth and another in which "the thing to do in ordinary social intercourse is to tell people whatever they wish to hear"? How does one choose between a culture that defines stealing as taking without permission what is not yours and a culture in which "a man may help himself to another's possessions as long as it is known who has taken them, and he may not have to return them until asked"?[17] Cultural relativism holds that one cannot choose—and should not.

Crisis Among Nonevangelicals

Scholarly writing and discussion of the past twenty-five years indicate that nonevangelicals have been consciously facing a crisis concerning biblical authority (see chaps. 3–5). On the eve of the centennial of the Society of

---

14. John S. Mbiti, "New Testament Eschatology in an African Background," in *Readings in Dynamic Indigeneity*, ed. Charles H. Kraft and Tom N. Wisley (Pasadena, Calif.: William Carey Library, 1979), 456.

15. *International Encyclopedia of the Social Sciences*, s.v. "Culture: II. Cultural relativism"; see also Melville J. Herskovits, *Man and His Works: The Science of Cultural Anthropology* (New York: Knopf, 1956), 61–78.

16. Robert B. Taylor, "Cultural Relativism for the Christian," *Practical Anthropology* 1 (1954): 109.

17. Robert B. Taylor, *Cultural Ways: A Concise Edition of Introduction to Cultural Anthropology*, 2d ed. (Boston: Allyn, 1976), 259.

Biblical Literature in 1980, the assessments of the state of biblical studies provided a vehicle for articulating the problem.

Some nonevangelicals view the crisis within the larger context of the current turmoil in the Western intellectual tradition. According to Douglas Knight, the person who faces the question "Why study the Bible?" in a university context faces a crisis in humanistic studies that has been with us since the seventeenth century. At the heart of the matter is "a sense of cultural relativism, or at least a disenchantment with any provincialism which grants prior preference to the achievements of a given cultural tradition, whether, e.g., the Greco-Roman world . . . or the Judeo-Christian heritage." Concomitant with that attitude is the desacralization of classical writings, including the Bible. Together these factors have created unresolved problems for humanistic studies: "the relation of past to present, of tradition to modernity, and of classical culture to general culture—all of this in an age which has seen the catchword 'relevance' elevated to the status of an ultimate argument for many."[18]

Knight sees the problem clearly, and he seeks to solve it from the perspective of moderate relativism. He calls for the humanities to become more inclusive, involving a range of cultures, and to address the basic issue of human existence. At the same time he warns against facile generalizations about human nature or a simplistic identification of human values with a single culture. He does identify the Bible as a work providing a classic vision able to speak to the present through dialogue which bridges the historical distance between the text and today. Yet, because it is a human product representing an ethnic experience, he cautions "against pressing the Bible too eagerly and facilely to our breasts, for a broad gulf in time and world-view exists between it and us. It remains a cultural deposit with its own identity and integrity, yet precisely because of that it can become a partner in conversation with those living in later periods."[19]

Walter Brueggemann also deals with the question "Why study the Bible?" but in a seminary context. He takes into account the issues raised in the university context and adds another—authority. Theological convictions about truth, ethics, divine-human relationships, and the nature of a called community which are derived from an authoritative Scripture must be reconciled with the results of humanistic studies, that is, with the findings of the historical-critical method. Only then can the Bible be understood properly and function authoritatively as the "life source" for the church.

Brueggemann attempts to reconcile authority and criticism by setting them on a razor's edge, balanced off against one another. Such an approach

---

18. Walter Brueggemann and Douglas A. Knight, "Why Study the Bible?" *Council on the Study of Religion Bulletin* 11 (1980): 77.

19. Ibid., 78.

to the Bible "involves authority and criticism, responding and questioning, and never permitting either to overwhelm the other." Scriptural authority functions in such a relationship as a continually energizing paradigm which, while admittedly having enduring claims, spurs on a continuing process in which the church both constructs and is disciplined by tradition (i.e., authoritative content). The concept of canon must be understood as "the general quest for authority and true standards, at potentially any and all points in the history of a people." Brueggemann concludes that this type of understanding "has a relativizing, or better, a broadening effect on canon as a theological problem."[20]

The current state of nonevangelical missiology, with its contextualized ethnic theologies (e.g., liberation, black, African, and Asian), often reflects a radical relativism. The contemporary context holds dominant control of the hermeneutical process, and Scripture ceases to be the sole or final authority (see chaps. 9–10).

The issue, as formulated by the nonevangelical, is how an interpreter, operating out of a framework of historical or cultural relativism, can find in the Bible, an ancient and culture-bound book, a meaningful and authoritative message for the contemporary world. Yet the issue actually lies much deeper because the interpretative problems created by historical and cultural relativism are so critical. As Knight's and Brueggemann's reformulations of the hermeneutical process and the concept of biblical authority clearly demonstrate, once historical and cultural relativism is accepted as a given, it becomes impossible to find a meaning for Scripture determined by Scripture alone and not in some sense conditioned by the interpreter's context. Consequently, Scripture's authority can never be viewed as universally valid and final. This situation suggests a much more basic question: If historical and cultural relativism has such distorting effects on the hermeneutical process and the concept of biblical authority, can these conceptual frameworks be valid? If not, can the hermeneutical process, as applied to Scripture, be redesigned to take fully into account the role of the ancient and contemporary historical and cultural contexts in communicating meaning, and at the same time maintain the integrity of Scripture's meaning and its final authority?

Crisis Among Evangelicals

Carl F. H. Henry stated the matter for evangelicals when he was interviewed for *Christianity Today's* twenty-fifth anniversary and was asked what he considered the key issues for the 1980s.

---

20. Ibid., 78, 80.

The problem of biblical authority will probably continue to disturb evangelicals very deeply. The issue will focus not simply on inerrancy, but also on interpretation as well, and especially on the culture-relatedness and culture-dependence of biblical revelation. Evangelicals insist that although the Bible was written in particular historical and cultural milieus, it speaks with binding authority to our different historical and cultural situations (for instance, on such a subject as marital faithfulness).[21]

At Summit II on Hermeneutics (1982), the International Council on Biblical Inerrancy issued the "Chicago Statement on Hermeneutics," defining the various aspects of the interpretation and application process in line with the belief in a fully inerrant and finally authoritative Scripture. Earl Radmacher, who chaired the meeting, expressed pleasure at the summit's achievements, but he was quick to indicate that there were areas which needed further investigation.

Where are the lines to be drawn in the use of cultural accommodation and critical techniques lest God's message to us in Scripture be evaporated? How can we prevent hermeneutical leakage from the gains we have achieved for biblical authority in the inerrancy debate? . . . In the process of determining the singular meaning of the text of Scripture, will we be equally aggressive in determining its significance for our own personal lives?[22]

The late Francis A. Schaeffer, evangelical apologist, termed the crisis "the great evangelical disaster." He identified the root cause as the accommodation many evangelicals have made to the prevailing world spirit on two key issues—truth and life. By truth he meant the issue of biblical authority. Some evangelicals have decided that scriptural statements on history and the cosmos and on the moral absolutes in the area of personal relationships are all culturally oriented. Consequently, the "Bible is made to say only that which echoes the surrounding culture at *our* moment of history. *The Bible is bent to the culture instead of the Bible judging our society and culture. . . . It is the obeying of the Scriptures which is the watershed! It is believing and applying to our lives which demonstrate whether we in fact believe it.*"[23]

These accommodationists have adjusted themselves to the contemporary spirit of "freedom from all restraints and especially rebellion against God's truth and moral absolutes," a spirit that sympathetic nonevangelicals

21. "The Concerns and Considerations of Carl F. H. Henry," *CT* 25 (1981): 323.

22. "Introduction," in *Hermeneutics, Inerrancy, and the Bible*, ed. Earl D. Radmacher and Robert D. Preus (Grand Rapids: Zondervan, 1984), xii–xiii. See also Norman L. Geisler, "Explaining Hermeneutics: A Commentary on the Chicago Statement on Biblical Hermeneutics Articles of Affirmation and Denial," ibid., 889–904 (esp. Articles 6–9); J. Robertson McQuilkin, "The Behavioral Sciences Under the Authority of Scripure," *JETS* 20 (1977): 37.

23. Francis A. Schaeffer, *The Great Evangelical Disaster* (Westchester, Ill.: Crossway, 1984), 60–61.

call liberation. Such a spirit is guided by the secular humanistic world-view which maintains that "we live in a universe that is ultimately silent, with no meaning and purpose, with no basis for law and morality, with no concept of what it means to be human and of the value of human life. All is relative and arbitrary." Schaeffer concludes that only a strong view of Scripture is sufficient to withstand "the pressure of an all-pervasive culture built upon relativism and relativistic thinking."[24]

The warnings of Henry, Radmacher, and Schaeffer come to the evangelical community at a time when there is a great deal of ferment in discussions of methodology, the historical and cultural factor in Scripture, and the role of the interpreter and the interpreter's context in the hermeneutical process.[25] Evangelicals are experimenting with tools from the historical-critical method and are taking different views on how their procedures and findings square with biblical inerrancy. In addition to honest questions and investigation, there is fresh concern for properly understanding and assessing the continuing validity of the historical and cultural factor in Scripture. Further, there is a heightened awareness of the interpreter's "horizon," the preunderstanding and thought-world one brings to the hermeneutical task of understanding and applying authoritative Scripture.[26] When such questions and issues are being wrestled with in a general intellectual climate of relativism, the challenge to uncover a methodology that will take into account contemporary concerns and at the same time permit Scripture to govern one's beliefs and conduct is clear.

Harvie Conn identified this crisis within evangelical missiological studies as early as the 1970s. He observed the streams from the disciplines of anthropology, theology, and missions converging in a new agenda—ethnotheology, of which Charles Kraft's proposed system is an example.[27] Some tools suggested for working with the new agenda are dynamic equivalence from linguistics and tagmemics, a grammatical concept for interdisciplinary bridge-building. Since ethnotheology sees "the process of doing theology . . . [as one] of human interaction with divine truth perceived and defined according to cultural, contextual settings," the issue of

---

24. Ibid., 32, 36, 48. Norman K. Gottwald describes the rise of the spirit of biblical studies as influenced by Renaissance humanism. Biblical studies had been dominated by myth and dogma—a domination shattered by introducing rational empirical inquiry into human subject matter. To study the Bible as a human product became an intellectually and culturally liberating experience. "And so it has been ever since" (*The Tribes of Yahweh: A Sociology of the Religion of Liberated Israel, 1250-1050 B.C.* [Maryknoll, N.Y.: Orbis, 1979], 8).

25. See Millard J. Erickson, "Biblical Inerrancy: The Last Twenty-Five Years," *JETS* 25 (1982): 387–94; Alan F. Johnson, "The Historical-Critical Method: Egyptian Gold or Pagan Precipice?" *JETS* 26 (1983): 3–16.

26. Anthony C. Thiselton, *The Two Horizons: New Testament Hermeneutics and Philosophical Description, with Special Reference to Heidegger, Bultmann, Gadamer, and Wittgenstein* (Grand Rapids: Eerdmans, 1980).

27. Conn, *Eternal Word*, 128; Charles Kraft, *Christianity in Culture* (Maryknoll, N.Y.: Orbis, 1979).

relativism comes immediately to the fore. Conn recognizes this and predicts that relativism will be a continuing agenda item for the future.[28]

While Conn agrees with Kraft's effort to seek some rapport with related disciplines, he disagrees with many of Kraft's findings. What Conn calls for is a *multiperspectival* approach to doing theology, one in which theology is hemmed in and bombarded by the normative perspective of the Bible, the situational perspective of cultural and social time and place, and the existential perspective of our humanity as images of God. "It does not fear relativism. The normative perspective is always there to provide balance. Rather, it embraces relativism in a creative sense. For interacting with the normative and balancing it are the situational and the existential angles to be considered and savored."[29]

On the other hand, because it poses a threat to biblical authority, evangelical missiologists such as J. Robertson McQuilkin take alarm that cultural relativism is a current agenda item: "If the hermeneutics of Scripture, the basis of interpreting Scripture, is from the perspective of cultural anthropology or naturalistic psychology, for example, Scripture is no longer the final authority. Cultural relativism, environmental determinism and other anti-Biblical concepts seep in and gradually take control."[30] Current missiological studies that seek to be under the functional control of Scripture are challenged to find a methodology which takes into account the cultural differences between the contexts of the ancient text, the missionary interpreter, and the evangelized hearer, and at the same time allows Scripture's message to be understood and applied as the biblical writer intended it to be.[31]

Response

Two major tasks are involved in interpreting and applying authoritative Scripture in an age of relativism. The first is a descriptive analysis of both

---

28. Conn, *Eternal Word*, 128, 330.

29. Ibid., 338, 167–76. See also Donald E. Hiebert, "Epistemological Foundations for Science and Theology," *Theological Students' Fellowship Bulletin* 8 (March/April 1985): 5–10; and idem, "The Missiological Implications of an Epistemological Shift," ibid. (May/June 1985): 12–18. He contends that Thomas Kuhn (*The Structure of Scientific Revolutions*, 2d ed. [Chicago: University of Chicago Press, 1970]) has identified a major paradigm shift to a pluralistic-relativistic conceptual scheme in postempiricist philosophy and history of science. Bernstein concurs that Kuhn's thought has been used to promote a relativistic understanding of the use of the scientific method in the natural sciences (*Beyond Objectivism*, 15). Hiebert points out that some philosophers of science have moved beyond the radical relativism of Kuhn to a critical realism, a position that I would label a moderate relativism. This he commends to missiologists as "a biblical approach to knowledge."

30. McQuilkin, "Behavioral Sciences," 36.

31. J. Robertson McQuilkin, "Problems of Normativeness in Scripture: Cultural Versus Permanent," in *Hermeneutics, Inerrancy*, 217–40; George W. Knight, "A Response to Problems of Normativeness in Scripture: Cultural Versus Permanent," ibid., 241–54; Alan F. Johnson, "A Response to Problems of Normativeness in Scripture: Cultural Versus Permanent," ibid., 255–82.

the roots and current state of biblical hermeneutics. We must trace the origin of the major thought-constructs in terms of which current hermeneutical discussion is conducted (see chap. 2). Our exploration will examine the presuppositions of the historical-critical method as they were first expressed in the thought of René Descartes and Gotthold Lessing, and also the foundational contributions of Immanuel Kant to epistemology and of Friedrich Schleiermacher to hermeneutics. It will entail analyzing Ernst Troeltsch's historicist metaphysic, which is based on the historical-critical method. In the descriptive analysis, our concern will be not only to uncover the origin of the major thought-forms and patterns in the contemporary hermeneutical discussion, but also to determine their relativizing impact on the concept of biblical authority. We will also consider the current state of discussion concerning biblical hermeneutics, particularly in the period 1971–1982 (see chaps. 3–12).

A summary of the International Council on Biblical Inerrancy's Summit II on Hermeneutics will provide a fitting conclusion to our discussion. The affirmations and denials regarding the process of interpretation and application provided the clearest and most comprehensive handling of the issue for evangelicals. The discussion between Robertson McQuilkin and Alan Johnson crystalized the main evangelical positions on how to approach the process of interpretation and application with reference to the historical and cultural factor in Scripture.

There were other significant meetings of biblical scholars at the turn of the decade, whose findings must be taken into account. For North American nonevangelicals, the centennial of the Society of Biblical Literature (1980) proved a time for describing and assessing the current state of biblical hermeneutics. In missiology, the evangelical Lausanne Committee concluded a major consultation on contextualization (chap. 12), and the World Council of Churches wound up its discussion of the nature of biblical interpretation and authority (chap. 9).

Discussion has of course continued briskly since then, and we will examine the latest currents as we develop our own position (chaps. 13–18). Our analysis of the current state of this discussion will focus on three concerns: (1) *presuppositions*, that is, how various thinkers have defined the nature and authority of Scripture and how they understand the nature of language, meaning, and truth; (2) *components and conduct of the process of interpretation and application*, that is, such factors as the ancient and modern cultural contexts, the interpreter's preunderstanding, the hermeneutical circle, and contextualization; and (3) *hermeneutical bridges*, that is, thought-constructs that enable one to interpret and apply Scripture across historical and cultural distances.

Many of these data will come from Western nonevangelicals who are wrestling with the challenge of historical relativism to biblical authority (chap. 3) and seeking ways to overcome the historical distance between the ancient text's message and its intelligibility and relevance to the modern context, a distance which the historical-critical method in itself is incapable of bridging (chaps. 4–5). We will analyze the ongoing evangelical discussion of how to properly understand and apply Scripture which contains historical and cultural elements and at the same time claims to be the eternally and universally authoritative Word of God (chaps. 6–8). In missiology, we will look at contextualization as practiced by nonevangelicals (chaps. 9–10), and we will examine the evangelical response as well as its experiments with anthropological thought-constructs in communicating biblical truth across cultures (chaps. 11–12).

The second major task is the development of a biblical theology of hermeneutics and culture, together with suitable guidelines for interpreting and applying the Bible. We will study *culture the context* (chap. 13), or what the Bible teaches about the nature and aspects of human culture, especially relativism, and about God's relationship to and evaluation of culture. We will consider in depth *the God who communicates* (chaps. 14–16) and thus determine what the Bible teaches about Scripture's nature and authority, the nature of truth and meaning in language, and the role of the Holy Spirit in the process of interpretation and application. To complete this biblical theology of hermeneutics and culture, we must look at *man the interpreter* (chaps. 17–18), asking what the Bible teaches about the interpretational process, and what sinful human beings bring to it, where the hermeneutical bridge is to be found, and what the components are in interpretation, application, and contextualization.

We will frame the hermeneutical guidelines emerging from such a theology to cover four basic aspects of the process of interpretation and application (chaps. 19–20). We will illustrate each guideline with examples from both Western and Third World contexts. We will suggest steps for dealing with an interpreter's cultural preunderstanding as he or she approaches the text and will propose ways to analyze and appropriate information about historical-cultural elements in Scripture. We will explore how to develop a coherent interpretation that communicates in, and speaks to, the contemporary cultural context, and we will consider a method for applying Scripture's content. In sum, we will seek to understand how the eternally and universally authoritative Bible may be intelligibly understood and relevantly applied in modern cultural contexts.

2

Some Roots of the Contemporary Hermeneutical Discussion

Contemporary hermeneutical discussion, whether conducted from a conservative orthodox position or from a thoroughgoing relativism at the other end of the spectrum, has deep roots that go back to the thought of the post-Reformation era, of the Enlightenment, and of the nineteenth-century philosophers. This fertile mix is the common seedbed for the tangled variety of issues and thought-constructs that vex present-day approaches to biblical interpretation.

Thinkers from every branch of philosophy, historians, theologians, and even some anthropologists engaged in an "objectivist project" from the dawn of the Enlightenment through the nineteenth century. They were searching for a fixed and permanent ahistorical matrix which could be appealed to in determining what is true, real, rational, right, and good.[1] The very fact of such a search and the intensity of it presupposed the existence of such an objective reference point.

There is an intriguing irony here, for these thinkers looking diligently for an objective, ahistorical absolute were neither relativists themselves nor

---

1. Richard J. Bernstein, *Beyond Objectivism and Relativism: Science, Hermeneutics, and Praxis* (Philadelphia: University of Pennsylvania Press, 1983), 8, 15; see also Harvie M. Conn, *Eternal Word and Changing Worlds: Theology, Anthropology, and Mission in Trialogue* (Grand Rapids: Zondervan, 1984), chaps. 1–3.

were they working from a relativist perspective, and yet they provided ideas and methods and raised questions and concerns that became the matrix for the relativism that is the climate of current hermeneutical discussion. For example, to pose such an ahistorical absolute as pure reason to provide the framework for understanding reality had the immediate effect of subverting the content and authority of all historical phenomena by relativizing them. The Bible as a historical phenomenon was submitted to such analysis.

The "objectivist project" is now considered a failure in Western intellectual tradition. But from this discredited philosophical stance the relativists appropriated propositions and ideas that have served them well. René Descartes supplied the concept of the "knowing self"; Gotthold Lessing, that of the "ugly ditch" of historical distance. Immanuel Kant explicated a distinction between knowledge of the noumenal and knowledge of the phenomenal; Friedrich Schleiermacher, "preunderstanding" and the idea of the "hermeneutical circle." These tools of the objectivists were seized by the relativists and are being used by them during the ascendancy they currently enjoy.

In addition, the combination of such concepts formed a foundation for the development of the historical-critical method so popular in current hermeneutics. Late in the nineteenth century Ernst Troeltsch devised a historicist metaphysic based on the method.

The Enlightenment

The Historical-Critical Method

Philosophers and biblical scholars of the Enlightenment, following their legacy of Renaissance thinking, maintained that autonomous human reason unaided by revelation was sufficient to know reality and to guide life. They fashioned an interpretational approach, the scientific historical-critical method hailed by succeeding generations of practitioners because it "freed biblical interpretation from the grip of supernaturalism and ecclesiastical dictates."[2] One ecclesiastical dictate with supernatural content was the belief that Scripture was divine revelation, fully inerrant and finally authoritative. In the exercise of the historical-critical method, liberated human reason may come to conclusions critical of Scripture's content. Although claiming to be objective and neutral in this operation, reason positions itself as an authority to judge and evaluate Scripture. Those who practice the historical-critical method acknowledge that that method will not submit to

---

2. Russell Pregeant, *Christology Beyond Dogma* (Philadelphia: Fortress, 1978), 15.

any higher authority. Edgar Krentz, Lutheran biblical scholar, concludes that the historical-critical method is inescapably ruthless. It changes everything and "finally destroys the dogmatic form of method that has been used in theology."[3]

The use of autonomous reason within the historical-critical method has other consequences for Scripture. Because it views the content of any historical phenomenon as relative and contingent, the Bible and Christianity as historical phenomena become relativized.[4] The method skeptically assumes that each individual historical phenomenon or event studied is uncertain. Ultimately, only events that can be understood through cause and effect *in relation to* other events are certain. Such scrutiny robs the Bible and Christianity of their independent uniqueness, for they can be comprehended only in relation to the whole of history.

Three principles of the historical-critical method lead to these consequences: the principles of criticism or methodological doubt, of analogy, and of correlation.[5] We have already alluded to some aspects of methodological doubt in the discussion of autonomous reason. This principle assumes that all knowledge is historically conditioned. In order to arrive at true historical knowledge, to recover what happened, the interpreter must scientifically test all evidence from whatever source, including Scripture. The level of certainty attainable is only probability.

The principle of analogy introduces the criterion for probability. Assuming that nature, society, and humanity possess a certain uniformity over time, we can use present experiences and occurrences to judge the probability of past events.[6] The final principle is correlation or mutual interdependence. All historical phenomena are so interrelated that a change in one phenomenon will necessarily spark a chain reaction of causes and effects. As commonly understood by practitioners of the historical-critical method, this principle when combined with the second principle allows for only natural explanations. God as a causative factor is excluded. The possibility that a historical phenomenon such as the Bible could be divine revelation

---

3. Edgar Krentz, *The Historical-Critical Method* (Philadelphia: Fortress, 1975), 55.

4. Robert L. Saucy observes that the hermeneutical ramifications of this autonomy include an "overwhelming historical consciousness. . . . If human reason is the final authority, it is only logical to understand truth in relativistic terms" ("A Response to Presuppositions of Non-Evangelical Hermeneutics," in *Hermeneutics, Inerrancy, and the Bible*, ed. Earl D. Radmacher and Robert D. Preus [Grand Rapids: Zondervan, 1984], 631).

5. Krentz, *Historical-Critical Method*, 55ff., following Ernst Troeltsch.

6. Krentz notes that when the principle of analogy is raised to a universal, it can become constricting, making inadmissible some legitimate evidence (ibid., 57). Royce G. Gruenler goes further and points out that this principle can become captive to the interpreter's preconceived notions of what is historically probable or improbable ("A Response to the New Hermeneutic," in *Hermeneutics, Inerrancy*, 585). Such a process is deceptive because interpreters think that they are describing only what actually happened, while they are in fact reflecting their own opinion of what qualifies as a historical event. In recent years historians have realized this dilemma.

that explains and authoritatively addresses all historical phenomena is excluded. The possibility of miracles is excluded. The place and role of every phenomenon, including the Bible, is determined by the process of historical development.

René Descartes

The philosophical underpinnings for this liberation of reason from dogma began with French philosopher René Descartes (1596–1650). He was searching for an epistemological method to provide knowledge that was certain, but when he surveyed the field of academic knowledge, he could not find any opinions which were "not in dispute and consequently doubtful and uncertain."[7] He "resolved to seek no other knowledge than that which I might find within myself, or perhaps in the great book of nature."[8] He devised a standard for evaluating knowledge: A conclusion provided certain knowledge if it presented itself "so clearly and distinctly to my mind that there was no reason or occasion to doubt it."[9]

This approach revolutionized Western thought by establishing the knowing subject as the starting point and an essential ingredient in the epistemological process.[10] This awareness of the subject over against the object in turn produced a sense of historical distance between the interpreter (subject) and the ancient text (object).

Descartes's framing of the epistemological process provided a foundation for several presuppositions of the historical-critical method. To attain certainty of knowledge about anything, he contended one must doubt, that is, set aside "customary and long-standing beliefs" about it.[11] This is the methodological doubt in the historical-critical method. Descartes's emphasis on the knowing subject as an essential ingredient in the epistemological process gave substance to the principle of analogy. If one acknowledges as historically true only those events that are analogous to what the knower perceives as possible in the present, then the knower is truly an essential and determinative ingredient in the process.

---

7. René Descartes, *Discourse on Method* and *Meditations*, trans. Laurence J. Lafleur (Indianapolis: Bobbs, 1960), 8.

8. Ibid. See Rule 3 of Descartes's *Rules for the Direction of the Mind* (trans. Laurence J. Lafleur [Indianapolis: Bobbs, 1961]): "Concerning the subjects proposed for investigation, we should seek to determine, not what others have thought, nor what we ourselves conjecture, but what we can clearly and evidently intuit, or deduce with certainty; for in no other way is knowledge obtained" (p. 8).

9. Descartes, *Discourse on Method*, 15.

10. "For the knowledge of objects, only two things need to be considered: we who know, and the objects themselves which are to be known" (Descartes, *Rules*, 44). See Helmut Thielicke, *The Evangelical Faith*, vol. 1, *Prolegomena: The Relation of Theology to Modern Thought Forms* (Grand Rapids: Eerdmans, 1974), 34.

11. Descartes, *Discourse on Method*, 79.

It is interesting to note that although Descartes's epistemological speculations provided principles on which to develop a method for subjecting Scripture to the critique of reason and ultimately to relativize it, Descartes himself never did so. "Having learned on great authority . . . that the truths of revelation which lead [to heaven] are beyond our understanding, I would not have dared to submit them to the weakness of my reasonings. I thought that to succeed in their examination it would be necessary to have some extraordinary assistance from heaven, and to be more than a man."[12] Descartes perceived that human reasoning alone does not have the capacity for examination and validation of the "truths of revelation" so that one may arrive at certain knowledge in this area.

Gotthold Lessing

When German literary critic Gotthold Lessing (1729–1781) applied the historical-critical method to the Scriptures, he made a surprising and unsettling discovery. Observing that miracles no longer occur, he applied the principle of analogy and came to the logical conclusion that the truth of New Testament miracles cannot be demonstrated. The consequences were more profound than simply the loss of miraculous content from Scripture. The miraculous authority for the truth of the metaphysical and moral teaching of Jesus had been undermined. Since reason based on his own experience could not demonstrate the truth of miracle, Lessing could not locate any binding authority in New Testament teaching:

> But since the truth of these miracles has completely ceased to be demonstrable by miracles still happening now, since they are no more than reports of miracles (even though they be narratives which have not been, and cannot be, impugned), I deny that they can and should bind me to the very least faith in the other teachings of Christ . . . *accidental truths of history can never become the proof of necessary truths of reason.*[13]

Lessing also dismissed the argument that inspired writers who could not err are proof of the truth of Scripture, since this assertion is not historically certain.

For Lessing, all Scripture is historically conditioned and by its very nature can never provide proof of its truthfulness to autonomous human reason. He says he would believe if the New Testament miracles occurred before his eyes, but since they have not, their force as proof of other truths is

---

12. Ibid., 7–8.
13. Gotthold E. Lessing, *Lessing's Theological Writings*, trans. Henry Chadwick (London: A. & C. Black, 1956), 55, 53 (emphasis added).

removed because of the nature of historical testimony. As a historical document the Bible can never give evidence that will prove a "necessary truth of reason." Lessing laments, "That, then, is the ugly, broad ditch which I cannot get across, however often and however earnestly I have tried to make the leap. If anyone can help me over it, let him do it, I beg him, I adjure him. He will deserve a divine reward from me."[14]

It should be noted that the yawning ditch is a seminal form of the question of relevance raised by the contemporary relativist. For Lessing, historical testimony, including the Bible, cannot be binding on his reason. Following a similar line of thought, the contemporary relativist concludes that a book out of an ancient setting cannot be decisive for contemporary problems. Historical distance has become a chasm we cannot cross. In fact, it seems to have widened: the relativist now raises the question of whether an ancient text can be intelligible, let alone relevant, to today's interpreter.

Immanuel Kant

German philosopher Immanuel Kant (1724–1804) took up the objectivist project in the face of empiricism and searched for the epistemological framework, the essential element, that would allow him to attain certain knowledge. He reasoned that judgments or propositions characterized by logical necessity and strict universality provide such knowledge.[15] He chose scientific procedure, not metaphysics, as his model for developing a method of critical inquiry. He thoroughly analyzed the subject (the reasoning mind) and the object (the phenomena of sense experience) of the epistemological process. He came to the conclusion that in pure reason, in the mind, the judgments or principles of certain knowledge are to be found. These a priori judgments are either analytic (i.e., logically necessary) or synthetic (principles in math and science and morality, e.g., "every event has a cause"). For Kant, a priori synthetic judgments are the essential ingredient that the knower, the mind, contributes to the epistemological process. They structure a person's perception of experience so that knowledge of objective reality is possible.

Kant emphasized that sense experience can never be the source of knowledge that is necessarily and universally certain. He maintained a strict disjunction between the phenomenal realm of sense experience and the transcendent noumenal realm of pure reason. He further concluded that the knower must realize the limits of reason and the kind of certain knowledge it can yield. Reason does not lead to knowledge of things in themselves. Thus metaphysics can never be an exact science, though it is a

14. Ibid., 55.
15. Immanuel Kant, *Critique of Pure Reason*, trans. J. M. D. Meiklejohn (New York: Dutton, 1934), 26.

natural disposition of the mind.[16] Rather, the universal and necessary propositions or judgments which a critique of pure reason yields are categories of the mind that can be applied only to the objects of sense experience, not to the objects in the transcendental noumenal realm.

If necessarily and universally certain knowledge is derived only from a critique of pure reason, how are the absolute truth claims of a divine revelation, the Bible, to be evaluated? Kant clearly holds that special revelation, because it is historical (i.e., a part of sense experience), cannot properly make universal truth claims.[17]

> A church dispenses with the most important mark of truth, namely, a rightful claim to universality, when it bases itself upon a revealed faith. For such a faith, being historical (even though it be far more widely disseminated and more completely secured for remotest posterity through the agency of Scripture), can never be universally communicated so as to produce conviction. Yet, because of the natural need and desire of all men for something *sensibly tenable*, and for a confirmation of some sort from experience of the highest concepts and grounds of reason . . . some historical ecclesiastical faith or other, usually to be found at hand, must be utilized.[18]

Kant's epistemological system affected his attitude toward interpretation of Scripture in three ways. First, since the Bible is historical, it cannot yield universal truth and so ceases to be the final authority for determining true belief and conduct. Kant adopts a condescending attitude toward those who need such a tangible authority. He asserts that though the content of the religion of pure reason can be found in the Bible, it can be discovered just as well by an analytical consideration of the a priori synthetic judgments of one's own reason. Second, the hermeneutic one brings to bear on Scripture should aim to support the religion of pure reason, namely, morality.[19] If a literal interpretation does not produce such a result, another should be tried. Third, reason cannot prove the divine origin of Scripture, though it can and should be used by scholars to show that "there is nothing in the origin of Scripture to render impossible its acceptance as direct divine revelation."[20]

Roy Howard, student of philosophical hermeneutics, asserts that Immanuel Kant's thought has been decisive for contemporary hermeneutics in two ways. First, by making the procedures of the natural sciences normative for all epistemological endeavors, Kant turns the unified field of knowing

---

16. Ibid., 189, 36.
17. Immanuel Kant, *Religion Within the Limits of Reason Alone*, trans. Theodore M. Greene and Hoyt H. Hudson, 2d ed. (LaSalle, Ill.: Open Court, 1960), 99.
18. Ibid., 100.
19. Ibid., 101.
20. Ibid., 103.

into a scientific realm, but "at the risk of making such knowing as was supposed to occur in the non-scientific realms theoretically untenable and only emotionally, psychologistically—in short, irrationally—tolerable."[21] These consequences manifest themselves in Kant's views about revelation. The truth claims of special revelation have been relativized because they are found in the Bible, which is a historical phenomenon. Any claims for the absolute reliability and inerrancy of the truth of Scripture are judged by such an epistemological system to be not just false, but inconceivable.[22]

Second, Kant described the knowing process with clearly defined roles for subject and object. So complete and convincing was his analysis that it established the autonomy of the rational knower using the thought-categories of pure reason. German theologian Helmut Thielicke sees the full implications of this view: "Since Kant discovered man's autonomy one can no longer accept a truth-claim or an imperative unless it has passed the censor of theoretical and practical reason."[23]

So revolutionary were Kant's assertions about the thought-categories of the mind as the essential ingredient in obtaining objective knowledge of reality that British biblical scholar Anthony Thiselton claims, on the one hand, that modern thinkers can no longer be satisfied with a correspondence view of truth.[24] British Old Testament scholar James Barr, on the other hand, feels free to dismiss fundamentalism (i.e., conservative evangelicalism) as a viable expression of modern Christianity because it does not follow Kant's view with regard to the categories of the mind.[25] Barr labels fundamentalism as pre-Kantian eighteenth-century empirical rationalism.

In Kant we have another thinker who was not himself a relativist. In fact, modern proponents of the sociology of knowledge strongly criticize Kant's contention that the a priori synthetic judgments or categories of thought of pure reason are absolute and universal.[26] Yet, in philosopher Richard Rorty's view, "the fashionable talk of alternative conceptual schemes is a linguistic, pluralistic development of Kant's claim that there is only *one*

---

21. Roy J. Howard, *Three Faces of Hermeneutics: An Introduction to Current Theories of Understanding* (Berkeley: University of California Press, 1982), 5.

22. W. David Beck, "A Response to Truth: Relationship of Theories of Truth to Hermeneutics," in *Hermeneutics, Inerrancy*, 65–66; see also James I. Packer, who says that Kant developed a "critical philosophy of mind . . . which silenced God by making it methodologically unphilosophical to suppose that he sends any messages by any means at all" ("A Response to the New Hermeneutic," ibid., 563).

23. Thielicke, *Evangelical Faith*, 1:38.

24. Anthony C. Thiselton, *The Two Horizons: New Testament Hermeneutics and Philosophical Description, with Special Reference to Heidegger, Bultmann, Gadamer, and Wittgenstein* (Grand Rapids: Eerdmans, 1980), 199.

25. James Barr, *Fundamentalism* (Philadelphia: Westminster, 1977), 272.

26. Steven W. Stall, "Sociology of Knowledge, Relativism, and Theology," in *Religion and the Sociology of Knowledge: Modernization and Pluralism in Christian Thought and Structure*, ed. Barbara Hargrove (New York: Mellen, 1984), 77.

human conceptual scheme which is specified by *the* table of categories."[27] Though anthropology may not have consciously developed from Kant its distinction between the real world and one's perception of it through a conceptual scheme, Rorty's observation is essentially correct. Such a distinction did not lead Kant into relativism, but it has that effect when used to analyze the epistemological process in diverse cultures. Anthropological theory contends that a human being perceives reality not directly but through the conceptual scheme, the thought-categories, provided by the culture. And these conceptual schemes, while they do not have universal validity, do function in the same way as Kant's categories. They help an individual determine what is true, right, or real—but only in that particular culture.

Friedrich Schleiermacher

German theologian Friedrich Schleiermacher (1768–1834) viewed the process of textual interpretation in a broad framework as the art of understanding. He asserted that understanding is basically a contextual operation. Humans understand something by comparing it to something already known. He maintained that "every child comes to understand the meanings of words only through hermeneutics."[28] Just as a child comes to understand a word's meaning by relating it to what he or she already knows, so the process of hermeneutics must proceed. By thus framing the interpretational process, Schleiermacher introduced two new foundational concepts: preunderstanding and the hermeneutical circle. Preunderstanding, which is the possession of the interpreter, is that minimum common ground, in terms of experience and categories of understanding between the interpreter and the text, which is essential for the interpreter to begin to understand the text.[29] The hermeneutical circle is the dynamic interaction between the whole and the part. "An individual concept derives its meaning from a context or horizon within which it stands; yet the horizon is made up of the very elements to which it gives meaning. By dialectical interaction between the whole and the part, each gives the other meaning; understanding is circular, then. Because within this 'circle' the meaning comes to stand, we call this the 'hermeneutical circle.'"[30]

---

27. Quoted by Bernstein, *Beyond Objectivism*, 76.

28. Friedrich Schleiermacher, *Hermeneutics: The Handwritten Manuscripts*, ed. Heinz Kimmerle, trans. James Duke and Jack Frostman, AAR Texts and Translation Series 1 (Missoula, Mont.: Scholars Press, 1977), 52.

29. Thiselton, *Two Horizons*, 105.

30. Richard E. Palmer, *Hermeneutics: Interpretation Theory in Schleiermacher, Dilthey, Heidegger, and Gadamer* (Evanston, Ill.: Northwestern University Press, 1969), 87.

Schleiermacher also contended that the understanding of a text includes both grammatical and psychological analysis. Grammatical analysis allows the interpreter to uncover the boundaries of the writer's thought. Psychological analysis is the sympathetic and imaginative understanding of the writer's inner life as he or she wrote the work. Both are necessary for interpretation, which is "the historical and divinatory, objective and subjective reconstruction of a given statement."[31]

The concepts of preunderstanding and hermeneutical circle have been influential in the contemporary hermeneutical enterprise and have led readily to a view that context is the origin and final determiner of meaning. This approach, in turn, has become in many instances a self-evident construct supporting an epistemological relativism.[32] The practice and findings of anthropology, sociology, psychology, linguistics, and related sciences are perceived by many as providing the scientific validation of this view.

Schleiermacher's emphasis on psychological analysis of the text is consistent with his understanding of the Christian faith as basically a feeling of subjective dependence on God and of Christian theology as "the descriptive verbalizing of corporate Christian experience (feeling, in the sense of emotionally-laden intuition)."[33] British evangelical theologian J. I. Packer asserts that this approach dealt a "knockout blow to every form of Christianity that seeks to live by words that proceed from the mouth of God."[34] It transformed Scripture's revelatory content into reports of religious experience and removed from interpreters any confidence in their ability to hear God speak in and by his Word.

Nineteenth-Century Historicism

The writings of German historian Ernst Troeltsch provide our most comprehensive description of the historical-critical method[35] and a well-developed synthesis of norms of value derived from its use.[36] He accepts both Lessing's ditch and Kant's characterization of the phenomenal and concludes that all historical phenomena are relative. Applying the principle of correlation, he concludes that all phenomena derive their meaning from being part of a network of cause and effect, a network that can be traced

---

31. Schleiermacher, *Hermeneutics*, 111.

32. Harry C. Stafford, *Culture and Cosmology: Essays on the Birth of a World View* (Washington, D.C.: University Press of America, 1981), passim.

33. Packer, "Response to the New Hermeneutic," 563; see also James B. Torrance, "Interpretation and Understanding in Schleiermacher's Theology: Some Critical Questions," *SJT* 21 (1968): 268–82.

34. Packer, "Response to the New Hermeneutic," 563.

35. See note 5.

36. Ernst Troeltsch, *The Absoluteness of Christianity and the History of Religions*, trans. David Reid (Richmond: John Knox, 1971), chap. 3.

through contexts of ever-increasing comprehensiveness until it encompasses all history, which amounts to all reality. This is Troeltsch's basic metaphysic. Values are also relative, since they must be expressed as historically conditioned phenomena. They exist as absolute and unchanging, not within history, but beyond history, where they can be perceived only in presentiment and faith. Inside history, however, absolutes remain temporally conditioned. It follows that Scripture as a historical phenomenon can communicate absolute truth only in a relative, temporally conditioned form.

Troeltsch introduces a factor into his framework which enables him to avoid a reduction of his historical relativism into materialism. He proposes that history itself, "the inexhaustible movement of life," is the ultimate reality. History is moving toward a goal but not in the sense that a prior law or idea controls an evolutionary process so that the goal may be realized.

> Evolutionary development means, rather, the eruption—at coexisting but discrete points—of dynamic orientations directed toward the absolute goal of the human spirit. Each orientation evolves the richness of potential granted to it, first in its own limited sphere. At length orientations come into contact. . . . Then in free religious and ethical encounter men take note of their gradations of value and strive to obtain a basis of judgment by drawing them together to form a philosophy of history.[37]

Troeltsch's metaphysic, then, has one primary characteristic—change. Its organizing principle is a relational and "process" paradigm of cultural and social evolution. The one certainty in the vast network is change.

Since history is moving toward a greater and greater synthesis—the realization of values that will fully actualize the human spirit—absolute values can be expressed only in relative form. They always represent a situationally informed striving toward a future goal, a goal not yet completely realized, not yet become absolute.[38]

Troeltsch proposes to uncover absolute values by exercising the historical-critical method on the stuff of history. He warns against smuggling in speculative metaphysical norms or supernatural dogmatic standards from other contexts to determine what the universal values are. Only such criteria as comprehensiveness and clarity are admissible when evaluating values, conditions, and presuppositions in order to determine which values promote the procession of history toward its goal. The values of various religions have a place in the evaluation, and Troeltsch places Christianity at the apex of the world religions. However, nothing in his method requires

---

37. Ibid., 101.
38. Ibid., 90.

this to be so. If, in time to come, values from another religion show greater comprehensiveness in promoting the realization of the human spirit, that religion will have pride of place as the best expression of absolute values.[39] In the end, all judgments of truth and value are subjective. They are personal, ethically oriented religious convictions acquired by comparison and evaluation using the historical-critical method.

Troeltsch sees the actualization of the human spirit, historically understood, as the goal of history and the criterion for judging values within it. His correlated metaphysic provides humans with the basis for an autonomous and self-sufficient way of explaining existence and judging values. For all this, Troeltsch should probably be classified as only a moderate relativist or soft perspectivist because he does seek to make judgments on what values in a given culture or period are moving history toward its ultimate goal.

---

39. Harvie Conn shows the withering effect of Troeltsch's relativism on missions and notes the defense that Gustav Warneck makes of Christianity's absoluteness (*Eternal Word*, 75–76).

Part 2

Hermeneutics and Culture

The Nonevangelical Perspective

3

Historical Relativism and Biblical Authority

Adeep crisis in biblical authority set the tone for the late 1960s, and as it intensified, it became obvious that neoorthodoxy and the biblical theology movement it fostered could not synthesize the relativity of the historical-critical method with the unique and final authority of Scripture. This approach collapsed so suddenly under the assault from skeptical hermeneutics that James Barr wondered whether questioning and doubt about the status of the Bible might not become normal in the life of the churches.[1]

---

1. James Barr, *The Bible in the Modern World* (New York: Harper & Row, 1973), 8. See also Brevard S. Childs, *Biblical Theology in Crisis* (Philadelphia: Westminster, 1970); idem, "The Search for Biblical Authority Today," *Andover Newton Quarterly* 16 (1976): 199–206; Robert T. Osborn, "The Rise and Fall of the Bible in Recent American Theology," *Duke Divinity School Review* 41 (1976): 57–72; Lesslie Newbigin, "Text and Context: The Bible in the Church," *Near East School of Theology Theological Review* 5 (1982): 5–13.

Peter Homans ("Psychology and Hermeneutics: An Exploration of Basic Issues and Resources," *Journal of Religion* 55 [1975]: 329) gives an excellent analysis of the origins of this relativity thinking, which has pervaded contemporary Western culture. Freud and Marx relativized the claims of tradition in the area of explanations of social and personal behavior. They employed positivism and science to show that an infrastructure of thought, whether developmental or economic, is the hidden basis of all behavior. Anthropology relativized religious tradition by showing that the mythic thought of primitive religion was simply an expression of social and ethnographic conditions. Further, the presence of Eastern religions challenged the absolutist and universalistic claims of Western thought; see Barr's comments that the ascendancy of historical relativism and the resulting crisis in authority were due in the English-speaking world to the presence of an empiricist philosophical tradition, a libertarian social

The loss of confidence in the authority of Scripture motivated even non-evangelical scholars to seek a solution and stimulated many to reexamine their reliance on historical and cultural relativism. During the 1970s there was a serious attempt within the relativist perspective to describe in what sense the Bible could still be authoritative.[2]

James Barr

James Barr undertook a detailed analysis of the effects of relativism on the church's view of biblical authority in the late twentieth century.[3] He found that the majority of church members experience relativism as a vague but pervasive questioning whether the Bible has any validity for today. They acknowledge the Bible's authority, but they are uncertain about what this means. A smaller group in the church questions the very concept of biblical authority. Barr identifies another minority who uphold the traditional views on the subject. These he classifies as the fundamentalists, but in his view dogmatic fundamentalism is not a live option in the mainstream of modern Christian thought, one reason being that fundamentalism does not take into account Kant's categories.

Other critics focus on the reverberations in contemporary culture at large. They see that the authority of the Bible is waning in our century because it is thought of as a book from a remote historical and cultural context. In addition, modern men and women view themselves as liberated from the archaic moral standards and myths of the past. They are free, as Harvard theologian Gordon Kaufmann sees it, to savor and enjoy to the full the possibilities of life in a new awareness of their autonomy. Responsible moderns will think through what the norms are for their lives and define themselves over against the past.[4]

James Barr isolates five questions with which relativism confronts the concept of biblical authority:

---

philosophy, the absence of a strong preaching tradition, and strong influence from the neoorthodox movement (*Bible in the Modern World*, 8).

Childs describes the situation: "For various and complex theological and cultural reasons, this [neoorthodox] way of understanding the Bible, in the opinion of many, proved inadequate to meet the new crises which exploded on American society in the late sixties" ("Search for Biblical Authority," 200). Barr considers the crisis so deep that the only way out is to redefine the idea of authority in general and of the Bible in particular ("The Old Testament and the New Crisis of Biblical Authority" *Interpretation* 25 [1971]: 38).

2. Barr, *Bible in the Modern World*, chap. 3; Dennis E. Nineham, *The Use and Abuse of the Bible: A Study of the Bible in an Age of Rapid Cultural Change* (New York: Barnes & Noble, 1976); F. Gerald Downing, "Our Access to Other Cultures, Past and Present (or the Myth of the Culture Gap)," *Modern Churchman* 21 (1977): 28–42; Joseph Runzo, "Relativism and Absolutism in Bultmann's Demythologizing Hermeneutic," *SJT* 32 (1979): 401–19.

3. Barr, *Bible in the Modern World*, 11.

4. Gordon D. Kaufmann, "What Shall We Do with the Bible?" *Interpretation* 25 (1971): 96.

(1) *How can material from that very different biblical situation be decisive for our problems?* Barr argues that a belief in the immutability of human nature from culture to culture has been the assumption on which the transhistorical and transcultural validity of the Bible was maintained. But from a relativist perspective, such a universal human nature is a fiction. The only reality that can be known is human beings as they have appeared in a great variety of quite different cultures. He concludes that to designate a book that is the product of one culture as a decisive authority for other cultures is simply irrational.[5]

Barr attempts to discredit transcultural and transhistorical biblical authority by pointing to the problems which such a use of Scripture generates: In the light of 1 Corinthians 11, must women wear hats in church? Does God, according to Thessalonians, still have a separate purpose for the Jews? When the Bible is "distorted, one-sided, inadequate, or *just plain wrong*," the interpreter who holds to biblical authority has the unenviable task of defending the text.[6]

Another problem for Barr is the diversity in Scripture, including the "polemics" of one biblical writer against another. As proof that the Bible's basic character is not unity but diversity, he points to the use scholars are currently making of this very conflict and diversity as helpful analytical tools.

In light of these difficulties, Barr urges recognition of Scripture's character as historically and culturally conditioned and asserts that only "when we give up the futile expectation that the Bible's utterances will express what is right and authoritative can we begin to face it for what it really is, something belonging to an environment entirely different from our own, in which the questions and answers also were entirely different."[7]

(2) *How can we expect that which was meaningful to the writers and audiences of biblical times to communicate the same meaning to us?* Barr contends that to expect direct communication between different cultural or historical contexts flies in the face of historical fact. Modern culture and its assumptions are different from biblical culture and its assumptions; therefore, the meaning we would assign to events must differ from the meaning biblical writers would assign to them.[8]

---

5. Barr, *Bible in the Modern World*, 42. Barr further argues that when the application process is undertaken with this assumption, there is no provision for identifying when the analogy between the situations in the Bible and modern life has been established. "How great does the similarity have to be, and how great a degree of difference can be tolerated," for us to make direct application of biblical content to the modern world (p. 47)?

6. Ibid., 42.

7. Ibid., 43. John Leith states quite emphatically that to identify the Bible as the only infallible rule with inerrancy is "now no longer a possibility. The Bible does contain errors of fact, and many of its statements of faith and practice are in error" ("The Bible and Theology," *Interpretation* 30 [1976]: 241). See also Schubert M. Ogden, "The Authority of Scripture for Theology," *Interpretation* 30 (1976): 257; Paul J. Achtemeier, *The Inspiration of Scripture: Problems and Proposals* (Philadelphia: Westminster, 1980).

8. Barr, *Bible in the Modern World*, 39.

The difference between first- and twentieth-century cultural outlooks is so radical that the problem is not simply that contemporary men and women see the biblical message as irrelevant and choose not to believe it—rather, they cannot even understand it. Dennis Nineham sees our present circumstances as proof of the radical difference. We live in a modern world of high technology, mass culture, and rapid change, and it is characteristic of such a period that in many spheres one can "no longer rely to any extent on the practice or opinions of the past for guidance on how things are best done in the present."[9]

A report from the Fourth World Conference on Faith and Order, held in Montreal in 1963, identified and located the problem more precisely when it said that this global civilization shaped by rapid technological advances is grounded in a scientific outlook that transforms our concept of the universe. "The new cosmology which is taking shape challenges our traditional conceptions of man and of nature, both in themselves and in their interrelationship with one another."[10]

Peter Baelz cautions that to accept the biblical message literally, still clothed in its ancient cultural expression, is to risk a kind of schizophrenia. "I as a child of the Enlightenment" cannot live with a first-century cultural outlook.[11] Gordon Kaufmann observes that "we would hardly be inclined—or even able—to subordinate or subject our own views on anthropology, cosmology, and ethics to those found in the Bible."[12] Barr offers the sense of sin and the longing for immortality as two samples of such categories.[13]

Nineham noted two additional aspects of the discontinuity between cultures in different historical periods. First, there is the difficulty of imaginative identification because interpreters tend to project their own concerns and perspectives into the past so that their way of seeing the past is historically conditioned. This, of course, is true when one studies a contemporaneous culture as well. Second, one does not have access to the presuppositions, the self-evident truths, of a historically distant culture. They are part of the implicit information of the text—assumed, but not explicitly expressed.[14]

---

9. Nineham, *Use and Abuse*, 9. See also Norman K. Gottwald, *The Tribes of Yahweh: A Sociology of the Religion of Liberated Israel, 1250–1050 B.C.* (Maryknoll, N.Y.: Orbis, 1979), 704.

10. Ellen Flesseman–van Leer, ed., *The Bible: Its Authority and Interpretation in the Ecumenical Movement*, Faith and Order Paper 99 (Geneva: World Council of Churches, 1980), 29.

11. Peter Richard Baelz, "Old Wine in New Bottles," *Theology* 76 (1973): 121. He offers the biblical presentation of demons as an example.

12. Kaufmann, "What Shall We Do?" 98. Nineham cites Lionel Trilling's judgment, "To suppose that we can think like men of another time is as much an illusion as to suppose we can think in a wholly different way" (*Use and Abuse*, 39).

13. Barr, *Bible in the Modern World*, 39.

14. Nineham, *Use and Abuse*, 24.

(3) *How can the Bible's insights be decisive for us in any way that is qualitatively different from that which attaches to other books and other times?*[15] Here Barr has raised the question of the finality and definitiveness of the Bible as canon. He describes the Bible as a limited set of books, chosen partly by accident from a limited segment of church history. In this view, the Scriptures appear as incomplete and inadequate.

(4) *How can the Bible be qualitatively different from other factors that come into mind when deciding faith and ethics?*[16] Barr would reply that it cannot be different, and he would find an ally in British New Testament scholar Dennis Nineham, who also sees the Bible as too historically and culturally conditioned to be appealed to in deciding matters of faith and ethics. Nineham insists that "there can be no possibility of a revelation which transcends culturally conditioned terms altogether and is given in terms which are not peculiar to any one culture but apply equally to all cultures . . . if there is to be divine communication to men who dwell in history, it will inevitably be historically conditioned."[17]

(5) *Do we not evade our responsibility or distort the biblical message if we take as our goal simply the restating or reinterpreting of the Bible?*[18] Barr says that our responsibility is, rather, to express for our contemporaries what the church and Christians believe today. We evade this responsibility when we simply make our thoughts dependent on what was believed in Bible times.

David Kelsey

Most nonevangelical theologians were keenly aware of the crisis created by their relativist perspective, but this did not drive them to despair. Rather, they accepted the crisis as a challenge to investigate in what sense and in what way the Bible could still be authoritative. A starting point was the conclusion that the traditional method, which employed the translation metaphor, must be discarded. Yale theologian David Kelsey made their position clear when he said that no one now supposes true theology can be straightforwardly read off from the pages of the Bible.[19] The Bible is not a

---

15. Barr, *Bible in the Modern World*, 10. Ogden argues that liberal Protestant theology is committed to using reflective critical inquiry to test whether theological assertions are meaningful and true ("Authority of Scripture," 243). The Bible as canon cannot provide sufficient authorization of the meaningfulness and truth of theological statements. Liberal Protestantism takes this position not only because of historical-critical findings, but because Scripture does not stand as a final norm. Rather, it derives its authority from God, who is the ultimate authority. See Lyman T. Lundeen, "Authority of the Word in a Process Perspective," *Encounter* 36 (1975): 282.

16. Barr, *Bible in the Modern World*, 10.

17. Nineham, *Use and Abuse*, 12.

18. Barr, *Bible in the Modern World*, 10.

19. David H. Kelsey, *The Uses of Scripture in Recent Theology* (Philadelphia: Fortress, 1975), 186ff.

problem solver. One does not come to it for answers. There is not a direct
relation between the meaning of the biblical text and a theological proposal
authorized by Scripture. In this matter Barr concurred.[20]

For Kelsey, the basic reason for discarding the traditional method is the
fact that it has already been discarded by many theologians of the modern
period.[21] The majority of theologians no longer operate from a "referential"
hermeneutic. They do not construct their theology from the ideas, events,
accounts, and truths referred to in the text of Scripture. Such prooftexting
has fallen into disfavor. Modern theologians work with an "intentionality"
hermeneutic. They get at the meaning of the text in an indirect way by
investigating the writer's purpose, context, and theology as well as the
thought-categories he used.

A similar pattern is being followed in the historical study of Scripture.
The conclusions about the introductory matters of a book are now decided
from an analysis of the ideas, motivations, and intentions extracted from the
"phenomena" of the book. These conclusions are then used to evaluate any
explicit or referential claims that appear in the text. Authorship of the pastoral Epistles is an example. Analysis of the vocabulary, theological themes,
and historical situation of the pastoral Epistles has led many to conclude
that Paul did not write them, and this scholarly analysis takes precedence
over the text's explicit witness to Paul's authorship.[22]

The same indirect approach is used with today's attempts to apply Scripture. Using the intentionality approach, theologians become aware of their
own contemporary context: the thought in which they must frame their
theological assertions if the latter are to be relevant. The object of doing
theology, according to Barr, is to make a constructive assertion of what the
church believes now. It does not regurgitate the Bible, but if it uses the Bible,
it incorporates these earlier thoughts by deciding that they can be appropriated and affirmed by us today.[23] The Bible becomes an instrument and
expression of faith, not an object of faith. Doctrinal and ethical positions are
no longer reached by applying inductive principles to the pages of Scripture. Doctrine and ethics have as their points of origin "a total vision, a
conception of what Christian life, action and society should be like. These
visions come from Christian men, informed by the Bible . . . [and] all sorts

---

20. Barr, *Bible in the Modern World*, 61, 90–91, 110–33.

21. Kelsey sees this reason as cogent because he wants the description of the way Scripture may
function as authority to be broad enough to include all the present approaches to biblical authority (*Uses
of Scripture*, 186). Since the traditional approach—translation metaphor—calls into question the appropriateness of other approaches, including relativism, it cannot be considered "theological position
neutral." Some other approach must be found.

22. Paul Feine, Johannes Behm, and Werner Georg Kummel, *Introduction to the New Testament*, trans.
A. J. Mattill, Jr., 14th rev. ed. (Nashville: Abingdon, 1966), 261–70.

23. Barr, *Bible in the Modern World*, 133.

of other influences which play upon their lives."[24] Biblical authority is exercised, but the operation is shifted to biblical critiques of the new positions.

---

24. James Barr, *The Scope and Authority of the Bible* (Philadelphia: Westminster, 1980), 62. Kelsey agrees and sees the theologizing process as beginning with the choice of a particular understanding of what Christianity is all about (*Uses of Scripture*, 166). That understanding will determine how one views the Bible as an authority.

4

The Historical-Critical Method and Hermeneutical Supplements

During the reevaluation occurring in the 1970s, some biblical scholars discovered serious deficiencies in the historical-critical method and set out on a radical restructuring.[1] Many searched for modes of thought that could serve to construct interpretational links from the past to the present better than the crisis theology of neoorthodoxy or the existentialism of Rudolf Bultmann.[2] The church as confessional interpreter, the Bible as canon, the phenomenological approach to the philosophy of language, and process philosophy were all proposed as hermeneutical supplements from which a transhistorical bridge could be constructed.[3] It should be noted that, at the least, a moderate relativism characterizes these various approaches.

---

1. E.g., Walter Wink, *The Bible in Human Transformation: Toward a New Paradigm for Biblical Study* (Philadelphia: Fortress, 1973); Peter Stuhlmacher, *Historical Criticism and Theological Interpretation of Scripture: Towards a Hermeneutic of Consent* (Philadelphia: Fortress, 1977); Daniel J. Harrington, "Biblical Hermeneutics in Recent Discussion: New Testament," *Religious Studies Review* 10 (1984): 7–9; David L. Bartlett, "Biblical Scholarship Today: A Diversity of New Approaches," *Christian Century* 98 (1981): 1090–94.

2. For examples of neoorthodox and Bultmannian hermeneutics, see Floyd V. Filson, "How to Interpret the Bible: The Interpreter at Work," *Interpretation* 4 (1950): 178–88; Otto A. Piper, "Principles of New Testament Interpretation," *TT* 3 (1946): 192–204; Rudolf Bultmann, "How God Speaks Through the Bible," in *Existence and Faith: Shorter Writings of Rudolf Bultmann*, trans. Schubert M. Ogden (Cleveland: World, 1960), 166–70; idem, "The Problems of Hermeneutics," in *Essays Philosophical and Theological*, trans. J. C. G. Greig (London: SCM, 1955), 234–61.

3. Stuhlmacher, *Historical Criticism*; Brevard S. Childs, *Introduction to the Old Testament as Scripture*

Recent Critique

Walter Wink, a biblical scholar at Union Seminary, New York, declared that biblical criticism was bankrupt because it had not achieved its purpose to interpret the Scriptures so that the past comes alive and illumines the present with "new possibilities for personal and social transformation."[4] Rather than providing the bridge it had promised, the method actually created historical distance between the contemporary context and the historical one of the ancient text. Peter Stuhlmacher, a German New Testament scholar, observes that this distancing has certain benefits which are welcome and tolerable as long as the goal is "the intellectual mastery of history and the emancipation from all inhibiting tradition."[5] In practice, this historical distance could not be confined to the method and became part of the end product. The interpreter set out to master a text as an object understood within its own ancient context. To do so, one had to remain removed from the ancient context and maintain oneself as subject, operating out of a contemporary context. Objective neutrality is the ideal, but in such a stance the interpreter is not free and cannot see how to overcome the historical distance and apply the text's message to the contemporary context.[6]

Moreover, such a stance is "incommensurate with the intention of the texts,"[7] for they intend to evoke a lived response of faith. It also flies in the face of the church's aim in using Scripture—a serious matter, for the church's "very identity stands or falls by its connection with Holy Scrip-

---

(Philadelphia: Fortress, 1979); *IDB Sup*, s.v. "Hermeneutics"; Hans-Georg Gadamer, *Truth and Method* (New York: Seabury, 1975); Paul Ricoeur, *Interpretation Theory: Discourse and the Surplus of Meaning* (Fort Worth: Texas Christian University Press, 1976); Russell Pregeant, *Christology Beyond Dogma* (Philadelphia: Fortress, 1978).

4. Wink, *Human Transformation*, 2. Stuhlmacher agrees. For scholars, pastors, and students, "historical criticism is the agent of a repeated and growing rupture of vital contact between biblical tradition and our own time" (*Historical Criticism*, 65).

5. Stuhlmacher, *Historical Criticism*, 62.

6. Gerhard Maier (*The End of the Historical-Critical Method*, trans. Edwin W. Leverenz and Rudolph F. Norden [St. Louis: Concordia, 1977]) contends that the difficulties of the historical-critical method lie not in communication between the ancient and modern contexts but in the paucity of positive results. "At fault was, rather, the objective impossibility of taking the few settlings of knowledge that remained in the sieve of critique and that bore the seal of approval and making them the foundation of practical life in the existing church, or for that matter, in any church. Ultimately, this is where remoteness and estrangement between theological scholarship and congregational life has its root, not in difficulties of communication" (p. 22).

7. Wink, *Human Transformation*, 2. Childs wholeheartedly agrees from his perspective of canon criticism. He observes that the hermeneutical gap has arisen in large measure from a disregard of canonical shaping. The historical-critical method seeks "to restore an original historical setting by stripping away those very elements which constitute the canonical shape. Little wonder that once the biblical text has been securely anchored in the historical past by 'decanonizing' it, the interpreter has difficulty applying it to the modern religious context" (*Introduction to the Old Testament*, 79).

ture."[8] Such emphasis on detached observation of phenomena, without the interference of emotions, will, consciousness, or interests, separates theory from practice and creates a trained incapacity for dealing with real problems of actual living persons in their daily lives.[9] To put it another way, when the historical-critical method has done its work in creating historical distance, the end result is finally to isolate each human individual in ethical and religious deafness.[10]

Even so, the strongest critics of the method continued to advocate its use.[11] There were insistent and recurring calls for new forms of thought to supplement the method as a hermeneutic bridge. The limits of the historical-critical method had been recognized, and its advocates set out to compensate for them.

Hermeneutical Supplements

Peter Stuhlmacher

The hermeneutical bridge proposed by Peter Stuhlmacher would engage the church as confessional interpreter. To the historical-critical study he proposes to add a dogmatic confessional stage, which would entail spiritual interpretation in the church. He recommends accomplishing this through a kind of dialogue which would involve continuous interaction between the critical exposition of the text and the confessional tradition (i.e., the way the Scriptures have been historically understood in the church). The two main pylons in this hermeneutical extension are the concepts of tradition and transcendence.

---

8. Stuhlmacher, *Historical Criticism*, 62.

9. Wink, *Human Transformation*, 2; David Lockhead frames the problem as objectivism, which in the end is really the exercise of private interpretation that does not engage in praxis ("Hermeneutics and Ideology," *Ecumenist* 15 [1977]: 84).

10. Robert W. Jenson, "On the Problem(s) of Scriptural Authority," *Interpretation* 31 (1977): 246. Pregeant goes further and says that a text cannot be viewed with absolute objectivity, for it is unintelligible to the interpreter apart from a point of contrast in the interpreter's experience (*Christology Beyond Dogma*, 15). It is always appropriated in the light of certain questions, values, and perspectives brought to it. This was Schleiermacher's point.

11. Wink, *Human Transformation*, 17; Stuhlmacher, *Historical Criticism*, 65; Pregeant, *Christology Beyond Dogma*, 15; see also Paul J. Achtemeier and Gene M. Tucker, "Biblical Studies: The State of the Discipline," *Council on the Study of Religion Bulletin* 11 (1980): 72–76. David L. Bartlett ("Biblical Scholarship Today," 1094) contends that historical-critical studies will be prerequisite for any new approach to handling the text, since all methods must depend on the historical understanding of the text. See also Edgar Krentz, *The Historical-Critical Method* (Philadelphia: Fortress, 1975), 87. Ernest Best terms the contributions of the method "an undoubted success" ("The Literal Meaning of Scripture, the Historical-Critical Method, and the Interpretation of Scripture," *Proceedings of the Irish Biblical Association* 5 [1981]: 24).

Stuhlmacher sees the biblical text as part of tradition, which he defines as the received truth from past times that does in fact impinge on our lives now. In the church, whose connection with the Scripture supplies its life-blood, this outlook is most appropriate. For "the intent of the biblical texts is disclosed to such an understanding—and only to such!—which allows itself to be led by the witness of those who heard the Scripture before us."[12] Thus it is appropriate to ask "what claim or truth about man, his world, and transcendence we hear from these texts."[13] The church benefits from this dialogue, and theology benefits as well from its interaction with the current tradition regarding its durability and need for transforming.[14] Tradition is a factor present in our modern consciousness, and so when Scripture and theology are understood as part of it, a connection is established between the ancient and modern contexts.

The second key factor is transcendence and the attendant stance of openness to it. One of the basic failings of the historical-critical method, according to Stuhlmacher, has been its objective naturalistic view of history. He is convinced that this perspective is no longer accepted as the only way, or even the best way, to view history. Though no longer so widely accepted, the basic attitude is maintained and encouraged by the modern scientific world-view, which sees itself as autonomous and untouchable by any thought outside itself, whether tradition from the past or revelation from above. Stuhlmacher does not hesitate to call insolent the attitude which this approach fosters. Such an interpreter considers every claim from tradition, from the present environment, or even from transcendence "an imposition or restriction on his right to freedom which he must resist."[15]

For Stuhlmacher, this issue is one of the essential anthropological and ontological questions of our time. Will we in the twentieth century succeed in "getting free of this absolutist stance toward emancipation and find our way to a new openness to the world, that is, a willingness to open ourselves

---

12. Stuhlmacher, *Historical Criticism*, 80; George M. Landes, "Biblical Exegesis in Crisis: What Is the Exegetical Task in Theological Context?" *USQR* 26 (1971): 275.

13. Stuhlmacher, *Historical Criticism*, 85. Brevard S. Childs gives five guideposts for how the Scriptures may be understood as authority: (1) In the church's worship we are confronted with the living presence of God. (2) In the church's peculiar language of faith, the Scripture is always the measure of how well we have learned it. (3) In the reading of the Bible we have the expectation that God will continue to address his people. The authority of the Scriptures also emerges (4) in a commitment to the tradition of the whole Christian canon and (5) in the seeking of the whole church to hear and respond to its message. "The authority of the Bible emerges only when it is used, and the simplicity and power of its self-authenticating truth is experienced by each person, individually and corporately" ("The Search for Biblical Authority Today," *Andover Newton Quarterly* 16 [1976]: 203–5).

14. Stuhlmacher, *Historical Criticism*, 85. Jenson agrees ("Problem[s] of Scriptural Authority,". 244). Theology bears fruit as propositions in general form. These must be tested by Scripture. Theology unaffected by Scripture is ideology. Theology that fights texts is in the process of refutation. Theology rather should liberate texts, pointing out the possibilities of meaning.

15. Stuhlmacher, *Historical Criticism*, 84.

anew to the claim of tradition, of the present, and of transcendence"?[16] The openness and receptiveness Stuhlmacher calls for, he identifies as faith, and the transcendent he identifies as the Holy Spirit, the power of faith, and true understanding working through the Scriptures.

Stuhlmacher stops short of affirming verbal inspiration of propositional revelation according to evangelical understanding, but he does see a role for the doctrine of inspiration. He calls scholars back to the Reformation model of the self-sufficiency of Scripture. The biblical texts have a truth that awakens faith, a process which lies beyond the scope of human possibility. The ultimate effect of Scripture's truth on the human will lies with that truth and not with the individual. To reject any possibility of the transcendent breaking in on us is to reject the impact of the Scriptures as God's truth. In consequence, exposition of the Scriptures is reduced to a reinterpretation of the ancient texts as history or perhaps as anthropology. For Stuhlmacher, when tradition and transcendence are firmly in place, they form pylons upon which the hermeneutical bridge can span the chasm. His system affirms that "the biblical texts can be fully interpreted only from a dialogical situation defined by the venture of Christian existence as it is lived in the church."[17]

Brevard Childs

Brevard Childs is a Yale Old Testament professor who stands in the tradition of the biblical theology movement. He and fellow Old Testament scholar James Sanders propose to construct a hermeneutic to bridge the centuries by emphasizing the nature of the Bible as canon. Canon criticism practices a historical and theological analysis of Scripture in its final form to discover "the divine imperative and promise to a historically conditioned people of God whose legacy the Christian church confesses to share."[18] This method still views the materials as historically conditioned, but it does provide a bridge between those times and these in two ways.

---

16. Ibid.

17. Ibid., 89. See also Robert G. Bratcher, "Toward a Definition of the Authority of the Bible," *Perspectives in Religious Studies* 6 (1977): 119. Charles F. D. Moule ("'Through Jesus Christ Our Lord': Some Questions About the Use of Scripture," *Theology* 80 [1977]) sees the hermeneutical link which transcendence provides in two parts. First, there is the background of the continuity of a common humanity: the constancy of human motives and emotions, and the nature of personal relations, throughout history. "What Jesus showed and practiced of relations between man and God and man and man still applies to us. Whatever the differences, the character of personal relations remains virtually unchanged" (p. 35). In parallel continuity the risen Christ enables the church to take the Scriptures and use them to give guidance to twentieth-century Christians. The resurrection is the basis, then, for a mediatorial Christology which makes the hermeneutical task possible. "Jesus transcends time in such a way as actually to go along with time. . . . And to be shown the Man of Nazareth in his ancient environment is to begin to find the very same person who is with us (paradoxically) as we read about him" (p. 36).

18. Childs, *Introduction to the Old Testament*, 77.

The first is to examine the patterns, or paradigms, for hermeneutics that the Scriptures themselves present. The Bible gives considerable evidence of how "authoritative traditions encountered ancient cultural challenges, were rendered adaptable to those challenges, and thus themselves were formed and reformed according to the needs of the believing communities."[19] And that evidence "gives indications of how to make again today the points originally made and then to move on in our contexts to further theological horizons (views of truth)."[20]

Such a paradigmatic use is possible because of several continuity factors: the Christians' covenant identity and their ability to remember the mighty acts of God, to find dynamic analogies with the ancient experiences of God's people, and to apply the biblical comfort or challenges to themselves. But there are also differences that must be reckoned with. One must study one's present context to know what type of message is needed from Scripture. The ambiguity of reality must be dealt with and the tendency resisted to view the canon as always right and its adversaries as always wrong. In making the application, the interpreter must not moralize, viewing the biblical characters as models of morality when they are actually "mirrors of identity." Any appropriation of Scripture's message must be first of all a "theologizing" focused on the prophetic declaration of the truth about God's character and saving activity.

The second way of providing a bridge is to appreciate Scripture's "canonical intentionality" as an essential factor in linking the biblical context to the twentieth century. Childs maintains that the purpose of the canonical process is to insure that "a tradition from the past be transmitted in such a way that its authoritative claims be laid upon all successive generations of Israel."[21] The canonical intentionality is the dynamic that renders the tradition accessible to future generations. This intentionality controlled the shaping of the traditions as they were handed on in the canonization process. The canonical concern is "built into the structure of the text itself, and reveals the enormous richness of theological interpretation by which to render the text religiously accessible."[22]

The interpreter who studies Scripture from the perspective of its canonical intentionality will be able to discern the text's function for the community of faith today and will also learn the boundaries in which exegesis should take place. Neither the historical-critical method nor any

---

19. *IDB Sup*, s.v. "Hermeneutics."

20. Ibid. Jenson agrees, seeing the apostle's theology as "guaranteed samples of authentic theologizing" ("Problem[s] of Scriptural Authority," 243). But as Sanders also points out (in *IDB Sup*, s.v. "Hermeneutics"), this does not mean we are simply to reproduce or to amplify the content deductively, since ancient concerns are not our concerns.

21. Childs, *Introduction to the Old Testament*, 78.

22. Ibid., 79. Sanders sees the richness in terms of the multivalent character which canonical material has ("The Bible as Canon," *Christian Century* 98 [1981]: 1252–53).

other will have absolute priority in the interpretation process because Scripture's nature as canon sets the limits within which these methods are practiced.

Hans-Georg Gadamer

German philosopher Hans-Georg Gadamer develops a descriptive philosophical hermeneutic which shares some of Martin Heidegger's perspectives and focuses on the types of experiences in which truth is communicated. For Gadamer, historical consciousness and the historical distance it entails pose no problem for hermeneutics; they simply clarify the situation and bring to the fore that element in the hermeneutical process which is the essential link between text and interpreter.[23] All interpreters perform their task from a position within history. This means that the gap between ancient and modern contexts is already bridged. It is filled with the continuity of custom and tradition, which determine the patterns of throught and language of the contemporary culture. In fact, the ancient text—in this case, the Scripture—is a part of that tradition.

This body of custom and tradition is present not only *externally* as one's cultural heritage, but *internally* as the content of the interpreter's preunderstanding. In that role it is prejudice, the thought-structure of one's mind, that has made certain judgments before all the elements that determine a situation have been finally examined. This preunderstanding is what we bring to the text, and it functions as a tool in trying to understand the text.

The meaning of a text is never identical with what the original writer intended to say to the original audience. The interpreter's horizon—internally his or her preunderstanding, and externally the ancient text's current position in the tradition—has a decisive role.[24] The real meaning of a text is also determined in part by the historical situation of the interpreter and consequently by "the totality of the objective course of history."[25]

---

23. Gadamer, *Truth and Method*, 264. See also Sandra M. Schneiders, "Faith, Hermeneutics, and the Literal Sense of Scripture," *Theological Studies* 39 (1978): 719–36. Walter Wink's psychoanalytic linguistic paradigm uses the same basic steps as does Gadamer: distancing and fusion (*Human Transformation*, 19ff.). See also Patrick Henry, *New Directions in New Testament Study* (Philadelphia: Westminster, 1979), 212ff.

24. According to Jenson, "every particular attempt to understand some part of the tradition is but an event in an antecedent and continuing shaping by the tradition, which shaping is the intellectual and moral given substance of the one who seeks to understand" ("Problem[s] of Scriptural Authority," 247). Prosper Grech ("The 'Testimonia' and Modern Hermeneutics," *New Testament Studies* 19 [1973]: 318–24) points to the New Testament writer's interpretation of the Old Testament within the context of tradition, with the perspective of salvation history, and with the conviction of the continuing witness of the Holy Spirit as a model for bridging the time gap. He proposes the same elements for modern hermeneutics, in which illumination by the Holy Spirit is present and "the evolution of the meaning of a text can be accounted for by reinterpretation within a tradition as well as by the evidence of new happenings in salvation history" (p. 324).

25. Gadamer, *Truth and Method*, 263.

The process of historical understanding, including construing the meaning of an ancient text, involves placing oneself back into a historical situation and is more than a matter of empathy or the application of one's own preunderstanding to materials of another time. It is the "attainment of a higher universality that overcomes, not only our own particularity, but also that of the other."[26] That higher universality has an ontological basis:

> The one great horizon that moves from within, and beyond the frontiers of the present, embraces the historical depths of our self-consciousness. It is, in fact, a single horizon that embraces everything contained in historical consciousness. Our own past, and that other past towards which our historical consciousness is directed, help to shape this moving horizon out of which human life always lives, and which determines it as tradition.[27]

Gadamer admits his debt to Georg Hegel for this idealistic metaphysic. All self-knowledge proceeds from what is historically pregiven, what, with Hegel, he calls substance. The historically pregiven is the basis of all subjective meaning and attitude, and hence prescribes and limits our understanding of any tradition. To pursue a philosophical hermeneutic Gadamer prescribes that we move back along the path of Hegel's phenomenology of the mind to discover in the subjective what substantiality has determined it.[28] The end result of Gadamer's hermeneutical model is the fusing of the horizon of the ancient text with that of the contemporary interpreter.

Historical consciousness with its awareness of historical distance characterizes the first phase in the process. During this phase the contemporary interpreter projects a historical horizon for that element of tradition being studied—in this case, Scripture. But the ancient text must not remain isolated within this projected historical horizon; it must continually be used to test the prejudices of the interpreter's own horizon so that the false will die away and the true may become the means by which new sources of understanding and unexpected elements of meaning continually emerge.[29]

The historical consciousness of the interpreter distinguishes the historical horizon for the text based on elements of tradition. But this very consciousness is laid over a continuing tradition. For this reason it recombines what has been discovered in order to become again one with itself within the historical horizon that it has acquired. That becoming one with itself is the fusion of horizons. It is the inherent dynamic of tradition, the stuff of reality. "This process of fusion is continually going on, for there old and new continually grow together to make something of living value."[30] When

---

26. Ibid., 272.
27. Ibid., 271.
28. Ibid., 269.
29. Ibid., 265–66.
30. Ibid., 273.

such fusion occurs, true understanding takes place, and the historical horizon of the text is overtaken by our own present horizon of understanding.

Gadamer is proposing a total fusion of horizons. In the early tradition prior to the Enlightenment, hermeneutics was viewed as a threefold process: understanding (what the text meant), interpretation (what the text means), and application (what the text means to me). Gadamer contends that from the Romantic period on, the inner unity of understanding and interpretation was recognized. He insists that application is integrally related to the other two steps. For understanding involves something like application of the text to the present situation of the interpreter.[31]

This argument reflects Gadamer's understanding of the hermeneutical process in general, a process which takes into account the way religious texts are intended and may be properly understood (i.e., according to their claim to exercise a saving effect on those who read them in their own particular situation). Application is so essential to understanding that it can never be viewed as an optional and subsequent act of relating a given universal to a specific case understood by itself. Understanding can take place only in the interpreter's concrete particular situation. Therefore, application is the process that yields "the actual understanding of the universal itself that the given text constitutes for us."[32]

The reader does not exist who,

> when he has his text before him, simply reads what is there. Rather, all reading involves application so that a person reading a text is himself part of the meaning he apprehends. He belongs to the text that he is reading. It will always happen that the line of meaning that is revealed to him as he reads it necessarily breaks off in an open indefiniteness. He can, indeed he must, accept the fact that future generations will understand differently what he has read in the text.[33]

Gadamer anticipates the charge that such a model is a reversion to pure subjectivity. He insists that, though the understanding may be described in part as understanding oneself in the text, the proper stance is one of subordination. We open ourselves to the superior claim the text makes and respond to what it has to tell us. We do not take control of the meaning it speaks but, rather, serve the text, letting its claims dominate our minds so that a valid interpretation and application issue forth.

This affirmation of the unity of the hermeneutical process (understanding, interpretation, application) forms Gadamer's hermeneutical bridge. "Our thesis is that historical hermeneutics also has a task of application to

---

31. Ibid., 276.
32. Ibid., 305.
33. Ibid., 304.

perform because it too serves the validity of meaning, in that it explicitly and consciously bridges the gap in time that separates the interpreter from the text and overcomes the alienation of meaning that the text has undergone."[34]

Paul Ricoeur

Paul Ricoeur is a French phenomenologist who often uses Heideggerian and Freudian constructs.[35] His hermeneutical bridge centers in a philosophy of language, especially metaphorical and religious language.

Ricoeur has long studied the nature of language and the way it functions in speaker-audience discourse, and he asserts that the meaning of language in discourse, or word-event, has a reality that transcends the event itself. The meaning exists in ideality as an ideal object. This ideal existence makes it possible for meaning in discourse to be identified and reidentified by different individuals at different times as being one and the same. "The sameness of sense in the infinite series of its mental actualizations constitutes the ideal dimension of the proposition." Now meaning consists of referent (what is being spoken about) and sense (what is being said about it), and it should be noted that Ricoeur applies his statements about ideality to the sense portion of meaning.[36]

The referent, however, does not have a sameness for all readers of a text because the nature of written text differs from discourse. When a written text is read by someone other than the original hearer and not in the presence of the writer, this tertiary reader does not share the here-and-now, spatiotemporal context of the original participants in the dialogue. That context was the matrix toward which the referents of the discourse pointed. For the subsequent reader, the ostensive character of the referents has been removed from the text's message. The text now has "semantic autonomy," being freed from the identifiable extralinguistic entities of the original. It projects a referential world which is independent of, and should not be confused with, the "real" world. This dynamic makes it possible for readers in historical and cultural contexts other than the original to understand the text. For it has overcome the bounds of original word-event and is free to engender other word-events in those who read it.

Metaphoric and religious language in poetic or fictional texts is especially suited to projecting worlds with which the reader can interact. Such a text "liberates a power of reference to aspects of our being in the world that

---

34. Ibid., 278. Note that Gadamer rejects the bridge of "connaturality"—the idea that interpreters can understand the work because they share the same nature with the original writer (p. 277).

35. Richard E. Palmer, *Hermeneutics: Interpretation Theory in Schleiermacher, Dilthey, Heidegger, and Gadamer* (Evanston, Ill.: Northwestern University Press, 1969), 43–45.

36. Ricoeur, *Interpretation Theory*, 90.

cannot be said in a direct descriptive way, but only alluded to, thanks to the referential values of metaphoric and, in general, symbolic expressions."[37] According to Ricoeur, metaphoric, poetic discourse fictionally redescribes reality.[38] Its basic referent, as with religious language, is human experience in all its wholeness. The indirect communication of meaning is characteristic of parable and metaphor. Such language applies a familiar label to a new object which at first resists and then surrenders to the application. "It is an eclipsing of the objective manipulable world, an illumining of the life-world, of non-manipulable being-in-the-world, which seems to me to be the fundamental ontological import of poetic language."[39] Because human experience is its basic referent and its mode of expression is indirect, metaphoric/poetic/religious language opens up many possible worlds which can be appropriated by the interpreter, who can then cross the hermeneutical bridge and continue to find meaning in the text.

Ricoeur believes he has found in metaphor and symbol a way not only to bridge Lessing's ditch, but also to link Kant's noumenal and phenomenal worlds.[40] The logical nexus between thought (the unknown categories) and knowledge (the known phenomena) is poetic language, functioning to redescribe and translate reality through metaphor. This discourse in symbol, parable, and myth is the indirect presentation of the unconditioned, the noumenal. But such symbols do not yield objective knowledge, and Ricoeur cautions that the symbols grounded in biblical narrative must remain paradoxically on the boundary of reason or they become idols. When biblical narratives are made subservient to rational philosophy, they are reduced to moral allegories. They must not move within reason's boundary lest they claim to add to our objective knowledge of reality. Thus, for Ricoeur, propositional revelation is not only not possible; it is idolatry.

Ricoeur's hermeneutic involves three steps: guess, explanation, and comprehension/appropriation. After a first naive grasping of the text's meaning as a whole (i.e., the guess), the interpreter moves on, seeking to validate that initial interpretation by the logic of subjective probability, analyzing the text to arrive at its sense. The last step is to comprehend and appropriate the meaning. By structural analysis of the depth of semantics, the interpreter

---

37. Ibid., 37.

38. Paul Ricoeur, "Biblical Hermeneutics," *Semeia* 4 (1975): 34, 127–28.

39. Ibid., 87. Ricoeur's concept of revelation parallels his high evaluation of metaphor (see his "Toward a Hermeneutic of the Idea of Revelation," in *Essays on Biblical Interpretation*, ed. Lewis S. Mudge [Philadelphia: Fortress, 1980], 93ff.). He takes as his basic model Exodus 3:13–15. The God who reveals himself is a hidden God, and hidden things belong to him. In none of the modalities or analogical forms of revelation may revelation be included in and dominated by knowledge. "To say that the God who reveals himself is a hidden God is to confess that revelation can never constitute a body of truths which an institution may boast of or take pride in possessing" (p. 95).

40. Ricoeur, "Biblical Hermeneutics," 145.

may arrive at the new nonostensive referent in the semantically autonomous text, and a kind of world is disclosed. This amounts to "an injunction
coming from the text, as a new way of looking at things, as an injunction to
think in a certain manner." A fully realized appropriation complies with the
injunction of the text and follows the "arrow" of the sense, and the interpreter tries to think accordingly. This initiates a new self-understanding. "In
this self-understanding, I would oppose the self, which proceeds from the
understanding of the text, to the ego, which claims to precede it. It is the
text, with its universal power of world disclosure, which gives a self to the
ego."[41]

Process Hermeneutic

Alfred North Whitehead and his followers view language according to
the metaphysic and epistemology of his process philosophy. The hermeneutic developed from this perspective seeks to remedy some of the
deficiencies of Bultmann's demythologizing. This hermeneutic is grounded
on an understanding of reality as process, a fluid environment of causal
nexus in which, by participatory involvement, humans are able to make
sense and meaning out of what they perceive. Language, then, is of necessity analogical, with no univocal or unanimous sense, no reference to absolutely definite objects. Reality does not consist of such discrete objects.
Language is inexact and fragmentary, and it speaks by way of abstraction
lifted out of the fluid process, reality. In process hermeneutics, language
has no univocal meaning; still, communication is possible and is guaranteed
by the fact that words are "spoken within the framework of an intelligible
universe."[42]

Process theologians construct their hermeneutical bridge from the actual
function of language. Language operates in propositions, but these serve as
lures toward "feeling," that is, toward "encounters with actualities and
potentialities that form the basis of all experience."[43] In order to perform
this function, language must by nature be value-laden, filled with many
potential meanings. These meanings have been generated by the specific
references and intentions and by the complex of feelings, presuppositions,
and metaphysical commitments that went into the choice of words to form a
proposition. Indeed, surface assertions point to this complex of feelings,
which in turn reveals a fundamental disposition to reality, the ultimate
claim to truth, on which the lure rests.

---

41. Ricoeur, *Interpretation Theory*, 88, 94.
42. Pregeant, *Christology Beyond Dogma*, 40.
43. Ibid., 36.

Language, especially religious language, can function in this way and can communicate with an interpreter in any historical context because "every human being has, by virtue of living in and experiencing the world, some feeling for the reference of religious symbols." All disclosures involve valuing, and that valuing points ultimately to the metaphysical ground of value. Religious language makes explicit the complex of feelings which is implicit in all other modes of speech. It presents "an understanding of and commitment to a particular vision of the ultimate nature of things." Religious language may present itself as literal, but it should not be taken that way. Rather, it should be understood as primal image, analogically functioning as the lure toward feeling. The religious text serves as image, a question, "an invitation to readers to re-examine their lives in the light of the symbol it conveys." The truth the text conveys is not doctrinal or literal but existential. A process interpretation of Matthew 16:15–16 would be framed as follows: "The real import, then, of the question, 'Who do you say that I am?' lies in its function as a concrete way of asking, 'Is that the way life is?' i.e., of asking whether or not one sees that his or her existence is pervaded by the transcendent presence of the radical grace and radical demand the Christ-image conveys."[44]

Process analysis insists that it does not reduce meaning simply to existential meaning, for an existential response implies a conceptual one. (One must conceptualize the image, clarifying the presuppositions which underlie it. The commitment of the intellect as well as the intentionality of the interpreter must be present when one responds to the lure toward the apprehension of reality as a whole.) Process hermeneutics sees interpretation as an ongoing process because, given the imprecise and abstract nature of language, conceptualization can never replace image. There must always be new encounters with the text and new attempts to allow its images to penetrate into the present. A process analysis does not attempt to reduce the word of the New Testament to a "meaning," but rather to expose more clearly the objective witness: "the *experience* of grace, the *act* of trust, the *deed* of mercy."[45]

The Bible does not exercise authority in such a hermeneutical framework by being the source of divine doctrinal and literal truth. Authority is "experienced importance," and since the function of language is to lure the interpreter toward the complex of feeling, it is more important that a proposition be interesting than true. Scripture's authority lies in its directionality, which enables its interpreters to live productively from the past into the present

---

44. Ibid., 40, 38, 165.
45. Ibid., 168.

toward the future. For process hermeneutics, then, "the authority of word and the scripture rests in its continuing capacity to generate motivating visions of possibility as a consequence of our interaction with God and one another."[46]

---

46. Lyman T. Lundeen, "Authority of the Word in Process Perspective," *Encounter* 36 (1975): 300.

5

Paradigms from the Behavioral and Language Sciences

Biblical studies among nonevangelicals continued in a state of upheaval throughout the 1970s as scholars wrestled with new questions that emerged and with old ones that resurged because they had never been fully answered. Yale New Testament scholar Leander Keck observed the disarray and fragmentation of the discipline's received tradition of historical-critical inquiry, and he asserted that nothing short of a complete reintegration of biblical studies into a different configuration could revitalize the discipline.[1]

In chapter 4 we examined in some detail the critiques of the historical-critical method made by Walter Wink and Peter Stuhlmacher and considered various proposals for rehabilitating the method by adding hermeneutical supplements. Suggestions for a more radical restructuring came from scholars who saw possibilities for resuscitating the interpretation process with transfusions obtained from the behavioral sciences (sociology and anthropology) and the language sciences (linguistics, literary criticism, and structuralism).[2]

---

1. Leander E. Keck, "On the Ethos of Early Christians," *Journal of the American Academy of Religion* 42 (1974): 435.

2. See Robert R. Wilson, "Anthropology and the Study of the Old Testament," *USQR* 34 (1979): 175–81; John W. Rogerson, *Anthropology and the Old Testament* (Atlanta: John Knox, 1979); Daniel J. Harrington, "Sociological Concepts and the Early Church: A Decade of Research," *Theological Studies* 41 (1980): 181–90; Robin Scroggs, "The Sociological Interpretation of the New Testament: The Present

Keck followed this activity with interest and saw as serious efforts to reconstitute biblical criticism the rising fascination with the nature of language, with linguistics, and with the many-sided structuralism, as well as the growing desire to reconstruct early Christianity according to "trajectories."[3] By the end of the decade, Paul Achtemeier noted that the major trends appeared to be employment of one or another linguistic paradigm and the use of sociological research. He saw these developments as "signs of life rather than decay."[4]

This reintegration, which amounted to a shift of paradigm, had inevitable consequences for the issue of biblical authority. First, these scholars continued to accept the results of a historical-critical method that relativizes Scripture's content. The new paradigms were being put to use in a post-critical age.

Second, this probing for new paradigms was being carried out in a different academic context. Robert Osborn pointed to the exodus during the 1960s "of many distinguished theologians from the more churchy halls of the seminary to the more objectively academic environs of the university."[5] These theologians included biblical scholars. They gathered students who in turn gathered others, so that more and more biblical studies were being carried out in a secular university environment. Such a setting does not

State of Research," *New Testament Studies* 26 (1980): 164–79; and David L. Bartlett, "Biblical Scholarship Today: A Diversity of New Approaches," *Christian Century* 98 (1981): 1090–94, for general survey and bibliography. James Barr sees sociology and anthropology and the contemporary discussion of their methods as the source of the cultural-relativism perspective (*The Bible in the Modern World* [New York: Harper & Row, 1973], 50). Examples of evangelical work in this area are Derek Tidball, *The Social Context of the New Testament: A Sociological Analysis* (Grand Rapids: Zondervan, 1984), and Edwin M. Yamauchi, "Sociology, Scripture, and the Supernatural," *JETS* 27 (1984): 169–92.

For the area of language sciences, see the following: Anthony C. Thiselton, "Semantics and New Testament Interpretation," in *New Testament Interpretation: Essays on Principles and Methods*, ed. I. Howard Marshall (Grand Rapids: Eerdmans, 1977), 75–104; Norman Perrin, "Eschatology and Hermeneutics: Reflections on Method in the Interpretation of the New Testament," *JBL* 93 (1974): 3–14; David Robertson, *The Old Testament and the Literary Critic* (Philadelphia: Fortress, 1977); Norman R. Petersen, *Literary Criticism for New Testament Critics* (Philadelphia: Fortress, 1978); Amos N. Wilder, *Theopoetic: Theology and the Religious Imagination* (Philadelphia: Fortress, 1976); Northrop Frye, *The Great Code: The Bible and Literature* (New York: Harcourt Brace Jovanovich, 1982); William G. Doty, *Contemporary New Testament Interpretation* (Englewood Cliffs, N.J.: Prentice-Hall, 1972); Alfred M. Johnson, Jr., ed. and trans., *The New Testament and Structuralism* (Pittsburgh: Pickwick, 1976); Daniel Patte and Aline Patte, *Structural Exegesis: From Theory to Practice* (Philadelphia: Fortress, 1978); Daniel Patte, *What Is Structural Exegesis?* (Philadelphia: Fortress, 1976); Robert Detweiler, *Story, Sign, and Self: Phenomenology and Structuralism as Literary Methods* (Philadelphia: Fortress, 1978). An example of evangelical work in the area of the Bible as literature is Leland Ryken, *Reading the Bible as Literature* (Grand Rapids: Zondervan, 1985).

3. Keck, "Ethos of Early Christians," 435. Paul J. Achtemeier and Gene M. Tucker ("Biblical Studies: The State of the Discipline," *Council on the Study of Religion Bulletin* 11 [1980]: 72–76) and Daniel J. Harrington ("Biblical Hermeneutics in Recent Discussion: New Testament," *Religious Studies Review* 10 [1984]: 7–9) have similar estimates.

4. Achtemeier and Tucker, "Biblical Studies," 74.

5. Robert T. Osborn, "The Rise and Fall of the Bible in Recent American Theology," *Duke Divinity School Review* 41 (1976): 60.

provide conditions in which to shape a new view of biblical authority. Scholars in such a situation take their categories for expressing biblical truth and imperatives from the behavioral sciences practiced in a pluralistic society. Brevard Childs warns that "the church cannot long survive in a healthy condition if it continues to play the role of the beggar with cup in hand, waiting for a few drops from the social sciences."[6]

Behavioral Science Models

In the early encounters with behavioral sciences, biblical scholars found much that was congenial and helpful. A study of the social world of ancient Israel and early Christianity provided additional information about the larger ancient social context for Old Testament Judaism and for the early Christian movement.[7] The interpreter could gain new insights through analyses using sociological and anthropological categories.[8] It was possible to gain a better understanding of the oral transmission process.

The Sociology of Knowledge

One particularly interesting tool offered by the behavioral scientists was their sociology of knowledge. The concept rested on scientific examination of the acquisition and comprehension of language and knowledge.[9] The

---

6. Brevard S. Childs, "The Search for Biblical Authority Today," *Andover Newton Quarterly* 16 (1976): 203.

7. Bruce J. Malina, *The New Testament World: Insights from Cultural Anthropology* (Atlanta: John Knox, 1981), 16; Robert R. Wilson, *Genealogy and History in the Biblical World* (New Haven, Conn.: Yale University Press, 1977), 17.

8. Gerhard Theissen, *Sociology of Early Palestinian Christianity* (Philadelphia: Westminster, 1978), 25. Norman Gottwald contends, ["Sociology's] virtue is that it can bring a higher order of inclusiveness, which permits a grasp of otherwise unrelated data." It can set the results of historical study in an entirely new contextual light. Since in historical study, topics, sources, and methods can be substantially changed according to the larger intellectual and social context in which one works, the use of divergent disciplines (sociology and history) on the same material will lead to reciprocal modification through the "incorporation of one another's angles of approach and methods of study" (*The Tribes of Yahweh: A Sociology of the Religion of Liberated Israel, 1250–1050 B.C.* [Maryknoll, N.Y.: Orbis, 1979], 12, 18). Robert R. Wilson is more cautious. In a discussion of the use of comparative anthropological studies in biblical interpretation, he gives these guidelines: The biblical text must be the controlling factor in exegesis. Comparative material must be used only to form a hypothesis that is to be tested against the text. The exegesis of the text will support, disprove, or modify the hypothesis. If exegesis does not provide conclusive evidence, the question must be allowed to remain open for that particular text (*Prophecy and Society in Ancient Israel* [Philadelphia: Fortress, 1980], 16).

9. For a social-construction theory of language acquisition, see Harry C. Stafford, *Culture and Cosmology: Essays on the Birth of a World View* (Washington, D.C.: University Press of America, 1981), 35. Cf. the preformationism/predeterminism theory, which says that there is an innate grammar in every human mind. Dianne E. Papalia and Sandy W. Olds describe this approach in *A Child's World*, 3d ed. (New York: McGraw, 1982), 213–14, citing the work of Noam Chomsky (e.g., *Language and Mind* [New

behavioral scientists maintained that the procedure had been empirically validated by careful analysis, measurement, and evaluation of the ways in which language is acquired, written material is comprehended, and knowledge is attained. Since the method was deeply meshed into a framework of epistemological relativism, this empirical validation lent credibility to that framework.

The sociology-of-knowledge perspective claims that "our conceptions of meaning, value, goals, truth, reality, duties . . . are not 'out there' as external entities. They are products of human creativity in the social order."[10] Each individual has a universe of perception, the norms of which structure one's subjective perceptions of reality into a meaningful, cohesive, and "objective" universe. This universe of perception is our own, colored by our unique personality and experiences, but at the same time is that of our society, "which is largely responsible for giving and maintaining all structures of meaning."[11] The meanings that individuals know and share are derived from their culture's thought-world, which in turn comes from the culture's social matrix.

This perspective has at least four consequences for biblical interpretation. First, with regard to divine revelation, the conclusion is plainly stated by Dennis Nineham: "There can be no possibility of a revelation which transcends culturally conditioned terms altogether and is given in terms which are not peculiar to any one culture but apply equally to all cultures . . . if

---

York: Harcourt Brace Jovanovich, 1968]) and others.

For the "scenario model" of reading comprehension, which supports a "sociology of knowledge" presupposition, see A. J. Sanford and S. C. Garrod, *Understanding Written Language: Explorations of Comprehension Beyond the Sentence* (New York: Wiley, 1981); G. Miller and P. Johnson-Laird, *Language and Perception* (Cambridge, Mass.: Belknap, 1976); and Bruce J. Malina, "The Social Sciences and Biblical Interpretation," *Interpretation* 36 (1982): 230. Sanford and Garrod also point out that there is evidence for the operation of the proposition model, in which the text evokes mental representation in a chain of propositions directly derived from the sentences which constitute the text (*Understanding Written Language*, 210–11). The reader parses and reconnects these propositions mentally and in that way comprehends.

For genetic epistemology, which in developmental psychology supports a sociology of knowledge, see Jean Piaget, *The Origins of Intelligence in Children* (New York: Norton, 1963).

For supporting findings from anthropology and sociology applied to biblical hermeneutics, see Malina, *New Testament World*; and Dennis Nineham, "A Partner for Cinderella?" in *What About the New Testament?* ed. Morna Hooker and Colin Hickling (London: SCM, 1975), 143–54.

10. John G. Gager, *Kingdom and Community: The Social World of Early Christianity* (Englewood Cliffs, N.J.: Prentice-Hall, 1975), 9. Peter L. Berger and Thomas Luckmann are often cited as the authoritative expositors of this perspective (*The Social Construction of Reality: A Treatise in the Sociology of Knowledge* [Garden City, N.Y.: Doubleday, 1967], 210).

11. Richard L. Rohrbaugh, *The Biblical Interpreter: An Agrarian Bible in an Industrial Age* (Philadelphia: Fortress, 1978), 23. Harry Stafford calls these constructs "psycho-social structures of consciousness." For completeness he would have us understand that there are also first-order structures of consciousness, the "psychological space-time" orientation derived from the organic structures of the human body (*Culture and Cosmology*, 3).

there is to be divine communication to men who dwell in history, it will inevitably be historically conditioned."[12]

Such a culturally conditioned nature of Scripture means that we cannot talk of the message of the Bible "as something which can be formulated in set terms and used as an authoritative touchstone of what Christians are, and are not, committed to believing."[13] Nineham goes even further: "I cannot hold . . . or be directly affected by [the ancient beliefs], in the precise form in which [the ancient person] held and . . . [was] affected by them."[14]

Second, a knowledge of the categories of meaning (i.e., of the cultural preunderstanding) with which the text was written and of the social context that spawned it is necessary for understanding an ancient text. But because the preunderstanding and social context form the substance of a shared view of reality, they are assumed more often than they are expressed in the text. This makes New Testament content fragmentary and contradictory in nature, and Nineham considers it unlikely that an interpreter could unearth from Scripture a full and coherent set of first-century Christian beliefs and values, the lodestone for a sociology of knowledge.[15]

Third, the contemporary social context is constantly changing; therefore, the meaning the interpreter is able to assign to the text will also change. Interpretation always takes place in terms of one's contemporary context.[16]

Some sociologists of religion modify this thoroughgoing relativity in interpretation. They contend that biblical content and religious symbols uncovered through scientifically informed study can be preserved and used in the contemporary context, though not in a way exactly identical to the ancient context. An accurate scientific understanding of the social and material conditions of today is the seedbed from which valid religious symbols may grow. In this view, validation of the truth of religious symbols becomes "a judgment on the promise of . . . particular religious symbols to further

12. Dennis E. Nineham, *The Use and Abuse of the Bible: A Study of the Bible in an Age of Rapid Cultural Change* (New York: Barnes & Noble, 1976), 12.

13. Nineham, "Partner for Cinderella," 150. Stafford agrees and points to an "ontological fallacy" in Western thinking, born of a weakness in the structure of Indo-European languages, which leads to the erroneous assumption that knowledge of words brings knowledge of things. Such thinking is the basis of "any system such as religious orthodoxy which asserts some 'absolute truth'" (*Culture and Cosmology*, 52). But words by their very nature have a mediatory and abstracting function and cannot express absolutes.

14. Nineham, *Use and Abuse*, 28. Gottwald agrees. To reaffirm the validity of Israel's religious symbols today is to do so in social and intellectual conditions that fundamentally alter the locus and import of early affirmations. They were socially progressive at their origin. Today they are reactionary. "To purport to believe the same things in different social and intellectual conditions is in fact not to believe the same things at all" (*Tribes of Yahweh*, 704).

15. Dennis E. Nineham, "The Strangeness of the New Testament, I," *Theology* 85 (1982): 173.

16. Rohrbaugh, *Biblical Interpreter*, 104. George S. Worgul describes an anthropological model for culture change: culture is spawned from conflict and exists with a dialectic of transformation ("Anthropological Consciousness and Biblical Theology," *Biblical Theology Bulletin* 9 [1979]: 5).

the evolution of social relations in a productive way for the maximum number of people."[17]

Fourth, there is today no unified world-view, no commonly accepted preunderstanding which both the writers of the ancient text and the modern interpreter embrace.[18] It is impossible, therefore, to identify the meaning enunciated in one's interpretation with the meaning of the text. To do so is to transfer "whatever normative quality we assume for the text to our interpretation of it."[19]

Hermeneutical Bridges

While sociology of knowledge maintains the gap between ancient text and modern context, other aspects of sociology and anthropology can provide hermeneutical bridges. Keck sees the sociological study of the relation of ancient text and context as yielding a pattern of interaction which is repeatable today. The pattern recurs when the Bible serves as a critic. The Bible not only grew out of an ethos, or social context, but its gospel critiqued that ethos. When those scriptural books were canonized, the church subjected itself in perpetuity to self-criticism. So the interpretational task is not to restate ideas but to reactualize the dialectical relationship between the text and the church. When the text's relationship to its original social context is understood in this fashion, Scripture is liberated so that it may confront today's church as critically as it confronted the early church.[20]

Theoretical models of social and cultural dynamics from the behavioral sciences offer possibilities for hermeneutical bridging. Structural functionalism, conflict theory, or symbolic model purports to set forth those "time- and culture-invariant principles [which] govern human conduct and association . . . there are patterns of action, associations of, or systems of, variables that also are inherent in human conduct and social interaction."[21] These provide a form of external control for analyzing the literary products of any culture.[22] They also provide the means for understanding a culture other than our own.[23] Analysis according to these models can be combined

---

17. Gottwald, *Tribes of Yahweh*, 706.

18. Nineham, *Use and Abuse*, 30.

19. Rohrbaugh, *Biblical Interpreter*, 105. Nineham contends that when Christians saw a given interpretation as the *meaning*, without realizing it they were simply making absolute what was relative. The absolutist presuppositions of Christian readers have been the presuppositions not so much of the biblical writers themselves as of the cultural situation of those who have interpreted the Bible in whatever periods—patristic, medieval, or Reformation (*Use and Abuse*, 37).

20. Keck, "Ethos of Early Christians," 450–51.

21. Brian W. Kovacs, "Philosophical Issues in Sociological Structuralism: A Bridge from Social Sciences to Hermeneutics," *USQR* 34 (1979): 155; Theissen, *Sociology*, 1ff.

22. Gager, *Kingdom and Community*, 3.

23. Malina, *New Testament World*, 18.

with an awareness that we can change social roles and empathetically perceive someone else's horizon and standpoint. That awareness includes consciousness of the actual differences and potential similarities between ourselves and others.

This combination of analysis and awareness offers the possibility of understanding biblical culture. The models that explain human social behavior, then, become the bridge for understanding a text from an ancient culture.

Language Science Models

Linguistics

Until the appearance in 1961 of James Barr's *Semantics of Biblical Language*, biblical studies evidenced little impact from modern linguistic theory.[24] Indeed, it is only in the decade of the seventies that the fruits of this discipline became available to scholars working in biblical studies. In order to understand the impact, we must consider the major trends in language theory and theory of meaning.

Louis G. Kelly, translation-practice historian at the University of Ottawa, identifies two basic streams of language theory in the twentieth-century West.[25] One is the *instrumental* approach, which sees language as a tool for communicating a message; this approach provides a foundation for the modern field of semantics, whose study is meaning and its communication.[26] The other is the *logos* approach, which sees language as a creative entity.

Within the instrumental approach Kelly finds two distinct theories of meaning. First is a traditional sign theory, stemming from Aristotle and Augustine, which locates meaning in language in two basic elements: the *sign*, or word, and the *signified*, a mental construct derived from a perception of reality. This perception involves both *referent*, what the sign is talking about, and *sense*, what the word is saying about it (see figs. 1–4).[27] There is

---

24. Thiselton, "Semantics," 75. Arthur Gibson has sought to carry on Barr's work (*Biblical Semantic Logic: A Preliminary Analysis* [New York: St. Martin's, 1981]).

25. Louis G. Kelly, *The True Interpreter: A History of Translation Theory and Practice in the West* (New York: St. Martin's, 1979), 2.

26. John Lyons comments, "Indeed, it is difficult to imagine any satisfactory definition of the term 'language' that did not incorporate some reference to the notion of communication" (*Semantics*, 2 vols. [Cambridge: Cambridge University Press, 1977], 1:32).

27. Ibid., 1:96. According to Eugene Nida, this semantic model is regarded at the present time as quite old-fashioned: "The semiotic model of Charles Peirce is a much more sophisticated and relevant model for thinking creatively about the social context of communication" (letter to author, 15 January 1987). The traditional model, however, is still accorded respect. Lyons uses it. William Callaghan in an essay on Peirce refers to it as a "celebrated model." One main difference between the basic semantic

Figure 1
A Basic Semantic Model

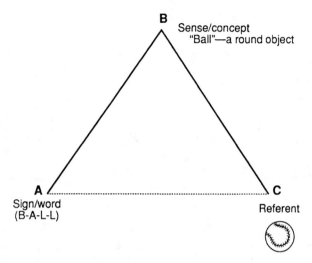

also a positivistic theory based on observation of behavior. According to Kelly, such theories reject traditional dualism and relate their object of meaning to three readily analyzable characteristics of language:

> relevance in the social situation in which the utterance is produced; role of the utterance within a unit of psychological behavior; and relationships of linguistic units to context. The philosophical background . . . is a fragmented one: in England, the primary source was Wittgenstein's ". . . the meaning of a word is its use in the language" (*Philosophical Investigations* 1.43); and in America, the behaviorist movement in psychology, which attempted to reduce all human actions to bodily processes [see fig. 4].[28]

Despite Kelly's neat characterization, modern linguistics has become very complex, exhibiting many schools of thought with regard to meaning; British linguist John Lyons identifies at least five (see fig. 4, which lists four of them).[29]

---

model (fig. 1) and that of Peirce is that Peirce conceives of the sense/concept portion of the triangle (point *B*) not as a single meaning but as a threefold meaning or interpretant: emotional, energetic, and logical (William J. Callaghan, "Charles Sanders Peirce: His General Theory of Signs—Review Article," *Semiotica* 61 [1986]: 136).

28. Kelly, *True Interpreter*, 10.

29. Lyons, *Semantics* 1:109–14, 120–38, 230–38, 245–50; 2:607–13.

Figure 2
Semantic Taxonomy: *Basic Elements*

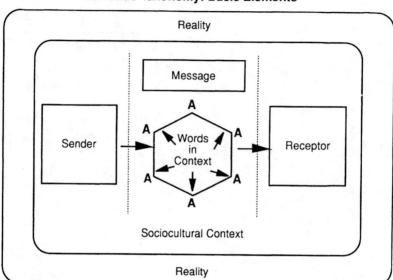

Key:
A – sign/word

Lyons terms the traditional sign theory "conceptualism" and has nothing but criticism for that approach. The structuralism that developed under the influence of Ferdinand de Saussure (1857–1913) is, according to Kelly, a type of the traditional sign theory of meaning. Yet, since it emphasizes the role of linguistic context as a determiner and, in some sense, a source of meaning, Kelly also seems to include this approach under the positivistic theories.[30] The behaviorist, functionalist, and contextualist theories could all be classified as positivistic. Linguists who do not consider themselves positivists will, while seeing the limitations of each approach, use valuable insights from them for constructing a more comprehensive theory of meaning and its communication.

A few things are certain in the current state of the discussion concerning theories of meaning in the field of semantics. Since "there are many different kinds or aspects of meaning that must be taken into account in the description of language-behavior . . . no single gloss or definition can be expected to capture all of these" (see figs. 2–4).[31] Further, any present theory of meaning is incomplete, since it can be criticized. It cannot explain

---

30. See also Thiselton, "Semantics," 81.
31. Lyons, *Semantics* 1:79–80.

Figure 3
Semantic Taxonomy: *The Process*

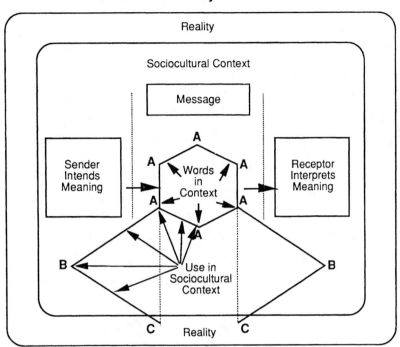

Key:
A – sign/word   B – sense/concept   C – referent (extralinguistic entity referred to)

all elements in the semantic process. This judgment also applies to the linguistic relativist approach.[32] The linguist and translator should take a selective approach, not opportunistically eclectic, but one that recognizes the complexity of the phenomena involved. As Jan de Waard and Eugene Nida observe, "Like metaphors, scientific theories are perspectives which provide important insights on certain aspects of complex relations. Accordingly, a translator should take full advantage of the significant contributions which have been made by scholars employing quite different theories about interlingual communication."[33]

Because of the fluid nature of the current discussion of the theory of meaning, it is wise to characterize semantics as a discipline whose theories of meaning and approaches to translation exist on a continuum (see fig. 4).[34]

32. Ibid., 246–47.

33. Jan de Waard and Eugene A. Nida, *From One Language to Another: Functional Equivalence in Bible Translating* (Nashville: Nelson, 1986), 185.

34. Ibid., 182–85.

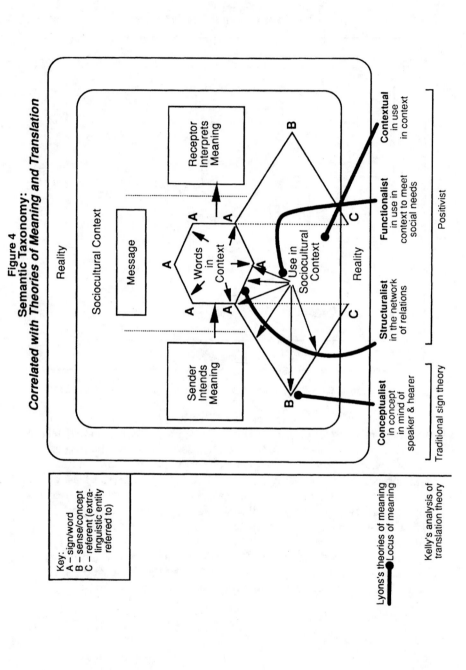

Figure 4
Semantic Taxonomy:
Correlated with Theories of Meaning and Translation

Key:
A – sign/word
B – sense/concept
C – referent (extra-
    linguistic entity
    referred to)

Reality

Sociocultural Context

Message

Receptor
Interprets
Meaning

Sender
Intends
Meaning

Words
in
Context

Use in
Sociocultural
Context

Reality

Conceptualist
in concept
in mind of
speaker & hearer

Structuralist
in the network
of relations

Functionalist
in use in
context to meet
social needs

Contextual
in use
in context

Traditional sign theory

Positivist

Lyons's theories of meaning
Locus of meaning

Kelly's analysis of
translation theory

At one end is a concern with the words of the text, the traditional sign theory of meaning. At the other end is an all-embracing approach which also includes the sociocultural context of the receptor or interpreter. In between fall concerns for the grammatical-literary context of the text and for the linguistic context of the receptor's language. Approaches to meaning are differentiated by their starting points on the continuum and by the relative value they give to various aspects of the process. It is possible to correlate approaches to meaning and approaches to translation (see fig. 4). Semantics has moved beyond thoroughgoing epistemological relativism; in the current state of inconclusiveness with regard to a theory of meaning, it finds itself operating in a climate of moderate epistemological relativism.[35] All these concepts and conclusions have implications for interpretation and particularly translation.

Linguistic theory, particularly semantics and translation theory, has been appropriated for the interpretation process in a number of ways. In 1972, J. F. A. Sawyer's *Semantics in Biblical Research: New Methods of Defining Hebrew Words for Salvation* directly applied linguistic theory to Old Testament word study. He concludes his study with the general semantic principle that "adequate definition of context must precede every semantic statement."[36] This step is necessary because semantic definition (i.e., meaning) is always supplied by context. Contextualization is the choosing of a situation in terms of which to understand the word. For Sawyer, the original context of the writer is not necessary to identify meaning. Any context will serve—for example, that of the modern worshiper, religious teacher, or preacher. Any context will allow the term to yield meaning because context is what supplies the meaning.

Also in 1972, Eugene Nida of the American Bible Society published a key article in the *Journal of Biblical Literature*, "Implications of Contemporary Linguistics for Biblical Scholarship."[37] Nida showed his agreement with the sociology-of-knowledge approach to epistemology by using the term "shared knowledge" in communication theory. One principle in communication theory is that knowledge necessary for understanding is omitted in matters shared within a culture. Such knowledge is nonspecified in a text but must often be brought out in a translation. This is why good translations are often 50 percent longer than the original text.

Nida also pointed out that the most effective way to understand meaning is to view a text or utterance on two levels. The surface structure is made up of words in their formal grammatical-literary relationships, the kernel of

---

35. Lyons, *Semantics* 1:245ff.

36. John F. A. Sawyer, *Semantics in Biblical Research: New Methods of Defining Hebrew Words for Salvation*, Studies in Biblical Theology, 2d ser., 24 (London: SCM, 1972), 112.

37. Eugene A. Nida, "Implications of Contemporary Linguistics for Biblical Scholarship," *JBL* 91 (1972): 73–89.

which contains the message. The work of translation must move from an analysis of surface structure to a study of the deep structure of the text in the original language. Then it must translate the dynamics of this deep structure into a surface structure in the receptor language.

If one has faithfully translated the text, the translation will evoke the same response in the receptor-language audience that it did in the original-language audience. This is the dynamic-equivalence approach to translation. But once response becomes the key for testing translation, we are no longer focusing on the text's meaning. In fact, we can never answer with certainty whether the same meaning is being communicated by both the original and the translation. Indeed, the surface structure/deep structure approach to meaning would affirm that it is impossible for "the average reader of a translation . . . [to] understand precisely what the original receptors understood."[38]

Linguistic theory has contributed to hermeneutical bridging. For example, the Old Testament as a religious text is, as Sawyer saw, "peculiarly fitted for contextualization in . . . almost [an] infinite number of situations" because its important vocabulary comprises words with exclusively religious application. Religious texts tend to minimize ambiguity, meaninglessness, and irrelevance, offering the possibility of continuous contextualization which bridges the gap between ancient and modern context.[39]

The concept of the deep structure of language offers rich possibilities. Nida identifies four principal semantic categories here, and they apply to any language: objects, events, abstracts (qualities or quantities of objects and events), and relations. He asserts that these universal features are increasingly "recognized by those working with the semantic structures of language."[40] If this deep structure is indeed a universal grammar in which all languages participate, then it can serve as a bridge between not only contemporaneous languages, but languages that are historically distant.

---

38. Ibid., 89. Kenneth Pike also admits category slippage in translation between languages. Yet he maintains that the loss is not such that the truth of the message is lost. "Human language is a sufficient vehicle for carrying communication from God in propositional form" ("The Linguist and Axioms Concerning the Language of Scripture," *Journal of the American Scientific Affiliation* 26 [1974]: 48).

In the mid-seventies two other articles appropriating linguistic theory for biblical studies appeared. Charles R. Taber covered much the same ground as Nida but with more illustrative material (*IDB Sup*, s.v. "Semantics"). Anthony Thiselton wrote an appreciative background essay but cautioned that when working through the transformational analysis process (from surface structure to deep structure and back to surface structure), one must make sure that what one judges is implicit and should now be made explicit is really there in the first place ("Semantics," 75–104).

39. Sawyer, *Semantics*, 113.

40. Nida, "Implications," 77. Sawyer speaks of semantic universals which operate in Old Testament Hebrew as much as in any other language (*Semantics*, 114).

Literary Criticism

A number of biblical scholars have found in literary criticism an inter-pretational tool to overcome the problem of historical distance in the histor-ical-critical method, which they term captivity to the genetic fallacy.[41] Literary critics are quick to acknowledge the Bible as an appropriate object for literary analysis. Northrop Frye, for example, characterizes Scripture as "oratorical, a combination of the poetically figured and the concerned, of imaginative and existential appeal."[42]

Norman Petersen and Hans Frei are convinced that the historical-critical method suffers from a common fallacy that is uncovered by literary analy-sis—the genetic fallacy. Its basic assumption is that the meaning of a text is explained by the background factors that gave rise to it in the original historical setting. Such an approach leads inevitably to misunderstanding, which further obscures the text's meaning. "The history-likeness or literal meaning of biblical narrative has been confused with its 'ostensive' refer-ence to actual historical events . . . the narrative shape and meaning of biblical texts have been eclipsed by the significance attributed to the events."[43]

Literary criticism seeks to offset the displacement of the effect (text) by the cause (historical background) and to overcome the eclipse of a narrative's meaning by the significance attributed to the events about which it speaks. Literary criticism does so by approaching classic works in general, and the Bible in particular, as literature—that is, as works that are an imitation of reality.

Everything in a piece of literature is essentially metaphoric and creates an alternative reality analogous to, but not identical with, the everyday world. A piece of literature, then, can be treated as a self-contained, self-regulated, self-referential system of metaphoric expressions. Its meaning may be un-derstood in terms of the functional relations of parts to one another and to the whole. A piece of literature is the product of imagination, which in-volves the construction of imaginative universes that contain within them-selves the rules and procedures by which they are interpreted.[44]

As for hermeneutical bridges, when one analyzes biblical language as metaphor or symbol, one discovers its ability to cross the gap between the ancient and modern contexts in two ways. First, as symbol in general, it "is

---

41. Petersen, *Literary Criticism*, 18ff.; Hans W. Frei, *The Eclipse of Biblical Narrative: A Study in Eighteenth and Nineteenth Century Hermeneutics* (New Haven, Conn.: Yale University Press, 1974).

42. Frye, *Great Code*, 216.

43. Petersen, *Literary Criticism*, 20. See also Frei, *Eclipse of Biblical Narrative*, 1–16.

44. Robertson, *Old Testament and the Literary Critic*, 5–8. Petersen (*Literary Criticism*, 33–48) gives a very helpful description of Roman Jakobson's modified communications model, a useful paradigm for such analysis.

a relatively stable repeatable element of perceptual experience, standing for some larger meaning or set of meanings which cannot be given, or not fully given, in perceptual experience itself."[45] Second, and more important than the familiarity of a symbol in human experience, is its power to point to a plurality of meanings. This quality frees the symbol to operate in an infinite number of contexts and to have meaning in each one.[46]

As metaphor, biblical language conjoins "two disparate entities in such a way that a third entity comes into linguistic expression." In addition, multiplicity of meanings, this time identified as "significations," can be apprehended. The interpretational process involves restoring plurality and richness of signification to biblical language comprehended as metaphor. William Doty distinguishes this literary interpretation from understanding biblical language as theology. The Bible "gestures in the direction of its meaning, but does not permit a 'literal' description of [it]."[47]

Northrop Frye calls imaginative literature "polysemous." Language expressed in metaphor has the power to expand beyond its original context and engage in a dialectic with new contexts of the interpreter's experience in a series of phases and stages of comprehension, thereby generating multiple meanings. It is not that the interpreter uncovers different senses; rather, the interpreter becomes aware of "different intensities or wider contexts of a continuous sense, unfolding like a plant out of a seed."[48]

As metaphor, biblical language also has the evocative force to bring to expression the appropriate signification in any given context. It teases the mind into ever-new perceptions of meaning. It spurs on Christian creativity, so that new worlds open themselves for participation not by coercion but by the virility of creative love.[49] In these two ways, then, biblical language understood as metaphor can have meaning in the contemporary context.

---

45. Perrin, "Eschatology and Hermeneutics," 10. In *Theopoetic*, Wilder contends that human nature and society are motivated more deeply by images and fabulations than by ideas. He urges that effective theology in any age must be creative and imaginative theology (p. 2). It should always be redefining itself "in relation to the dominant myths, dreams, images of the age, that is, with the contemporary quest-patterns of a changing world" (p. 25). It is not simply a matter of communication, but of effective authority. Only when theology comes to terms with the ruling metaphors and idioms of the age can it awaken "a deep resonance in the hearts of men" (p. 27). He mentions Paul as an example of one who "took hold of the readers at this deep level, through all the potent layers of the self, especially the unconscious and the prerational" (p. 26).

46. Jay G. Williams comments that Scripture does not have one recoverable meaning but many, which enables it to speak diversely to many different generations ("Exegesis-Eisegesis: Is There a Difference?" *TT* 30 [1973]: 220).

47. Doty, *Contemporary New Testament Interpretation*, 112, 150.

48. Frye, *Great Code*, 221.

49. Perrin, "Eschatology and Hermeneutics," 10. See Robert P. Carroll, "The Sisyphean Task of Biblical Transformation," *SJT* 30 (1977): 512. He describes metaphor as a linguistic process in which a shift takes place in the use of words, and aspects of one word are carried over to another word. The result is that we are allowed to escape the limited horizons of reality and our imaginations are allowed to work. See also Frye, *Great Code*, 218.

Literary genre can create its own bridge between text and context. The interpreter identifies a piece of literature as an example of a particular genre. When the text is studied according to its unitary structure and the rules of that genre, it yields a comprehensive meaning. This is what Northrop Frye is getting at when he describes the Bible as "a gigantic myth, a narrative extending over the whole of time from creation to apocalypse, unified by a body of recurring imagery that freezes into a single metaphor cluster, the metaphors all being identified with the body of the Messiah, the man who is all men, the totality of *logoi* who is one Logos, the grain of sand that is the world."[50] A text studied this deeply can be compared and contrasted with texts of a similar genre regardless of their space-time relationship.

"Without question, one of the handsome dividends of literary study of the Bible is the meaningful connections that can be made between biblical texts and texts that have little or no connection in space and time with biblical culture,"[51] says David Robertson, who gives as example comparison of the Psalms with Vedic literature, which would find a receptive audience because of current interest in Eastern religion. In this way too the hermeneutical gap is crossed.

Literature as imitation of reality has a meaning which may be understood only in reference to the fictional universe the text has created. There are no referents in reality to which a piece of literature directly points. The literary critic can affirm the same thing of Scripture, even though there is a recognition that the Bible does in some sense indirectly point to reality.[52] The measure for the truth of a text is its "fit." Is it appropriate within the world created by the work?

Can the study of the Bible as literature offer a way of crossing the hermeneutical bridge? The literary critic would say yes, given the function of imaginative literature in the life of humanity. As an imitation of reality and as nonutilitarian, "the corpus of world literature can be viewed as authored by the human race as a means of practicing how to live, of finding what will suffice to make our lives meaningful and valuable."[53] Frye affirms that the study of imaginative literature enables us to make contact with the level of vision that is beyond faith, a level that pushes human beings to the limit not just of the actual, but of the conceivable. To study the Bible as a product of imaginative play is to arrive at its contemporary relevance.

Robertson, however, argues that literary analysis of Scripture places a limit on its power. When the interpreter reads the Bible as literature, not as

---

50. Frye, *Great Code*, 224.

51. Robertson, *Old Testament and the Literary Critic*, 10.

52. Frye, *Great Code*, 228. This is why Martin and Mary Hull Mohr ("Interpreting the Text and Telling the Story," *Dialogue* 21 [1982]: 102–6) and others prefer to call the biblical narrative "story" rather than "history."

53. Robertson, *Old Testament and the Literary Critic*, 15.

Scripture, the Bible has a power finite not infinite, "power to aid rather than to save. It joins the likes of Homer's epics and Shakespeare's plays in literature's grand symphony of imaginative speech that offers temporary order, insight, and peace."[54]

An important contribution of literary criticism to the hermeneutical task has been the proposal of an interpretational paradigm based on the semantic autonomy of the text. A text's meaning may be understood independent of reference to anything outside itself. One may try to relate the text to other texts and to the extrinsic world of knowledge, but this is preliminary or subsequent to identifying the sense of the text in terms of itself and the imaginative universe which it projects.[55] For the literary critic, "the meaning of a work of art is not exhausted by, or even equivalent to, its intention [understood as a cause]. As a system of values, it leads an independent life [i.e., it constitutes a 'world' separate from the real world in which it was produced]. The total meaning of a work of art cannot be defined merely in terms of its meaning for the author and his contemporaries."[56]

The semantic autonomy of the text is maintained as a reality because of two logical fallacies that become evident when we seek to tie the meaning to something or someone external to the text. The *intentional fallacy* (a variety of the genetic fallacy) explains the meaning of an effect (the text) in terms of its cause (what the writer intended to say). Literary critics point out that the meaning of the text may be wholly different from what the original writer intended. The writer may not have succeeded in what he or she hoped to accomplish. Ambiguities and false meanings may have been introduced, or the discourse may have been fraught with many more implications than the author was aware of.

The *referential fallacy* construes the sign as referring directly to the real-world object without regard for the "signified."[57] Petersen illustrates with a communications model in which a sign consists of the physical signifier, the letters that make up a word (e.g., *c-a-t*), and the conceptual signified, *cat*, which must be distinguished from a real, live cat. A signifier, or word,

---

54. Ibid.

55. Petersen, *Literary Criticism*, 29ff.; Frye, *Great Code*, 229.

56. René Wellek and Austin Warren, *Theory of Literature*, rev. ed. (New York: Harcourt, Brace & World, 1956), 42, as cited in Petersen with bracketed comments. Petersen also notes Murray Krieger's picture of semantic autonomy. The text is like "an enclosed set of endlessly faceted mirrors ever multiplying its maze of reflections but finally shut up within itself" (*Literary Criticism*, 28).

Discourse analysis follows this approach in a modified way. It involves studying the text itself to construe the meaning that can be arrived at "by competent judges with sufficiently extensive knowledge of the linguistic context, discourse context, and the situation context shared by the speaker and his intended audience" (Vern S. Poythress, "Analyzing a Biblical Text: Some Important Linguistic Distinctions," *SJT* 32 [1979]: 126; see also Peter R. Jones, "Biblical Hermeneutics," *Review and Expositor* 22 [1975]: 147).

57. Petersen, *Literary Criticism*, 39. See also Umberto Eco, *A Theory of Semiotics* (Bloomington: Indiana University Press, 1976), 58–66.

might be referring to a metaphoric entity not existing in the real world. The referential fallacy misses such a possibility by always identifying the word directly with an object in the real world. But literature is an imitation of reality, and such a serious misunderstanding of the nature of referents can only confuse interpretation.

Structuralism

Structuralism climaxes the nonevangelical wrestling with behavioral and linguistic concepts during this period. The basic insights of the new hermeneutic and of literary criticism that language has power to evoke meaning are accepted. The interpreters move beyond these insights to appropriate methodology from anthropology and linguistics to study the structure of language and how meaning is produced.

Structuralism is an exegetical method which focuses on that part of the dialectic between humanity and language where the person receives significations, or meanings, imposed by language and text. The method contends that there are a number of structural levels that interact to create a meaningful effect. Daniel Patte, a New Testament scholar at Vanderbilt, labels the first two levels as structures of enunciation and cultural structures,[58] which may be studied with traditional exegetical methods. The third level is the deep structure, which contains frames of meaning that characterize "man *qua* man." Since these are universal, they provide the basis for a hermeneutical bridge.[59]

From the terminology used, it is evident that the constructs of modern linguistics have been appropriated. A linguistic process of decoding to uncover the deep structure is followed. The text is viewed synchronically and is studied in isolation from the original writer's intention.[60] According to the structuralist, uncovering the deep structure of a text leads to some measure of clarity as one understands the meaning of the text in its own terms through comprehending the various relationships of its constituent elements.

But structuralists acknowledge that the process can lead to uncertainty. One source of uncertainty is that the code or categories for understanding the text are imposed by the interpreter's culture. The interpreter uses this code in reading and deciphering the text. So the decoding is actually a recoding of the text in the interpreter's cultural code. This cannot be

---

58. Patte, *What Is Structural Exegesis?* 25. For Patte, *structure of enunciation* is "the constraints brought about by the author as an individual or as a group, and his situation in life."

59. Ibid., 34. Patte observes that we presuppose these same structures in our own discourses.

60. Ibid., 15. In *Meaning in Texts: The Historical Shaping of a Narrative Hermeneutics* (Philadelphia: Fortress, 1978), Edgar V. McKnight contends that "the intention of a text can never be completely defined as the identification of its elements with factors in the real world" (p. 274).

avoided, since the categories of one's own cultural code are the only ones available by which to understand the text. So the handing on of a text from one cultural context to another happens in endless permutation, where every decoding is a recoding.[61]

The only way the interpreter can hope to arrive at a valid meaning is to aim at identifying in the deep structure (1) the correlation of various elements of meaning, (2) the relations of these elements to the whole, and (3) the rules for reading them. The structuralist must establish the understanding of the text on the basis of those correlations, relations, and rules.

But all this care does not provide final certainty about the one valid meaning of the text. Because of the very nature of language, interpretation involves an infinite dialectical movement between the surface structure and the deep structure. The relation of the surface structure to any given reading (interpretation) of the text adds meaning to the text—infinitely. So the text becomes "denser" from all its readings and obtains meaning endlessly. This infinite dialectic creates the uncertainty. The text has no one fixed, definite meaning.

How does interpretation take place in such a situation? Structural study of a text uncovers in its deep semantic structure a presupposed semantic universe—a set of convictions which the text accepts as self-evident truths. The interpreter is also aware that one's own culture has a semantic universe. The interpretation of a text can take place when an interrelationship of the text's universe and the semantic one of the interpreter is established, or when an extension of some portion of the text's semantic universe occurs in the interpreter's new interpretational discourse related to the text.

Interpretation is also affected by whether the text is sacred or profane. A sacred text is one in which, after analysis, the primary narrative level presupposes values more fundamental than those presented on the writer's interpretive level. The Gospel of Matthew is proposed by Patte as an example of a sacred text.[62] In a profane text, the opposite is true. For example, the Gospel of Mark on the narrative level can be considered a profane text, for it speaks of relations between elements in human society. On the interpretive level, however, it is more fundamental and treats of values placing God opposite humankind.

When a narrative is a sacred text, the hermeneutical discourse, which extends the text's semantic universe, accepts that semantic universe as its own and absolutizes its values. The text is accepted as a complete, final revelation, and the hermeneutical discourse simply "proposes a new series of mediated oppositions . . . that prolongs the demonstration of the validity

---

61. Louis Marin, "A Conclusion," in *The New Testament and Structuralism*, ed. Alfred M. Johnson, Jr. (Pittsburgh: Pickwick, 1976), 236.

62. Patte and Patte, *Structural Exegesis*, 104.

of the semantic universe of the text in the hermeneut's discourse (and life)."[63] In the end, a hermeneutic exercised on a sacred text identifies the interpreter's story with the text in such a way that the interpreter's story is only a variant of the text's story.

The hermeneutic of a sacred text involves two steps. First, the retelling of the story in various forms according to the type of experiences and situations brought to the text by the interpreter. Then there is the expression of a new discourse which, while presupposing the revelation of fundamental values, manifests their implications for various aspects of human experience.

When the narrative is a profane text, it "is interpreted in such a way that it demonstrates the validity of the system of values of the hermeneutical discourse which prolongs it."[64] The interpreter's semantic universe takes precedence, and the text is used to justify it. Admittedly one begins with the text as "canon," a respect for the text's semantic universe. But the interpreter who projects the text onto the contemporary story reads the text as containing the types and promises that provide a key to understanding contemporary events. Events in the interpreter's current experience are then viewed as acts of God. For example, by such a hermeneutic apocalyptists of early Judaism discovered "the fundamental values that gave meaning and authenticity to their lives *in the events of their contemporary history* and not in the biblical text or in the biblical events."[65]

Hermeneutics on profane texts is practiced by retelling or reinterpreting the interpreter's present story or history in terms of the categories of the biblical text. The interpreter discovers fundamental values in surrounding events—new revelation—portions of the current semantic universe through which one can discover one's true identity as chosen for a specific vocation.[66] A second step involves simply living life and carrying out one's vocation on the basis of these fundamental values. The biblical text offers various models to follow, but the interpreter is not bound to follow them when Scripture is treated as a profane text. The interpreter's duty in this case is to satisfy the demands of the new election or vocation.[67]

---

63. Ibid., 97.

64. Ibid. This approach may also be used on sacred texts, which then are no longer viewed as having the character of absolute revelation.

65. Ibid., 106.

66. Such a discovery of true identity does not involve the same process or yield exactly the same result as does existentialist interpretation. François Bovon points out that the structuralist method maintains the proper distance between text and interpreter, whereas Bultmannian existentialism does not ("French Structuralism and Biblical Exegesis," in Roland Barthes et al., *Structural Analysis and Biblical Exegesis: Interpretational Essays*, Pittsburgh Theological Monograph Series 3 [Pittsburgh: Pickwick, 1974], 7). E. V. McKnight observes that the existentialist approach is too limited and limiting, since it defines meanings in only one important area: concern about the meaning of human existence. Structuralism sets no limits, so that no area of human concern is left out (*Meaning*, 275).

67. Patte and Patte offer Jesus in his freedom from the Mosaic law as an example of practicing such a hermeneutic (*Structural Exegesis*, 127 n. 14).

There are dangers here for the integrity of the hermeneutical process, and Patte recognizes them. The fundamental values expressed in the hermeneutical discourse belong to the interpreter's semantic universe, not to the biblical text. This means that the interpreter can easily betray the text, no longer respecting the integrity of its semantic universe. The way would then be open for an unbridled subjective interpretation. The structuralist counters that since the hermeneutic is grounded in structural exegesis which seeks to uncover the semantic universe in the text's deep structure, this exegetical method is itself the means for verifying the legitimacy of the hermeneutic, the extension of the text's semantic universe into a new discourse.[68] It should also be noted that structuralists see real strength in working from the interpreter's hermeneutical discourse and semantic universe to the text, recognizing here a process for hermeneutical bridge-building. Edgar V. McKnight describes its essence:

> The text presents and invites reactions to and attitudes toward the real world of the reader, which may include versions of the world of Jesus, the tradition, and the church, and it is these reactions and attitudes that constitute the meaning and reality of the text for the reader. . . . The text as a "performance utterance" causes the reader to create meaning for himself which is as compelling as the meaning which inspired the author.[69]

Another danger in the hermeneutic of a profane text is that it opens itself to the uncertainties of a multiplicity of interpretations, something Patte describes as "a constant change in fundamental values attuned to the rhythm of the ever-changing experiences 'retold' in the hermeneutical discourses."[70] Here again, this uncertainty and multiplicity is regarded by structuralists as strength, not weakness. For them it means the text in all its semantic potentialities remains ever open, ever alive for the appropriation of meaning by the person bringing personal experience to it. Advocates of literary criticism and of structuralism insist that a text maintains its relevance across historical contexts (i.e., it stays alive and relevant) by continuing to produce or obtain new meaning.

---

68. Ibid., 107. Marin insists that structuralism, though it may have an infinite number of correlations of elements and structures, depending on the interpreter, should not be confused with subjectivity or cultural relativism ("Conclusion," 236).

69. McKnight, *Meaning*, 274–75.

70. Patte and Patte, *Structural Exegesis*, 107.

Part 3

Hermeneutics and Culture

The Evangelical Perspective

6

Hermeneutical Presuppositions and Interpretational Method

The rumblings of debate and theorizing that vibrated through the scholarly world of biblical criticism had a sharp impact on evangelicals, whose scholarship was no less profound but was pursued in a more cautious way. They were not willing to open the hermeneutical door to unchecked winds of change; they sensed the danger that everything they valued would be swept away before they could take stock or count the cost.

However, evangelicals unavoidably addressed the question of hermeneutics and culture with increasing urgency during the decade of the seventies. Basic texts in biblical hermeneutics from this period all deal with the cultural factor in understanding and applying the Bible. During this decade evangelicals interacted vigorously with the contemporary hermeneutical discussion, questioning the presuppositions of radical and moderate relativist approaches, and probing into the basic issues raised by the deliberations. The roles of the interpreter's preunderstanding and of the original writer's intent in the hermeneutical process were carefully considered, particularly in their implications for the evangelical view of Scripture as inerrant verbal propositional revelation.

Some evangelicals adopted the basic constructs of the contemporary approach to hermeneutics, despite the relativizing consequences for Scripture's content. Those thinkers who were convinced that biblical language is in essence culture-bound were faced with the problem of denying or redefining inerrancy, while at the same time continuing to affirm Scripture's inspiration and authority.[1] Throughout the hermeneutical discussions, evangelicals offered suggestions for spanning the hermeneutical gap, proposing as vital links between the culture of the message and that of the hearer the nature of God, humankind, language, and Scripture.

Hermeneutical Presuppositions

In their critique of historical relativism, evangelicals shifted the discussion from the doctrine of the inspired Scripture as eternally valid propositional revelation to a critical analysis of historical relativism itself and its implications for such basic concepts as revelation, truth, meaning, inspiration, and authority.[2] Carl F. H. Henry contends that a radical historical relativism, in which verbal communication of meaning is impossible from one age to another, deintellectualizes and dehumanizes humankind.[3] He sees the existential hermeneutical approach as essentially nihilistic because it destroys the normativity of any and all communication and so in the end is self-destructive of even existential theory. W. Harold Mare criticizes radical historical relativism, saying that generally we recognize that an authority with maturity of mind can write literature with a message which is essentially meaningful for people in his or her own day and a time one hundred or two hundred years removed. We assume this is true for Plato and Aristotle. Why not the Bible?[4] In criticizing Dennis Nineham's historical relativism, Anthony Thiselton says that Nineham's difficulty with the category of miracle is not just a matter of historical distance (differences of worldview) but a theological difference between Scripture and himself over the nature of reality. Thiselton too makes a comparison with classical studies and says classicists would not tolerate radical historical relativism.[5]

If the interpreter's present-day self-understanding becomes decisive for the text's meaning, then the interpreter's subjective response to the text, rather than the text itself, determines the message that comes through.

---

1. James D. G. Dunn, "The Authority of Scripture According to Scripture," *Churchman* 96 (1982): 99–122, 201–25.

2. See the essays in the following works for the content of the previous evangelical discussion: Carl F. H. Henry, ed., *Revelation and the Bible* (Grand Rapids: Baker, 1959); Ned B. Stonehouse and Paul Woolley, eds., *The Infallible Word* (Philadelphia: Presbyterian Guardian, 1946); Merrill C. Tenney, ed., *The Bible, the Living Word of Revelation* (Grand Rapids: Zondervan, 1968).

3. Carl F. H. Henry, *God, Revelation, and Authority*, 6 vols. (Waco, Tex.: Word, 1976–1979), 4:304.

4. W. Harold Mare, "The Meaningful Language of the New Testament," *WTJ* 37 (1974): 95–105.

5. Anthony C. Thiselton, *The Two Horizons: New Testament Hermeneutics and Philosophical Description, with Special Reference to Heidegger, Bultmann, Gadamer, and Wittgenstein* (Grand Rapids: Eerdmans, 1980), 57, 60. See also Henry A. Virkler, *Hermeneutics: Principles and Processes of Biblical Interpretation* (Grand Rapids: Baker, 1981), 22–24.

There is no meaning independent of the interpreter's preferences. For Henry, the Christian response to such an approach is to "champion the indispensable importance of historical and philological exegesis in identifying the content of the scripturally given revelation, and . . . acknowledge the authorial cognitive intention is ultimately definitive for textual meaning."[6]

Henry also criticizes historical relativism as self-contradictory. If the theory of historical relativism is true, it logically follows that its primary assertion must be false, for relativism, by definition, denies that there is transcendent objective truth. Yet, to assert that relativism is valid is to make such a truth claim. The proponent of relativism must claim a special privilege for the theory, asking one to accept as absolute the proposition that all human statements are historically relative.[7]

Henry argues that nothing in history or culture precludes transhistorical truth; hence the absolutists have grounds as valid as do the relativists for their claims concerning the particular character of truth. In fact, the absolutists' grounds are stronger because of transcendent divine revelation. God has demonstrated the reality of historically transcendent truth by intelligibly disclosing in the Scriptures his transcendent will to human beings.

Truth and Meaning

The issue of truth also had to be addressed. Some scholars identified the root philosophical difference between those who hold to full inerrancy and those who do not as the rejection or acceptance of Kant's dualism, since this difference seems to determine one's view of truth. For the evangelical holding to full inerrancy, true statements are those that correspond to the facts, to reality, and the Bible communicates just such true verbal propositions. Others, as W. D. Beck describes them, argued that "the Bible is eternal, religious truth known only to faith."[8] The definition of truth in this case is faithfulness, or lack of deception. Proponents of this view hold that the Bible may err in the sense of being historically or scientifically inaccurate.

---

6. Henry, *God, Revelation, and Authority,* 4:314. John S. Feinberg also argues that the use of a conventional (positivist) or contextual approach to meaning is unsatisfactory: "There needs to be some kind of referential element in order to tie language to the world. Without it there seems to be no reason other than pure convention as to why a certain utterance and not another is appropriate for performing a given speech act. . . . My utterance might be nothing more than a reflection of what is going on in my mind, and it is that lack of necessary relation between language and world which troubles me about use theories" ("Truth: Relationship of Theories of Truth to Hermeneutics," in *Hermeneutics, Inerrancy, and the Bible,* ed. Earl D. Radmacher and Robert D. Preus [Grand Rapids: Zondervan, 1984], 35).

7. Henry, *God, Revelation, and Authority,* 4:53.

8. W. David Beck, "A Response to Truth: Relationship of Theories of Truth to Hermeneutics," in *Hermeneutics, Inerrancy,* 66.

However, in the biblical understanding of the term, the Bible does not err. It is faithful—that is, not "swerving from the truth and upsetting the faith."[9]

Proponents of full inerrancy challenged this concept of Scripture's truth. They proposed that for the biblical writers "the correspondence theory in some form seems to be foundational to what they wrote . . . [i.e.,] statements are true or false, and what makes them so is their congruity or incongruity with states of affairs. Truth is relation between word and world."[10] Still other evangelicals viewed the biblical concept of truth as having a polymorphous character, including both faithfulness and correspondence with reality.[11]

A variety of approaches to semantics also developed as evangelicals sought to deal with the complexity of that issue and, at the same time, to choose the theory of meaning that identified the locus of meaning most useful for interpreting the words. Carl Henry, Norman Geisler, and Walter Kaiser appear to assume the traditional sign theory, as they discuss the nature of meaning.[12] Geisler's exposition of the International Council on Biblical Inerrancy affirmation of Scripture's single, definite, and fixed meaning illustrates this view, and his explicit statements on theory of meaning strongly contend that the conventionalist (functionalist) theory (i.e., the meaning of words is a product of public behavior, normal usage in a given cultural context) is false and inconsistent with inerrancy.[13]

Carl Henry has demonstrated the role of context in the communication of meaning, pointing out that when considered in isolation, words carry a range of possible meanings. This is the *usus loquendi* of the sociocultural context in which they function as part of the culture's vocabulary stock. The grammatical-literary context must be engaged to determine a word's meaning in any given statement. Henry goes on to contend that when words are employed in statements, they gain a precise meaning that is single, fixed, definite, and an expression of the writer's intent. According to John Feinberg, such meaning requires an extralinguistic referential component.[14]

---

9. Gerrit Cornelis Berkouwer, *Holy Scripture* (Grand Rapids: Eerdmans, 1975), 181.

10. Feinberg, "Truth," 18, 8. Norman Geisler contends that the correspondence view of truth is indirectly taught in Scripture ("A Response to Truth: Relationship of Theories of Truth to Hermeneutics," in *Hermeneutics, Inerrancy,* 55; see also Roger Nicole, "The Biblical Concept of Truth," in *Scripture and Truth,* ed. D. A. Carson and John D. Woodbridge [Grand Rapids: Zondervan, 1983], 287–302; Norman L. Geisler, "The Concept of Truth in the Inerrancy Debate," *BS* 137 [1980]: 327–39).

11. Thiselton, *Two Horizons,* 411–15; Alan F. Johnson, "A Response to Problems of Normativeness in Scripture: Cultural Versus Permanent," in *Hermeneutics, Inerrancy,* 260.

12. Henry, *God, Revelation, and Authority,* 3:389ff.; Norman L. Geisler, "Explaining Hermeneutics: A Commentary on the Chicago Statement on Biblical Hermeneutics Articles of Affirmation and Denial," in *Hermeneutics, Inerrancy,* 893. Walter Kaiser's emphasis on an author's single intended meaning also seems to be built on such a theory (*Toward an Exegetical Theology: Biblical Exegesis for Preaching and Teaching* [Grand Rapids: Baker, 1981], 24–34, 44–45, 106–14); see also Geisler, "The Relation of Purpose and Meaning in Interpreting Scripture," *GTJ* 5 (1984): 230–31.

13. Geisler, "A Response to Truth," 54–55.

14. Feinberg, "Truth," 35.

Such an element makes intelligible communication and valid interpretation possible by tying language to the world. The author's language is pointing to something outside itself to which the hearer can refer and so receive the communication. The extralinguistic factor also provides a basis for validating interpretation, which in the final analysis is a check to see whether the hearer understands the verbal statements in the way the author intends them to be understood.

Moisés Silva investigates the usefulness for hermeneutics of the referential (traditional sign theory) and the structuralist approaches to meaning.[15] He observes that only a small number of words in a culture's vocabulary stock—such words as proper names (*Julius Caesar*) and technical terms (*sin, law*)—refer to only one thing and so can be fully understood by analyzing that referent. The majority of words, while having a more or less precisely defined referential dimension, can be understood best through structural analysis of the linguistic context. The interpreter identifies meaning by analyzing the relationship of the sense of one word to the sense of other words in the grammatical-literary context (syntagmatic relations) and the sense of similar words in the vocabulary stock (paradigmatic relations). For example, one would learn the meaning of "the woman is running quickly" by analyzing the paradigmatic relation of "woman" to "man" and "boy," and the syntagmatic relation it is in as the subject of "is running."

Anthony Thiselton detects the severe limitations in a referential theory of meaning and contends that the functionalist approach is the most fruitful one.[16] A word's meaning is located in its *use* in a given linguistic context within a given "language game," the set of life surroundings in which it is spoken. Public behavior provides the currency of meaning, for the structure of language is determined by the particular functions it has to perform to meet human and social needs.[17] Thiselton is quick to point out that such an approach should not be applied to biblical content in a way that reduces it to the terms of this narrow area of meaning, public human behavior. The referential dimension of meaning still has an important part to play, because New Testament writers make truth claims that go beyond "merely functional considerations." Indeed, questions of reference remain an important factor in hermeneutical inquiries.

John Feinberg concludes with John Lyons that no single theory is entirely satisfactory. Any account of meaning must include "the notions of reference, use within a context, the performance of a speech act, and the idea of conventions of language."[18]

---

15. Moisés Silva, *Biblical Words and Their Meaning* (Grand Rapids: Zondervan, 1983), 105–9.
16. Thiselton, *Two Horizons*, 123–24.
17. John Lyons, *Semantics*, 2 vols. (Cambridge: Cambridge University Press, 1977), 1:249.
18. Feinberg, "Truth," 35.

In the matter of relating theories of meaning to theories of truth, there were again several approaches. For John Feinberg, "no theory of meaning necessitates any particular theory of truth."[19] Geisler disagrees; he sees a definite connection. Since only meaningful statements may be judged true or false, the nature of the meaning of a statement does have a necessary influence on the nature of its truth.[20] And though he does not explicitly indicate which theory of meaning he considers foundational, he does insist that it cannot be a theory in which the meaning of statements is arbitrary or conventional.[21] It must be an approach that affirms meaning as objective and essential. Thiselton, as we have seen, qualifies his functionalist approach so that the truth claims of Scripture can be properly dealt with, his chief concern being that theories of meaning not be so extended in their use as to make judgments about the truth claims of the biblical text.

Biblical Inspiration and Authority

The evangelical affirms that the Scripture's meaning is conveyed by the ordinary communication processes, through human language. But with this affirmation comes the challenge to explain how the Bible, developed in a given language system, can claim to be divinely inspired and authoritatively valid for people of all language systems. In answer, Vern Poythress proposes that divine inspiration is congruent with the human verbal communication. A particular verbal meaning is generated by choices the original writer makes within the structures and constraints that are the contextual features of a given language system. "The doctrine of verbal inspiration, then, says that in the case of the Bible the choices of word-sequences are all choices that God made. Of course, it is true in addition that the human author made the choices. At the same time God takes responsibility for those choices of the human author."[22]

In the face of relativism, which would treat all biblical content as culturally conditioned, evangelicals affirmed the full scope of scriptural authority. Carl Henry, while insisting that the main concern of Scripture is God's self-revelation of his nature and will, and that therefore its authority is basically theological and ethical, goes on to assert that the scope of scriptural authority coincides with what the inspired writers teach, no matter the

---

19. Ibid., 40.
20. Geisler, "A Response to Truth," 55.
21. Geisler, "Relation of Purpose," 230–31.
22. Vern S. Poythress, "Adequacy of Language and Accommodation," in *Hermeneutics, Inerrancy,* 363.

subject. If it impinges on astronomy, botany, economics, geography, history, or politics, it is trustworthy, though not comprehensive. "On whatever themes it speaks in God's name, Scripture is not to be relativized."[23]

It was acknowledged throughout the discussion of presuppositions that one's view of Scripture determined the direction of one's hermeneutic.[24] The point of difference was whether that view was determined by Scripture's teaching about itself[25] or by the interpreter's evaluation of the phenomena of Scripture.[26]

Interpretation

The Context of the Ancient Text

Evangelical interpretation of Scripture manifested increasing precision with regard to cultural factors. There was also a growing awareness of the need to study the implications of the "biblical world" for interpretation—that is, the writer's literary, historical, and cultural setting and the general historical situation facing author and audience.[27] The components of this world were identified as thought-forms, expectations, fears, tensions, as well as institutions, laws, social customs, and religious practices—in short, all cultural factors that made up the original writer's preunderstanding. As evangelical interpretation recognized more and more that "biblical writers were influenced by their culture and reflected its effect upon them,"[28] the interpreter's task broadened "to genuinely appreciate the factors involved in the mentality of the ancients."[29]

23. Henry, *God, Revelation, and Authority*, 4:42–43. Dunn disagrees because he finds cultural relativity in the content of Scripture: "We must recognize that what was the Word of God in and to a culture and time very different from ours (New Testament as well as Old Testament) may well no longer be the Word of God to our culture and time. In such cases, the normative force of the scripture will lie more in *how* God spoke to their situation and context than in *what* he said" ("Authority of Scripture," 217).

24. James I. Packer, "Hermeneutics and Biblical Authority," *Themelios* 1 (1975): 3–12; Alan F. Johnson, "History and Culture in New Testament Interpretation," in *Interpreting the Word of God Today*, ed. Samuel J. Schultz and Morris A. Inch (Chicago: Moody, 1976), 130.

25. John W. Wenham, "Christ's View of Scripture," in *Inerrancy*, ed. Norman L. Geisler (Grand Rapids: Zondervan, 1979), 3–38; and Edwin A. Blum, "The Apostles' View of Scripture," ibid., 39–56.

26. Dunn, "Authority of Scripture," 201ff.

27. J. Julius Scott, Jr., "Some Problems in Hermeneutics for Contemporary Evangelicals," *JETS* 22 (1979): 73; Alan F. Johnson, "History and Culture," 143; C. Hassell Bullock, "Introduction: Interpreting the Bible," in *The Literature and Meaning of Scripture*, ed. Morris A. Inch and C. Hassell Bullock (Grand Rapids: Baker, 1981), 16; Virkler, *Hermeneutics*, 79.

28. Bullock, "Introduction," 16. Note that Virkler refers to a "philosophical gap" in interpretation, since views of life, circumstances, and the nature of the universe differ among various cultures (*Hermeneutics*, 16).

29. James E. Jennings, "Interpreting the Historical Books: 2 Samuel 1:17–24; 2:1–4, 12–16," in *Literature and Meaning*, 47.

R. C. Sproul presented his concerns about the cultural factor in Scripture in a series of questions: Does Scripture reflect views of life, the history, and the cosmos of antiquity? Does that mean it teaches outmoded views as true? Is the cultural perspective part of the essence of Scripture's message? Or does "reflect" mean that the interpreter should read between the lines, understanding such things as phenomenological language and perceiving the cultural setting in which a culture-transcending message is placed? The ultimate question then becomes: "To what extent is the Bible's relevance and authority limited by changing human structures and perspectives in the biblical text?"[30] Gordon Lewis answers the difficulty: The inspired writers used their own powers of self-transcendence and received God's transcendent guidance in writing Scripture. Therefore the biblical message is not culture-bound.[31]

Most discussions in evangelical circles focused on ways in which background data could help explain the meaning and significance of ancient cultural customs and practices recorded in Scripture,[32] and even of scriptural injunctions. Not many evangelicals recognized the full implications of such a procedure: how the examination and assessment of biblical content in the light of extrabiblical cultural information could lead to the undermining of biblical authority. In fact, some evangelical scholars used extrabiblical cultural information to indicate the differences between ancient and contemporary cultures, and in that way sought to demonstrate the inappropriateness of directly applying some scriptural injunctions.[33] Labeling certain parts of the Bible as cultural practices had definite implications for scriptural authority.

The increased historical interest served to call attention to the diverse and culturally particular character of the literary genres in Scripture.[34] Previously, evangelicals had distinguished between teaching sections (the Epistles), which may be directly applied, and historical sections (the Gospels and Acts), which could be applied only on the level of principles. Now this

30. R. C. Sproul, *Knowing Scripture* (Downers Grove, Ill.: Inter-Varsity, 1977), 103.

31. Gordon R. Lewis, "Response to Presuppositions of Non-Evangelical Hermeneutics," in *Hermeneutics, Inerrancy*, 619.

32. Bullock, "Introduction," 16; Virkler, *Hermeneutics*, 79. Evangelicals were also aware of the potential contribution of linguistics to word study (Simon Kistemaker, "Current Problems and Projects in New Testament Research," *JETS* 18 [1975]: 17–28; Silva, *Biblical Words*).

33. Gordon D. Fee, "Hermeneutics and Common Sense," in *Inerrancy and Common Sense*, ed. Roger Nicole and J. Ramsey Michaels (Grand Rapids: Baker, 1980), 175. Fee gives the example of the lack of educational opportunities for women in ancient times as explaining in part the need for the prohibition against women teaching in church (1 Tim. 2:9–15). Since the cultural situation no longer exists in Western cultures, Fee suggests that the prohibition may be no longer binding. Note Carl Henry's judgment concerning the cultural factor in general: "Yet we know too little about sociological conditions in the first century Greco-Roman world to draw up any confident listing of what must or must not have been merely cultural behavior on the part of the early Christians" (*God, Revelation, and Authority*, 4:56).

34. Scott, "Some Problems," 74; see also Fee, "The Genre of New Testament Literature and Biblical Hermeneutics," in *Interpreting the Word*, 105–27.

distinction was breaking down. The Epistles began to be viewed by many as occasional literature written with a particular purpose to a particular people in a particular situation. Some transcultural principles may be clearly identified in Scripture, but most have to be uncovered by separating them from the specific applications in which they are presented.

The implications for biblical authority when a genre of Scripture is characterized as occasional are clear. If the intended direct application is understood as culture-specific, that is, limited to the particular situation, its present-day application is diminished to the level of broad ethical principle.

Study of the genre of gospel narrative raised issues concerning the nature of Scripture's truth. In his commentary on Matthew, Robert H. Gundry concluded that many portions of that Gospel were midrashic, following the pattern of a Jewish religious exposition combining history and nonhistory—in this case, first-century history and Matthew's theological and instructional embellishment. Gundry reasoned that since historical and non-historical material can communicate truth separately, it follows that they can do so in combination, "provided their mixture was a recognized and accepted mode of communication. Ancient midrash and haggadah show that it was. . . . Hence, 'Jesus said' or 'Jesus did' need not always mean that in history Jesus said or did what follows, but sometimes may mean that in the account at least partly constructed by Matthew himself Jesus said or did what follows."[35] Ancient cultural expectation and practice provide the basis for concluding that Scriptures may contain factual fabrication and still be considered true.

Evangelical reaction to Gundry's views followed at least two lines of thought. Douglas Moo, even though he rejected the idea that Matthew was midrash, declared that midrash could not be ruled out a priori as a genre found in inerrant Scripture, because inerrant meaning exists within the limits of the literary genre used.[36] In fact, it would be inappropriate to apply modern historical methods to midrash because that form is not history. Norman Geisler, on the other hand, argues that midrash, by definition, violates inerrancy, "because in practice Gundry's midrash view rejects a correspondence view of truth implied in an inerrancy commitment (a report of an event must be factually true, especially an inspired report)."[37]

35. Robert H. Gundry, *Matthew: A Commentary on His Literary and Theological Art* (Grand Rapids: Eerdmans, 1982), 630.

36. Douglas J. Moo, "Matthew and Midrash: An Evaluation of Robert H. Gundry's Approach," *JETS* 26 (1983): 32. See D. A. Carson's discussion of midrash, in *Matthew, Mark, Luke*, EBC 8 (Grand Rapids: Zondervan, 1984), 39–41.

37. Norman L. Geisler, "Is There Madness in the Method? A Rejoinder to Robert H. Gundry," *JETS* 26 (1983): 102.

Throughout these exegetical discussions, evangelicals continued to maintain that the original writer's intention, as recovered by the grammatical-historical-literary method, governs the text's meaning.[38]

The Interpreter's Context

The second part of the interpretation process, communicating the text's meaning in the interpreter's context, challenged evangelical thinkers. In defining the hermeneutical task in general, they took into account the role the interpreter's preunderstanding and presuppositions play in the enterprise. They also conceived of the hermeneutical bridge as already formed and in place because of the nature of God, humankind, language, and Scripture.

The Hermeneutical Task

Anthony Thiselton conceived of the interpretational task as an active, meaningful engagement between interpreter and text, leading to a fusion of the horizons of both.[39] In the process, the interpreter's own horizon is corrected, reshaped, and enlarged. The Bible can and does speak today, but this does not mean that the horizons of the text and the interpreter will fuse and become identical. There is a clear distinction between the *exegetical* and *hermeneutical* meaning of the text, between the text understood in terms of its own horizon and the text understood in terms of the interpreter's horizon. And though the lines of understanding meet at points, and sometimes even intersect, they remain distinct and separate.

Gordon Fee and Douglas Stuart proposed another link between the meanings extrapolated from the two horizons. For them the exegetical meaning of the text as recovered by grammatical-historical-literary analysis controls the hermeneutical meaning for the present time. The Bible cannot mean now what it never could have meant to its author and readers.[40]

For Carl Henry and Walter Kaiser the interpretational task involves discovering the single meaning of Scripture. "The truth of God can be stated in all cultures," writes Henry; "it does not need to be *re*stated in any culture

---

38. I. Howard Marshall, "How Do We Interpret the Bible Today?" *Themelios* 5, no. 2 (1980): 9; Fee, "Hermeneutics and Common Sense," 168. Donald Bloesch disagrees, saying that "the ultimate norm is not simply what the human writer intends but what God intends . . . though there is always a certain congruity between the latter and the former" ("Crisis in Biblical Authority," *TT* 35 [1979]: 460).

39. Thiselton, *Two Horizons*, xix. Gordon D. Fee and Douglas Stuart claim that biblical interpretation is demanded by "the tension . . . between [Scripture's] *eternal relevance* and . . . *historical particularity*." There is a two-step process: finding out "what it meant," its historical particularity, and "what it means," its eternal relevance (*How to Read the Bible for All Its Worth: A Guide to Understanding the Bible* [Grand Rapids: Zondervan, 1981], 19).

40. Fee and Stuart, *How to Read the Bible*, 27.

except by way of linguistic translation and repetition." By "restated" he means a conscious adaptation of biblical thought-forms to those of a modern culture. He points to Rudolf Bultmann's imposing the category of myth upon, and the liberation theologians' injecting Marxist ideology into, the interpretation process as examples of a "comprehensive subordination of Scripture to a culturally rooted conceptuality." The danger here is that a regard for the whole or part of the intellectual *Zeitgeist* "as indispensable to the biblical view will only admit into the circle of revelation what is unstable and inadequate as a foundation for life and society."[41] For this reason evangelical concern should never be to Africanize Christian theology, for example, but rather to biblicize it so that the universal validity of the Christian revelation may be maintained. The Christian interpreter's task should be simply to state "by way of linguistic translation" the biblical message for the contemporary culture.

Walter Kaiser fully agrees: "*To interpret we must in every case reproduce the sense the Scriptural writer intended for his own words.* The first step in the interpretive process is to link only those ideas with the author's [words] that he connected with them. The second step is to express these ideas understandably." Kaiser sees his personal reception and application of an author's words as a secondary and separate act from the initial understanding of those words. Kaiser here follows closely the distinction between meaning and significance made by E. D. Hirsch. But Kaiser warns of the danger of thinking that what the text *means* and what the text *meant* are not identical. Such a conclusion would reduce all knowledge "to the horizon of one's own prejudices and personal predilections. This is true whether it is done for 'spiritual' or for philosophical reasons; both approaches usurp the author's revelatory stance and insert one's own authority for his."[42]

The Interpreter's Preunderstanding

A key factor in the hermeneutical process is the interpreter's horizon or preunderstanding—one's world-view, presuppositions, and personal predilections. All evangelical exegetes acknowledge the importance of this element. The interpreter's preunderstanding, according to Thiselton, particularly one's prior understanding of the subject about which the text speaks, is a necessary condition for any understanding of the text to take place, for no one comes to the task of expounding a text without a frame of reference, a pattern of assumptions derived from sources outside of Scripture. The interpreter's preunderstanding or horizon is the context in terms of which the text's meaning is understood.[43]

---

41. Henry, *God, Revelation, and Authority*, 4:53, 59–60.

42. Walter C. Kaiser, Jr., "Legitimate Hermeneutics," in *Inerrancy*, 118, 122. See also E. D. Hirsch, Jr., *The Aims of Interpretation* (Chicago: University of Chicago Press, 1976), 1–13, 79–81.

43. Thiselton, *Two Horizons*, 114.

Because the interpreter's preunderstanding derives largely from extra-biblical sources, many evangelicals contended that this faculty must submit to a critique by Scripture before it can be effectively used in interpretation. Gordon Lewis suggests that all interpreters—evangelicals and non-evangelicals alike—should test their presuppositions against the criteria of truth. Presuppositions must exhibit coherence with the teaching and refer-ents of Scripture without logical contradiction. They must also fit em-pirically and be experientially viable. In such a climate, Lewis is confident, a dialogue could open up among interpreters that would bring them out of their hermeneutical circles. This would be a true breaking out of *the* her-meneutical circle because an interpreter's preunderstanding would be con-firmed or disconfirmed. Lewis proposes a hypothesis-verification approach, in which the biblical data are accepted as primary sources of theology and the human mind is viewed as self-transcendent, that is, so constituted as to understand and also assess the truthfulness of one's presuppositions. Such an approach would provide common ground on which interpreters of all persuasions could work and interact with one another. The interpreter would no longer simply assert his or her presuppositions but rather would propose them and then test to see if they make a coherent fit with the biblical data.[44] It should be noted in passing that preunderstanding would include the interpreter's traditional interpretations of the text.

Just how does one critically evaluate and correct one's preunderstanding so that it may function efficiently in the hermeneutical process? As Fred Klooster counsels, the interpreter must try to detect presuppositions from the contemporary *Zeitgeist* that distort or silence the message of Scripture.

> Every synthesis of Christianity with Aristotle, Plato, Common Sense philoso-phy, idealism, existentialism, process thought, or any other type of non-Christian thought, must be eradicated so that the Christian preunder-standing will fully conform to the Word of God. . . . Every interpreter . . . must be alert . . . to the constant danger of a fusion of horizons that results even if one unwittingly reads Scripture through the spectacles of the *Zeitgeist*.[45]

James Jennings demonstrates how this distorting or silencing can take place unconsciously in the interpreter. All readers interact with written history in terms of their understanding of how that history occurred. This

---

44. Lewis, "Response to Presuppositions," 623, 625. Lewis derives his method from epistemological studies in his *Testing Christianity's Truth Claims* (Chicago: Moody, 1976). He applies it in *Integrative Theology: Historical, Biblical, Systematic, Apologetic, and Practical* (Grand Rapids: Zondervan, 1986), vol. 1, chap. 1. Millard J. Erickson presents similar steps for developing presuppositions ("Presuppositions of Non-Evangelical Hermeneutics," in *Hermeneutics, Inerrancy*, 610).

45. Fred H. Klooster, "The Role of the Holy Spirit in the Hermeneutical Process: The Relationship of the Spirit's Illumination to Biblical Interpretation," in *Hermeneutics, Inerrancy*, 464–65.

means blocking out matters one knows little about or does not appreciate and focusing on what one readily identifies with. Unless one becomes consciously aware of this mental filter—the preunderstanding through which the text passes—and acts to correct it, one probably will misinterpret and misapply the text's content. It is necessary to attempt consciously to divest oneself of the contemporary mental baggage that hinders comprehension of the ancient documents and make every effort to genuinely appreciate the factors involved in the ancient mentality.[46]

Klooster offers a positive suggestion in this matter. "Scripture must be interpreted through the spectacles of Scripture; the pre-understanding with which the interpreter approaches Scripture must wholly conform to Scripture. This hermeneutical circle must be consciously embraced."[47]

Royce Gruenler proposes two indispensable elements for Christian preunderstanding: a personal relationship with Jesus Christ, enabling one to enter the story from the inside, and an acceptance of the authoritative witness of the Evangelists. This will enable the interpreter, by the power of the Holy Spirit, to understand Scripture as God's "own interpretation of the deep grammar of nature, history, and of human existence."[48]

This may sound at first like reasoning in a circle, but it is not. The biblical message has essential meaning located in the extralinguistic referents; the biblical message is true in the sense that its statements correspond to reality. This enables it to make contact with life beyond the language. In addition, an interpreter's preunderstanding is brought more and more into conformity with the biblical data during the sanctification process, particularly when the interpreter stands beyond the hermeneutical circle and is impacted by it. Finally, the illumination of the Holy Spirit guides in the proper interpretation and application of the text, and through it all, authoritative Scripture impacts the interpreter's horizon and exercises functional control.

Hermeneutical Bridges

For most evangelical interpreters, the hermeneutical bridge is already in place, held there by the nature of God and the nature of his dealings with his creatures. Walter Kaiser contends that the nature of God, the biblical concept of truth, and the fact that human beings are created in the image of God provide the objective grounding and reference points for the "possibility for *adequate* . . . transcultural communication."[49] If God in his nature is

---

46. Jennings, "Interpreting the Historical Books," 46–47.

47. Klooster, "Role of the Holy Spirit," 465; see also Erickson, "Presuppositions," 610; and Lewis, "Response to Presuppositions," 624.

48. Royce G. Gruenler, "A Response to the New Hermeneutic," in *Hermeneutics, Inerrancy*, 588.

49. Walter C. Kaiser, Jr., "Meanings from God's Message: Matters for Interpretation," CT 22 (1979): 1321; see also George W. Knight, "A Response to Problems of Normativeness in Scripture: Cultural Versus Permanent," in *Hermeneutics, Inerrancy*, 252; Eugene A. Wilson, "Homiletical Application of Old Testament Narrative Passages," *Trinity Journal* 7 (1978): 86.

unchanging faithfulness and truth, then the interpreter may expect his message to be understandable from one historical time to another. The work of God the Holy Spirit in illuminating the modern believer's mind to understand the biblical message guarantees communication of meaning.

Evangelicals who view Scripture as given in culture-bound or time-bound language hold that the Holy Spirit serves as teacher and guide to bridge the gap.[50] Peter Richardson interprets the continuing activity of the Spirit to mean that no final and authoritative interpretation or principle of interpretation is possible. The interplay of the text and the Spirit provides a solid basis for individuals to hear God's Spirit speaking to them.[51]

James Dunn perceives this interplay as a union of strictly historical exegesis and prophetic openness to the Spirit speaking now. In this interaction each factor serves to stimulate and check the other. This dialogical approach, described by Dunn in personal communication (3 October 1986), seeks to hear again the Word of God in its original authority and to recognize the degree to which that authority was conditioned by culture or a specific situation, acknowledging that continuing authority may well be limited by such factors. The "directive authority," the guidance on what to do in a particular situation, is not found in the original message of Scripture recovered by historical exegesis. Rather, it is to be found in the Spirit's speaking through, but also oftentimes apart from, Scripture, as when the Spirit produces the mind of Christ in the context of the church. "It is in this interaction between the Spirit's inspiration then, and the mind of Christ now, that the authoritative Word of God is to be heard speaking to particular situations today."[52]

God's dealings with humankind in every age provide ample evidence that meaning can be conveyed transhistorically. J. I. Packer contends that Scripture as "inspired material stands for all time as the definitive expression of God's mind and will."[53] In applying this message to a given time, we can assume that God deals the same way with men and women in every age, which makes the transhistorical understanding and application of the message possible. Paul Wells also sees God's dealings with human beings, particularly in a covenant-communion relationship, as a key for grasping the transcultural nature of the Scripture message.[54]

The nature of humankind and our fallen condition provide further spans in the hermeneutical bridge. Walter Kaiser sees the human creature in the

---

50. Bloesch, "Crisis," 462; idem, *Essentials of Evangelical Theology*, 2 vols. (San Francisco: Harper & Row, 1978), 1:73–74; Kenneth Hamilton, *Words and the Word* (Grand Rapids: Eerdmans, 1971), 83; Dunn, "Authority of Scripture," 219.

51. Peter Richardson, "Spirit and Letter: Foundation for Hermeneutics," *Evangelical Quarterly* 45 (1973): 218.

52. Dunn, "Authority of Scripture," 220.

53. Packer, "Hermeneutics," 4.

54. Paul R. Wells, *James Barr and the Bible* (Phillipsburg, N.J.: Presbyterian & Reformed, 1980), 354ff.

image of God and the doctrine of creation as sufficient grounds for trans-cultural communication.[55] Gordon Lewis suggests that the image of God in all people of all times includes the capacities for self-transcendence, moral discernment, and linguistic communication.[56] For Robin Nixon, the basis for transcultural communication rests on the principles of human nature, conduct, and relationships that do not change from age to age.[57] This continuity makes it possible to translate New Testament ethical principles into the contemporary situation.

According to W. Harold Mare, the sameness of the human sinful con-dition throughout history accounts for the continuing relevance of Scrip-ture's message of salvation from that condition. "Since man is the same now in regard to his sin and need as he was in ancient times, those ethical and soteriological terms ring true for the twentieth-century man."[58] George Knight sums up the perpetual significance of the biblical message for hu-mankind:

> Since the message of the Scripture is addressed primarily to man as man, to man as sinner, to man as saved, to man as the one who must be obedient to the God who is the same yesterday, today, and forever, and not to man primarily because of or in a culturally distinct or unique situation, we may appropriately expect that its message will apply to man in the cultures of this day and age and in the cultures of tomorrow.[59]

Paul Wells contends that the breakdown in communication between God and human beings, which the hermeneutical bridge seeks to remedy, is not a matter of God's being infinite and our being finite; it is a matter of the human race's falling away from covenant communion with God into covenant-breaking sin. The interpreter who begins with communion with God as the basic perspective and traces its revelation in history (from creation through fall, incarnation, and redemption) is in a position to understand how the Scriptures can and do speak across history. The Holy Spirit serves

---

55. Kaiser, "Meanings," 1321.

56. Lewis, "Response to Presuppositions," 618.

57. Robin E. Nixon, "The Authority of the New Testament," in *New Testament Interpretation: Essays on Principles and Methods*, ed. I. H. Marshall (Grand Rapids: Eerdmans, 1977), 345; see also Dan R. Johnson, "Guidelines for the Application of Old Testament Narrative," *Trinity Journal* 7 (1978): 82. Winfried Corduan, using phenomenological analysis, argues that "entailed in my existence is a facet of communality with the rest of humanity, viz. that intersubjectivity is given within my subjectivity" ("Philosophical Presuppositions Affecting Biblical Hermeneutics," in *Hermeneutics, Inerrancy*, 504). This is a link to the community of origin of any proposition the interpreter wants to understand.

58. Mare, "Meaningful Language," 103. Gordon Lewis agrees: "Across the centuries-gap people are human, persons possess inherent human rights, demand justice, need forgiveness, desire loving acceptance and seek faithfulness to what is and to one another in deed and word" ("Response to Presuppositions," 618). Winfried Corduan also cites the ontology of all historical events as creating another link ("Philosophical Presuppositions," 508).

59. Knight, "Response to Problems," 252.

as the divine energizing link, as he was at the origin of communion between God and human beings. As Redeemer Spirit, he is the author of incarnation and inscripturation, and he energizes the renewal of human beings' communion with God, in which the restoration of the divine image takes place. Such a restoration depends on and is interpreted by the new relationship in which the Christian stands, savingly connected to the incarnation and the inscripturated Word. So faith in Christ and the Scriptures is the essence of this communion. The Spirit takes human words into his service to produce the Scriptures, and they become "divinely authorised to seal the covenant communion."[60]

Additional materials for the hermeneutical bridge were detected in the nature of language. Evangelicals identified two characteristics of language that allow it to communicate across time and culture. First, the successful practice of translation shows that truth can be communicated across such gaps. For a translation to succeed, rules of logic and thought-forms must transcend cultural bounds.[61] After comparing the thought of the biblical writers and that of modern scholars, I. H. Marshall concluded that their thought is not so different as to make translation impossible.[62]

Second, Carl Henry bases his argument for transhistorical communication on the creation accounts. "Language is possible because of man's God-given endowment of rationality, of a priori categories and of innate ideas, all of which precondition his ability to think and speak. . . . Human language is adequate for theological knowledge and communication because all men are divinely furnished with certain common ideas."[63] The meaning of language has the capacity to become significant for any perceptive reader outside the original audience. A text's significance is the relationship between its single meaning and the reader, situation, or idea brought to the text. Those applications of the text are in line with the original meaning.

Walter Kaiser is confident that both interpretation and application are possible in any historical period. He illustrates the process by pointing to Paul's use of Deuteronomy 25:4 in 1 Corinthians 9:8–10. He concludes that communication can continue and the Scriptures can be appropriated as the authoritative Word of God, as long as interpreters leave the final court of appeal for determining normative theological content "in the original writers' hands, in their single meaning and principle for each text, in their contextual settings, in the theology that informs their writings and in the faithful naming of new relationships between that original meaning and contemporary persons, conceptions and situations."[64]

---

60. Wells, *James Barr*, 370.

61. Henry, *God, Revelation, and Authority*, 4:53, 59; Lewis, "Response to Presuppositions," 618.

62. Marshall, "How Do We Interpret?" 10.

63. Henry, *God, Revelation, and Authority*, 3:389; see also Poythress, "Adequacy of Language," 352. Henry emphasizes, e.g., that the *imago Dei* universally underlies the idea of God.

64. Walter C. Kaiser, Jr., "The Current Crisis in Exegesis and the Apostolic Use of Deuteronomy 25:4 in 1 Corinthians 9:8–10," *JETS* 21 (1978): 18.

Anthony Thiselton, using a descriptive semiotic analysis of language informed by Wittgenstein, gives a number of reasons why biblical content need not be viewed as inescapably culture-relative. He begins with his functionalist understanding of language as a system of interrelated symbols. The rules governing the interrelationships and the meaning that flows from them are learned in one's culture, and the whole system may be called a language game. As Wittgenstein analyzed language games, he noted that there are certain statements (grammatical utterances) that are not culture-relative. He labels these second-class grammatical utterances. These are axiomatic statements so fundamental to one's thinking that one can say, "If I am wrong about *this*, I have no guarantee that anything I say is true." Examples of such assertions are statements in Paul such as, "Let God be true, and every man a liar. . . . God is not unjust if he bears wrath, is he?" Rom. 3:4–5). In these statements the justice and truthfulness of God are assumed as unshakable axioms. These statements express these fundamental conceptions and thus articulate "the scaffolding of our thoughts." Thiselton contends that such class-two statements "regularly occur in the context of an appeal which presupposes a given religious or ethical 'common understanding.'"[65] That is, they derive from a theological tradition that can be differentiated from the culture in which they are spoken (an additional reason why class-two statements should not be considered culture-relative). Thiselton identifies New Testament witness to Old Testament authority as class-two statements.

Thiselton next considers why noncognitive accountings for biblical language and explanations that place everything within the framework of cultural relativism are not adequate. He argues that before biblical authority can be experienced within a language game, there must be a propositional aspect to revelation—that is, it must somehow communicate objective truth. "The dynamic and concrete authority of the Bible rests, in turn, on the truth of certain states of affairs in God's relation to the world. . . . For performative language to function effectively, 'certain statements have *to be true.*'" In its authoritative functioning, Scripture must also provide paradigms "in the light of which given concepts or experiences may be *identified* as genuinely 'Christian,' or otherwise." Basic Christian concepts derived from Scripture have transhistorical and transcultural authority, and to redefine them in such a way as to undermine the Bible would be to "saw off the branch on which I am sitting" as a Christian.[66]

Thiselton completes his argument by asserting that some biblical content functions as axiomatic class-two grammatical utterances, and these are derived from religious and theological, not cultural, tradition. One must assume objective propositional truth in order for Scripture to function authoritatively and provide paradigms for what it means to be a Christian.

65. Thiselton, *Two Horizons*, 392, 397.
66. Ibid., 437–38.

7

Application of Biblical Material

During the period 1971–1982, whenever evangelicals addressed the problem of applying biblical material—statements, injunctions, and concepts—to twentieth-century Christian living, two questions dominated. What possibilities exist for applying biblical injunctions and statements of truth that are infused with cultural elements? And what guidelines are there for determining which biblical content is intended to establish moral, spiritual, and social norms and standards?

Mandates and Principles

Before looking at these areas, it would be well to note the four basic components of biblical imperatives: the practice or teaching advocated, the principle or meaning that the action expresses, the rationale for the action, and the cultural context in which the action takes place and is understood. The issue for evangelical interpreters was how to apply a specific mandate with a particular meaning in its ancient cultural context to a contemporary context where the same teaching might have a completely different meaning or no meaning at all. Is it possible to be precisely obedient to the original writer's commands when applying his direction in a contemporary setting?

R. C. Sproul presents four general approaches for applying biblical material which contains cultural elements.[1] Taking 1 Corinthians 11:2–16 as an example, he identifies as the meaning the injunction that women are to be submissive to men. The form or practice for expressing that principle is the wearing of a head covering, which was a cultural sign of that submission. One approach, unacceptable to most evangelicals, would treat both form and meaning as custom, as culturally relative to Paul's time and therefore without continuing binding authority.[2]

A second approach treats both form and meaning as principle, and therefore eternally valid. Walter Kaiser says that this is often true of biblical content. The modern application, then, would keep both the meaning and the cultural-historical expression of that meaning.[3] Though evangelicals generally recognized that at any given place in Scripture both form and meaning could be potentially normative, in practice they showed a great deal of selectivity. Some materials could be applied easily and directly; other passages had to be adjusted. Gordon Fee and Douglas Stuart note that those who deny that cultural values are relative do not succeed very well in adopting first-century culture. It is extremely difficult to be consistent because "there is no such thing as a divinely ordained culture."[4] Evangelicals were ambivalent about consistently following this second approach.

A third approach focuses on the principle in the directive. Richard Longenecker asserts that Scripture's declared principles, or meanings, have continuing validity, but the practices, or forms, that implement them are only "signposts at the beginning of a journey which point out the path to be followed if we are to reapply that same gospel in our day." In his view, contemporary interpreters need to undertake a project of reapplication rather than adopting biblical practices. The biblical writers only began to work out the implications of the gospel for the situations they encountered; we must "endeavor to follow the path that they marked out for the application of those gospel principles, seeking to carry out their work in fuller and more significant ways."[5]

---

1. R. C. Sproul, *Knowing Scripture* (Downers Grove, Ill.: Inter-Varsity, 1977), 106.

2. See, however, James D. G. Dunn, "The Authority of Scripture According to Scripture," *Churchman* 96 (1982): 217.

3. Walter C. Kaiser, Jr., "Legitimate Hermeneutics," in *Inerrancy*, ed. Norman L. Geisler (Grand Rapids: Zondervan, 1979), 141.

4. Gordon D. Fee and Douglas Stuart, *How to Read the Bible for All Its Worth: A Guide to Understanding the Bible* (Grand Rapids: Zondervan, 1981), 65; see also Henry A. Virkler, *Hermeneutics: Principles and Processes of Biblical Interpretation* (Grand Rapids: Baker, 1981), 222.

5. Richard N. Longenecker, *New Testament Social Ethics for Today* (Grand Rapids: Eerdmans, 1984), 27–28; see also J. I. Packer, "Exposition on Biblical Hermeneutics," in *Hermeneutics, Inerrancy, and the Bible*, ed. Earl D. Radmacher and Robert D. Preus (Grand Rapids: Zondervan, 1984), 912–13.

At Summit II on Hermeneutics (1982) of the International Council on Biblical Inerrancy, Robertson McQuilkin challenged this approach on the grounds that it is nowhere enunciated in Scripture. "To set aside any specific teaching of Scripture, allowing only the principle deduced from the particular(s) to be normative, is to impose an extra-biblical notion and violate the authority of Scripture."[6] Alan Johnson, on the other hand, expressed support for Longenecker's approach, suggesting that it allows the whole of biblical phenomena to instruct us and "includes the necessary recognition that language and practice are culturally related and are *not* universal at certain levels of expression."[7]

The final approach holds that both the principle and the practice are normative, though the specific cultural expression of the practice may vary. In the case of 1 Corinthians 11, the principle of submission is still in force and the symbolic act of covering the head is specifically prescribed. However, the article for covering may vary from culture to culture.

Henry Virkler, focusing specifically on modification, points out that "since a given behavior in one culture may have a different meaning in another culture, it may be necessary to change the behavioral expression of a scriptural command in order to translate the principle behind it from one culture and time to another."[8] Walter Kaiser notes that there is "scriptural precedent for such cultural replacements." Paul, for example, replaces the death penalty (Lev. 20:11; see also 18:7) with excommunication (1 Cor. 5) as the punishment for incest. "The cultural *form* of a command may be modified even though the principle of that form remains unchanged for all subsequent readers."[9]

It is clear that evangelicals tackled the problems of application with vigor, and yet the decade of the seventies was characterized by a growing tentativeness. It appears that the unspoken consensus concerning which biblical commands were cultural and which were transcultural had begun to break down.

R. C. Sproul represents a case in point, for after advancing with precision the four approaches for application, he withdraws into uncertainty when confronted with the problem of stating which is most pleasing to

---

6. J. Robertson McQuilkin, "Problems of Normativeness in Scripture: Cultural Versus Permanent," in *Hermeneutics, Inerrancy,* 228; see also Richard N. Longenecker, "The Hermeneutics of New Testament Social Ethics" (unpublished paper, n.d.).

7. Alan F. Johnson, "A Response to Problems of Normativeness in Scripture: Cultural Versus Permanent," in *Hermeneutics, Inerrancy,* 270.

8. Virkler, *Hermeneutics,* 224; Grant R. Osborne adds another circumstance in which commands may be modified. "Those commands that have proven detrimental to the cause of Christ in later cultures must be reinterpreted" ("Hermeneutics and Women in the Church," *JETS* 20 [1977]: 340).

9. Kaiser, "Legitimate Hermeneutics," 142; see also I. Howard Marshall, "How Do We Interpret the Bible Today?" *Themelios* 5, no. 2 (1980): 11; J. Julius Scott, Jr., "Some Problems in Hermeneutics for Contemporary Evangelicals," *JETS* 22 (1979): 75.

God: "I certainly do not know the final answer to the question."[10] J. Julius Scott was also frank to admit that very little had been done to distinguish between those commands based on norms that transcend culture and those that are culturally conditioned. Carl Henry summed up the situation: "The problem of biblical content and cultural context is rapidly becoming a central concern in current evangelical discussions of Scripture, since more and more theologians hold that the New Testament writers in some respects teach as doctrine what in fact reflects the cultural milieu in which they live. . . . To distinguish the supercultural from the cultural is a fundamental concern of hermeneutics."[11] The question then becomes, What are the guidelines for determining what is truly normative in Scripture?

Guidelines for Normativeness

The probing and deliberations of scholars during this period established five basic criteria for determining which biblical content is normative: (1) similarity in situations, (2) the nature and rationale of the directive, (3) the form of the directive, (4) the analogy of faith, and (5) the intent of the author.

Similarity in Situations

Obviously, striking similarities between first-century and twentieth-century situations give impetus for applying biblical commands. "Whenever we share comparable particulars (i.e., similar specific life situations) with the first-century setting, God's Word to us is the same as His Word to them."[12]

By the same token, great cultural differences, and sometimes subtle ones, may indicate that directives set forth in cultural terms are no longer in effect.[13] For example, sufficient cultural difference to neutralize a precept may exist when the first-century situation does not and is not likely to occur in the twentieth century. Great cultural difference is also present when the scriptural first-century issue is no longer an issue in the twentieth century. In addition, significant cultural differences may be present that are not immediately obvious.[14] A directive might be based on cultural circum-

---

10. Sproul, *Knowing Scripture*, 107–8.

11. Carl F. H. Henry, *God, Revelation, and Authority*, 6 vols. (Waco, Tex.: Word, 1976–1979), 4:63, 57.

12. Fee and Stuart, *How to Read the Bible*, 60.

13. Gordon D. Fee, "Genre of New Testament Literature and Biblical Hermeneutics," in *Interpreting the Word of God Today*, ed. Samuel J. Schultz and Morris A. Inch (Chicago: Moody, 1976), 113–14.

14. Fee and Stuart, *How to Read the Bible*, 60, 68; Edwin M. Yamauchi, "Christianity and Cultural Differences," *CT* 16 (1971): 903.

stances which, though not explicitly stated in the text, are precisely what gave meaning and purpose at the time the teaching was written. For example, Is scriptural proscription against women as ministers no longer valid now that women have more educational opportunities to equip themselves for church leadership? Is head covering still required for women, or is decency of dress shown today in some other way?

As could be expected, numerous evangelical scholars cautioned against making similarity between cultures the test for normativeness.[15] Because societies and cultures are the product of sinful human beings, Scripture's role is to challenge a culture's values and standards of behavior. When certain principles are no longer at issue, it may be because the whole of society has accepted a practice or an attitude that is against God's will as revealed in Scripture. Twentieth-century ideas and practices concerning divorce spring immediately to mind.

The Nature and Rationale of the Directive

A different approach was suggested by those scholars who undertook to distinguish the essential moral and theological material in Scripture from the nonmoral and nontheological content that is wholly tied to a cultural situation and hence is not timeless in itself.[16] There is no authority in a directive which was the only option in a given first-century cultural situation. It is teaching that transcends the cultural biases of both the author and the readers that is normative.[17] Paul's teaching on unity in Christ, which supersedes ethnic, sexual, and socioeconomic distinctions (Gal. 3:28), transcends the cultural biases of the first century and is a clear example of a true norm.

One way of getting at the inherently moral and theological material is to explore the rationale with which it is presented. One recurring rationale is an appeal to the creation order and to God's relationship with people as people. Viewed in such a light, Jesus' directive concerning divorce (Matt. 19:6) is normative and binding for all time. These "creation ordinances are normative unless explicitly modified by later biblical revelation."[18]

---

15. Robin E. Nixon, "The Authority of the New Testament," in *New Testament Interpretation: Essays on Principles and Methods,* ed. I. H. Marshall (Grand Rapids: Eerdmans, 1977), 346; Harold Lindsell, "Biblical Infallibility from the Hermeneutical and Cultural Perspectives," *BS* 133 (1976): 312–18. H. Dermot McDonald expresses this same concern with reference to the Christian message. It may lose its distinctiveness when totally reinterpreted in terms of the cultural vogue, "the shibboleths of the hour" ("Theology and Culture: An Evangelical Correlation," in *Toward a Theology for the Future,* ed. Clark H. Pinnock and David F. Wells [Carol Stream, Ill.: Creation House, 1971], 254).

16. Fee, "Genre of New Testament Literature," 113; Scott, "Some Problems," 75.

17. Osborne, "Hermeneutics and Woman," 339–40; Fee and Stuart, *How to Read the Bible,* 68.

18. Sproul, *Knowing Scripture,* 111; Kaiser, "Legitimate Hermeneutics," 143; John Jefferson Davis, "Some Reflections on Galatians 3:28, Sexual Roles, and Biblical Hermeneutics," *JETS* 19 (1976): 206.

A second rationale lies in the nature of God. Scriptural directives against murder, thievery, lying, and similar offenses are based upon God's unchanging nature (Gen. 9:6; see also Exod. 20:1–20). Such commands have permanent relevance for all believers in all times.[19] The same holds true for prohibitions against pagan cultural practices; they are an offense to God's moral nature. Walter Kaiser makes the point that even in our contemporary culture such practices as bestiality, homosexuality, transvestism, and public nudity are forbidden. They offend the society of human beings made in God's image. It follows that Christ in his person, nature, and action also provides the basis for evaluating the authority of directives. The instruction for conduct in marriage in Ephesians 5:22–33 becomes unquestionably binding when seen as a reflection of Christ's relation to the church.

God's redemptive activity in the world provides a third rationale. In his saving activity, God enters into a covenant relationship with human beings that is uniquely transcultural, a covenant involving particular obligations and behavior patterns. These are much more than transitory, adaptable cultural expressions of eternal principles. As John Jefferson Davis puts it, "These patterns are understood as essential to a positive, dynamic, and missionary-oriented thrust toward secular culture." He contends that there is a discernible Christian ideology which must be integrated in distinctive, redemptively based forms of social life.[20]

Such a contention is based on the biblical understanding that God, working through the structures of human freedom, sovereignly and providentially controls all cultural development. He has the capacity to choose cultural patterns, whether they are Old Testament patriarchal structures of society or marriage regulations transformed by Jesus Christ (Matt. 5:27–32). Since these cultural patterns are grounded in the creation order, the culturally conditioned character of a biblical command becomes a subsidiary matter.

In critiquing the matter of rationale, Robertson McQuilkin sees the need to establish where in Scripture such criteria have been explicitly stated. He views the matter of rationale as an extrabiblical principle imported into the application process, thereby undermining biblical authority. Furthermore, the criteria cannot be applied to all explicit teachings in Scripture, for not all have a discernible rationale, nor can it be demonstrated that all are moral or theological. This means that some normative teachings would not be discovered, for they fail these tests.[21] Alan Johnson counters that, though Scripture may not explicitly establish these criteria, the biblical point of view,

---

19. Kaiser, "Legitimate Hermeneutics," 142.

20. Davis, "Some Reflections," 207 n. 19; see also idem, *Foundations of Evangelical Theology* (Grand Rapids: Baker, 1984), 276–79.

21. McQuilkin, "Problems of Normativeness," 228–29.

taken as a whole, does. He finds them not only workable, but helpful in avoiding "extreme cultural fundamentalism."[22]

The Form of the Directive

A third guideline is the directive's form. As J. Julius Scott suggests, if it is a precise command stated in universal terms, then it is normative. If it is "case law," the application of an unstated principle to a specific situation, then the specific application is not binding, but the principle is. If the principle is stated explicitly elsewhere in Scripture, then we can identify the culturally expressed material as a specific application of the principle.[23]

The Analogy of Faith

The hermeneutical principle of the analogy of faith becomes a fourth guideline. Scripture is best interpreted by Scripture, and this principle can show whether a command is normative. First, there is the matter of repetition. Roy Zuck contends that those situations, commands, or principles that are repeatable, continuous, and unrevoked, that pertain to other theological subjects, and that are repeated elsewhere in Scripture are normative and may be transferred directly for application.[24] Second, there is the matter of proportion and harmony with the larger context. A comparison of subject matter will either extend or limit the application and hence indicate the continuing authority of a given command. If the command is linked to the central core of the Bible's message or the central purposes of a given writer, then it should be viewed as normative. A teaching that is properly viewed as binding will be in harmony with the general message of the biblical writer and of Scripture as a whole.

Harold Lindsell considers the scriptural command concerning a wife's submission to her husband to be just such a norm. He asserts that this teaching is "so integral a part of the total presentation [of Ephesians and Colossians] that its nullification would impair or imperil the other major teachings of these epistles."[25]

---

22. Johnson, "Response to Problems," 272.

23. Scott, "Some Problems," 75. Osborne asserts that redaction criticism could be of use in distinguishing the primitive teaching of the early Christian tradition from the later temporal application to specific problems ("Hermeneutics and Women," 339).

24. Roy B. Zuck, "Application in Biblical Hermeneutics and Exposition," in *Walvoord: A Tribute*, ed. Donald K. Campbell (Chicago: Moody, 1982), 30; note Fee's guideline that a normative command should be part of uniform New Testament witness on the point ("Hermeneutics and Common Sense," in *Inerrancy and Common Sense*, ed. Roger Nicole and J. Ramsey Michaels [Grand Rapids: Baker, 1980], 174).

25. Lindsell, "Biblical Infallibility," 314.

Kenneth Kantzer, on the other hand, disputes the lasting authority of such passages as 1 Corinthians 11, 14, and 1 Timothy 2 in matters of a woman's role in the church. "If we were to universalize [the] prohibitions [of 1 Tim. 2:11–12 and 1 Cor. 14], we would extend the passages beyond the scope the apostle intended. It would conflict with other Scriptures, Paul's own clear statements in Corinthians, and his general teaching. . . . [Those who prohibit women's ordination] fail to see exactly the total thrust of Scripture in this matter."[26]

The concept of the larger context can also be employed in the framework of progressive revelation.[27] Some interpreters argue that unless a biblical injunction is explicitly modified or done away with by later biblical revelation, the injunction remains in effect; that is, only Scripture can limit or modify the authority of Scripture.[28] Other interpreters contend that "all of the Old Testament law is still the Word of God for use even though it is not still the command of God to us."[29] In this view, the Old Testament law is the old covenant whose obligations expired with the coming of Christ (Luke 16:16–17; Rom. 6:14–15); consequently, unless an Old Testament precept is restated or reinforced in the New Testament, it is no longer directly binding on God's people.

McQuilkin takes strong exception to this approach as being at odds with Christ's and the early apostles' view of the Old Testament as the authoritative Word of God. It would eliminate from consideration prohibitions that are not repeated in the New Testament, such as those against bestiality and rape. Though he acknowledges that there are problems in interpreting and applying the Old Testament, to disallow its normative nature "is certainly an attack on the authority of the majority of Scripture."[30]

The Intent of the Author

The final criterion is the intent of the original author. In uncovering this element, the interpreter can make a judgment concerning the extent of application. J. Julius Scott observes that when an author gives directives dealing with local customs or a particular situation, these injunctions may not be normative, though the principles behind them are. Indeed, the

---

26. Kenneth S. Kantzer, "Women's Role in Church and Family," CT 25 (1981): 254–55.

27. Eugene A. Wilson would have us ask these questions as we apply Old Testament narrative: Where in God's redemptive history do we find ourselves in relation to the people of the narrative? What added perspective of God's nature and work do we have as people living after Christ? Does God relate to us in the same way? ("The Homiletical Application of Old Testament Narrative Passages," Trinity Journal 7 [1978]: 89).

28. Sproul, Knowing Scripture, 110; Lindsell, "Biblical Infallibility," 313.

29. Fee and Stuart, How to Read the Bible, 139.

30. McQuilkin, "Problems of Normativeness," 230. Alan Johnson ("Response to Problems," 272) agrees with McQuilkin.

interpreter should be alert to "other indicators of the presence of historically or situationally controlled materials."[31] Scott gives as examples of directives that are situationally or culturally conditioned 2 Timothy 4:11 ("Get Mark and bring him with you") and Romans 16:16 ("Greet one another with a holy kiss"). R. C. Sproul recommends that the interpreter distinguish between cultural institutional structures (such as the monarchy) that Scripture simply recognizes to exist and those like monogamous marriage that the Bible institutes and endorses.[32]

Historical narratives, Gordon Fee contends, present many opportunities for distinguishing which factors are simply reported and which are normative.[33] Here again, the author's intention is the key. In Acts one may find incidental principles reflecting the author's theology. However, if they are not part of his basic message, they should not be given primary importance. For example, the strong Servant-Messiah Christology in the early preaching is incidental to Luke's overall purpose (Acts 3:26; 4:25, 30). Such incidental material may provide secondary support for what is taught elsewhere. Historical material does not become authoritative historical precedent unless the author intends it so, as is clearly the case in Jesus' and the apostles' two-stage experience: born of the Spirit, then baptized in the Spirit (Luke 1:35; 3:22; Acts 2:1–4). However, using the historical incident of Jesus' cleansing of the temple (Matt. 21:12–13) to justify selfish anger masquerading as righteous indignation is improper application, since selfish anger is not approved in Scripture.

Even patterns without normative foundation may have value for personal Christian experience. Where there are diverse patterns—for example, in the author's presentation of the relationships between conversion, baptism, and the coming of the Spirit (Acts 2:38–41; 8:17–18; 10:44–46; 19:6)—it is necessary to establish the pattern to be taken as binding. This can be done by finding where else in Scripture the principle behind the pattern is explicitly taught.

During the decade of the seventies no consensus was achieved in methods for uncovering the Bible's normative commands. This may explain why the dominant plea was for interpreters to address these issues, while interacting in a Christian manner with those with whom they may differ. R. C. Sproul called for humility in areas of uncertainty where it is hard to decide whether the biblical content is binding. Gordon Fee asked for charity, forgiveness, and open communication between those of differing opinions.[34]

---

31. Scott, "Some Problems," 75.

32. Sproul, *Knowing Scripture*, 109.

33. Fee, "Genre of New Testament Literature," 117–19; see also idem, "Hermeneutics and Historical Precedent—A Major Problem in Pentecostal Hermeneutics," in *Perspectives on the New Pentecostalism*, ed. Russell P. Spittler (Grand Rapids: Baker, 1976), 118–33.

34. Fee, "Hermeneutics and Common Sense," 176.

In suggesting how to handle uncertainty in a way that balances the interpreter's tentativeness with commitment to a fully authoritative Scripture, Sproul counsels that overscrupulousness may be wise for a mandate of uncertain authority. Yet the interpreter must stop short of unnecessarily binding the conscience of another. This means, Sproul counsels, that the interpreters must do their analytical homework before making absolute statements about normative content.[35]

---

35. Sproul, *Knowing Scripture*, 111–12.

8

International Council on Biblical Inerrancy

Two conferences were sponsored by the International Council on Biblical Inerrancy, in 1978 and 1982, providing a forum in which North American conservative evangelicals could articulate their understanding of the nature and authority of Scripture and the implications for the hermeneutical task.

The Chicago Statements

Summit I

At the first conference Scripture was defined as the fully inspired, inerrant, and authoritative Word of God. A statement was published defending this position, and in the process the implications of inerrancy for hermeneutics were stated, thus creating the theological context for discussion of hermeneutics and culture at the next conference. That statement declared that Scripture is "to be believed, as God's instruction, in all it affirms; obeyed, as God's command, in all that it requires." The Bible is to be received as truth in all matters on which it touches, and its authority must in no way be "limited or disregarded, or made relative to a view of truth contrary to the Bible's own."[1]

---

1. "The Chicago Statement on Biblical Inerrancy," in *Inerrancy*, ed. Norman L. Geisler (Grand Rapids: Zondervan, 1979), 494.

One possibility for limitation exists when the thought-patterns of the interpreter's culture are permitted to stand in judgment over the content of Scripture. To guard against this, the statement denied that any scientific hypothesis about earth history may be used to overturn scriptural teaching on the creation and the flood. It also noted that the nature of progressive revelation makes it impossible for subsequent revelation to correct or contradict prior revelation.

The Summit I statement also addressed the standards of truth that are to be applied to Scripture. The paper distinguished between the standards of literary convention and truth norms, pointing out that an absence of modern technical or scientific precision, irregularities of grammar and spelling, the use of figurative and poetic language, and topical arrangements of material in no way diminish the truthfulness of Scripture. In the exposition there is the further explanation that such literary conventions as were customarily acceptable and did not violate the expectations of the ancient writer's culture should not be faulted. Rather, Scripture is inerrant in achieving "that measure of focused truth at which its authors aimed."[2]

The Chicago statement described the nature of Scripture's inerrant meaning in terms of both ancient text and modern interpretation, affirming that human language, before and after the fall, is adequate for God's use as a means of revelation to human creatures made in his image. Moreover, inspiration guarantees the truthfulness of the biblical writers in all matters on which they speak. Even in their finite and fallen state, the biblical writers were preserved by God's sovereign providence from introducing distortion or falsehood into the inspired text. Ancient culture and convention in no way limit the presentation of God's truth.

This being the case, how does one approach the biblical text to interpret it for today? The interpretational process outlined in the statement follows the grammatical-historical method, taking into account literary forms and devices and employing the analogy of faith—that is, using Scripture to interpret Scripture.[3] The twentieth-century interpreter who desires to affirm biblical inerrancy will avoid presuppositions and methods that relativize, dehistoricize, or discount the teaching or claims to authorship of the text. Skepticism toward basic Christian tenets, whether from agnosticism, rationalism, idealism, or existentialism, makes a faithful interpretation of Scripture impossible. In the matter of application the statement affirmed that although Holy Scripture is nowhere culture-bound in the sense that its teaching lacks universal validity, it is sometimes culturally conditioned by

---

2. Ibid., 501.
3. The principle of the analogy of faith is based on "the unity and internal consistency of Scripture," which the statement affirms (ibid., 497). It also points out that unresolved alleged errors and discrepancies do not vitiate the truth claims of Scripture.

the customs and conventional view of a particular period, so that the application of its principles today calls for a different sort of action.[4]

Summit II

At Summit II, the delegates set to work on the details of the hermeneutical implications, addressing such issues as the nature of truth, the meaning of language, and the problem of distinguishing the permanent from the cultural in Scripture when one applies its teaching. Building on the first summit's definitions, the second conference enunciated the definitional presuppositions and hermeneutical guidelines for faithful interpretation and application.

Biblical truth is by nature propositional, objective, and absolute and corresponds to reality; and, as Norman Geisler points out, these qualities are critically significant for contemporary hermeneutical discussion.[5] Scripture as absolute truth cannot accommodate epistemological relativism, moderate or radical; as objective truth, it leaves no room for subjectivism; as truth that corresponds to reality, it resists dilution from existential or pragmatic ideology.

Once again human language was affirmed as adequate to convey divine revelation without error. The second conference also considered the nature of meaning, undertaking to refine and extend its definition. Meaning in Scripture was declared to be single, definite, and fixed. Single, because multiple meanings and modifications arising from the interpreter's context are not admissible; definite, because the author's written expression determines the limits; and fixed, because the meaning so delineated is unchanging. This careful analysis of language and meaning was intended to underscore that the meaning of a scriptural passage comes from the words themselves and not from the interpreter's understanding.

Summit II considered and offered guidelines for translating inspired and authoritative Scripture. The nature of language as previously defined ensures the possibility of communicating the knowledge of God via translation across all temporal and cultural boundaries. Nor is meaning so tied to the ancient culture that it cannot be accurately conveyed to another culture. Truth is transcendent and not culture-bound; this means that it can be reexpressed in another language without impairing the message. Great care must be exercised, of course. Linguistic equivalents must be sensitively selected to preserve the original content and meaning.

---

4. Ibid., 501.

5. Norman L. Geisler, "Explaining Hermeneutics: A Commentary on the Chicago Statement on Biblical Hermeneutics Articles of Affirmation and Denial," in *Hermeneutics, Inerrancy, and the Bible*, ed. Earl D. Radmacher and Robert D. Preus (Grand Rapids: Zondervan, 1984), 889–904.

For the hermeneutical process, the Chicago statement recommends interpreting the text according to its literal or normal sense, that is, the grammatical-historical meaning expressed by the writer, and giving full weight and appreciation to any figures of speech or literary conventions that are present. On the other hand, any method developing a meaning which through a generic category negates historicity or goes beyond what the literal sense can support is to be rejected. It was recognized that extrabiblical data can often be useful in clarifying a scriptural teaching or correcting a faulty interpretation. However, extrabiblical sources should not be used to dispute the teaching or undermine its authority.

Several conference statements acknowledged with appreciation the role of contemporary context in hermeneutics and also the contributions made by the social sciences. These are the components of an interpreter's pre-understanding, components that the interpreter must be willing to measure by Scripture's teaching and submit to Scripture's correction. Faithful interpreters must be aware of any presuppositions that might distort their perceptions, making sure that they are not viewing the text through lenses focused by "naturalism, evolutionism, scientism, secular humanism, and relativism."[6]

A highly positive role was envisioned for the interpreter in the area of application. The statement affirms that hermeneutics deals not only with what biblical revelation means, but with how it bears on lives. This part of the hermeneutical task should include active involvement with the Holy Spirit, a process enabling the interpreter to understand the spiritual implications of a passage. The Holy Spirit infuses the interpretational task faithfully performed in such a way that the truth discovered can be applied to Christian living. Still, there is the warning not to let the need or desire for specific application so color one's interpretation that the interpreter's horizon provides the text's meaning.

The 1982 Chicago Statement of Hermeneutics advanced evangelical thinking markedly:

We affirm that the Bible contains teachings and mandates which apply to all cultural and situational contexts and other mandates which the Bible itself shows apply only to particular situations.

We deny that the distinction between the universal and particular mandates of Scripture can be determined by cultural and situational factors. We further deny that universal mandates may ever be treated as culturally or situationally relative.[7]

---

6. Ibid., 901.
7. Ibid., 893.

Clearly, the universal teachings are seen to transcend culture even when they speak to, and are expressed within, a particular culture; and Scripture itself will determine which teaching applies only to a particular situation. The commentary accompanying the paper points out that cultural and situational factors can aid in discovering right application, but these do not determine what is normative, since God's law is not situationally determined.

Robertson McQuilkin

A highlight of the second conference was a paper by Robertson Mc-Quilkin, formerly a missionary to Japan and currently the president of Columbia Bible College and Seminary. Long concerned with the issue of biblical authority and cultural interpretation, McQuilkin has repeatedly warned that such antibiblical concepts as cultural relativism and environmental determinism were seeping from the behavioral sciences into evangelical hermeneutics and taking functional control of the interpretational process.[8] He saw the behavioral sciences erecting constructs for application in space that theologians had failed to fill. Calling into question current evangelical practices of cultural interpretation, he proposed guidelines for taking into account both the ancient and modern cultural factor in interpretation and application.[9] His conference paper, "Problems of Normativeness in Scripture: Cultural Versus Permanent," contained a comprehensive exposition of his fully developed thought.[10]

From the outset McQuilkin affirms the full verbal inspiration and inerrancy of Scripture as well as its total and independent divine authority. This inspiration and authority extend so deeply into the very words of Scripture that form and meaning become part of the permanent revelation of God's truth. Thus "the words . . . inspired to convey the meaning God intended, constitute the permanent revelation of God's truth."[11] McQuilkin has great confidence in locating the authoritative content of the text in its "plain meaning."

8. J. Robertson McQuilkin, "The Behavioral Sciences Under the Authority of Scripture," *JETS* 20 (1977): 31–43.

9. J. Robertson McQuilkin, "Limits of Cultural Interpretation," *JETS* 23 (1980): 113–24; idem, "Biblical Authority Made Functional" (paper presented at the annual meeting of the Evangelical Theological Society, Deerfield, Ill., 27 December 1978).

10. "Problems of Normativeness in Scripture: Cultural Versus Permanent," in *Hermeneutics, Inerrancy*, 217–40. McQuilkin has also incorporated his views in a college text, *Understanding and Applying the Bible* (Chicago: Moody, 1983).

11. McQuilkin, "Problems of Normativeness," 222. McQuilkin finds the authoritative content of Scripture by asking three questions: Who said it? What did he say? What did he mean? ("Biblical Authority," 1).

In a vigorous response to this paper, Alan Johnson questions whether McQuilkin's understanding of the relation of revelation and language is adequate for the task of interpretation and application, contending that to wed the meaning of God's truth to its ancient cultural form, the words of Scripture, eliminates the possibility of expressing that same meaning in any other historical or cultural situation. Words change meaning from cultural context to cultural context and sometimes even within a single context. He uses the text "man shall not live by bread alone" (Deut. 8:3) as an example. The word *man* should be changed because in our culture it is used less and less in its generic sense and more and more to point exclusively to males. For Johnson, interpretation means allowing "the biblical message to be heard in meaningful terms that correspond as clearly as possible with the understanding the original hearers would have received."[12]

Johnson also faults McQuilkin for failing to distinguish between the effects of the cultural factor in doctrinal teaching and its effects in behavioral teaching.[13] Johnson asserts that the interpreter should recognize that doctrinal teaching—what the writer reveals about himself, human beings, and the world—though expressed in culture-laden human language, transcends the culture. In behavioral teaching, on the other hand, moral universals and general moral principles are normative, but the culturally specific expression of these principles is not. The interpreter must find a functional equivalent to express the basic principle in contemporary cultural terms.

In the matter of application McQuilkin asserts Scripture's independent authority over each step of the process, a process that identifies in the biblical teaching the recipient intended and the response called for. This determination is grounded in Scripture, of course, and not imposed from an external source. McQuilkin acknowledges that though an understanding of biblical and contemporary cultural forms may be helpful, they must not contradict the plain meaning of the authoritative text; "meaning, recipient, and application must be established within the limits set by the data of Scripture."[14]

Johnson qualifies this position in two ways. (1) He sees the rejection of the decisive influence of extrabiblical data as flawed because it fails to take into account general revelation, God's truth present in creation. Scripture is better viewed as the supreme and final authority among other authorities. (2) He disputes McQuilkin's assumption that there is a clear and unambiguous "plain meaning" to Scripture and points out that the Reformers made no such assumption. For them, Scripture's perspicuity applied only to its central message of salvation.

---

12. Alan F. Johnson, "A Response to Problems of Normativeness in Scripture: Cultural Versus Permanent," in *Hermeneutics, Inerrancy,* 261.

13. Ibid., 262–63.

14. McQuilkin, "Problems of Normativeness," 222.

For Johnson, the plain meaning of the text is determined by the whole literary, cultural, and historical context in which the biblical authors wrote. An objective meaning is sought through study of the whole ancient context of the passage. Claiming to know the plain meaning apart from the ancient context amounts to imposing one's own perspective on the text, and that, Johnson points out, has a distorting influence. Johnson, following Charles Kraft, sees the individual's preunderstanding as providing a context for the meaning of the text. Those who cannot distance themselves self-critically from the text will "discover" a plain meaning that accords with their contemporary preunderstanding, not with the ancient author's. Indeed, unless scriptural statements are very general, the unreflective interpreter arrives at misleading meanings.

While insights from ancient and modern cultural concerns or preunderstandings can clarify the text, they must do more. The interpreter should let them modify and even change his or her understanding of certain biblical teaching. "Otherwise, we are bound to human ecclesiastical traditions and our own provincial view of Scripture."[15]

McQuilkin also asserts that "a fully authoritative Bible means that every teaching in Scripture is universal unless Scripture itself treats it as limited."[16] Because Scripture is the fully authoritative, inspired, inerrant Word of God, the interpreter should treat all its teaching as universal for all people and all times, unless Scripture itself shows that the teaching is intended to have a limited application.

Again Johnson challenges the thesis. He sees the principle as self-defeating because Scripture itself states no such principle, though he grants that the thesis would stand or fall on the basis of the direction in which the whole of scriptural phenomena points. Johnson, however, does not test this thesis or its converse (which could equally be true) that every teaching of the Bible is a specific word of God limited to its historical-cultural context unless Scripture teaches that it is universal.[17]

---

15. Johnson, "Response to Problems," 267. Note that Harvie Conn also criticizes McQuilkin on this point, charging that his appeal to the plain sense of the text comes in part from a static view of culture born of functionalism (*Eternal Word and Changing Worlds: Theology, Anthropology, and Mission in Trialogue* [Grand Rapids: Zondervan, 1984], 121–22). Conn's analysis should be questioned, since McQuilkin seems to be more indebted at this point to the hermeneutical heritage of the Reformation than to anthropological functionalism (see John Calvin, *Commentaries on the Epistles of Paul to the Galatians and Ephesians,* trans. William Pringle [Grand Rapids: Eerdmans, 1957], 135).

16. McQuilkin, "Problems of Normativeness," 230; idem, "Limits," 123. Henry A. Virkler agrees when he says that there is a need to develop criteria for distinguishing cultural universals which are logical and consistently applied, the "nature of which is either drawn from Scripture or, at least, is consistent with Scripture" (*Hermeneutics: Principles and Processes of Biblical Interpretation* [Grand Rapids: Baker, 1981], 223).

17. Johnson, "Response to Problems," 259–60. Harvie Conn also points out a danger in the kind of approach which promotes biblical priority: "The danger in saying this is that we do not mean 'biblical priority' so much as 'theological priority.' Theology, after all, is one more scientific discipline. And, like any other, it too misreads" (*Eternal Word,* 175).

McQuilkin proposes seven questions to aid in determining whether Scripture has limited a teaching:[18]

(1) *Does the context limit the recipient or application?* Taking Paul's comments on celibacy in 1 Corinthians 7, McQuilkin refers to Matthew 19:12 and 1 Corinthians 7:8 and concludes that "the teaching is addressed not to all Christian men but to those so gifted."[19]

Johnson basically agrees with this principle, but asserts that all New Testament literature is occasional, and that "the larger context including the historical, cultural, and theological situation must be brought to bear on questions of meaning and normativeness even when the text itself does not explicitly mention all these factors."[20] George Knight responds that the real issue is the significance of this occasional character for the communication of universal and normative truth. Either the biblical literature is so occasional that it contains no normative and universal truth, or God can communicate his universal and normative truth in occasional situations.[21] Using Exodus 20:17, "Thou shalt not covet," Knight suggests that "here we see occasional character and universality side by side, but with the occasional character concretizing and communicating the universal, not delimiting the truth or making it a captive to that culture and time."[22]

(2) *Does subsequent revelation limit the recipient or the application?* This criterion applies primarily to Old Testament law. McQuilkin notes that Jesus modified the old law on divorce (Matt. 5:31–32; 19:8–9) and set aside the structure of civil government for his people (Matt. 16:18; 26:52; John 18:36), as well as the sacrificial system and dietary laws (Mark 7:19; Acts 10:15).

(3) *Is this specific teaching in conflict with other biblical teaching?* When apparent conflict arises, it may indicate that a teaching is limited in regard to the recipient or the application. Unity may be restored by applying each teaching within its proper limits, and help from the cultural background may be sought to clarify those limits. In his 1978 paper McQuilkin concluded that when the conflict remains unresolved, the stronger, clearer, more enduring teaching of Scripture is to be received as having the wider application. His 1982 exposition asks whether extrabiblical cultural background may properly be used to clarify meaning in situations where there are conflicts. He concludes that cultural factors may be used when one's aim is to defend Scripture's authority, but one should not use extrabiblical cultural background to avoid application of passages with uncontested meaning.

---

18. McQuilkin, "Problems of Normativeness," 230–40.

19. McQuilkin, "Biblical Authority," 3. In fact, the structuring of the criteria of this paper under two general headings, "Identify the Recipient; Identify the Response," more clearly lays out the issues.

20. Johnson, "Response to Problems," 273.

21. Johnson says that he is in agreement with this characterization of biblical content (letter to author, November 1986).

22. George W. Knight III, "From Hermeneutics to Practice: Scriptural Normativity and Culture, Revisited," *Presbyterion* 12 (1986): 100.

Women's silence versus women's speech in church is a case in point (1 Cor. 14:34; 1 Tim. 2:11; 1 Cor. 11:5; Acts 2:17–18), as is the Nazirite vow versus the shame of long hair on males (Num. 6:5; 1 Cor. 11:14).[23]

George Knight in responding suggests restating the criterion. Is *my understanding* of this specific teaching in conflict with other biblical teaching?[24]

On the grounds that "every word from God comes in ordinary human language and addresses itself to specific historical situations," Alan Johnson challenges McQuilkin's restrictions on using cultural factors.[25] Johnson points to the conflict between Galatians 3:28 ("there is neither male nor female") and 1 Timothy 2:12 ("I permit no woman to teach or to have authority over men! She is to keep silent") as an indication of Scripture's historical and cultural character. Would McQuilkin permit cultural features to resolve the difficulty?

John Jefferson Davis makes an interesting point in commenting on Galatians 3:28, where Paul's Christian egalitarianism seems to conflict with his teaching on woman's subordinate role in the family. Davis locates the source of conflict in the contemporary interpreter's imposition of modern egalitarian social ideas upon Paul, rather than in the apostle's rabbinic eisegesis of hierarchialism. Modern interpreters often fail to understand that ontological equality and mutual dependence do not conflict with the economic or social subordination in the creation order. In fact, there seems to be a basic contemporary misunderstanding of the nature of authority relationships as presented in Scripture.[26]

(4) *Is the reason for a norm given in Scripture, and is that reason treated as normative?* In cases where no rationale is given for a norm, the proper response is faith and obedience. When a rationale is provided, it must be tested to see whether it is universal and normative ("comfort one another because Christ will return," 1 Thess. 4:18) or cultural ("work with your hands, in order to have a good reputation before those who value such labor," 5:12–13). The universal and normative has continuing authority.

In addressing the problem passage of 1 Corinthians 14 McQuilkin warns against introducing an external cultural rationale that has the effect of setting aside the passage's teaching. For example, we would be wrong to argue that women were to keep silent in the first-century church because they did not have education and that, since contemporary society affords them educational opportunities, the restriction no longer applies. Such reasoning has

---

23. McQuilkin, "Problems of Normativeness," 231–32; idem, "Behavioral Sciences," 37; idem, "Biblical Authority," 4–5.

24. George W. Knight III, "A Response to Problems of Normativeness in Scripture: Cultural Versus Permanent," in *Hermeneutics, Inerrancy,* 247.

25. Johnson, "Response to Problems," 274.

26. John Jefferson Davis, "Some Reflections on Galatians 3:28, Sexual Roles, and Biblical Hermeneutics," *JETS* 19 (1976): 204–5; see also Knight, "From Hermeneutics to Practice," 100.

potential for almost limitless setting aside of Scripture. McQuilkin acknowledges the difficulty that exists when a passage such as 1 Corinthians 11 contains obvious cultural reasons for behavior, indicated by such terms as "traditions," "dishonor," "shame," "you all judge," "seemly," "the natural thing," and "custom," together with theological reasons.[27] When cultural factors reinforce theological reasons, the commands are obviously normative. If, however, the theological base is present in a clearly delineated and specific cultural setting, it seems permissible to apply the same theological truth differently in a different cultural setting.

Respondent George Knight argues that 1 Corinthians 11 gives an authoritative norm with regard to length of hair. His thorough exegesis emphasizes that the term *nature* as used by Paul refers not to cultural perception of what is appropriate but to the created order, and therefore the command is normative.

Alan Johnson responds more generally, contending that the Bible gives no instruction about which rationales are cultural and which are universal. To illustrate the usefulness of extrabiblical cultural information, Johnson points out that in first-century pagan worship, women impersonated men. He concludes that Paul commands long hair and head covering in 1 Corinthians so that women might be distinguished from men in public worship. No universally normative roles for men and women are intended here; rather, Paul is outlining a culturally recognized form for distinguishing female and male in worship. Johnson argues that in Western culture the wearing of dresses would sufficiently distinguish women from men.

(5) *Is the specific teaching (as well as the principle behind it) normative?* McQuilkin insists that specific teaching is normative "unless the condition of the teaching is not mandated in Scripture and it does not exist in the situation at hand." "Condition" refers to those circumstances that must be present for one to obey the specific teaching. The instructions for footwashing in John 13:14–15 provide an example: "Wash your brother's feet if they are dirty and someone ought to. But serve him in other ways if he does not need your help with his feet at the moment."[28]

The prohibition of homosexuality is put forward as a command whose condition is mandated. It is therefore normative. The promiscuousness of a particular culture may not be introduced to limit the prohibition of homosexual relationships, because this brings in extrabiblical information to set aside biblical authority. The Bible prohibits homosexuality universally. The conditions in which this teaching is to be obeyed admit of no exceptions across time or culture. There are no circumstances in which it is not normative.

---

27. McQuilkin, "Problems of Normativeness," 233.
28. Ibid.

Though Alan Johnson agrees that Scripture prohibits homosexuality, he has several questions about this guideline for application. How does one distinguish between mandated and nonmandated conditions? Knowledge of the larger ancient context would, in Johnson's opinion, reveal the implicit cultural assumptions of the writer and his intent with regard to the universality or cultural limitation of a specific command. Johnson also agrees that if the situation no longer exists, the specific command is not normative. However, on the basis of his understanding that meaning is located in the context, he suggests that even when conditions for fulfilling a given command still exist, the action may have a different meaning in the contemporary cultural context. The command to "greet one another with a holy kiss" (Rom. 16:16) is such an action; "the changed social-cultural meaning attached to expressions of kissing (especially homosexual) within the present American culture would lead us to forego kissing and instead exchange vigorous handshakes."[29] Therefore, even though one could literally fulfil the command, it would be better to find a functional equivalent. The same principles can be applied to biblical teaching on family, church, societal governance, and male-female relationships.

(6) *Does the Bible treat the historic context as normative?* McQuilkin's view is that historical context, either actions or words, is not normative unless Scripture indicates otherwise, and the biblical writer's approval of the action and an accompanying rationale are strong indicators. If only the writer's approval is present, a rationale needs to be found elsewhere in Scripture to establish the action as normative. When clear teaching, such as that of Jesus or the apostles, is present in historical narrative, it should be regarded as normative unless the context itself indicates historical limitation.

Johnson considers such a distinction between teaching and historical portions of Scripture to be artificial. In his view, every literary genre in Scripture can be a vehicle for God's normative revelatory truth. Biblical history is not simply the accurate report of events, but is an interpretive theological and kerygmatic account intended to convey authoritative truth concerning God's purposes for the world.[30]

(7) *Does the Bible treat the cultural context as limited?* By culture McQuilkin means human behavior, morals, values, the way things are done; he holds that biblical teaching concerning culture is normative unless Scripture itself limits the recipient or the response. An interpreter should not be surprised to find that most references to culture are in teaching passages, since God is

---

29. Johnson, "Response to Problems," 276; see also Grant R. Osborne, "Hermeneutics and Women in the Church," *JETS* 20 (1977): 340; Virkler, *Hermeneutics*, 227–28.

30. See Gordon D. Fee, "Hermeneutics and Historical Precedent—A Major Problem in Pentecostal Hermeneutics," in *Perspectives on the New Pentecostalism*, ed. Russell P. Spittler (Grand Rapids: Baker, 1976), 124.

out to change culture. Human behavior is the object of revelation, and God has given his revelation in propositional form so that the chief element of culture—which is language, both word and meaning—can be used to embody that revelation. McQuilkin is not concerned with incidental and transient Eastern customs mentioned in Scripture; his definition of culture is behavioral.

McQuilkin argues strongly for considering the cultural context as binding unless Scripture itself sets limits. He laments that in recent years many interpreters have used the term *cultural* to label and set aside content in Scripture not congenial to contemporary culture. This practice makes culture an external authority over Scripture and is potentially destructive of biblical authority.

> To set aside any of Scripture simply on the basis that it is cultural and therefore valid only for one specific cultural setting is to establish a principle that can be used to set aside any or even all biblical teaching. The interpreter thus becomes the authority over Scripture, establishing as normative for human belief or behavior only those elements of Bible teaching or those principles deduced from Bible teaching which prove universally valid relative to some cultural criteria.[31]

Alan Johnson responds by asking just how cultural context is to be distinguished from historical context. For Johnson, the authority of Scripture is undermined when the interpreter treats as culturally absolute what God never intended as universal, thus creating "a nonbiblical fundamentalism that ultimately imprisons portions of the Word of God within ancient cultural forms irrelevant to the contemporary world." The way to avoid relativizing Scripture is to develop and apply "consistently careful guidelines designed to honor the evidence of the full biblical context including an understanding of the historical occasion and the cultural language."[32]

---

31. McQuilkin, "Problems of Normativeness," 238.
32. Johnson, "Response to Problems," 277.

Part 4

Hermeneutics and Culture
The Missiological Approach

9

Culture Impacts Theology

For missiologists, the impact of culture on theology is a compound one, for they face the problem of communicating the Bible's message to a diversity of modern cultures. Some see a possibility for using data from anthropology and other behavioral sciences to understand the cultures involved, both ancient and modern. Others fear that introducing such elements into the hermeneutical process might undermine biblical authority.[1] On the whole, however, missiologists view the contribution of anthropological and sociological insights as positive and consider how to integrate the content of biblical revelation with the presuppositions, methods, and conclusions of anthropology.[2] The result has been an outpouring of articles, monographs, and consultations.

The ecumenical movement set the agenda at the Faith and Order Conference in Louvain (Belgium) in 1971. The statement "Authority of the Bible" asserted that contemporary cultural context determines the meaning,

---

1. J. Robertson McQuilkin, "The Behavioral Sciences Under the Authority of Scripture," *JETS* 20 (1977): 31–43; Paul G. Hiebert, "Missions and Anthropology: A Love/Hate Relationship," *Missiology* 6 (1978): 165–80; Bruce J. Nicholls, *Contextualization: A Theology of Gospel and Culture* (Downers Grove, Ill.: Inter-Varsity, 1979), 13.

2. Charles H. Kraft, "Can Anthropological Insight Assist Evangelical Theology?" *Christian Scholar's Review* 7 (1977): 165–202; G. Linwood Barney, "The Challenge of Anthropology to Current Missiology," *International Bulletin of Missionary Research* 5 (October 1981): 172–77.

interpretation, and application of Scripture. Scriptural authority was presented as a "relational concept"[3]—the Bible demonstrates its authority by submitting to reciprocal questioning between itself and the contemporary context.

The staff of the World Council of Churches (WCC) Theological Education Fund enthusiastically affirmed the priority of contemporary context and coined the term *contextualization*. They called for a renewal in theological education for mission which would take "contextuality seriously by discerning God's mission for man in history . . . [through] heeding the signs which are God's way of talking to us in our time and context."[4]

Among evangelicals, Charles Kraft addressed the issue of hermeneutics and cultural context most consistently throughout the decade.[5] He views the hermeneutical task from Eugene Nida's "relative relativism" perspective, affirming a divinely inspired Scripture given in the cultural forms of ancient peoples, but relevant and applicable to culture-bound contemporary interpreters.[6] The problem becomes how to understand and apply scriptural meanings presented in the forms of particular ancient cultures to the lives of contemporary peoples immersed in other cultures. Kraft proposes an ethnolinguistic method that takes into account the cultural immersion of text and interpreter, an approach he calls ethnotheology.

Role of the Behavioral Sciences

Robertson McQuilkin presented a critical analysis of the relationship of behavioral sciences to an authoritative Scripture at the 1975 annual meeting of the Evangelical Theological Society, asserting that whenever an academic discipline deals with subject matter which is the concern and focus of Scripture, Scripture should exercise functional control. "The functional control of Scripture over any discipline will vary in direct proportion to the overlap of that discipline with the substance of Biblical revelation." The "control" operates when an idea from a given discipline is faced with a

---

3. "The Authority of the Bible—Text," *Ecumenical Review* 23 (1971): 419–37.

4. TEF Staff, *Ministry in Context: The Third Mandate Programme of the Theological Education Fund (1970–77)* (Bromley, Kent: Theological Education Fund, 1972), 30; see also Bruce C. Fleming's description and critique (*Contextualization of Theology: An Evangelical Assessment* [Pasadena, Calif.: William Carey Library, 1980], 5ff.). For further description and critique, see Nicholls, *Contextualization*, 21ff.; and Harvie M. Conn, "Contextualization: Where Do We Begin?" in *Evangelicals and Liberation*, ed. Carl E. Armerding (Nutley, N.J.: Presbyterian & Reformed, 1977), 90–119.

5. Charles H. Kraft, "Toward a Christian Ethnotheology," in *God, Man, and Church Growth*, ed. Alan R. Tippett (Grand Rapids: Eerdmans, 1973), 109–27; idem, "Ideological Factors in Intercultural Communication," *Missiology* 2 (1974): 295–312; idem, "Interpreting in Cultural Context," *JETS* 21 (1978): 357–67; idem, *Christianity in Culture* (Maryknoll, N.Y.: Orbis, 1979).

6. Eugene A. Nida, *Customs and Culture* (New York: Harper, 1954), 48–52.

contrary idea from Scripture; an inerrant Bible will never be wrong, but the methods and conclusions of human disciplines may be. The highest level of overlap occurs with subject matter which should be derived from Scripture alone. McQuilkin places the disciplines of theology and Christian philosophy at this level. In the second level are the behavioral sciences—psychology, sociology, and anthropology. At this level, "overlap with revelation is great though not complete, so that subject matter should be derived from Scripture but extended by empirical research and experimentation."[7]

McQuilkin sees the behavioral sciences as at this level because their basic focus is human behavior, and the main purpose of Scripture is to change human behavior (2 Tim. 3:15–17). He is careful to point out that overlap is not complete, since Scripture does not profess to be a textbook on the behavioral sciences. It is proper to extend the understanding of human nature and relationships by empirical research and experimentation.

McQuilkin's analysis would be everywhere accepted and followed if it were not for one other factor—sin. Human beings are in rebellion against God. The effects of sin are so deeply engrained in the human mind that people will resist God's authority either by disregarding the evidence of biblical revelation or by reinterpreting it in terms of their own thought-constructs as they develop humanly autonomous behavioral sciences. As a result, any understanding of human nature and relationships is necessarily flawed. Human finiteness also plays a part in the inevitable distortion present in the behavioral sciences.

McQuilkin contends that currently the behavioral sciences are outside the functional control of Scripture, as is demonstrated by comparative studies of the religious commitment of professors in various disciplines.[8] Such studies reveal an inverse relationship between the degree of religious conviction of professors in a given discipline and the level of overlap between that discipline's subject matter and the Bible's. Teachers of home economics, agriculture, and medicine showed a 90 percent religious-affiliation rate, though their disciplines have the least overlap with Scripture's subject matter. McQuilkin places them at the fifth level of overlap. This correlation contrasts with the 44 percent for teachers of anthropology, a second-level discipline. Overall, only 7 percent of instructors in the social sciences believe that the Bible is the revealed Word of God, and only 19 percent affirm that God is the Creator. They see religious convictions as unrelated to their discipline. Since it can be documented that in childhood they experienced religious socialization in line with the national average, the researchers

---

7. McQuilkin, "Behavioral Sciences," 32.

8. Malcolm G. Scully, "Faculty Members, Liberal on Politics, Found Conservative on Academic Issues," *Chronicle of Higher Education*, 6 April 1970; Fred Thalheimer, "Religiosity and Secularization in the Academic Professions," *Sociology of Education* 46 (Spring 1973): 186.

conclude that somewhere in their academic development these social scientists encountered a conflict or dissonance between the content of biblical revelation and their discipline. This they chose to resolve either by compartmentalizing or by redefining biblical content in terms of their discipline's presuppositions, methods, and conclusions.

Promoting anthropology as a useful discipline for missiology, G. Linwood Barney touches on this problem: "Probably most members of the discipline of anthropology would not want to address some of the topics that follow. When metaphysical or supracultural matters are considered, their agnostic posture would assert that since these cannot be empirically verified they are outside the purview of anthropology."[9] According to Barney, most members of the discipline compartmentalize—that is, they practice anthropology without reference to the content of biblical revelation.

As evangelicals undertook to integrate the social sciences for missiology, many were aware that anthropological insights might gain authoritative control over scriptural interpretation. They warned against an unguarded exposure of anthropology which has virtually relativized the essentials of Christianity, "as if Christianity were but one of the myriad of cultural expressions of religion."[10] Such cultural relativism, when combined with a thoroughgoing empiricism, creates compartmentalization. Perception then operates in an epistemologically closed system where there is no room for the direct apprehension of the supracultural. Since the supracultural does not invade the cultural, there can be no such thing as inscripturated divine revelation. Indeed, if divine revelation is considered, its origin and nature are reinterpreted. The empirical factors within the closed system account for all cultural formation, including religion. Therefore, the anthropologist following such an approach will conclude that all "claims to knowledge of supra-cultural realms are themselves a product of the system."[11]

Barney suggests that the current state of anthropological studies provides a way to avoid radical reinterpretations of biblical revelation.[12] The discipline has moved from omnibus definitions of culture through the functional/structural schools with their dynamic, though closed, systems to an "insider" definition. James Spradley, for example, defines culture as "the acquired knowledge that people use to interpret experience and generate social behavior."[13] Barney argues that for Christians acquired knowledge has as one primary source their relationship with God or their experience of

---

9. Barney, "Challenge," 173.

10. Kraft, "Christian Ethnotheology," 112.

11. Nicholls, *Contextualization*, 13.

12. Barney, "Challenge," 173.

13. James R. Spradley and David W. McCurdy, *Anthropology: The Cultural Perspective* (New York: Wiley, 1975), 5.

Christ. For this reason it is appropriate to discuss metaphysical or supracultural matters as part of cultural analysis.

Evangelicals in general vigorously maintain the reality of a supracultural realm in which God speaks absolute truth, which can be adequately expressed in a variety of cultural contexts.[14] They point to the shift of anthropological thinking away from a thoroughgoing cultural relativism to a recognition that there are similarities among cultures. For example, Melville J. Herskovits recognized a degree of formal similarity: language, religion, family, technology, morality, truth, beauty, good and evil.[15] Walter Goldschmidt saw similarity of drives: dissatisfaction, selfishness, exploitativeness, conflict, tension, desire to escape.[16] Paul G. Hiebert observes that most forms of cultural relativism are almost dead.[17] Anthropologists are now searching for universals in the areas of generative processes of language, structures of the mind, and common-sense functions. Mathematical anthropology looks for universals in the fundamental order inherent in the universe itself.

Barney defines the supracultural as that which has its source outside the sphere of culture, that which is universal, not limited to any one culture, and capable of penetrating culture.[18] The two sources for the supracultural are God and Satan. The gospel, faith, the essential nature of the church, the fruit of the Spirit, the gifts of the Spirit, sin, and evil are supracultural elements. The supracultural may be defined as that which is absolute, underived, and unchanging, while the cultural is relative, derived, and subject to change. If reality consists of two spheres containing such opposite elements, how can there be penetration of one sphere by the other? The incarnation of God into the natural world indicates that the supracultural can penetrate the cultural. The absolute in the supracultural sphere, according to Barney, is God alone; only he is underived and unchanging. The "constant" entities form a second category in the supracultural sphere; they are unchanging by nature, but may be derived. God initiates and affirms in covenant and redeeming acts these spiritual

---

14. Lloyd Kwast, "Christianity and Culture: Biblical Bedrock," in *Crucial Issues in Missions Tomorrow,* ed. Donald A. McGavran (Chicago: Moody, 1972), 159–74; G. Linwood Barney, "The Supracultural and the Cultural: Implications for Frontier Missions," in *The Gospel and Frontier Peoples: A Report of a Consultation, Dec. 1972,* ed. R. Pierce Beaver (Pasadena, Calif.: William Carey Library, 1973), 48–57; Nicholls, *Contextualization,* 11ff.

15. Cited by Kwast, "Christianity and Culture," 165.

16. Ibid. Kwast reports Goldschmidt's observation that since culture is a necessary device set up to preserve society against the essential self-interest of the individual, we are led to the conclusion that people are more alike than cultures.

17. Hiebert, "Missions and Anthropology," 175. Walter Goldschmidt saw relativism as a necessary phase through which anthropology had to pass so it could free itself from the habit of evaluating cultures according to the anthropologist's own culturally determined predilections (reported in Kwast, "Christianity and Culture," 166).

18. Barney, "Supracultural and the Cultural," 50.

realities: the gospel, faith, the essential nature of the church, the gifts and fruit of the Spirit. He brings salvation into culture.

Culture, however, is a product of human beings who are alienated from God. There is a vicious cycle in which humanity both makes culture and is shaped by it in each new generation. "Each society has its own peculiar patterns of man-oriented culture which tends to alienate each generation from God and screen out any God-oriented perspective and life-style."[19] Culture, then, is derived, dependent, changing, and relative. The response of individuals to God's saving initiative will be in forms tied to their particular culture. The expression of their faith and the way they live out their relationship with God will always be relative.

In Barney's view, the category of "constant" entities in the supracultural sphere enables one to escape cultural relativism in a very fundamental way. Biblical truth, though expressed in language forms of a particular culture, is a supracultural constant and is not relative or contextual in its source. God the Holy Spirit is the guide and power bringing this supracultural constant into the ethical behavior and lifestyle of every believer. The Spirit's power not only guarantees the possibility of such inculturation, but his guidance guarantees that though the expression of our response to the supracultural is cultural and relative, "the essential nature of these supracultural components should neither be lost nor distorted but rather secured and interpreted clearly through the guidance of the Holy Spirit in 'inculturating' them into this new culture."[20]

Donald McGavran seeks to overcome the dichotomy between supracultural and cultural by pointing to the inspiration of Scripture, a factor that frees biblical writers and content from being in any sense culture-bound. "What it says speaks to men in all cultures as if it had been (as indeed it was) voiced especially for them." The Spirit's role is to provide "a new understanding of what God has already said in the Bible and of its implications and extensions." McGavran rejects the concept of a vague unchanging supracultural "something" and changing cultural forms. He cautions that one must make sure that changing the form does not impoverish or distort the biblical function.[21] The function of a form is determined by the plain meaning of Scripture, and any change must be in close conformity to biblical norms.

Lloyd Kwast integrates biblical revelation and anthropology by asserting the transcultural nature of biblical truth. "The true, intended meaning of biblical revelation as delivered to an ancient Hebrew and Greek culture can be clearly and correctly understood by Spirit-directed men in every human

---

19. Ibid.

20. Ibid.

21. Donald A. McGavran, *The Clash Between Christianity and Cultures* (Washington, D.C.: Canon, 1974), 53, 55, 64–65.

culture today." The cross-cultural nature of biblical revelation is established by its author, the supracultural God, and by its aim to effect change in persons of all cultures. Because of its character and perspicuity, Scripture intends to and can communicate with individuals in all cultural environments.[22]

The hermeneutical principles for discovering this cross-cultural revelation focus on the qualifications of the interpreter and the capabilities of biblical language. Kwast emphasizes that an interpreter must be indwelt by the Spirit of God and desire to know and obey Scripture. By exercising reverent faith and depending on the Holy Spirit for guidance, the interpreter can come to a correct understanding of God's truth in biblical revelation.[23] Though Kwast sees human languages as thought-forms to which God accommodated himself when he anthropomorphized his eternal truth, their limitations do not make communication of God's message among cultures impossible. Kwast insists that the grammatical-historical method can uncover the meaning of Scripture because all peoples use language to think and conceptualize, all essential truth in Scripture is clearly presented, and God chose particular thought-forms to convey precise meanings.

In considering application, Kwast characterizes the Bible as a book of principles, not a catalog of minute directions, which would necessarily be culture-bound, provincial, and relative. "For example, biblical teaching on women in the church, cutting of hair and wearing of veils are purely cultural teaching, but yet hold spiritual principles for Christians of all cultures, that is, that women should avoid all appearance of immodesty, and be chaste and dignified in dress and behavior."[24]

By the end of the decade the debate over relativism had shifted; anthropologists are wrestling today with what Paul Hiebert calls philosophical relativism.[25] In the area of epistemology, for example, the questions are, What is truth? How does one thought-system claiming to be true relate to other thought-systems? Such questions are prompted by a shift away from a correspondence view of truth, or *naive realism*. Anthropologists no longer view themselves as passive observers discovering laws about reality. Scientific knowledge is not considered as a photograph of external reality. Rather, their theories and laws are humanly constructed maps or understandings of reality. The test of a good map is its fit with reality (i.e., the degree to which it conforms to our experience), its usefulness, inclusiveness, uniformity,

---

22. Kwast, "Christianity and Culture," 167, 157ff.

23. Ibid., 168–69.

24. Ibid., 170.

25. Hiebert, "Missions and Anthropology," 176ff.; see the more developed discussion in idem, "Epistemological Foundations for Science and Theology," *Theological Students' Fellowship Bulletin* 8 (March/April 1985): 5–10; idem, "The Missiological Implications of an Epistemological Shift," ibid. (May/June 1985): 12–18. See also Harvie M. Conn, *Eternal Word and Changing Worlds: Theology, Anthropology, and Mission in Trialogue* (Grand Rapids: Zondervan, 1984), 315ff.

simplicity, and aesthetic beauty and balance.[26] Obviously the observer contributes his or her knowledge to the map of reality. This approach is *critical realism*. Hiebert welcomes this shift because it brings Christians "closer to the biblical perspective of the limits of human knowledge and of the importance of faith."[27] And anthropologists find this approach congenial with the idea of being a participant-observer who understands and is able to describe a culture from the inside and from without. For the anthropologist, part of the order perceived in knowledge exists in the external world, part is imposed by the senses, and part is created by the mind. Hiebert concludes that a most difficult question facing science is to distinguish between these three.

WCC Approaches to Hermeneutics and Culture

Ever since its founding after World War II, the World Council of Churches has assigned the topic of hermeneutics to one of its study units. The 1967 Bristol conference on "The Significance of the Hermeneutical Problem for the Ecumenical Movement" drew some basic conclusions that have widespread implications.[28] The conferees presented a hermeneutical method that treated the Bible, not as unique, but as a collection of human writings. They emphasized the diversity of content in Scripture, including the possibility of contradiction. The challenge that these conclusions posed for the traditional understanding of biblical authority prompted the conference to call for a study on that subject.

The 1971 Louvain Statement

The 1971 Louvain statement of the Faith and Order Commission, "The Authority of the Bible," crystalizes the issues for nonevangelicals. The crisis in biblical authority has three roots. First, in a time when the mood of society at large is to rebel against authority, the automatic acceptance of the Bible as a standard has been shaken, a problem compounded by a hermeneutic that treats the Bible like any other book. Second, the contradictions in Scripture uncovered by the historical-critical method make it difficult, if not impossible, to decide which statements are to be taken as authoritative. Third, the historical distance between the ancient text and the

---

26. In personal correspondence Hiebert clarifies that by "fit" he means truthfulness understood according to a correspondence view of truth. "I argue strongly for a retention of the word 'Truth' with regard to knowledge carefully tested against reality" (letter to author, November 1986).

27. Hiebert, "Missions and Anthropology," 177.

28. Ellen Flesseman–van Leer, ed., *The Bible: Its Authority and Interpretation in the Ecumenical Movement* (Geneva: World Council of Churches, 1980), 5ff.

modern context raises the question of how any relevance can be claimed for the Bible at all.[29]

The WCC statement specifically rejects the evangelical solution to these problems. Although it is ambivalent about asserting that the Bible is inspired, the statement rejects the presupposition that the inspiration of Scripture serves as a basis for claiming unique and final authority. It asserts, rather, that the content of Scripture must prove itself authoritative. The report opts for a historical-critical method that yields a Scripture full of contradictions and scoffs at those who fear that the methods of historical criticism may destroy the authority of the Bible and with it the Christian faith itself. "The fear is ultimately baseless. But clearly historical and critical scholarship has resulted in a new encounter with the biblical records and therefore makes a fresh account of biblical authority necessary."[30]

Those who assume "almost unquestioningly an attitude of contemporaneity with the Bible and feel no need to attach any great importance to its historical character" are censured, as are those who would use the Bible "as a standard to which we must conform in all the questions arising in our life."[31] The charge is that fundamentalists and those who attempt to formulate the biblical view on every topic under discussion press the Bible too far, turning it into law. The Scripture then becomes a norm imposed on the church from the outside.

The statement proposes a relational concept that Scripture does have authoritative force as a literary document that occupies an important place in the history of humankind, and as the historical document that, in a most trustworthy form, preserves the witness on which the church is founded. But it is the fact that "men are arrested by the message of the Bible, the fact that they hear God speaking to them from the Bible," that gives the Bible its authority.[32]

Inspiration can be affirmed of the Bible, not as a presupposition, but because in the Bible God's claim is experienced in a compelling way. Such inspiration can also be affirmed of great Christian theologians and preachers who throughout church history have done a work of interpretation leading to "the Bible's speaking once again with fresh authority."[33]

The hermeneutic of the statement allows the perceived contradictions in Scripture to stand, asserting that such contradictions are really a collection

29. Ibid., 43ff.

30. Ibid., 45.

31. Ibid., 46, 56. The 1978 Bangalore report, "The Significance of the Old Testament in Its Relation to the New," continues to caution against any hermeneutic which would assume such contemporaneity, whether it be liturgical, a close literary reading of the text, the African Independent Church's interpretation, or liberation and materialist theology's political interpretation of the Scripture (ibid., 61, 62 n. 6).

32. Ibid., 47.

33. Ibid., 55.

of diverse interpretations of God's action in history, each addressed to a particular, historically conditioned situation. The statement does not propose discarding any content from the Scriptures, but it does assert that one can distinguish between contradictory interpretations by identifying one as more important, and therefore more authoritative, than another, and by asking "to what extent an interpretation interprets a central saving event attested in the scriptures and is rooted in that saving event."[34]

The report then introduces another question to determine the authoritative functioning of a given interpretation in the contemporary context. Does the biblical content succeed or fail in speaking authoritatively to today? The success or failure depends on how closely the ancient historical situation and the contemporary situation coincide. Since the contemporary historical context is constantly changing, one need not discard biblical content that does not speak now, for there may come a new and altered situation to which it may once again speak. Accepting the diverse and often contradictory interpretations of saving events in Scripture, then, allows the interpreter to understand not only the historically conditioned character of the material, but also its great potential for speaking authoritatively to the diversity of an ever-changing contemporary situation.

The report suggests two approaches for bridging historical distance:

> Some hold that, as God's Word, the Bible has a timeless claim on every generation and that its message can speak directly to the men of all times provided it is set free from the historically conditioned forms in which it is clothed. Man with his questions remains fundamentally the same and, since the Bible answers his deepest questions, it is still relevant for today. But others believe that God's action in history to which the Bible bears witness continues further and that the present situation is primarily to be understood not as analogous to that earlier time but as its fruit.[35]

Though the report uses elements from both options, it clearly favors the latter. The interpreter and the biblical writer are in analogous situations in the sense that both are seeking to interpret God's revelatory action, but it is an analogy of "dynamic," not of "content." The interpreter is not looking for analogies between the current situation and the Bible in order to appropriate and apply an authoritative biblical interpretation to the contemporary context. The interpreter must accept responsibility for interpreting God's action in the world now, and the Bible's role is to submit to questions from the contemporary situation and to address its own questions to that situation. Though the report acknowledges that the Bible has authority to pose questions to the contemporary context and to reject questions to which it

---

34. Ibid., 50.
35. Ibid., 46.

does not speak, "the situation with its given elements and open problems determines the perspective within which the biblical witnesses must be read and interpreted."[36] The report claims that this is not a matter of introducing bias into the interpretational process. It consistently maintains that the only way the Bible can demonstrate its authority is through an interplay of text and contemporary context.

Wherever this situation-conditioned hermeneutic is adopted, the Bible may be put to authoritative use, for Scripture, with its often widely divergent interpretations, is "an invitation to us to attest in our own words the message which it contains." The interpreter should read expectantly, since "the decisive importance of its message for all times is only rightly acknowledged when its testimony is read in anticipation of its disclosure to us of the ultimate sense of our world and of our own lives." The Bible can be used as a critical authority to which the church must "constantly defer and from whose judgments not even the developments taking place in our world are exempt." The Bible speaks most effectively when it is read in the context of corresponding controversies in the contemporary situation. This authoritative use is not intended to yield final judgments, however, since the contemporary interpretive process functions to extend the interpretive process begun in the Bible. "Only by constantly renewed interpretation does the one message remain a living Spirit and not a dead letter."[37]

The WCC report concludes with two confident assertions: (1) understanding the interpretive process as a continuation of the hermeneutical task begun in Scripture sheds new light on the right relationships between unity and diversity and between norm and change; and (2) as the ecumenical movement continues to face these questions afresh and use the Bible aright, the Bible will demonstrate its power anew.[38]

Contextualization and Missions

Historically, Christian missions were devoted to translating biblical teaching on faith and life into culturally relevant forms in order to create a truly indigenized church in a particular society, a church which would be self-governing, self-supporting, and self-propagating. This missiology was addressed to traditional Third World cultures and operated on the assumption

---

36. Ibid., 51–52.

37. Ibid., 56–57.

38. Ibid. The report begins with the question, "How are we to approach the Bible so that, through the biblical text, God may speak to us authoritatively today?" (p. 43). It ends with the questions, "How can the Bible prove its authority in the face of the changes of our time which lead to so radical a criticism of traditional claims to authority? How can we interpret the message of the Bible in such a way that, at one and the same time, its authority is respected and it sets us free to understand the demands and opportunities of our present time?" (p. 57).

that the Bible is the source of an eternal and universally applicable message about what to believe about God and how to live in a way pleasing to him. Indigenization was a matter of communicating this message in culturally appropriate forms; the culture might provide the forms, but the Bible always provided the content, the meaning.

The situation-conditioned hermeneutic advocated by the agencies of the WCC introduced the concept of contextualization into the work of missions. Contextualization was to move beyond indigenization by taking into account "the process of secularity, technology, and the struggle for human justice, which characterize the historical movement of nations in the Third World." In this view the contemporary context—the Third World society interrelating with the processes of modernity—is the source of theological truth. The church needs to heed "the signs [of the times] which are God's way of talking to us in our time and context. Relevance takes contextuality seriously by discerning God's mission for man in history."[39] Though the Bible still has a role to play, it is now placed in dialectical relationship with the contemporary context, and the result is a process which is "always prophetic, arising always out of a genuine encounter between God's Word and His world, and moves toward the purpose of challenging and changing the situation through rootedness in and commitment to a given historical moment."[40]

At the WCC Ecumenical Institute, Anthony O. Dyson contrasted contextual and dogmatic theology, and in the process emphasized the new primacy given to analysis of the historical moment or the contemporary cultural context. "The contextual approach has an inductive character which should encourage fraternal relations with the empiricist approach in the human and natural sciences." He likened the method of contextual theology to that of liberation theology. Each begins with a technical understanding of the present situation, and subsequently certain theological motifs are connected to it. In terms of a starting point for the dialectic, Scripture is secondary, as is the theological material derived from Scripture. "We shall have to ask what kind of difference the introduction of theological motifs could make to a conclusion based on complex and often technical evidence" concerning the contemporary situation.[41]

---

39. TEF Staff, *Ministry in Context*, 20, 30. Shoki Coe, chairman of the fund, describes contextuality as the "discernment of the signs of the times, seeing where God is at work and calling us to participate in it" ("In Search of Renewal in Theological Education," *Theological Education* 9 [1973]: 241). Daniel von Allmen sees the contextualization process operative in New Testament times ("The Birth of Theology: Contextualization as the Dynamic Element in the Formation of New Testament Theology," *International Review of Missions* 64 [1975]: 37–52). See Nicholl's evangelical critique of von Allmen, which asserts that von Allmen absolutizes local culture and reduces theology to a comparative study of different Christian cultural traditions (*Contextualization*, 26–27).

40. TEF Staff, *Ministry in Context*, 20.

41. Anthony O. Dyson, "Dogmatic or Contextual Theology?" *Study Encounter* 8, no. 3, SE 29 (1972): 5.

By the end of the decade Ellen Flesseman–van Leer had a more positive estimate of the role of the Bible in contextual theologies.[42] She was convinced that Louvain's emphasis on contemporary context in the authoritative use of the Bible made it possible to take a constructive biblical approach to emerging contextual theologies—black, feminist, and liberation.

Ethnotheology of Charles Kraft

The most comprehensive contextual theology among evangelicals is the ethnotheology of Charles Kraft. Although his full exposition, *Christianity in Culture: A Study in Dynamic Biblical Theologizing in Cross-Cultural Perspective*, did not appear until 1979, he was writing and refining throughout the decade, and his influence began to be felt as early as 1974.

Kraft's ethnotheology may be properly classed as an approach to contextual theology because it shares an affirmation of cultural relativism,[43] though in the relativized form advocated by Eugene Nida. Also it has a dynamic understanding of Scripture's nature and authority as well as a conviction of the importance of the contemporary context for hermeneutics. Yet there are differences.

Though he sees a continuity between God's revelatory action today in "inspiring" people to respond to his truth and his past action in the production of inspired Scripture, Kraft's basic hermeneutic is not a matter of "prolonging the interpretational process" by analyzing God's work in the contemporary context.[44] Rather, the primary source for theology is the inspired casebook, the Scriptures. And the object of theologizing "is to come to ever more adequate, accurate, understandable (by the group in focus), and communicable perceptions of the glimpses of God's absolute Truth (with a capital T) embedded in the inspired casebook."[45]

The contemporary context plays a vital role because it is the receiver of God's truth and conditions the way the content is communicated. Kraft urges that we "need to be open to what [God] seeks to say to contemporary hearers in contemporary cultural contexts,"[46] but he does not regard the current context as the starting point and primary source for discovering God's message to modern men and women.

---

42. Flesseman–van Leer, *The Bible*, 12.
43. Nicholls mentions Kraft in his description of existential contextualizing as over against dogmatic contextualizing (*Contextualization*, 25).
44. Kraft, *Christianity in Culture*, 212.
45. Ibid., 301.
46. Ibid., 302.

Kraft's ethnotheology appears to grow out of the first approach to the historical-distance problem noted in the Louvain report (see p. 138). For Kraft agrees that the Bible has "a timeless claim on every generation and that its message can speak directly to the men of all times provided it is set free from the historically conditioned forms in which it is clothed."[47] And Kraft would add that the Bible's message needs to be clothed in forms appropriate to the particular contemporary culture in which the interpreter seeks to communicate it.

As the word indicates, ethnotheology combines two disciplines, Christian theology and anthropology, and is an interpretive approach to the study of God, humankind, and divine-human interaction. From anthropology it draws culturally relative truths and perceptions about how meaning is communicated within a culture and between cultures, and from theology come culturally relative understandings of absolute supracultural truths about God's provision for human need and the supracultural condition for receiving that provision—faith.[48]

Kraft acknowledges the distinction, developed by William A. Smalley, between the supracultural and the cultural. He views humanity as so culture-bound that any knowledge, including knowledge of God's truth, can be understood or communicated only in terms of a particular culture. Absolute supracultural truth, God's revealed will for human salvation, exists, but it can be perceived and communicated only in terms of culture. Culture-bound knowledge of supracultural truth can be adequate but never absolute in the sense that one knows it directly, apart from cultural perception of it. The line between supracultural truth and cultural expression is uncrossable this side of heaven.[49]

Ethnotheology asserts that the incarnation and the accounts of divine-human interaction in Scripture give us evidence that God in a moderately relativistic way respects the differences between cultures and hence the integrity of any given culture. Though Kraft sees cultural change as the end product of the gospel's penetration of a culture, his axiomatic starting point affirms "that a supracultural God is willing and anxious to accept any culture (without pre-condition) as a vehicle of His interaction with culture-bound man."[50]

---

47. Flesseman–van Leer, *The Bible*, 46.

48. Kraft, "Christian Ethnotheology," 110, 124.

49. Kraft, *Christianity in Culture*, 120, 122; see also William A. Smalley, "Culture and Superculture," *Practical Anthropology* 2 (1955): 58–71; Kraft, "Christian Ethnotheology," 120. Kraft details five factors which limit our understanding of supracultural truth: (1) God's control over the extent of revelation; (2) human finiteness; (3) human sinfulness; (4) cultural conditioning—one perceives all reality in terms of one's culture; and (5) individual psychological and experiential conditioning. "Though we are not totally unable to see beyond what such cultural structuring channels us into, our tendency is to gravitate toward and to most readily understand those portions of supracultural truth that connect most closely with life as we already perceive it" (*Christianity in Culture*, 130).

50. Kraft, "Christian Ethnotheology," 124.

In working out the implications of this approach for soteriology, Kraft concludes that God takes into account the relativity of the human situation and that human accountability is relative to the extent of revelational material received. God adjusts his expectations to the cultural patterns of each society.[51]

Kraft uses constructs from communication theory to explain the transmission of God's absolute supracultural truth into cultures and between cultures, asserting that meaning is "that which the receiver of a message constructs within his head and responds to."[52] In the communication process, a sender with a certain meaning in mind chooses symbols, such as words, to encode that meaning. The receiver hears the message, decodes the symbols, constructs in his or her mind the meaning, and responds to it. The basic assumption here is that the human mind within its cultural context is the locus of meaning.

Since any given symbol derives its meaning from participation in a particular cultural context, an encoding and decoding process within or between cultures is necessary. The correspondence between the sender's and the receiver's meanings depends on the "extent of agreement between communicator and receptor concerning what the cultural symbols signify."[53] Do they share a common cultural context which assigns to the given symbol the same meaning? Kraft contends that because a symbol's meaning is governed by its context, the receiver of a message in one culture never understands exactly what the communicator from another culture intends. This is particularly true when the communicator is a written document like the Bible. Contemporary receivers cannot ask the writers to verify their understanding of the message; they are separated not only by language and cultural context, but by the impersonal nature of the vehicle. Contemporary receivers do not share with the ancient biblical context all the same meanings for cultural symbols. Such an appropriation of communication theory has implications for understanding and applying an authoritative Scripture.

View of Scripture

Kraft formulates his understanding of revelation and inspiration within the framework of absolute supracultural truth and its culturally relative expression and perception; the result is an understanding broader than the evangelical characterization of the Bible as verbal propositional revelation. He contends that the behavioral insights developed in recent years enable the interpreter to better understand the dynamics of God's past and present

---

51. Kraft, *Christianity in Culture*, 125–28.
52. Kraft, "Interpreting," 359.
53. Ibid.

revelational activity. He finds it difficult to accept what he considers the static and past-oriented views of "closed" conservatives such as Harold Lindsell, John W. Montgomery, or Francis Schaeffer. With this understanding of God's communication in Old Testament and New Testament times as a dynamic revelatory process of divine-human encounter, Kraft does not find it reasonable "to believe that as soon as the last New Testament document was committed to writing, [God] totally changed in his method of operation to such an extent that he now limits himself to the written record." In Kraft's view, revelation is still occurring—one can participate today in the continuing dynamic process by which God communicates not only information but also himself. He continues to provide a revelational (divine) stimulus, usually through a human agent, in such a way that the information, whether from general or special sources, has the intended impact on the receptor.[54]

For Charles Kraft, the Bible is the record of a very important part of the revelatory activity of God. It is an "inspired classic casebook," a collection of case studies portraying and interpreting instances of divine-human encounters that highlight more widely applicable principles of God's interaction with human beings. These cases are time-tested and have been found to be of enduring value. This is not to deny that there is historical and theological systematization in the Bible, but rather to emphasize that the materials there present are basically of a case-study nature, as opposed to a textbook format, for they are part of "a specific presentation . . . dealing with the problems and participants in a specific context."[55]

Kraft points to a uniqueness in the biblical revelation, not present in the revelation of other divine-human interaction, no matter how effective or authentic. This uniqueness is confirmed by the fact that "God has led the church . . . to preserve and employ these particular materials in a unique way in their attempts to discern and follow God's leading."[56]

The church or the individual Christian is to use the Bible as an authority, as a yardstick or as a tether. In testing whether a postbiblical revelation or contemporary divine-human encounter is of God, the interpreter should use the Bible as a yardstick. The Bible reports a range of behavior and belief from the ideal, to the subideal but acceptable, to the unacceptable; the interpreter should judge by this yardstick the behavior and belief presented in a contemporary "revelation." "If contemporary behavior is functionally equivalent in meaning within its cultural context to what the Bible shows to have been acceptable (even though, perhaps, subideal) behavior in its cultural context, the measurement has proved positive."[57] The interpreter

---

54. Kraft, *Christianity in Culture*, 212, 396.
55. Ibid., 201, 398.
56. Ibid., 213.
57. Ibid., 187.

may also use the Bible as a tether to determine the limits within which behavior and belief may be considered biblical. The Bible as a standard pronounces negative judgment on contemporary behavior that parallels behavior the Bible records as unacceptable.

Kraft stresses that cultural analysis of the biblical text is necessary for correct understanding and contends that anthropology and linguistics are sharper tools for the task than are history and philology, as they provide categories for analysis such as form and meaning, universal and specific.[58] They offer a method for putting biblical material into a communicable form for contemporary culture and a means for identifying two common errors in interpretation.

The first error occurs when biblical exegetes attempting to communicate cross-culturally operate from a monocultural approach to interpretation by working with the ancient text and a single cultural context, their own. Since their interpretation is in terms of their own culture, there is a temptation to view it as more adequate to convey meaning than is the biblical culture. Rudolf Bultmann's demythologizing of Scripture was based on such a conviction. It is disastrous to take this, usually Western, contemporary interpretation and treat it as the meaning of the biblical text for translation into a Third World cultural context. Anthropology and linguistics provide tools and insights to expose the ethnocentrism in such approaches and to locate the meanings embedded in the cultural forms and thought-patterns of the biblical authors. These are the meanings that must be communicated in the third cultural context and expressed in terms of that equally valid worldview.

Another frequent error in interpretation is the assumption "that arriving at most supracultural truth is simply a matter of accepting the 'clear' or 'plain meanings' of Scripture." Meanings and the cultural symbols attached to them are contextually derived; so when interpreters claim to understand the "plain meaning" of the text, the meaning they are supplying to cultural symbols in the text is from their own context. It is the plain meaning to them only because they understand it clearly in terms of their own cultural context. But no two cultures are exactly alike. Moreover, it is a characteristic of written communication that meanings for cultural symbols shared by the writer and original readers are not made explicit, but are left implicit and must be supplied by the reader. When interpreters read the text, they will supply the meanings from their own context. These facts convince Kraft that what "are to us the plain meanings are almost certain to be the wrong meanings unless the statements are very general."[59]

---

58. Kraft, "Interpreting," 358.
59. Kraft, *Christianity in Culture*, 131, 133.

The situation can be remedied. The interpreter must realize that though the contemporary context may use many of the same cultural symbols as did the biblical authors (e.g., fox, lamb), the same meanings no longer attach to them. And since meanings agreed on by people conditioned in the same culture are not expressed in a text, "we, as readers, may not understand major portions of what is going on at all, since we don't know the cultural agreements." Once these differences and deficiencies are acknowledged, cultural analysis can be used to uncover the meaning the original author (and God) intended, the emic intent understood in terms of the original context. Such exegesis includes the ferreting out of cultural assumptions shared by the writer and the original audience. Exegetes need to identify with the author psychologically, trying to "think his thoughts" as if they were part of the original context. Kraft offers a practical suggestion: "Contemporary exegetes [should] . . . experience life in contemporary cultures similar to those of biblical times. There is not ordinarily enough livingness to library-based exegesis to enable one to achieve the kind of personal identification with the scriptural authors in their cultures that such exegesis demands."[60]

The Hermeneutical Bridge

Kraft conceives the hermeneutical bridge between Scripture and contemporary cultures as containing three pylons:

> Because, beyond the diversity of human frames of reference, human beings participate in a pervasive common humanity, because the perceptions recorded in the Scripture focus on the same unchanging message from God, and because God's Spirit is active in guiding people into God's truth, the study of this inspired casebook yields understandings adequate for human salvation and sanctification.[61]

On the basis of anthropological study Kraft concludes that all human beings, whatever their culture, have the same biological, psychological, sociocultural, and spiritual needs. Physically, they need food, shelter, air, sex, excretion, and health. Psychologically, they need meaning and the conditions that maintain the individual psyche. Socioculturally, people need to communicate, to provide for children, to transmit the culture, and to maintain the social system. Spiritually, there is a need to understand and relate to supracultural beings and factors. Each culture develops a worldview—a web of meanings, ideas, beliefs, and values—that functions to

---

60. Ibid., 132, 302.
61. Ibid., 300.

meet these needs. These meanings are then attached to certain behavior patterns or customs (forms). Cultures are very creative in the development of forms to express these meanings, and a great diversity of cultural forms is the result. We must not conclude, however, that cultures or human beings have nothing in common, for the great common denominator is that the world-view of each functions to meet the same needs. In fact, the "surface level forms of cultures differ more from each other than do the deep-level meanings (worldviews) and functions they express."[62]

For Kraft, one message—the basic meaning God is seeking to communicate to human beings—remains constant throughout the Bible and history. Though there is significant cumulative increase of information concerning God and his works, none of this is a precondition to salvation. The essential message of salvation is the same from the beginning of time, and the biblical casebook allows for a variety of informational starting points for one's relationship with God. A Christian witness may thus find Third World peoples who are "informationally B.C." (i.e., pre-Christ in the information available to them) and therefore better able to understand and respond to God's message through the Old Testament than to those messages that assume a detailed knowledge of Jesus and his part in the plan of salvation. People of today who are informationally B.C. can be saved by committing themselves to God in faith as Abraham did, who was chronologically B.C.[63] Kraft is confident that in spite of the cultural hindrances to accurate interpretation, Christians approaching Scripture from any cultural background may, under the leading of the Holy Spirit, "come to know something of how he desires us to live out these truths in terms of our cultural forms."[64]

Interpretation and Application

For interpretation and application, ethnotheology follows the dynamic-equivalence model of translation, asserting that theological truth "must be re-created like a dynamic-equivalence translation or transculturation within the language and accompanying conceptual framework of the hearers if its true relevance is to be properly perceived by them."[65] After doing exegesis (including cultural analysis) of the text and decoding the essential elements of the message, the interpreter reencodes the material in the receptor's

---

62. Ibid., 81–102; the quotation is from p. 89.

63. Ibid., 254.

64. Kraft, "Interpreting," 367.

65. Kraft, *Christianity in Culture*, 297; see also idem, "Ideological Factors," 295–312. Norm Mundhenk, a proponent of the dynamic-equivalence approach, is convinced that it is only individual subjective unease with the anachronism of translating all elements in terms of modern culture which prevents translations from being thoroughly dynamically equivalent ("The Subjectivity of Anachronism," in *On Language, Culture, and Religion: In Honor of Eugene A. Nida*, ed. Matthew Black and William A. Smalley [The Hague: Mouton, 1974], 259–73).

language and rewrites the material in an appropriate style to produce a dynamically equivalent effect on the hearers.

The two standards are the Bible as a yardstick and the contemporary cultural context as a guide. The Bible maintains the communicational (revelational) focus on a fairly small number of items, the deep-level core constants: "the existence of God, human sinfulness, God's willingness to relate to humans on certain conditions, the necessity of a human faithfulness response to God as preconditional to salvation."[66] The Bible also records the historical outworkings of these constants in the historical contexts of Israel, Jesus' ministry, and the early church. Neither the core constants nor the historical outworkings are debatable; they are the basic material of biblical revelatory activity. The Bible, as the inspired casebook, records various inspired interpretations of these constants, and contemporary interpretations will fall inside or outside Scripture's range of acceptable variation as determined by the biblical author's intent. Once a contemporary interpretation has been formulated, it is the interpreter's responsibility to express it in a receptor-oriented, emically valid way, using the thought-constructs of the culture to which he or she is communicating. When the theologizing process is understood in this way, many contemporary and ancient differences of theological interpretation, even many of those labeled heresies, can be seen to be simply differences in cultural understanding.

In applying scriptural teaching to behavior, ethnotheology makes a distinction between cultural form and its meaning. The dynamic-equivalence translation model again comes into play, as Kraft suggests a five-step process for creating dynamically equivalent church life. Steps one and two involve a cultural analysis of the behavior patterns of New Testament church life and a decoding from them of the essential meanings conveyed by those forms. Step three is an analysis of the forms in the contemporary culture to discover which convey meanings similar to those decoded from Scripture. In step four the interpreter determines which contemporary culture forms "can be used and transformed for Christian purposes in a way dynamically equivalent to the usage illustrated in the New Testament." The final step is "transculturation of the essential Christian functions into the form appropriate to communicate meanings equivalent to the New Testament meanings" in the contemporary culture.[67] For example, greeting one another with a holy kiss functioned to communicate affection in the New Testament culture. In contemporary North American culture a hearty handshake has a similar function. Dynamically equivalent obedience to the culture-specific New Testament command appropriately takes a different form.

---

66. Kraft, *Christianity in Culture*, 189.
67. Ibid., 327.

The amount of adjustment between biblical context and contemporary context depends on the level of abstraction at which the biblical command is given.[68] Kraft sees three levels: culture-specific commands (e.g., the head-covering command, 1 Cor. 11:10–12); general-principle commands (e.g., the prohibition against coveting anything that is one's neighbor's, Exod. 20:17); and human-universal commands (e.g., the commandments to love God and neighbor, Mark 12:29–31). General-principle and human-universal content in Scripture may be aligned with the deep level of world-view. Though in both cases their meaning will be quite general, they can be applied immediately from culture to culture, for by their nature such commands apply to every person in every culture at all times. This universality is indicated by content that is not dependent for its meaning on its application within the first specific cultural context. "Do not steal" as a general-principle command requires fewer culturally agreed meanings than "wear a head covering," which assumes a shared understanding of what the head covering meant in Greek culture.

Culture-specific commands communicate the value of a specific cultural action, but the shared understanding of the meaning of such an action is assumed, not expressed. In order for such a command to be carried out with the same meaning in another culture, it must be recast in a culture-specific form appropriate to that people's understandings. Because forms change meaning from culture to culture, the same form or type of behavior will not necessarily express the same biblically intended function. And so, whether the biblical content is a human-universal, a general-principle, or a culture-specific command, all can and should be expressed in contemporary culture in a dynamically equivalent way so that the effect on and response of the receptor will be as close as possible to that of the original audience.[69]

---

68. Ibid., 139–43. Kraft gives several principles for evaluating our reflexes when interpreting and applying biblical material of various levels of abstraction: (1) If the culture of the original at any given point is very similar to ours, our cultural reflexes serve us fairly well. (2) If the biblical material is a cultural universal, our interpretational reflexes enable us to get close to the intended meaning. (3) If the biblical material relates to experiences common to all humankind, our interpretational reflexes are of considerable help. (4) If the biblical material is very specific to cultural practices different from ours, our interpretational reflexes are of limited help (pp. 133–34).

On a similar note Karl J. Franklin sees three types of values in Scripture: those taught within Jewish culture, those not restricted to Jewish culture, and those that are supracultural. One identifies those values limited to Jewish culture by the fact that they are spoken of insultingly in Scripture and elsewhere. Franklin identifies the supracultural as values specified in Scripture and redundantly specified in a given society ("Interpreting Values Cross-Culturally," *Missiology* 7 [1979]: 355–64).

69. Cf. the views of Eugene Hillmann, who contends that Christianity supplies spirit but not content to the ethical systems of human culture ("Pluriformity in Ethics: A Modern Missionary Problem," *Missiology* 1 [1973]: 59–72).

10

Contextual Theology

Contextual theology flourished in the decade of the seventies, and evangelicals made their initial response at the Lausanne Congress on World Evangelization in 1974. The congress explored the topic of "The Gospel, Contextualization, and Syncretism,"[1] but the fruit of this discussion and the content of other papers revealed a lack of clarity about the issues raised, particularly the primacy of contemporary culture. Evangelicals in this period tended to treat contextualization as not very different from indigenization. While some sensed that contextualization was a threat to the core of the gospel and sought ways to identify Scripture's universal, transcultural core content, most were content to inquire about the limits of the contextualization process.

In 1975 the National Council of Churches sponsored the Detroit Conference on Theology in the Americas. It provided a showcase for contextual theologies—black, liberation, and feminist.[2] Third World theologians in

---

1. "The Gospel, Contextualization, and Syncretism Report," in *Let the Earth Hear His Voice*, ed. James D. Douglas (Minneapolis: World Wide, 1975), 1224–28.

2. Sergio Torres and John Eagleson, eds., *Theology in the Americas* (Maryknoll, N.Y.: Orbis, 1976). See also James H. Cone, "Biblical Revelation and Social Existence," *Interpretation* 28 (1974): 422–40; José Miguez-Bonino, *Doing Theology in a Revolutionary Situation* (Philadelphia: Fortress, 1975); Juan L. Segundo, *Liberation of Theology* (Maryknoll, N.Y.: Orbis, 1976); Elizabeth S. Fiorenza, "Feminist Theology and New Testament Interpretation," *Journal for the Study of the Old Testament* 22 (1982): 32–46.

Africa and Asia contributed contextual theologies.[3] In each, a contemporary cultural context provided the starting point: the oppressive poverty in the North American black ghetto, the Latin American shantytown, or the religiocultural heritage of emerging Third World Africa and Asia. This contextual theologizing laid great stress on the ideological control exercised by the world-view of the majority culture, whether oppressor or Western, over the interpreter's hermeneutic. Through a "hermeneutic of suspicion" and engagement with text and context, these theologies contrived ways for the biblical text to serve contemporary praxiological concerns, especially liberation.

The Lausanne Congress on World Evangelization

The Lausanne Congress had a year earlier issued a covenant setting out a formal evangelical consensus. It was a statement of faith and commitment to action and contains a representative view on the nature and authority of Scripture, affirming the Bible as divinely inspired and without error and as containing God's unchangeable revelation addressed to all humankind. The nature of the revealed message leaves no room for any syncretism or dialog with other religions as equals. On the issue of contemporary application of the gospel message in various cultures, the covenant relies on the Holy Spirit's illumination: "He illumines the minds of God's people in every culture to perceive [Scripture's] truth freshly through their own eyes and thus discloses to the whole church ever more of the many-colored wisdom of God."[4]

On the issue of evangelism and culture, the covenant places Scripture in functional control of culture because it evaluates all cultures according to its own criterion of truth and righteousness. Some of human culture is rich in

---

3. John S. Mbiti, "Christianity and African Culture," *Journal of Theology for Southern Africa* 20 (September 1977): 26–40; Kwesi A. Dickson and Paul Ellingworth, *Biblical Revelation and African Beliefs* (London: Lutterworth, 1969); Edward W. Fasole-Luke, "The Quest for an African Christian Theology," *Ecumenical Review* 27 (1975): 259–69. For the evangelical approach see Tite Tienou, *The Theological Task of the Church in Africa* (Achumota, Ghana: Africa Christian Press, 1982); Byang H. Kato, "Black Theology and African Theology," *ERT* 1 (1977): 35–48; Tokunboh Adeyemo, "Towards an Evangelical African Theology," *ERT* 7 (1983): 147–54.

Emerito P. Nacpil, "The Critical Asian Principle," in *What Asian Christians Are Thinking*, ed. Douglas J. Elwood (Quezon City: New Day, 1976), 3–6; and Wesley Ariarajah, "Towards a Theology of Dialogue," *Ecumenical Review* 29 (1977): 3–11. For the evangelical approach see Bong R. Ro, "Contextualization: Asian Theology," *ERT* 2 (1978): 15–23; Bong R. Ro and Ruth Eshenaur, eds., *The Bible and Theology in Asian Contexts: An Evangelical Perspective on Asian Theology* (Taichung, Taiwan: Asia Theological Association, 1984); Sunand Sumithra and Bruce Nicholls, "Towards an Evangelical Theology of the Third World: An Indian Reflection," *ERT* 7 (1983): 172–82.

4. "Lausanne Covenant," in *Let the Earth Hear His Voice*, 3.

beauty and goodness because it is a product of human beings created in God's image, but all is still tainted with sin because of our fallen state. Moreover, some of culture is positively demonic.

As we suggested earlier, one study group confronted the issue of "The Gospel, Contextualization, and Syncretism." Byang Kato presented a paper in which he defined contextualization as a cross-cultural communication process "making concepts or ideals relevant in a given situation. . . . It is an effort to express the never changing Word of God in ever changing modes for relevance."[5] He expresses an ambivalence to the process. On the one hand, he sees contextualization as right and necessary in light of the incarnation and the fact that the mode of expression of the gospel message is not inspired, though the message is. On the other hand, he sees the constant danger of syncretism.

Kato suggests two goals in the communication of the gospel: faithfulness to the content of the Word of God and relevance in meaningful expression to the receptors. But he is convinced that one can be so concerned with relevance that the gospel can be compromised and theological meanings sacrificed on the altar of comprehension. To avoid this pitfall he advocates biblical translation in terms faithful to the original historical context, even when there is no precise equivalent in the receptor's culture. For example, in the parable of the mustard seed, the seed should remain a mustard seed in translation, even though there is no such seed in Africa. Explanation should come in the teaching about the parable, not in the translation of the word. In Nigeria he would explain that a mustard seed is like *acha* (Hausa for "a small seed").

The summary report of this particular study group manifests tensions concerning the relationship of the core message of the gospel and culture. Kato's model assumed that it is possible—indeed, desirable—for the content of the gospel message and its theological meanings to move unchanged from one culture to another. Then a second model emerged, contending that whenever the essential core of the gospel moves from culture to culture, it takes on additional meaning. Thus when the core of the gospel, with its Western cultural accretions, is shared by a Westerner with

---

5. Byang H. Kato, "The Gospel, Cultural Contextualization, and Religious Syncretism," in *Let the Earth Hear His Voice*, 1217. Josphat K. Yego reflects the same approach as Kato ("Appreciation for and Warnings About Contextualization," *Evangelical Missions Quarterly* 16 [1980]: 153–56). Harvie Conn's evaluation of Kato at Lausanne and the general evangelical response to contextualization is that it is very thin theologically, it shows little interaction with the conciliar debate, and it is largely negative when it does address the issue ("Contextualization: Where Do We Begin?" in *Evangelicals and Liberation*, ed. Carl E. Armerding [Nutley, N.J.: Presbyterian & Reformed, 1977], 98). It should also be noted that in the follow-up symposium to the Lausanne Congress, the discussion of evangelism and culture again approached the issue in terms of cross-cultural communication (Jacob A. Loewen, "Evangelism and Culture," in *The New Face of Evangelism: An International Symposium on the Lausanne Covenant*, ed. C. René Padilla [London: Hodder & Stoughton, 1976], 177–89).

another contemporary culture, the essential core is somewhat changed. In this second model the basic elements of the gospel may well have been retained throughout the movement from ancient to modern context, but it is the Holy Spirit's illumination which ensures the final communication of the gospel from the early church to the entire world. This means that the modern receptors may "turn directly to the Scripture under the guidance of the Holy Spirit, to search the original message for themselves and in turn rediscover elements of the gospel lost in the transmission by the carrier [i.e., the Western missionary]."[6]

In these deliberations a number of important questions regarding the gospel and contextualization surfaced:

1. Which key biblical principles of hermeneutics identify clearly and objectively the gospel core?
2. What criteria can be used to isolate the elements of the gospel core from other biblical elements?
3. What is the gospel? Is there an unchangeable core?
4. How does one define contextualization? How does one isolate it from indigenization?
5. Does contextualization take in only the physical expressions of the culture, e.g., musical instruments and liturgical clothing, or does it include thought-forms as well?
6. What biblical guidelines should one observe to contextualize the gospel message to generate a healthy, growing church loyal to God and to evangelization of the world?
7. Are contextualization and syncretism the same thing on a continuum, or are they two different things?
8. Should each cultural zone have its own theology?
9. Who should undertake the task of contextualization?[7]

In the end the group defined contextualization as "meaningful communication in forms that are real to the person, and his full response to the Lord in repentance and obedience of faith that affects his whole life-style, his attitude, and his values, etc."[8] Syncretism was defined as the loss of critical and basic elements of the gospel in the process of contextualization and their replacement with religious elements from the receiving culture.

Though the group fell short of dealing with the source for theological truth, it seemed in still another way to be aware of the issue as it wrestled to fashion guidelines for contextualizing. These guidelines followed anthropological and linguistic models but made a concerted effort to keep the

---

6. "Gospel, Contextualization, and Syncretism Report," 1225.
7. Ibid.
8. Ibid., 1226.

Bible in functional control of the process. The group was very cautious about changing the form of the biblical message. Any new form adopted should not confuse or contradict the biblical message. Several categories of forms are identified. Those words, symbols, and analogies that lack deep value can be changed without loss of meaning. More care must be exercised when the form (e.g., lamb) has historical value, and in some cases the message is so essentially tied to the form that the form must be carried over if the meaning is to be communicated. The cross is an example of this type. Words, symbols, and analogies that carry a theological idea or have teaching value must be distinguished from those that merely describe visible reality.[9] A good deal of attention was devoted to knowing the receptor's world-view and thought-forms. How does the contemporary culture understand space-time dimensions, social structures, authority patterns, socioeconomic factors of class and economy, and relationships?

The group was unable to come up with hermeneutical principles to identify the gospel core and separate it from cultural elements in Scripture. They considered John H. Yoder's identification of linguistic, cultural, ideological, and existential layers in Scripture,[10] but to no avail. Their final statement reveals the intensity but also the stalemate of their efforts.

Five geographical groups—African, Asian, Latin American, European, and the Anglo-Saxon world—separately discussed the topic "How to Evaluate Cultural Practices by Biblical Standards in Maintaining Cultural Identity in (Area X)." After hearing a paper that followed the relative relativism of Charles Kraft, the Asian group reacted by affirming the superiority of the Hebrew and Greek cultures because they were vehicles of revelation.[11] The Latin American group heard a paper that scored liberation theologies for their sociopolitical approaches to certain topics of biblical theology.[12] The Marxist flavor and the European theological terminology of such approaches indicate that their thought is archaic and foreign. In the clearest statement of the congress, the Latin American group then called for a comprehensive treatment of the same issues within a totally biblical framework. The Anglo-Saxon group heard a thorough critique of cultural relativism and recommended that study be carried out to determine which matters are fundamental and which are cultural and can be done away with. "Too often biblical truth is saddled with concepts which are purely social and yet people cling to them eagerly."[13]

---

9. Ibid., 1227.

10. Ibid., 1227–28.

11. "How to Evaluate Cultural Practices by Biblical Standards in Maintaining Cultural Identity in Asia Report," in *Let the Earth Hear His Voice*, 1249.

12. Pablo M. Perez, "Biblical Theology and Cultural Identity in Latin America," in *Let the Earth Hear His Voice*, 1251–62, especially 1260.

13. Neville P. Anderson, "Biblical Theology and Cultural Identity in the Anglo-Saxon World," in *Let the Earth Hear His Voice*, 1289.

Liberation Theology

Liberation theologies developed largely within the Roman Catholic Church and have been appropriated by the conciliar movement. These theologies make a given contemporary context the starting point, criterion, and principal source of content for theologizing. Since Latin American liberation theology has set out most intentionally to practice the contextual theological method, its proponents are most representative of this method and so bear study.[14]

These theologians identify their presuppositions in four areas: epistemology, truth, meaning, and world-view or ideology. Liberation theologians are radical historical relativists, as can be seen from statements such as Hugo Assmann's "The Bible and the whole Christian tradition do not speak directly to us in our situation."[15] They contend that traditional theology maintains a separation from the contemporary context. In their view, traditional theology has consciously tied itself to a book out of the past and to the sciences used to study the past and has asserted its independence from sciences that study the present.

Juan Segundo accuses traditional theologians of holding "the naive belief that the word of God is applied to human realities inside some antiseptic laboratory that is totally immune to the ideological tendencies and struggles of the present day." Liberation theologians see society as constantly changing, raising new questions for theology and, more fundamentally, for interpretation of Scripture. Thus it is very wrong to interpret Scripture in isolation from the contemporary context and then expect to find relevant application in the contemporary context. Traditional interpreters respond to questions from the contemporary context by leaving them unanswered or by giving old, conservative, unserviceable answers. Theology that leaves the contemporary context out of interpretation will always be conservative because it lacks a "here and now" criterion for judging the present situation. Its guidelines are even more ancient and outdated because its source is an ancient book, the Bible, and its interpretation is in the past tradition. Not only is such interpretation irrelevant, it does positive harm. The interpreter

---

14. See Daniel J. Harrington, "Some New Voices in New Testament Interpretation," *Anglican Theological Review* 64 (1982): 362–70, for a discussion of contextual theologies. See examples in *Mission Trends No. 3: Third World Theologies*, ed. Gerald H. Anderson and Thomas F. Stransky (Grand Rapids: Eerdmans, 1976). Cf. the evangelical discussion and proposals in the area of Third World theologies in *ERT* 7, no. 1 (April 1983).

15. Hugo Assmann, "A Statement," in *Theology in the Americas*, 299. Segundo asserts that the only absolute for the Christian over against the relativities of history is faith. He defines it as our subjective free absolutizing—focusing "our whole being on some value which it declares unconditional." The content of that absolute faith is always relative (*Liberation*, 177).

cannot avoid literalism, and that produces ideological justification for oppression. All types of oppression can be justified by an appeal to the plain teaching of Scripture.[16]

José P. Miranda, himself a liberation theologian, argues that liberation theology takes the Bible far more literally than does conservative theology. He insists that literal interpretation of Scripture calls for a socialist system.[17]

The radical historical relativism of liberation theologians forces them to conclude that there is no direct access to the truth of Scripture that can then be immediately applicable. The blockages of the past stand in the way, as previous interpretations conditioned by the mindsets of the previous historical situations. Accordingly, the contemporary context, not Scripture, must be treated as the basic text.

Liberation theologies cross the hermeneutical bridge from the side of the contemporary context, using a dynamic rather than a conceptual view of truth. They see the biblical concept of truth as a dynamic "creative act, a history-making pronouncement." Truth is action or orthopraxy, rather than thought or orthodoxy. The truth of an action is judged by its "efficacy in carrying out God's promise or fulfilling his judgment." One responds to truth by "obedient participation—whether in action or in suffering—in God's active righteousness and mercy."[18]

The liberation theologian uses a sociology-of-knowledge approach to the origin and nature of meaning and a Marxist analysis of the socioeconomic situation, seeing it as inevitable class struggle. Western thought-systems are viewed as ideologies developed by a given class to justify itself within the bourgeois capitalist system. Any interpretation of the biblical text will share the same character.

The liberation theologian accuses traditional theology of claiming an interclass reading of Scripture, one that sees the Bible addressing all socioeconomic classes, when, in reality, this ideological hermeneutic is the work of the ruling class and is intended to legitimize the oppressor and offer little comfort to the oppressed other than the counsel of pious resignation.[19] The liberation interpreter joins with the poor struggling for freedom

---

16. Segundo, *Liberation*, 7, 30.

17. José P. Miranda, *Communism in the Bible*, trans. Robert R. Barr (Maryknoll, N.Y.: Orbis, 1982), 1–20.

18. Miguez-Bonino, *Doing Theology*, 89. Segundo asserts that truth is truth only when it serves as a basis for genuinely human attitudes (*Liberation*, 32); Fernando Belo contends that since the basic question today is whether the faith is an ideology that contradicts praxis aimed at liberation, it is necessary that Christian theology be reframed and then reevaluated not as words, but as actions or praxis (*A Materialist Reading of the Gospel of Mark*, trans. Matthew J. O'Connell [Maryknoll, N.Y.: Orbis, 1981], 1–2). J. Severino Croatto sees such a hermeneutic that concentrates on praxis as derived from Hans-Georg Gadamer's and Paul Ricoeur's emphasis on history as the basic matrix in which hermeneutics takes place (*Exodus: A Hermeneutic of Freedom* [Maryknoll, N.Y.: Orbis, 1981], 1–3). See also Charles V. Vicencio, "The Use of Scripture in Theology," *Journal of Theology for Southern Africa* 37 (December 1981): 3–22.

19. Sergio Rostagno, "Is an Interclass Reading of the Bible Legitimate? Notes on the Justice of God," *Communio Viatorum* 17 (1974): 1–14.

from oppression and analyzes Scripture from the standpoint of political, socioeconomic liberation. This focus allows the interpreter to become involved in action for liberation, for loving the poor and giving them hope.[20]

Such a stance is justified for three reasons: (1) it allows for active involvement (orthopraxy); (2) it unmasks the supposedly neutral interclass reading of the text;[21] and (3) it conforms to the condition in which and to which the Scriptures were originally written. Robert McAfee Brown calls this "the view from below."[22] He contends that the Scripture was written by and for oppressed people, with the promise from God that oppression would be overcome.

Interpreting the text from the position of an outsider, an oppressed and marginalized person, necessarily involves a healthy measure of ideological suspicion. Since traditional theology and interpretation is developed by those in power to legitimize their actions, the interpreter must uncover what is tendentious in it. The interpreter is then free to interpret afresh and let the text speak for itself.

Liberation theologians readily admit they are more concerned with method than content. Segundo describes the hermeneutical process as movement around a circle.[23] The interpreter begins by scientifically analyzing the historical situation in such a way that questions arise concerning basic issues like life, death, epistemology, and sociopolitical values and realities. These questions generate an ideological suspicion of the established beliefs of his world. Next the interpreter applies these questions to that world-and-life view, paying particular attention to those aspects that impact his theology. The interpreter then develops answers and uses them in reformulating his theology to make it a more accurate interpreter of the present reality. Finally, the interpreter uses the results of this new evaluation of reality to create exegetical suspicion. Application of the reformulated theology raises more questions and exposes the fact that the interclass reading is biased and has not taken into account important data from the biblical text itself. This leads to a "poverty hermeneutic," or the "view from

---

20. Beatriz M. Couch, "Statement," in *Theology in the Americas*, 305. Couch places hermeneutics in the broader context of existential concerns. She defines proper hermeneutics as "the most adequate in this moment for understanding human existence." Such a hermeneutic is born in suffering and conflict as the struggle to survive as free human beings.

21. Assmann, "Statement," 300. Paul Ricoeur associates this Marxist ideological suspicion with the three nineteenth-century masters of hermeneutical suspicion: Nietzsche, Freud, and Marx ("Two Essays by Paul Ricoeur: The Critique of Religion and the Language of Faith," trans. R. Bradley De Ford, *USQR* 28 [1973]: 203–24).

22. Robert M. Brown, "Theology in a New Key: Resolving a Diminished Seventh," *USQR* 33 (1977): 29; see also Frederick Herzog, "Liberation Hermeneutic as Ideology Critique?" *Interpretation* 28 (1974): 400.

23. Segundo, *Liberation*, 9. See also J. Emmette Weir, "The Bible and Marx: A Discussion of the Hermeneutics of Liberation Theology," *SJT* 35 (1982): 337–50.

below," which searches out liberation themes in the Bible. The new interpretation is admittedly partial to a given perspective, that of the poor, but is
justified "because we must find, and designate as the Word of God, that *part*
of divine revelation which *today*, in the light of our concrete historical situation, is most useful for the liberation to which God summons us."[24]

Robert McAfee Brown's interpretation of the parable of the sheep and the
goats (Matt. 25:31–46) is an example of this hermeneutical process.[25] He
begins with a Marxist-scientific analysis of the cause of poverty. People are
poor because what is rightfully theirs has been withheld from them. They
are oppressed. This conclusion challenges the life-view of most North
Americans, which contends that laziness or unfortunate circumstance
causes poverty. This new understanding impacts a person's theology or
ethic, so that he or she no longer sees giving to the poor as an act of charity
but as an act of justice, restoring to the poor what is rightfully theirs.
Coincidentally, exegetical suspicion has been aroused toward the customary
interpretation of the Matthew passage. The righteous are not righteous
because of Christ's saving work, which gives them a heart to help "the least
of these my brethren." That is, the righteous are not Christian missionaries
or evangelists.[26] The righteous are, rather, the just, who show that they are
just by doing justice to the economically poor, not as charity, but as restoration of what is rightfully theirs. This new interpretation has emerged from
the view from below.

So far the liberation hermeneutic has consistently used the contemporary context to discover what is theologically and exegetically true. The
movement of thought has been from the present context to the ancient text.
Now the question arises, How can the interpreter move from the ancient
text back to the contemporary context? Can the hermeneutical circle be
completed in such a way that Scripture comes in contact with the contemporary situation?

The radical relativism of liberation theology rejects a direct application of
the Bible to the contemporary context, for it does not perceive the content of
Scripture as law or precedent. Accordingly, what is presented by Scripture
as a correct faith response to a biblical situation, even if the contemporary
situation and the biblical situation correspond, cannot be accepted as a
normative faith response today. The gap between past and present is too
huge and is accelerating every day.[27] What the Scriptures can provide is

---

24. Segundo, *Liberation*, 33.

25. Robert M. Brown, *Unexpected News: Reading the Bible with Third World Eyes* (Philadelphia:
Westminster, 1984), chap. 9.

26. George E. Ladd, "The Parable of the Sheep and the Goats in Recent Interpretation," in *New
Dimensions in New Testament Study*, ed. Richard N. Longenecker and Merrill C. Tenney (Grand Rapids:
Zondervan, 1974), 191–99.

27. Miguez-Bonino, *Doing Theology*, 103; Segundo asserts that the approach of finding a biblical
situation akin to our present day and accepting the ideology Scripture presents as the correct response
of faith becomes more unrealistic and unscientific as time goes on (*Liberation*, 117).

help in rephrasing the questions or concepts growing out of one's analysis of the contemporary situation.[28] To achieve any correlation between the biblical situation and the contemporary situation, the interpreter must see that the biblical text moves in only one direction—in the direction of liberation, shalom, love. The Bible, so interpreted, offers no key for Christian obedience, but only suggests a framework for it. The Bible provides a place to exercise faith, which for the Christian is "learning how to learn." This learning how to learn in and through the Bible is a continuing process. One continues to give absolute value to objective Christian tradition by repeating the experiences of the biblical tradition. What is absolute in the end is the process. "Faith incarnated in successive ideologies constitutes an ongoing educational process in which man learns how to learn under God's guidance. We will never be able to reduce the faith to [a specific dogma, Bible, creed]. . . . All of these things point out *the road to be travelled* by faith, but never provide us with the journey completed."[29]

One may question how much guidance liberation theologians expect the Scripture to provide, since construction of ideologies or theologies to deal with the contemporary situation involves no correlation with the biblical text. The sequence seems to be for interpreters to devise an ideology which they think will be compatible with a contemporary gospel message. "It is becoming more and more obvious to Christians that *secular* inventiveness and creativity is more appropriate and fruitful" for this creative, imaginative, contemporary formulation of the gospel message than is scriptural content.[30]

Evangelical Critiques

Evangelical critiques of liberation theology have noted both benefits and liabilities. Stephen Knapp cites several benefits. For example, he finds useful the contention of liberation theology that all theology is ideology, that is, culturally conditioned. For him this assertion exposes the myth of objective exegesis, which equates its results with revelation.[31]

Knapp also contends that defending Scripture against theological relativism by appealing to the doctrine of inerrancy is outdated, or at least beside the point, because the contemporary hermeneutical discussion assumes the culturally conditioned nature of the interpretational process. A more fruitful approach for establishing Scripture's authority is to emphasize

---

28. Couch, "Statement," 306.
29. Segundo, *Liberation*, 181.
30. Ibid., 117.
31. Stephen C. Knapp, "A Preliminary Dialogue with Gutierrez' *A Theology of Liberation*," in *Evangelicals and Liberation*, 18–20.

either the work of the Holy Spirit or the context of the multicultural Christian community in interpretation.

Harvie Conn sees this emphasis on the culturally conditioned nature of interpretation as a vindication of Cornelius Van Til's presuppositional approach to apologetics, and he welcomes its expansion to include socioeconomic preconceptions. He asserts that accusing liberation theology of the socialization of theology is too often the result of uncritical assumptions about the objective neutrality of theology, for "even constructions based on the given of an inerrant Bible can be controlled by unbiblical presumptions regarding society and human relations."[32]

J. Andrew Kirk acknowledges the existence of modern preunderstandings, including socioeconomically conditioned ones, which produce culturally conditioned interpretations. He insists that these can and must be identified and justified to the degree that they conform to the biblical message. There are two objective poles in interpretation: the contemporary human situation scientifically analyzed and the biblical message understood by its own criteria. Our sinful disposition is to interpose between these poles hidden motives or obstacles of subjectivity and to limit the human context so as to neutralize the prophetic impact of the text. Kirk concludes that "only as man ceases to look for his identity within his own subjectivity, apart from these two poles, will he ever face the demand for radical renewal and transformation."[33]

The basic evangelical criticism of liberation theology centers on its refusal to view the Bible as the final authority in the interpretation process.[34] Kirk argues that since neither the church nor any ideological framework, such as Marxism or capitalism, can be identified with the kingdom, none can have ultimate authority in the interpretation of Scripture.[35]

Liberation theology excludes Scripture as its final authority because it adopts the wrong starting point for its hermeneutic. By beginning with a Marxist scientific analysis of the contemporary situation, it makes that analysis the canon on which theology is built. As Conn observes, "The theology of liberation is grounded on a situational canonicity in which the present practice becomes the norm for discovering the will of God in the practice of

---

32. Harvie M. Conn, "Theologies of Liberation: Toward a Common View," in *Tensions in Contemporary Theology*, ed. Stanley N. Gundry and Alan F. Johnson, 3d rev. ed. (Chicago: Moody, 1979), 413. Alan Johnson echoes this thought when he contends that, as a starting point for doing theology, an uncritical adoption of the free-enterprise system or Western individualism is just as unacceptable as Marxism ("A Response to Problems of Normativeness in Scripture: Cultural Versus Permanent," in *Hermeneutics, Inerrancy, and the Bible*, ed. Earl D. Radmacher and Robert D. Preus [Grand Rapids: Zondervan, 1984], 268).

33. J. Andrew Kirk, *Liberation Theology: An Evangelical View from the Third World* (London: Marshall, Morgan & Scott, 1979), 193.

34. J. Robertson McQuilkin, "Problems of Normativeness in Scripture: Cultural Versus Permanent," in *Hermeneutics, Inerrancy*, 224; Johnson, "Response to Problems," 268.

35. Kirk, *Liberation Theology*, 187.

truth."[36] Such an approach prevents the Bible from authoritatively determining the truth—in this instance, the truth among competing ideologies—and Knapp asks, "Haven't we simply transferred the verification question from biblical interpretation and theology to a 'scientific' analysis of reality?"[37] A further difficulty with the scientific analysis of the contemporary situation is that it does not take sin into account. Kirk contends that the Bible confronts human beings much more radically than does Marxism.[38]

For evangelicals, the whole approach of liberation theology leaves Scripture without any meaningfully authoritative role.[39] The hermeneutics of poverty and liberation, as it searches for what works, practices an autonomous dilution of what is distinctively Christian in Scripture. Kirk points out that "the truth of revelation, because it depends upon God who reveals, is true independently of whether it is acted upon or not. Nevertheless, it demands a consistent practice, [and] will be judged by that practice."[40] Liberation theology, though dealing with biblical themes, refuses to submit its praxis to the authoritative control of Scripture.

36. Harvie Conn, "Theology of Liberation," *Presbyterian Journal* 34 (23 July 1975): 9. Knapp holds that we should not grant the status of special revelation to ecclesiastical tradition and practice or to the sociopolitical analysis of our situation ("Preliminary Dialogue," 20).

37. Knapp, "Preliminary Dialogue," 25.

38. Kirk, *Liberation Theology*, 192–93.

39. Conn, "Theology of Liberation," 9; Knapp, "Preliminary Dialogue," 22; Conn, "Theologies of Liberation," 416.

40. J. Andrew Kirk, "The Meaning of Man in the Debate Between Christianity and Marxism," *Theological Fraternity Bulletin* 2 (1974): 19, cited in Conn, "Theologies of Liberation," 417.

11

Contextual Theology
The Evangelical Response

Trinity Evangelical Divinity School Consultations

In 1976 and 1979, Trinity Evangelical Divinity School sponsored consultations on theology and mission, and at each a study section was devoted to contextualization.[1] By and large, the papers and discussions of the consultation treated contextualization as an issue of cross-cultural communication. But there was growing awareness that the critical issue raised by contextual theology was precisely where the source of theological truth is located.

At the second conference David J. Hesselgrave approached the issue, suggesting that "the degree to which culture is held to be determinative in the revelatory process in biblical times, and in the missionizing process in modern times, is, in turn, determinative of the approach one takes to contextualization."[2] At one end of the continuum he placed orthodoxy, where culture is important but does not determine the biblical message. Contextualization in the orthodox setting may be characterized as apostolic

---

1. David J. Hesselgrave, ed., *Theology and Mission* (Grand Rapids: Baker, 1978), 71–130; idem, ed., *New Horizons in World Mission* (Grand Rapids: Baker, 1979), 199ff.
2. David J. Hesselgrave, "Response to Archer and Hiebert," in *New Horizons,* 234; see also idem, "The Contextualization Continuum," *Gospel in Context* 2, no. 3 (July 1979): 4–11.

accommodation, the process of taking the apostolic truth—supracultural biblical truth— and teaching it in culturally appropriate forms. On the other end of the spectrum is liberalism, which practices syncretistic accommodation. Here culture is the determinant, and contextualization is conceived as a dialogical process for seeking truth. In between these poles are neo-liberalism and neoorthodoxy, both of which practice a prophetic accommodation, seeking to discern what cultural forms the biblical message will take at any existential moment. Culture is not the sole determinant, but is involved in dialectical process with the biblical material. Hesselgrave's analysis set the deliberations in perspective.

Hesselgrave's student Bruce Fleming highlighted the difference between the evangelical and ecumenical approaches by describing the evangelical approach as "context-indigenization" to distinguish it from ecumenical contextualization. "By use of insights gained from anthropology and related social sciences, and missiology, evangelicals seek to indigenize the gospel in the modern context."[3]

Fleming emphasized that the ecumenical and evangelical approaches to contextualizing separate over their opposing views about the source of theological truth. For the evangelicals the Bible is the source of all theologizing:

> The practice of historical-grammatical exegesis in conjunction with context-indigenization allows the Bible to speak for itself, guarding against the imposition of certain motifs which contradict the teachings of the whole of Scripture . . . if evangelicals implement the dialectical approach of technical contextualization, they will denigrate the Bible by equating it with something less than God's special revelation. . . . Popular contextualization's failure to distinguish between God's authoritative text and other "words," must also be avoided by evangelicals as an unnecessary abandonment of God's revelation in an attempt to make His evertimely will "relevant." Properly speaking, evangelicals do not, and should not, contextualize the gospel.[4]

Deliberations on the issue of the relation of authoritative Scripture to the contextualizing process were lively indeed. Norman Ericson proposed that the Bible itself was more or less a product of the contextualizing process, particularly the New Testament, where "patterns . . . give us direction as to the nature of acceptable contextualization, indicating both imperatives as well as limitations."[5] Paul's instruction concerning "food offered to idols" is

---

3. Bruce C. Fleming, *Contextualization of Theology: An Evangelical Assessment* (Pasadena, Calif.: William Carey Library, 1980), 78.

4. Ibid.

5. Norman R. Ericson, "Implications from the New Testament for Contextualization," in *Theology and Mission*, 71.

an example (1 Cor. 8:1–10:22). Gleason Archer observed that since there was a continual tendency toward syncretism in Israel's history, contextualization was not a conscious concern in the Old Testament. Indeed, Joseph and Daniel, who followed the will of God in an alien culture, gained cross-cultural credibility by being different, by not contextualizing themselves.[6]

As for the limitations on the extent of adaptation to context, Ericson said that they are determined by the nature of the scriptural content. He identified four kinds of biblical content and suggested a contextualizing approach for each. First there is *the core*, the revelation and salvation effected in Jesus Christ. In addition, there is *the substance*, the gospel tradition as transmitted by the apostles; there is also *the application*, exhortations addressed to particular people; and finally there is *the expression*, descriptions of the quality of life in a cultural setting.

> The core and substance of the gospel are to be constant; only the linguistic and conceptual patterns may vary from one language to another. The application will be universal in those exhortations which deal with personal qualities and Christian virtues, but will be entirely contextualized when dealing with matters of social custom or economic arrangements. Similarly the quality of life must exhibit universal Christian virtues, but in contextualized manners which deliver the message in meaningful cultural behavior.[7]

Archer urged that contextualization be practiced within limits. While admitting that Christian culture may vary from context to context, he asserted that the clear intention of biblical absolutes must be retained. In thought, no basic element of the gospel is to be undermined. In life, no basic rule of a godly life and no part of the basic moral law is to be set aside by the contextualizing process.[8]

There was no consensus on these issues at the Trinity consultation. Here, as at Lausanne, some contended that inerrancy is violated if in cross-cultural communication one alters in any way the forms of Scripture. R. J. Davis so argued, saying that effective cross-cultural communication is the work of the Holy Spirit.[9] Others, such as Samuel Rowen, asked how the core of the gospel can be identified in Scripture.[10] James Buswell traced out a full description of contextualization by delineating three levels on which it functions in a different culture. First there is *inculturation*, the contextualization of the witness. Next there is *indigenization*, the contextualization of the

---

6. Gleason L. Archer, Jr., "Contextualization: Some Implications from the Life and Witness of the Old Testament," in *New Horizons*, 200.

7. Ericson, "Implications," 83.

8. Archer, "Contextualization," 215.

9. R. J. Davis, "Response to Buswell and Ericson," in *Theology and Mission*, 116. James Buswell strongly critiques Davis's position (see n. 12).

10. Samuel Rowen, "Response to Buswell and Ericson," in *Theology and Mission*, 114.

church and its leadership. Finally there is *ethnotheology,* the contextualization of theology by indigenous theologians.[11] Buswell acknowledges that contextualization is too often carried out by those "who are less meticulous in preserving the essentials of Christian orthodoxy." Accordingly, he finds fault with the evangelical reservations about contextualization in general, charging that many are uncomfortable with any method from a nonevangelical source. "Somehow, evangelicals must be more willing to appraise new procedures, methods, and theory in terms of their direct applicability to efficient and effective communication of the gospel no matter in whose camp they originated or who may be employing or applying them to less than evangelical ends."[12]

The Trinity consultants next set about analyzing the implications of contextualization for the hermeneutical process. As a first step, they affirmed the importance of cultural context, both ancient and modern, for the task of interpretation and contextualization.[13] They also recognized the potential advantages of a cross-cultural hermeneutic, in which modern interpreters seek to communicate the biblical message to a culture other than their own. As Norman Ericson noted, traditional hermeneutic has tended to be monocultural. "There is even a kind of inbreeding. Our Western hermeneutic has its roots in the origin of our Western society. We therefore fail to see that our applied hermeneutic may be based more on our Western cultural tradition than on the message of the New Testament."[14] Throughout the deliberations the evangelicals continued to set limits for legitimate hermeneutics by insisting that the absoluteness of the Word of God must not be undermined by a hermeneutic that finds multiple meanings in any given text.

For all these efforts, when the conferences ended there was an awareness that the implications of contextualization for hermeneutics had not been fully worked out. There was a continuing concern that contextualization not dim the absolute uniqueness of the gospel nor obliterate the clear distinction between truth and error.[15] Rowen left this unfinished agenda: "We must be able to determine what is normative and what is descriptive. What are the biblical norms for hermeneutics? Can hermeneutical norms be found within each culture? It is here that the critical differences between legitimate contextualization and syncretism will be determined."[16]

---

11. James O. Buswell III, "Contextualization: Theory, Tradition, and Method," in *Theology and Mission,* 90–98.

12. James O. Buswell III, "Reply," in *Theology and Mission,* 126.

13. Davis, "Response," 115; Norman R. Ericson, "Reply," in *Theology and Mission,* 122–23.

14. Ericson, "Reply," 122.

15. Hesselgrave, "Response," 235.

16. Rowen, "Response," 114.

David Hesselgrave

David Hesselgrave picked up this agenda in part at Summit II of the International Council on Biblical Inerrancy. "Contextualization is the process whereby representatives of a religious faith adapt the forms and content of that faith in such a way as to communicate and (usually) commend it to the minds and hearts of a new generation within their own changing culture or to people with other cultural backgrounds."[17] After formulating this working definition, Hesselgrave concentrated on the epistemological preunderstandings of the world's great religions as indicated by the genre of their special revelation. Shintoism employs "myth"; Hinduism and Buddhism, "the writings of the enlightened"; Islam, "divine writing"; Christianity, "inspired writings." Many approaches to the contextualization of Scripture are wrong because they tend to reflect a genre that is characteristic of other religions. Rudolf Bultmann and Paul Tillich treat Scripture as myth. The dynamic equivalence of Eugene Nida and Charles Kraft treats Christian Scripture in a way that resembles the Hindu and Buddhist approach to their scripture as "writings of the enlightened." Evangelical proponents of the majority text treat Scripture as "divine writing," much as the Muslim approach to the Koran. Hesselgrave cites Bruce Nicholls's approach as properly balanced, since he starts from a truly biblical revelational epistemology, a preunderstanding that treats Scripture as "inspired writing."

Hesselgrave takes care to note that biblical inerrancy requires that the contextualizer pay attention to words and not just to the nonverbal functions of a message. While he is willing to affirm that meanings are located in people and in the sociocultural context, he says to take it with a grain of salt that meanings are not in words, "because language constitutes the primary means whereby meanings are conveyed from one person to another."[18] For Hesselgrave, words and meaning, form and function, go together. All must be taken into account in translation and contextualization. Context can never be the sole locus of meaning. Culture is not a key to unlock meaning; rather, it is simply one number in a combination that unlocks the meaning of the ancient context. Hesselgrave urges evangelicals to use their revelational epistemological preunderstanding to "effect a much more complete system of contextualization, one that is truly worthy of the historic orthodox evangelical commitment that it reflects."[19]

---

17. David J. Hesselgrave, "Contextualization and Revelational Epistemology," in *Hermeneutics, Inerrancy, and the Bible*, ed. Earl D. Radmacher and Robert D. Preus (Grand Rapids: Zondervan, 1984), 694.

18. Ibid., 733.

19. Ibid., 730. In his "Response to Contextualization and Revelational Epistemology" (in *Hermeneutics, Inerrancy*), Morris A. Inch agrees (p. 749); see also Hesselgrave's exposition of cross-cultural (contextualized) communication, *Communicating Christ Cross-Culturally* (Grand Rapids: Zondervan, 1978).

Bible Translation

The implications of Bible translation practices for communicating the gospel message across cultures have been appreciated by evangelical scholars. One of the most significant contributions was made by John Beekman and John Callow of Wycliffe Bible Translators. Their *Translating the Word of God* gives a comprehensive survey of the methods, materials, and aims of good translation.

Basic to the theory of meaning Beekman and Callow develop is their definition of a word as "a symbol which represents an area of experience or a part of one's environment."[20] They then put forward three propositions regarding the structure of all language; this common structure makes translation possible. (1) All languages consist of words that may be analyzed according to their components of meaning, allowing one to classify each word as thing, event, abstraction, or relation.[21] Each word has a generic component of meaning that fits into one of these categories. (2) All languages have generic and specific words, and words are flexible, having a number of potential meanings. The word *table*, for example, may be a verb which expresses an event, or a noun which expresses a thing. (3) All languages have words which are semantically related by sharing in a generic component of meaning.[22] Such words form a semantic set. These last two characteristics of language make it possible for the translator to isolate a word's meaning by relating it to other words in a hierarchy of generic-specific terms. For example, "chair" relates to furniture, which relates to human artifacts. The word can then be distinguished from other terms in the same semantic set to determine its precise meaning as a chair rather than a table or bed, or some other piece of furniture.

Context also plays an important role in this process. "It becomes quite evident that *context*—more specifically, the collocates of the word under analysis—is basic in determining whether a word has a meaning consisting of several senses or of only one."[23] For example, the specific meaning of "chair" in such phrases as "to chair the committee" or "set the chair down" is indicated by other words in the context. Context functions to determine meaning by eliminating other potential meanings that cannot stand in this grouping of words.

Some critics have complained that the structure of language as proposed by Beekman and Callow is not universal at all, but is actually an arbitrary

---

20. John Beekman and John Callow, *Translating the Word of God* (Grand Rapids: Zondervan, 1974), 67.

21. See Eugene A. Nida and Charles R. Taber, *The Theory and Practice of Translation* (Leiden: E. J. Brill, 1974), 37.

22. Beekman and Callow, *Translating*, 78.

23. Ibid., 75.

scheme imposed by them. They respond that it is possible for native speakers, by a process of inductive questioning, to "classify with an expression any real-world distinction which they observe and want to make."[24] This can be done even though the native language may not distinguish and classify items in the same categories as does the translator. In fact, a native speaker can accept innovative classifications if they are implicit in the language, or if they can be conceptualized as legitimate groupings. On this basis Beekman and Callow maintain that the categories which translators use in their analysis of language are not arbitrary but exist objectively in the real world to which language points. The structure of the native language and the native speaker's judgment in determining legitimate groupings for words also play an important role for translators, according to Beekman and Callow. The groupings give evidence for the view that the extralinguistic referent is essential for meaning and the assurance that meaning can be conveyed from one linguistic cultural context to another.[25] These groupings form the basis for a solid linguistic pylon in the hermeneutical bridge.

In their book Beekman and Callow define a faithful translation as one that "transfers the meaning and the dynamics of the original text." "Meaning" in this definition indicates historical and didactic information. The translator has a responsibility to communicate historical information, even unfamiliar historical information, faithfully into the receptor language. Didactic information is interpretation of historical facts, "relating them to the needs of man and applying them to the kind of conduct and life appropriate to these facts. Scripture is therefore replete with commands, illustrations, parables, and similitudes, all of which have a didactic function which in faithful translation must be preserved."[26] This didactic information must be communicated according to the original writer's intention, whether the receptor audience agrees with it or not. "Dynamics" in this definition indicates that the translator makes use of the natural structure of the receptor language so that the message can be understood with ease.

Beekman and Callow point out that these criteria for fidelity sometimes compete with each other. When confronted with a historical detail for which there is no equivalent in the receptor language, the translator may fail to communicate or may miscommunicate. If the historical detail is part of a figure of speech (e.g., a metaphor such as "you are the salt of the earth") and one translates it literally, then didactic fidelity as well as dynamic fidelity is lost. To overcome this problem Beekman and Callow suggest an

---

24. Ibid., 73.

25. Kenneth L. Pike uses the universal characteristics of language as an argument for the possibility of moral universals, i.e., the constraints of conscience which are translatable into each culture ("Christianity and Culture I. Conscience and Culture," *Journal of the American Scientific Affiliation* 31 [1979]: 11).

26. Beekman and Callow, *Translating*, 33, 36.

order of priority. Fidelity to meaning, whether historical or didactic, takes precedence over fidelity to dynamics (i.e., ease of communication). If translating a figurative statement with historical fidelity results in wrong meaning, then didactic fidelity must take precedence, but one must be very cautious about making any adjustments that disregard historical fidelity.

When there is no lexical equivalent in the receptor language for the original term, Beekman and Callow recommend using a descriptive modification. The term *Passover*, for example, would become "the feast when God delivered the Jews." Only as a last resort do they suggest "the use of a real-world referent from the receptor culture for an unknown referent of the original, both of the referents having the same *function*." Though cultural substitutes are not to be used with historical references, they are permissible as a last resort in didactic passages. Similar functions may be indicated by different forms in different societies; the function is constant, but not the form. For this reason an adjustment in form may still communicate the same function. The word *foxes*, for instance, might become *coyotes* in Mexico at Matthew 8:20. "It is also a fact that there are places in the Scriptures where form is not in focus, but only the function served by the particular form. It is in these contexts, then, that it is sometimes permissible to substitute a form from the [receptor] culture whose function is identical or nearly so to the function associated with the form used in the original."[27] An example would be "sowing" in Matthew 6:26 or John 4:37, where it is not the focus and can thus accommodate a cultural substitute. However, in Matthew 13:1–9 "sowing" is the focus, and at that place must be translated with historical precision.

Extrabiblical cultural factors can also seep into a translation through drawing on the cultural context of the document. This context lies outside the text itself and includes such things as the circumstances of the writers, the readers, and their relationship. Occasionally, the translator has to draw on extrabiblical information about material objects, geography, religion, and culture in formulating a translation. Should such information be made explicit in a translation? According to Beekman and Callow, only when the receptor language requires it to maintain fidelity to the meaning of the text.[28] Here again they exercise a great deal of caution. Information contained in the text's immediate context is the most tempting candidate for explicit expression. The more remote context of the text and the ancient cultural context expressed by extrabiblical information are less likely sources of information which should be made explicit in translation.

---

27. Ibid., 201–2.
28. Ibid., 48ff.

Harvie M. Conn

Writing in a volume published between Lausanne and Willowbank, Harvie M. Conn presents a trenchant analysis of conciliar contextualization and especially of liberation theology.[29] He expresses dismay at the lack of informed and effective evangelical response to these movements and makes specific suggestions for dealing with this issue.

Conn perceives that in conciliar contextualization the primary "text" for hermeneutics has become the modern historical context. The most serious consequence is that the Bible becomes unnecessary for an authoritative interpretation of revelatory events and as a guide for discerning the work of Christ in the past and his ongoing work in contemporary history.[30] There is no longer an objective, absolute message from God that addresses the modern historical context.

Conn devotes equal space to the missiology of the World Council of Churches and that of evangelicals, but his critique of evangelicalism is of primary concern here. It points to a failure of evangelical missiology to engage the issue fully and effectively.[31] By treating contextualization as simply a matter of effective communication of the gospel to a different cultural context, evangelicals had frozen their response at a stage of the controversy already past. Conn sees contextualization as the process of "conscientization of the whole people of God to the hermeneutical obligations of the gospel."[32] This means that the people of God will consciously apply the Scriptures as judge and savior to the whole texture of their culture-bound lives.

Evangelicals failed in this area because their understanding of the hermeneutical task was distorted by influences from Western intellectual tradition. Unconsciously borrowing from the distinction made in nineteenth-century German idealism between language as brute fact and language as interpretation, they had assumed that language can exist independent of its cultural context. This led to a further assumption that the interpreter can

---

29. Harvie M. Conn, "Contextualization: Where Do We Begin?" in *Evangelicals and Liberation*, ed. Carl E. Armerding (Nutley, N.J.: Presbyterian & Reformed, 1977), 90–119. See also Conn's analysis of evangelicals' handling of the issues at Willowbank and beyond (*Eternal Word and Changing Worlds: Theology, Anthropology, and Mission in Trialogue* [Grand Rapids: Zondervan, 1984], 179–84).

30. Conn, "Contextualization: Where Do We Begin?" 102.

31. Some notable exceptions are F. Ross Kinsler ("Mission and Context: The Current Debate About Contextualization," *Evangelical Missions Quarterly* 14 [1978]: 23–30) and George W. Peters ("Missions in Cultural Perspective," *BS* 136 [1979]: 195–205). In his comments about revelational absolutism and cultural relativism, Peters observes and warns, "No doubt absolutism versus relativism is becoming one of the most serious struggles in world Christianity today. Yet few evangelical scholars are wrestling with it in depth and fewer missionaries are prepared to be of real help to the struggling churches. . . . Evangelical and biblical guidelines are urgently needed in this matter" (p. 196).

32. Conn, "Contextualization: A New Dimension for Cross-Cultural Hermeneutic," *Evangelical Missions Quarterly* 14 (1978): 43.

understand a text independent of his or her own cultural context. Evangelicals relied on the historical-grammatical-literary method to yield the objective meaning of the text without any interference from the interpreter's own cultural context. By locating the objective meaning within a framework of interpretation and application that is based on a Cartesian distinction between abstract theoretical cognition and concrete application, evangelicals have missed the essential link between the two.

As a consequence, evangelicals have found themselves in either irrelevant isolation or blind cultural captivity. Understandably fearful of existentialist rejection of biblical authority, they narrowed themselves to scientific exegesis until they could not participate with ease in the contemporary hermeneutical debate, where the whole issue is the relation of text and modern context.

> In this isolation from life's cultural contexts, western theology takes on a mythic character as a final refuge against theological relativism. In the process, we lose the nerve center of theology as "simply the application of Scripture to all areas of human life," involvement in the human dialogue over the answers of the inerrant word of God, and the questions implicit and explicit in the variety of the world's cultures.[33]

The hermeneutics of the Reformation, to which evangelicals are heirs, developed in a monocultural situation where the role of the interpreter's culture was never taken into account in the process of interpretation. Still, that culture was at work. Within itself every culture has preserving and integrating capacities, those hidden methodologies to which man as culture bearer is always liable.[34] This is why evangelicals have been consistently plagued by ethnocultural blindness to the cultural ingredients that play a formative part in their exegesis. They tend, for instance, to acculturate the Bible by allegorizing it. Such unself-critical evangelical exegesis promotes the goal of middle-class upward mobility.

Conn shows himself to be in essential agreement with two tenets of contextualizing theology: (1) theory and practice are inextricably bound together; and (2) Western hermeneutics is culture-bound—it has not exercised ideological suspicion. However, his remedy for this situation is much different. As a Reformed theologian, he points to "covenant" as a key biblical concept which will correct the deficiencies in both contextual and evangelical theology. "Covenant" reaffirms the absolute priority and sovereignty of God, the Creator, who has inscripturated a divine word of covenant responsibility that his creatures must live out in concrete historical

---

33. Ibid., 42.
34. Ibid., 45.

circumstances. In this one conceptual framework the denial of scriptural authority and the separation of absolute truth (interpretation) from historical action (application) are overcome. The contextual hermeneutic that Conn advocates is "the covenant conscientization of the whole people of God to the hermeneutical obligations of the gospel in their culture."[35] It involves answering two basic questions:

> How are the divine demands of the gospel of the kingdom communicated in cultural thought forms meaningful to the real issues and needs of the person and his society in that point of cultural time? How shall the man of God, as a member of the body of Christ and the fellowship of the Spirit, respond meaningfully and with integrity to the Scripture addressing his culture so that he may live a full-orbed kingdom lifestyle in covenant obedience with the covenant community?[36]

For Conn, the obligations of the gospel are covenant responsibilities within one's cultural context; thus biblical truth and action are brought together. Looking at Scripture and at the current historical circumstances with the same covenant conscientization, one experiences "a critical and growing self-awareness of his restored covenant relationship to the cosmos" because "the kingdom as a sign of liberation and of judgment must bring believers to a covenant conscientization of their witnessing responsibility to the demands of the life of the kingdom in every situation."[37]

But how does one escape the danger of cultural captivity? By following the hermeneutical principle that Scripture should interpret Scripture. Conn is convinced that this principle will free the biblical message from a form of expression and interpretation determined by the modern culture. Scripture will then be able to address that culture authoritatively. Such an independent authority will free those who bind themselves to it to exercise their covenant expression of life in the modern culture, for they will have an authoritative guide in the "struggle against cultural idols, against our repression of the divine questions."[38] "The Bible's own understanding of its

---

35. Ibid., 43. Paul R. Wells also suggests "covenant" as the center of a hermeneutical answer to James Barr's historical relativism (*James Barr and the Bible* [Phillipsburg, N.J.: Presbyterian & Reformed, 1980], 354–79). Conn's developed thought proposed six criteria for doing theology: biblical-theological, covenantal, culture-specific, confessional, communal, and prophetic (*Eternal Word*, 224–60).

36. Conn, "Contextualization: A New Dimension," 43.

37. Conn, "Contextualization: Where Do We Begin?" 109.

38. Conn, "Contextualization: A New Dimension," 45; idem, "Contextualization: Where Do We Begin?" 113. Andrew F. Walls argues that the gospel liberates us from our culture through the "pilgrim principle." Via a "universalizing factor," incorporation into the church brings one into association with a new set of family relations from various cultures. One is adopted into the church's history and receives a whole new set of ideas, concepts, and assumptions that do not necessarily square with the rest of life's cultural inheritance ("The Gospel as the Prisoner and Liberator of Culture," *Missionalia* 10 [1982]: 93–105).

hermeneutical role in the process of contextualization forbids us the bondage of abstractionism and any culturally privileged status quo. It calls us to the task of the renovation of creation in the name of the last Adam."[39]

39. Conn, "Contextualization: Where Do We Begin?" 113.

12

The Willowbank Consultation

In 1978, a section of the Lausanne Committee for World Evangelization sponsored a consultation on gospel and culture in Willowbank, Bermuda, for the express purpose of developing an "understanding of the interrelation of the Gospel and culture with special reference to God's revelation, to our interpretation and communication of it, and to the response of the hearers in their conversion, and their churches and their life-style."[1] The report issued by the consultation provided the most comprehensive statement to date of the evangelical consensus on the relation of hermeneutics and culture.[2]

---

1. William A. Smalley, "Foreword," in *Gospel and Culture*, ed. John R. W. Stott and Robert T. Coote (Pasadena, Calif.: William Carey Library, 1979), vii. Bruce J. Nicholls proposes that Willowbank had the practical purpose of getting evangelical theologians and anthropologists to begin to talk and listen to each other. They had previously been conducting the contextualization process on two levels: (1) cultural institutions and behavior and (2) theological world-view and ethical values. They were suspicious of one another for "they speak different languages, approach culture from different perspectives and look for different sets of results" (*Contextualization: A Theology of Gospel and Culture* [Downers Grove, Ill.: Inter-Varsity, 1979], 24).

2. "The Willowbank Report," in *Gospel and Culture*, 433–61. In 1982 and 1983, five other evangelical consultations were held at which contextualization was discussed or practiced:

In March 1982, the First Conference of Evangelical Mission Theologians from the Two-Thirds World was held in Bangkok, Thailand, to discuss the emerging Christologies of the Two-Thirds World. The conference issued its findings under the title "Towards a Missiological Christology in the Two-Thirds World." Among the items on the agenda and the accomplishments of the conference:

(3) We affirmed the crucial importance of the Scriptures as normative for Christology, and the

174

A number of Willowbank participants contributed to the discussion, not only in their papers, but also in other writings. In arguing for contextualized theology using the constructs of communication theory built on semantics, Charles R. Taber specifies how one's own culture conditions one's understanding of a text.[3] Bruce Nicholls develops a case for the uniqueness of divine revelation, presenting a theological understanding of the cultural factors present in the giving of revelation, its interpretation, and its application in a contemporary cultural context.[4] C. René Padilla expounds an evangelical understanding of the hermeneutical circle.[5]

---

necessity for a careful and obedient hermeneutic, true to the whole of Scripture, and sensitive to our contexts.

(4) We discussed in what ways our various contexts ought to be judged and tested by Scripture. We sought to grapple with the ways in which the life and mission of the Church are continuous with our various cultures and to explore how they are discontinuous. . . . We also examined ways in which the nature of Christ himself transcends cultural boundaries and enables us to do so in the power of the Spirit. ["Conference Findings: Towards a Missiological Christology in the Two-Thirds World," in *Sharing Jesus in the Two-Thirds World: Evangelical Christologies from the Contexts of Poverty, Powerlessness, and Religious Pluralism*, ed. Vinay Samuel and Chris Sugden (Grand Rapids: Eerdmans, 1984), 279]

In the summer of 1982, the Asia Theological Association, the Theological Commission of the Association of Evangelicals in Africa and Madagascar, and the Latin American Theological Fraternity sponsored a consultation in Seoul, Korea, on the subject "Theology and the Bible in Context." It produced the "Seoul Declaration" (see *ERT* 7 [1983]: 3–12), which critiques both Western theology and Third World contextual theologies. It affirms the primacy of Scripture in the task of theologizing: "No other sources stand alongside" (p. 10). It sets out various theological agendas for the different contemporary Third World contexts. The declaration sums up its understanding of theologizing: "As we theologize, we will seek to be faithful to the Word of God in spelling out the meaning and significance of biblical truth within our own particular contexts for the sake of obedience that comes through faith and to the glory of God" (p. 12).

The Faith and Study Unit of the World Evangelical Fellowship met in Cambridge, England, in November 1982, to consult on the hermeneutical problems relevant to understanding the nature, scope, and mission of the church in various cultures. This was an exercise in evangelical contextualization, the results of which are available in D. A. Carson, ed., *Biblical Interpretation and the Church: The Problem of Contextualization* (Nashville: Nelson, 1984).

Also in November 1982, Summit II of the International Council on Biblical Inerrancy had a study section on contextualization.

In November 1983, scholars from Latin America and North America met near Cuernavaca, Mexico, under the sponsorship of the Latin American Theological Fraternity and the Theological Students Fellowship (Inter-Varsity Christian Fellowship) to discuss "Context and Hermeneutics in the Americas." The conversations ranged over a wide spectrum of theological issues focusing on the effects of contemporary cultural context on interpretation and theologizing. No general statement was issued (see Mark Lau Branson and C. René Padilla, eds., *Conflict and Context: Hermeneutics in the Americas* [Grand Rapids: Eerdmans, 1986]).

3. Charles R. Taber, "The Limits of Indigenization in Theology," *Missiology* 6 (1978): 53–80; idem, "Hermeneutics and Culture: An Anthropological Perspective," in *Gospel and Culture*, 109–34; idem, "Is There More than One Way to Do Theology?" *Gospel in Context* 1, no. 1 (January 1978): 4–10; idem, "Author's Response to Comment on: Is There More than One Way to Do Theology?" ibid., 37–39.

4. Nicholls, *Contextualization*.

5. C. René Padilla, "Hermeneutics and Culture: A Theological Perspective," in *Gospel and Culture*, 83–108; idem, "The Interpreted Word: Reflections on Contextual Hermeneutics," *Themelios* 7 (1981): 18–23.

The Willowbank Report

The twenty-eight-page Willowbank Report comprehensively addresses culture in biblical revelation, in interpretation, and in application. At the revelation stage inspiration controlled the role played by ancient culture:

> The process by which the biblical authors borrowed words and images from their cultural milieu, and used them creatively, was controlled by the Holy Spirit so that they purged them of false or evil implications and thus transformed them into vehicles of truth and goodness. . . . God used the knowledge, experience and cultural background of the authors (though his revelation constantly transcended these), and in each case the result was the same, namely God's word through human words.[6]

Addressing the form-meaning distinction, the report stresses that for the sake of communication in translating and interpreting, the form of the words may be changed as long as the meaning is retained. It also affirms that the forms may have a certain normative quality, since God himself chose them as appropriate vehicles of his revelation.[7] This is especially true of important recurring symbols in Scripture. "Each fresh formulation and explanation in every generation and culture must be checked for faithfulness by referring back to the original."[8]

The Willowbank Report understands the interpretation phase as involving the cultural context of the contemporary reader as well as the cultural context of the biblical text. In this way a dialog develops, and "out of the context in which his word was originally given, we have God speaking to us in our contemporary context, and we find it a transforming experience."[9]

Though the term *dialog* is used and a process of dynamic interplay between text and interpreter is sketched out, this contextual approach and the conciliar contextualizing hermeneutic differ radically in the place they assign to Scripture. According to the Willowbank Report, "Scripture remains always central and normative."[10] Therefore, the dialogical process is not

---

6. "Willowbank Report," 435–36.

7. Ibid., 437; Nicholls states strongly that whereas symbolic forms (figures of speech) may be adjusted, conceptual forms—terms that are ontologically essential to the message because these forms are consistently used throughout Scripture—may not be changed ("Towards a Theology of Gospel and Culture," in *Gospel and Culture*, 75).

8. "Willowbank Report," 437.

9. Ibid., 439.

10. Ibid. Feliciano V. Carino's critique notes that the Willowbank Report's understanding of contextualization is still framed in terms of communicating the gospel's content instead of realizing that the meaning of the gospel is to be found in the contemporary concrete contexts. Evangelicals are too defensive of certain preconceived notions of the normative elements of the Christian faith and the essential meaning of the gospel. They must be willing to "let go of any dogmatic preconceptions about the meaning of Christian faith and life, to reduce . . . the inherited areas of certainty in favor of an openness to the work and presence of a living God in the varied but concrete contexts in which we find ourselves" ("The Willowbank Report: A Critical Response," *South East Asia Journal of Theology* 19, no. 2 [1978]: 43).

conducted among equally authoritative partners. Contemporary interpreters come to the biblical text with an awareness of concerns stemming
from their particular cultural background, personal situation, and responsibilities to others. The biblical text provides answers, but it also addresses
questions to the contemporary context. The interpreters' culturally conditioned presuppositions are challenged, and the very questions they ask
are corrected. In response they are compelled to reformulate their questions
and come up with new ones. The results of such an upward-spiraling
dialog are a continuously deepening knowledge of God and his will, and a
need to respond obediently. And the more we respond, the more God
makes himself known. Application and interpretation are integrally bound
together. In this dialogical process neither the Scripture's meaning nor application is determined by the contemporary cultural context; Scripture
remains central and authoritative.[11]

In applying the Bible to life, the report appropriates the form-meaning
distinction to handle the "cultural conditioning" of Scripture. It affirms "that
some biblical commands (e.g., the one regarding the veiling of women in
public and washing one another's feet) refer to cultural customs now obsolete in many parts of the world." There is no room for slavishly literal
obedience or for irresponsible disregard of the biblical text. What is called
for is "a critical discernment of the text's inner meaning and then a translation of it into our own culture."[12] When a biblical command in the form of a
cultural custom has become obsolete, there is a continuing responsibility to
find an equivalent behavior pattern, a cultural transposition so that one can
live out the inner meaning of the command. This approach is recommended for identifying the form the church should take in any given
culture. The Bible provides the principles or meaning, and the local culture
supplies the appropriate forms. Where Scripture is silent on a particular
feature of contemporary culture, the Holy Spirit will guide the church in
searching the Scriptures for precedents and principles that will enable her to
know the mind of Christ in these matters.

The report follows this same pattern when applying Scripture to the
Christian's personal lifestyle.[13] There are moral absolutes in Scripture that

---

11. C. René Padilla's background paper sketches the basic framework of this hermeneutical process
("Hermeneutics and Culture," 83–108).

12. "Willowbank Report," 437.

13. Charles R. Taber in a background paper distinguishes between permanent and relative
prescriptive statements in Scripture. "It seems to me *prima facie* evident that some NT teaching—I take it
that this is the material most Christians would consider relevant—is explicitly intended to be
theological and therefore universal and permanent in import; while some is explicitly or implicitly
conditioned by existing circumstances and therefore relative" ("Hermeneutics and Culture," 125). He
takes 1 Timothy 2:9–15 as an example of the latter category. It should be noted that Taber's definition
and distinctions depend on the majority vote of modern Christians, who determine what is normative
and permanent. This approach makes ethics vulnerable to the ideological and cultural blindness which
often afflicts the interpreters of Scripture.

directly encounter and judge such inhuman cultural practices as cannibalism, widow strangling, infanticide, patricide, and the like. Converts are expected to adopt these moral absolutes and renounce the cultural practices they condemn. Churches that study the Scriptures should not find it difficult to discern what belongs to this so-called direct-encounter category.

The report identifies another category of cultural practices—some marriage customs, initiation rites, festivals, and musical celebrations involving song, dance, and instruments—in which the moral issues are not so clearcut. These must be evaluated by scriptural principles under the Holy Spirit's guidance.

Charles R. Taber

The Origin of Meaning

Charles R. Taber begins with one simple concept about the origin of meaning and builds a contextual hermeneutic around it. Like Charles Kraft, he contends that, according to recent linguistics and cultural anthropology, meaning does not inhere in words, but is socially assigned.[14] The polysemy and homonymity of language and the concept of social convention support this conclusion. A single word or form can have a variety of meanings, and two words can sound the same but have different meanings. Social convention arbitrarily assigns meanings to words through usage.[15] Those who send a message do so by encoding in words the message they intend to convey. That is, they choose words and select a meaning for each from the potential range of meanings supplied by their sociocultural thought-world. They signal their selection by the arrangement of each word in relation to the others in a discourse context. To understand the message, the receptors carry out the reverse process. They decode the message by assigning meaning from their own cultural thought-forms and understandings. For Taber, meaning comprises the receptors' total perception of the response called for by the message. Interpretation, then, is the process by which receptors assign meanings to the words of the message. Understanding occurs when receptors assign essentially the same meaning to the message as the senders did when they formulated it. This hermeneutic is appropriate for Scripture, not only because this is the only way in which communication takes place, but also because when God gave us the Holy Spirit to interpret

---

14. Taber, "Hermeneutics and Culture," 119; see also Eugene A. Nida, *Exploring Semantic Structures* (Munich: W. Fink, 1975), 14.

15. Charles R. Taber, letter to author, October 1986.

Scripture, he did not "by-pass normal human approaches to interpreting messages." These approaches are conditioned, colored, and limited by our human finiteness, our human sinfulness, and our human cultural, social, and historical contexts.[16]

Basic evidence that meaning is socially assigned to words and done so independently by sender and receptor is found in the character of the two basic components of any verbal message: explicit and implicit information. Explicit information, the meaning denoted as well as connoted by the conceptual components, can be misunderstood. There may be a slippage between the message the sender intends and the meaning the receptor assigns to the communication. Such misunderstanding would not take place if the meaning were inherent in the words that bear the message.[17]

Implicit information has meaning which by its very nature must be supplied from the sociocultural context. Implicit information is that part of the message which is left unsaid. Senders assume that receptors share the meanings of their cultural context, so that they can rely on the receptors to supply from their own thought-forms and cultural understandings the implicit information necessary for understanding the message. Taber concludes that the meaning of the complete message, including explicit and implicit information, is socially assigned independently by author/sender and interpreter/receptor as each relates to the message within his or her own cultural context.

The Process of Interpretation

Receptors are responsible to supply from their own cultural context the implicit information and the meanings they know for the explicit terms. They are responsible for assigning denotative and connotative meaning to the terms of the message, and finally they must identify those referents in reality to which the message points.

Since the meaning of any message flows from the person, whether sender or receptor, how can one tell when correct communication has taken place? In Taber's judgment, a valid interpretation has occurred when the receptor assigns to the message essentially the same meaning as the sender did.[18] The integrity of interpretation is also affected by the backgrounds and points of view shared by the sender and receiver, assigning a sense for each word without adding information to the message. We must realize, of

---

16. Taber, "Hermeneutics and Culture," 110.

17. Taber comments, "Scholars sometimes seem to labor under the misapprehension that senses inhere in words, so that using 'the right word' becomes a shibboleth, without regard to how the eventual [receptor] will understand it" (ibid., 119).

18. Ibid.

course, that there is no perfect understanding, only "pragmatic degrees of similarity" between the sender's intent and the receptor's interpretation.

Taber notes that human beings are able to wonder, fantasize, empathize, and so interact with diverse thought-worlds. Consequently, he concludes that communication is possible between human beings in the same culture and also between human beings in different cultures. Multiple subcultures are often present within one's indigenous culture, and communication can take place among these. Humans participate in many asymmetrical social relationships: parent-child, teacher-student, employer-employee. These involve at least two viewpoints, and communication still occurs; this shows that it is possible for a person to interpret a message from an alien culture. Moreover, messages once understood have consequences for living and thinking and can transform culture.

Taber describes those factors from the receptor's personal and cultural context which assign meaning to the message. They are particularly significant in the area of discerning the implicit information required by the text. On the most general level, senders often assume they share beliefs, values, and world-view with the receptor and therefore do not explicitly express this information. The interpreter who is not sensitive to this implicit information may pass over and miss many cultural allusions. Biblical interpreters who do not recognize the gap between contemporary and ancient cultures may assign wrong meanings from their own culture's world-view, or they may simply think the people of the ancient world peculiar.[19] On the level of personal or systemic relationships, interpreters must take social, economic, political, and situational factors into account. The sender's and the receptor's perception of these factors will inevitably affect the interpretation process.

Taber insists that even the presuppositional foundation of any hermeneutic is a part of the interpreter's cultural context and is clearly related to cultural assumptions about the complex interrelations between truth, truthfulness, facticity, happenedness, precision, objectivity, and the like. Whether we like it or not, these assumptions and equations are not universal. Consequently, if we want to claim that our approach to hermeneutics is universally normative, we must make a case for our claim and not simply take it for granted.[20]

Taber launched the journal *Gospel in Context: A Dialogue on Contextualization,* in which he printed responses to his editorial "Is There More than One Way to Do Theology? Anthropological Comments on the Doing of Theology." He focused on the question, At what point and in what form does the Bible confront human cultural reality validly and fairly?

---

19. Taber, "Limits of Indigenization," 70.
20. Taber, "Hermeneutics and Culture," 116.

Any theology, any hermeneutic, is and must be profoundly conditioned by the culture in which it arises; it *is*, because those who develop their diverse expressions of faith are themselves conditioned by their own enculturation; it *must be*, because it must speak to other persons also profoundly enculturated so as to motivate and transform them. . . . And all theologies, western or non-western, must be continually brought into subjection to the inspired Scriptures, responsibly interpreted.[21]

Helpful responses come from Andrew Kirk and René Padilla. While both recognize the culturally and historically conditioned nature of theologizing, they question Taber's approach as "too dependent on a culture in which relativism has become an absolute."[22] Padilla suggests that we could draw from the New Testament a number of pointers to help us do theology without falling into the trap of either Western theological absolutism or Western anthropological relativism. According to Kirk, a major difficulty in overemphasizing the cultural conditioning of theology is that one is left with no way to challenge any given contextual theology.

One corrective would be to recognize that normative content is a given in the theologizing process and is present from the beginning in the gospel proclamation. Another would be to affirm that all cultures and cultural features are not equally valid. Some approximate more or less the values of the kingdom; others do not. Kirk comments on the theologizing task: "The task of distinguishing positive, creative additions to universal human culture from apostate expressions is a continuing one for theological hermeneutics in permanent dialogue with the relative disciplines. Fortunately, perhaps, we are not able to offer any easy answers."[23] Taber sees himself as representing the strain of evangelical missiology that uses "the specialized perspectives of anthropology and linguistics to help gain a more balanced perspective on what human beings can and cannot do with language and culturally conditioned concepts."[24]

---

21. Taber, "Is There More than One Way?" 10.

22. C. René Padilla, "Comments on: Is There More than One Way to Do Theology?" *Gospel in Context* 1, no. 1 (January 1978): 31; note J. Andrew Kirk's warning, "We must be careful not to transform cultural relativity into a virtue" ("Comments on: Is There More than One Way to Do Theology?" ibid., 26. Richard B. Gaffin offers a way to overcome the relativism: "The ultimately relevant and decisive context of [the church's] existence in all its enculturated particularity is the period between the exaltation and return of Christ in which the Church has its identity as the new and final wilderness community ([Heb.] 3:7ff.). This macro-historical and -cultural outlook is integral to the Gospel" ("Comments on: Is There More than One Way to Do Theology?" ibid., 22).

23. Kirk, "Comments," 26.

24. Taber, "Author's Response," 39. Carl F. H. Henry draws out the implications of Taber's views for the content of Scripture this way: "To hold, however, that the theology of the inspired prophets and apostles is such that none of its cognitive content transcends their cultural setting and is supracultural is to destroy the cognitive content of transcendent divine revelation" ("Comments on: Is There More than One Way to Do Theology?" *Gospel in Context* 1, no. 1 [January 1978]: 22).

Bruce J. Nicholls

Bruce Nicholls is executive secretary of the Theology Commission of the World Evangelical Fellowship and a missionary in India. He occupies a strategic position for evaluating theologically the whole contextualization discussion, and he provides more than critical analysis of the whole spectrum of contextualization. His theology of gospel and culture indicates how cultural factors can be present in the giving of divine revelation without robbing that revelation of its unique authority. Among the questions he raises are, "In what way and to what extent is the message of the Bible itself conditioned by the cultural setting of its authors? To what extent is the biblical message trans-cultural and how can this 'gospel core' be clearly identified and objectified? What was the nature of God's control over these culturally conditioning factors in the inspiration of the writing of the Scriptures?"[25]

Nicholls enters the hermeneutical circle at the point of the interpreter's preunderstanding, noting that preunderstanding has three elements: an ideological element, consisting of the interpreter's world-view and system of values; a cultural element, comprising the influence of society's institutions and customs; and the supracultural element, "either conversion to Christ and the acceptance by faith of his lordship over creation and history, or rejection of Christ in favor of secular humanism or Marxist atheism, or a turning to other religious gods, principalities and powers." By positing the reality of the supracultural, "the phenomena of cultural belief and behavior that have their source outside of human culture,"[26] Nicholls has opened the possibility for supracultural truth to impact a given culture.

Nicholls reasons that a Christian interpreter's preunderstanding begins with the supracultural factor of a living relationship with Jesus as Lord of all; this includes faith in the authority of Christ, who declares the Scriptures authoritative. Next comes construction of the ideological factor—one's world-view and system of values about the nature and authority of Scripture—from Scripture's teaching about itself. He affirms the Lausanne Covenant statement on the Bible as the inspired Word of God and asserts that behind such an affirmation "stand supra-cultural verities which are inherent in the Word of God itself."[27] The Scriptures manifest an essential unity, rationality, and perspicuity as correlates of inspiration; this means that Scripture can be understood on its own terms (i.e., Scripture interprets Scripture).

---

25. Nicholls, *Contextualization*, 38; see also idem, "Towards a Theology," 69–82.
26. Nicholls, *Contextualization*, 40, 13.
27. Ibid., 43.

Any cultural conditioning of inspired Scripture occurred under the sovereign control of God. "God the Holy Spirit overshadowed the cultural forms through which he revealed his word in such a manner that these cultural forms conveyed what God intended to be revealed. He controlled the use of [human culture] for his particular purpose of revelation."[28]

As a consequence, the supracultural content and the cultural form in which it is expressed have an inseparable relationship. The cultural form chosen by God to convey the content has such a decisive influence on the content that to radically change the form would be to change the content. Both content and form carry their own objectivity as integral parts of a unique divine revelation. Old Testament and New Testament cultures uniquely bear the marks of the divine-human interaction. Not only did the original historical-cultural forms have a decisive influence on the revelatory content, but as the Hebrew culture became the carrier of the divine message, it experienced progressive deculturalization: the elimination or transformation of any elements in conflict with that message. The prophets were persistent agents of deculturalization as they called the people back to faithfulness to the message. The history of Israel is the account of "divine sovereignty preserving the Word of God against the corrupt conditioning of pagan culture."[29]

The biblical message was undeniably conditioned by the author's cultural setting, but not in such a way as to distort or relativize the message. Indeed, the supracultural content of the message transformed the cultural form, even though the form was decisive for the expression of the content; both the form and the content have their own objectivity. God's control over the cultural factors kept them from undermining the perspicuity of Scripture, its intelligibility on its own terms, and its authority.

In the hermeneutical method advocated by Nicholls, faith commitment is the starting point for interpretation. The believing community is the corporate context in which interpretation should be practiced. Mission-in-the-world, which maintains the distinction between the world and the church, is the goal of this task.

Nicholl's objective-subjective principle involves a comprehensive hermeneutical pattern that maintains the balance between the objective au-

---

28. Nicholls, "Towards a Theology," 74; see also W. A. Visser't Hooft, "Accommodation—True or False," *South East Asia Journal of Theology* 8, no. 3 (1967): 11; John Jefferson Davis, "Some Reflections on Galatians 3:28, Sexual Roles, and Biblical Hermeneutics," *JETS* 19 (1976): 206; Vern S. Poythress, "Adequacy of Language and Accommodation," in *Hermeneutics, Inerrancy, and the Bible*, ed. Earl D. Radmacher and Robert D. Preus (Grand Rapids: Zondervan, 1984), 362.

29. Nicholls, *Contextualization*, 47.

thority of the Word of God and the subjective, culturally conditioned experience of interpretation. Interpreters relate to the Word of God by a two-way process of distancing and fusion. In the distancing they undertake a critical and reflective study of the text, using the grammatical-historical method to discover what the text says. This analysis involves a conscious distancing of the interpreters' thought-world from that of the biblical text to ensure that their preunderstanding will not be unconsciously read into the message of the text. Interpreters then use the text's content to correct their own ideological and culturally conditioned world-view, values, attitudes, and behavior. The next step is fusion—interpreters identify with the message they have discovered, receiving the Word as God's Word to their own heart.

When interpreters seek to communicate the message of Scripture to another culture or to their own, they must follow the same distancing-and-fusion process. In distancing, interpreters employ the prophetic principle demonstrated in the Old Testament, using the message of Scripture to critically judge their "own culture and pre-understanding and also the cultural assumptions and behavior of those to whom the message is being proclaimed."[30] Then by fusion they seek to identify the message with the culture to achieve a contextualized theology true to the objective authority of Scripture and also intelligible and authentic to the culture.

Nicholls contends that this contextualized theology is relative because even though it may be true to the gospel, no formulation can claim to comprehend the totality of the revealed Word of God. Moreover, all attempts are colored by the receiver's preunderstandings. But the relative nature of theologizing does not prevent the interpreter from judging their truthfulness or validity. Under the lordship of Christ and the illumination of the Holy Spirit, the method of distancing and fusion should promote an ever-closer approximation to biblical truth. "The truer [theological formulations] are to the givenness of biblical theology, the more complementary and the less contradictory they become."[31] Nicholls's hermeneutic for scriptural commands stresses that in matters of moral absolutes and principles for church life, the Scriptures provide content, but he gives no guidelines for handling biblical commands that contain cultural elements.

---

30. Ibid., 50. The prophetic principle is based on the premise that though some portions of culture are good, reflecting the image of God in human beings, because of the fall all culture is tainted with sin in every aspect. Culture is never neutral but always reflects the conflict between the kingdom of God and Satan. Furthermore, when the gospel comes, it comes as a given culture's judge and redeemer. The prophetic principle simply outlines four aspects of this work. The prophet will deculturalize accretions to biblical faith, judge and condemn elements of culture contrary to the Word of God, re-create and transform for the kingdom's use elements consistent with God's revelation, and bring new elements into the culture (Nicholls, "Towards a Theology," 82).

31. Nicholls, *Contextualization*, 54.

C. René Padilla

C. René Padilla, general secretary of the Latin American Theological Fraternity, develops his hermeneutical method on the basis of three premises about meaning. The first is that meaning is contextual and "cannot be separated from a specific context—either that of the writer or that of the readers. Meaning can never be separated from reality." This sets the dynamic-equivalence goal of transposing "the message from its original historical context into the context of present-day readers so as to produce the same kind of impact on their lives as it did on the original hearers or readers." It also makes application an integral part of meaning: "The Bible can only be properly understood as it is read with *participatory involvement* and allowed to speak into one's own situation. Ultimately, if the text written in the past does not strike home in the present it has not been understood."[32]

His second premise deals with the problem of meaning in cases where the Bible does not answer the questions that the contemporary situation is asking, for which Padilla proposes *sensus plenior,* a "fuller meaning." "The meaning of the original events in Scripture may go beyond that which was in the mind of the original writers—a fact that can hardly be denied by anyone who regards Scripture as the Word of God which transcends a specific historical situation and is relevant to the whole of human history."[33]

Padilla's final premise is that the meaning of Scripture is forged in the dialectic of the impact of Scripture and culture on each other. He sees great potential here as Scripture impacts culture by correcting one's world-view and providing a deeper and richer understanding of the historical situation. When this happens, a person can restate the questions addressed to the text, and the theology formulated will be more relevant to the situation. "Such theology will be relevant to the particular situation to the extent to which it is expressed in symbols and thought forms which are part of that situation, and it addresses itself to the questions and concerns which are raised in that context."[34] The faithful approach to Scripture called for by a given historical situation can bring to light aspects of the biblical message less visible or even hidden in other situations, for different facets of the message will be more meaningful in one situation than in another. Padilla sees the text and the historical context mutually enlightening each other as "a deeper and richer understanding of the historical context leads to a greater comprehension of the biblical message from within the concrete situation, through the work of the Holy Spirit."[35]

---

32. C. René Padilla, letter to author, October 1986; idem, "Interpreted Word," 18–19.
33. Padilla, "Hermeneutics and Culture," 100.
34. Ibid., 97.
35. Ibid., 102.

Padilla concedes that certain elements in culture conspire against the proper understanding of God's authoritative Word. "Whenever in the process of interpretation any of the values or premises of the interpreter's historical situation which are incongruent with the biblical message become a part of the interpretation, the result is syncretism." But he also contends that every historical situation has positive elements favorable to understanding the biblical message. "The hermeneutical task is not completed until the whole of reality is placed under the Word of grace and judgment."[36] When this occurs, people are able to hear God's Word from within their own historical situation.

Padilla develops a hermeneutical circle which encompasses (1) the interpreter's historical situation, (2) the interpreter's world-and-life view, (3) Scripture, and (4) theology. The historical situation includes language, patterns of thought and conduct, methods of learning, emotional reactions, values, interests, and goals. These elements provide the frame of reference within which God's message can become meaningful. The interpreter's world-view, one's religiously determined way of apprehending reality, furnishes the background for one's interpretation of Scripture. Without a biblically corrected world-and-life view, "there can be no proper understanding either of reality or of Scripture." Not surprisingly, Padilla sees a dynamic historical dimension in the Scriptures. "God who spoke in the past and whose Word was recorded in the Bible continues to speak today to all mankind in Scripture."[37] Scripture is to be interpreted objectively via the grammatical-historical method and with a view to conscientious response so that its message may be heard plainly and fully. The final element in the hermeneutical circle is theology; it is here that the horizons or contexts of the historical situation and the text merge.

> The interpreter progressively approaches Scripture with the right questions and from the right perspective, and his theology is in turn more biblical and more relevant to the situation. He goes from this concrete situation through his (increasingly biblical) world-and-life view to Scripture, and from Scripture through his (increasingly relevant) theology to his situation, to and fro, always striving for a merging of his own horizons with those of Scripture.[38]

This distinctive emphasis on the vital role of the historical situation and the possibility for concrete Christian obedience within it leads Padilla to the confident conclusion that there is the possibility for changing the prevailing

---

36. Ibid., 90, 98.
37. Padilla, "Interpreted Word," 20.
38. Padilla, "Hermeneutics and Culture," 102.

world-view to bring it into line with the biblical world-view. As interpreters come to understand Scripture better, their theology, interpretation, and application will be more relevant and responsive to "the burning issues which we have to face in our concrete situation."[39]

---

39. Padilla, "Interpreted Word," 23.

Part 5

Biblical Theology
of Hermeneutics
and Culture

13

Culture the Context

The foregoing exploration of the history of biblical interpretation since the Reformation and examination of the staggering variety of the harvest—the diverse qualities of the wheat and the inevitable mixture of tares—have brought matters to a point that demands synthesis. The analysis of the hermeneutical enterprise in particular raises several specific problems. The historical gap and the inescapable cultural bias that have presented such barriers for contemporary exegetes must be faced for the challenges they are, and the tools for dealing with them must be assessed. Several questions suggest themselves in such a situation. If there were a metahistorical and metacultural framework, one could stand above different historical periods and cultures and compare the world-views of different eras and translate between them, and such a framework would provide the much-sought hermeneutical bridge from which to interpret and apply Scripture's message across time periods and cultures.[1] Does such a framework exist? Where may its lineaments be found? Can such a framework be used to evaluate the hermeneutical proposals previously described?

The thesis of this book is that such a framework does exist and can be known from a systematic exposition of the Bible's own teaching about hermeneutics and culture. The Bible as divine revelation has its source a priori

---

1. Paul G. Hiebert, "Critical Contextualization" (Fuller Theological Seminary, Pasadena, Calif., 1986, Photocopy), 13.

outside any given culture. Its very words are "God-breathed" (2 Tim. 3:16). Moreover, the message proclaimed in Scripture is by its very nature intended to be universally and eternally valid. It presents the one way of salvation (Acts 4:12). It is the all-sufficient source of God's will concerning what to believe and how to act (2 Tim. 3:16–17). Its message is for every human being, regardless of culture or historical era. Time—a creation of God—cannot invalidate his promises, warnings, or commands, for "the word of the Lord stands forever" (1 Peter 1:25). Our culture cannot disqualify us from being addressed; God's Word "commands all people everywhere to repent" (Acts 17:30). His salvation is promised not only to the Jews and their children, but to all who are far off—it is "for all whom the Lord our God will call" (2:39).

Such an origin and such a purpose qualify this unique book, the Bible, as the source for a metahistorical and metacultural framework within which one can understand and communicate across historical eras and cultures. The Bible claims to be the norm of truth by which all human thought is tested (Heb. 4:12–13; John 10:35). Consequently, it qualifies also as arbiter of the truth and legitimacy of all hermeneutical proposals.

The plan here is to organize a biblical theology of hermeneutics and culture under three headings: culture the context (chap. 13); God the Communicator (chaps. 14–16); man the interpreter (chaps. 17–18). The biblical view of human culture is significant because the Bible was written in a variety of particular ancient societies. This fact is often used as grounds for dismissing all or part of biblical content as culture-bound. Therefore, an investigation of the Bible's understanding of culture and God's relation to it is essential to clarify the nature of the Bible's authority in any given culture, including one dominated by relativism. To understand the Bible's metacultural framework and authoritative message with regard to culture, it will be necessary to discover its attitude toward the human cultures to which it speaks and above which it stands.

After developing a comprehensive definition of human culture and a taxonomy of its constituent elements, we will sketch the biblical history of God's interaction with human cultures and study its teaching about their various components. God's relationships—both positive and negative—will be investigated, along with the implications these have for the Christian.

Definition and Taxonomy

Culture is that integrated pattern of socially acquired knowledge, particularly ideas, beliefs, and values (ideology) mediated through language, which a people uses to interpret experience and generate patterns of behavior—technological, economic, social, political, religious, and artistic—

so that it can survive by adapting to relentlessly changing circumstances.[2]

Several features of this definition need to be kept in mind as we look at the biblical teaching on culture. There seems to be an anthropological consensus that culture is basically ideational; that is, the essence of a culture is its ideology or world-view rather than its observable behavior patterns. Ideology (meaning) is primary, while behavior (form) is secondary.

Language is the primary medium for acquiring, using, and transmitting culture. Individuals acquire culture by learning from significant others around them. They learn ideas, or thought-structures for perceiving the world; beliefs, or convictions about the nature of things; and values, or convictions about what should happen. The sum total of this knowledge forms an ideology. It provides us with categories in which to make intelligible and acceptable interpretations of experience within our cultural context. One finds out how to act within the acceptable range of behavior. Because of constantly changing circumstances to which one must respond, everyone needs a framework with which to interpret and cope with that change. Culture provides that framework. Since culture is an integrated system, adjusting to change in one aspect of the culture will affect to some degree all other aspects. (The basic aspects of culture are depicted in fig. 5.)[3]

Historical Framework

To understand the biblical teaching on culture and language, it will be helpful to consider the cultural and linguistic contexts within which God carried out his revelatory and saving activity. The best approach is to trace that activity in historical sequence.

Creation

At creation (Gen. 1–2) there was one language. God used it to call aspects of creation into being (e.g., 1:3, 6, 9, 11, 14), and with it he addressed information, commands, and blessing to humankind made in his image (vv. 28–30; 2:16). Adam used it to name animals (2:19) and to utter an exclamation in the hearing of Eve and God (v. 23). Eve also used this language in addressing the serpent (3:2).

At creation there was also one culture, a God-ordained culture that had

2. In formulating this definition, several recent anthropological works were consulted: Peter B. Hammond, *An Introduction to Cultural and Social Anthropology*, 2d ed. (New York: Macmillan, 1978), 2; William A. Haviland, *Cultural Anthropology*, 3d ed. (New York: Holt, Rinehart & Winston, 1981), 28; Paul G. Hiebert, *Cultural Anthropology* (Philadelphia: Lippincott, 1976), 25. See also Anastasios Yannoulatos, "Culture and Gospel: Some Observations from the Orthodox Tradition and Experience," *International Review of Missions* 74 (1985): 185.

3. This taxonomy was composed using the following sources: Philip K. Bock, *Modern Cultural Anthropology: An Introduction*, 2d ed. (New York: Knopf, 1969), 311, 354, 431; Hammond, *Cultural and Social Anthropology*, 318, 320, table of contents; Hiebert, *Cultural Anthropology*, 25; Charles H. Kraft, *Christianity in Culture* (Maryknoll, N.Y.: Orbis, 1979), 53; Robert B. Taylor, *Cultural Ways: A Compact Introduction to Cultural Anthropology* (Boston: Allyn, 1969), 129–30.

Figure 5
Cultural Taxonomy

Definition: Culture is a socially acquired ideology, or world-view, which is mediated through language (phonology, grammar, and semantics) and generates particular structures and behaviors.

I. Culture Is a Socially Acquired Ideology

Myths of origin, power, and destiny generate or support

Ideas (what may be known)

Epistemology (knowledge)

Thought categories for

Evaluating perception;
e.g., truth, truthfulness, facticity,
happenedness, precision, objectivity

Ordering perception;
e.g., cause and effect,
logic, reasoning

The Universe

Origin;
e.g., creation, evolution

Structure

Destiny;
e.g., second coming,
nuclear holocaust

Cosmology;
e.g., earth round,
flat, bounded by water

Kinetology—
nature of power; e.g., how it operates, how events are caused and
controlled, curses and blessings

Immediate Environment;
e.g., weather, geography, time,
ethnobotany, zoology

Beliefs (what is)

Metaphysics (reality)

**Thought categories for
understanding reality**

Man

Basic nature,
reason for being, relations to
others, the world, and the universe

Values (what is desirable)

Ethics (conduct)

Distinctions in commands;
e.g., universalistic (all human beings) vs.
particularistic commands, absolute (all times
and all places, though possibly limited to a
particular group) vs. situational commands

II. This Ideology or World-View (Ideas, Beliefs, Values),
Mediated Through Language (Phonology, Grammar, Semantics),
Generates Particular Structures and Behaviors

Technological

Tools
Techniques
Technical Structure
Skills and use

Artistic

Economic

Systems of
production and
distribution

Political

Authority systems
Law
Organized aggression (war)

Social

Marriage and
domestic groups, roles, and
authority structures
Associations
Social differentiation and stratification

Religious

Ritual
Power control
Magic
Witchcraft
Application of judgment using values

specific tasks: filling, subduing, and ruling the earth (Gen. 1:28), and working and taking care of God's physical creation (2:15). There were also values
and behavior patterns, such as obedience to God under threat of punishment (vv. 16–17), and structures, including the family social order (vv. 18,
23–24).

The Fall to the Flood

After the fall one language continued—God, Adam, and Eve had no
difficulty communicating verbally (Gen. 3:9–13). Cultural tasks and social
structures remained the same, though the effects of the curse began to be
felt (vv. 16–19). The man would wrest his food from the soil with difficulty,
and there would be ongoing tension in husband-wife relationships.

Up to the flood (Gen. 4–5) one language prevailed, though the begin-
nings of cultural differentiation are discernible. Genesis 4 reports that
Adam's sons fulfilled the cultural task of "ruling over" the physical creation
in different ways. "Abel kept flocks, and Cain worked the soil" (v. 2). It
further describes Jabal the nomadic herdsman, Jubal the musician, and
Tubal-Cain the metalworker (vv. 20–22). Such cultural differentiation seems
to have been part of God's design when he instructed human beings to "fill
the earth" (1:28; see also Deut. 32:8; Acts 17:26).

The families of the earth, however, were united in their sinful rebellion
against God (Gen. 6:5–7), a rebellion that moved God to punish all humankind through the flood and in his mercy to save Noah and his family. Even
after giving the human race a new start after the flood, God perceived that
the human heart was still sinful; but he declared that he would not act to
wipe out humankind in each generation, and he set his rainbow in the sky
as a promise of merciful forbearance from generation to generation (8:21–22;
9:12–17).

After the Flood

After the flood God once more gave instructions to fill the earth (Gen.
9:1). The plan involved diverse clans living in various places on the earth,
each developing its own culture (10:5, 20, 31–32). Everyone still spoke the
same language (Gen. 10 shows signs of having been written from a post-
Babel perspective). This fresh start after the flood included additional
divinely ordained cultural structures and behavior patterns: capital punishment as appropriate for murder and the prohibition of eating blood (9:1–5).[4]
The event at the Tower of Babel (11:1–9) completed the process and created
circumstances still found in contemporary life. In an act of rebellion against
God, humankind refused to disperse over the earth and instead banded

---

4. Richard W. Engle, "Contextualization in Missions: A Biblical and Theological Appraisal," *GTJ* 4
(1983): 91.

together to build a tower and make a name for themselves. God squelched their rebellion by confusing their language. He generated a multiplicity of languages that were not mutually understandable, so that the earth was filled with diverse languages, the media of diverse cultures. God did instantaneously what would have happened gradually had humankind been obedient to the command to fill the earth.

many cultures
God's original
plan

Abraham to Christ

God in his redemptive plan selected a particular man, Abraham, from a particular culture with its particular language. He addressed that man and called him out of that culture so that God could make him a nation, that is, a new culture (Gen. 12:1–4).[5] Abraham obeyed, and he and his immediate descendants subsequently lived the life of nomads in the midst of various cultures in Canaan. Finally they settled in still another culture, in Egypt. The oppression of his people moved God to act to demonstrate his supracultural power by redeeming a particular culture from within another. He provided living space for his people in Canaan by judging and dispossessing the cultures that lived there (2 Sam. 7:23), in the process creating a culture like no other on earth—Israel. Moses made this point clear when he addressed the Israelites in the desert:

> Observe [God's decrees and laws] carefully, for this will show your wisdom and understanding to the nations, who will hear about all these decrees and say, "Surely this great nation is a wise and understanding people." What other nation is so great as to have their gods near them the way the LORD our God is near us whenever we pray to him? And what other nation is so great as to have such righteous decrees and laws as this body of laws I am setting before you today? [Deut. 4:6–8]

Throughout Israel's history God commanded them through apostle, judge, and prophet to keep only to his ways and to avoid defiling themselves with the idolatrous practices of their neighbors (Deut. 12:30–31; 2 Kings 17:13). But Israel continually rebelled and was finally exiled among the pagan cultures (Ezek. 11:12; 20:1–44).

Israel allowed itself to be pulled always in a direction away from God. There was the syncretizing, and finally apostatizing, pull of the idolatrous religions of the cultures in whose midst they lived. The people were

---

5. It is appropriate to understand the Hebrew term *gôy* (usually translated "nation") as "culture," since the major aspects of race, government, and territory are all involved in the term (G. Johannes Botterweck and Helmer Ringgren, eds., *Theological Dictionary of the Old Testament*, rev. ed. [Grand Rapids: Eerdmans, 1974–], s.v. *gôy*). These characteristics closely parallel elements found in anthropological definitions of culture.

tempted to worship the deities of their forebears in Ur and Egypt (Josh. 24:14–15; Ezek. 20:6–7). God's dealing with Israel unfolds itself as a de-culturalization process in which he repeatedly said, "Throw away the gods your forefathers worshiped beyond the River and in Egypt, and serve the LORD" (Josh. 24:14). Even when the Israelites did so, however, the attraction of the pagan gods persisted, and they were tempted to dilute, or even renounce, their faith (e.g., Judg. 3:7; 2 Chron. 24:17–18; Jer. 2:11–13). But there was still the pull of God, who challenged them to a life of covenant faithfulness, a life in which they would follow his decrees and show themselves a unique people living out the model culture intended by God (Exod. 19:3–6). When they watered down or rejected their special privilege, God called them to repent (Ezek. 14:6) and consistently warned them of judgment to come from such sin (Deut. 28:20; 1 Kings 9:8; 2 Kings 22:17).

God focused his attention on Israel as the model nation and culture, but he also had a word of hope for the other cultures of the earth. Even though they were developed by people who had no knowledge of the one true God (Ps. 147:19–20), the salvation of that Most High God would extend to them. God promised to Israel a Messiah whose saving power would reach beyond Israel to all the cultures of the earth (Isa. 2:2, 4; 11:10; 42:1, 6; 49:6).

Christ to the End

God fulfilled his promise by the incarnation (John 1:10–13). He sent his Son to be born in a single culture, first-century Judaism, whose roots were the God-ordained Old Testament pattern for national culture. But Jesus came with a message for all. His death and resurrection secured salvation for many human beings, no matter what their culture (Acts 4:12). He commissioned his disciples to go to men and women everywhere and make disciples (Matt. 28:18–20). That discipleship involved repentance from past worship of the gods and idols of one's culture (Acts 14:15–17; 17:29–31). This supreme God forbore, because of the Noahic covenant, to judge each generation and provided a divinely given set of beliefs, values, structures, and patterns for behavior to constitute a God-pleasing culture—the faith, life, and work of the people of God (Rom. 12:1–2; 1 Peter 2:9).

Unlike Israel (the original form of God's model culture), the church (the second form) is instructed to live out its earthly existence as a participant within the diversity of human cultures. The church is in but not of the world—that is, the given culture in which its members find themselves (John 17:11, 15; 1 John 4:17).[6] These are the basic historical facts to be kept in

---

6. Many New Testament instances of the term *kosmos* are appropriately understood as "culture" used in a general sense (I. Howard Marshall, "Culture and the New Testament," in *Gospel and Culture*, ed. John R. W. Stott and Robert T. Coote [Pasadena, Calif.: William Carey Library, 1979], 39).

mind about the relation of language and culture to God's past and present dealings with humankind. They provide insight into the biblical approach to the nature of culture and, more important, into biblical teaching about God's relationship to human culture and its implications for a Christian's own role in it.

The Bible and Culture

Some scholars conclude that the Bible does not address culture, since there is no single biblical word for it.[7] From a study of several terms, however, we have ample evidence to piece together a composite picture. The chief Old Testament term is *gôy*, "nation." Used to describe political, ethnic, or territorial groups of people, it is an appropriate term to follow in discovering the Bible's teaching about various aspects of a culture.[8] In the plural the term has a specialized meaning, "Gentiles—all noncovenant and nonbelieving peoples," a usage that can be interpreted as an Israelite ethnocentrism, since the Gentiles are almost always evaluated negatively. However, anthropological definitions of culture normally exclude divine revelation in describing the thought and activity of human beings, a circumstance that provides discernible parallels between the biblical description of Gentile cultures and the anthropologist's cultural definition and taxonomy. The Old Testament word *gôyim* and the New Testament *ethnē* are translated "Gentiles," and both provide evidence of Scripture's views on human cultures.[9] Additional information comes from examining such terms as *ḥōq* and *ḥūqqâ*, "statutes"; *derek*, "way"; and *mišpāṭ*, "judgment," all of which are used in reference to cultural customs. Also relevant are the various terms for "shame"—*kālam, qālôn, bôš*).

In addition to *ethnos*, the New Testament has the spatial and temporal terms *kosmos*, "world," and *aiōn*, "age," which can stand for human culture.[10] As with "Gentile," these terms used in the singular, given the predominantly negative evaluation of them, could be viewed as value-laden ethnocentrisms; they also refer to human cultural thought and activity separated from divine revelation. For this reason, they are appropriate for probing into the phenomenon the anthropologists have defined as culture.

a negative view of other cultures

---

7. Walter A. Elwell, ed., *Evangelical Dictionary of Theology* (Grand Rapids: Baker, 1984), s.v. "Christianity and Culture."

8. *TWOT*, s.v. *(gôy)* nation, people (326e).

9. Note the observation in *TDNT* that of all the Greek words used to describe a people, *ethnos* "is the most general and therefore the weakest of these terms having simply an ethnographical sense and denoting the natural cohesion of a people in general" (s.v. ἔθνος, ἐθνικός). See also Nils A. Dahl, "Nations in the New Testament," in *New Testament Christianity for Africa and the World: Essays in Honour of Harry Sawyerr*, ed. Mark E. Glasswell and Edward W. Fasole-Luke (London: S.P.C.K., 1974), 54–68.

10. *TDNT* comments, "The sense of 'time or course of the world' can easily pass over into that of the 'world' itself, so that αἰών approximates closely to κόσμος (s.v. αἰών, αἰώνιος).

Other terms that yield pertinent information are *ethos*, "custom"; *paradidōmi* and *paradosis*, "tradition"; *physis*, "nature"; *atimazō*, *aischynō*, *entrepō*, and cognates, "shame"; *timaō* and cognates, "honor"; *anēkō*, *prepō*, *euschēmōn*, *aidōs*, *semnos*, *axios*, and cognates, "fitting" or "worthy."[11]

Before pursuing the scriptural view of culture further, it would be helpful to consider biblical teaching concerning cultural relativism. Does the Bible view cultural pluralism as the basic reality? That is, does it concur with many anthropologists that there is no solid ground beyond the world-views and behavior patterns of particular cultures, no position that offers a comprehensive overview, a position from which the observer can make comparisons and judgments of various cultures?

The Bible clearly teaches that the unity of humankind derived from their first parents is more basic than the diversity of cultural expression. Paul states the proposition succinctly: "From one man he made every nation of men" (Acts 17:26). The creation accounts of our first parent, Adam, in Genesis 1 and 2, describe man made in the image of God. Following the empirical method, anthropologists and psychologists have also discovered a unity in humankind, a commonality which they locate in the felt needs and functional, perceptual, and intellectual operations that are constant from culture to culture. Scripture assumes as much from the very beginning and concentrates on God's dealing with man as man throughout history.[12] Not only does God address cultural tasks to man as man (Gen. 1:28; 9:1–3), he calls and directs individuals as key leaders in his saving work irrespective of their culture. Abraham is called out of Ur (12:1–3). Moses, born a Hebrew slave, raised an Egyptian prince, and living as a Midianite herdsman, is called to lead one cultural group out of the midst of another (Exod. 3:7–10). Through Moses God delivers to his model nation a moral law framed in eternal and universal terms, setting forth our duty to God and to our neighbor (20:1–17). Paul, born a Hellenistic Jew in Tarsus in Asia Minor, trained in strict Pharisaic Judaism in Jerusalem, is called to carry a universal message of God's saving activity to people of all nations (Gal. 1:15–16; Acts 9:15).

The unity of humankind created in God's image, so unequivocally maintained from beginning to end in the Bible, flies in the face of the epistemological and moral cultural relativism that characterizes such hermeneutical approaches as James Barr's and Dennis Nineham's. These approaches postulate an uncrossable gap between historical periods and cultures. The gap is impossible to bridge because inhabitants of a particular

---

11. See Michael Darton, ed., *Modern Concordance to the New Testament* (Garden City, N.Y.: Doubleday, 1976) for a helpful topical arrangement of related terms.

12. See John Jefferson Davis, *Foundations of Evangelical Theology* (Grand Rapids: Baker, 1984), 277.

historical period and culture can interpret data from another period or culture only in terms of their own thought-forms. However, if there is such a thing as human nature unified by reason of its creation in God's image, then radical epistemological or moral relativism based on irreconcilable cultural diversity is false. As human beings we have a commonality that enables us to interpret and apply ideas and patterns and forms from other cultures and time periods. This unity provides the framework within which God communicates truth, and this operation, so visible in his dealings with the vast procession of generations and nations, calls into question the foundations of a relativistic approach.

The Great Commission, which gives specific divine instructions for witnessing across cultural boundaries, provides a transculturally normative form—baptism. Disciples from all the ethnic groups are to be baptized as their initiation into the people of God (Matt. 28:19–20). The relative relativism of Eugene Nida and Charles Kraft distinguishes between supracultural truth (meaning) and cultural expression (form) and does not recognize the transculturally normative form as a category. Consequently, Kraft, while correctly interpreting the meaning of baptism as initiation, sees no reason why other forms symbolizing initiation should not be experimented with "if contemporary incorporation into the people of God is to have an impact on today's people equivalent to that of baptism on New Testament peoples."[13]

The concept of cultural relativism has been promoted by anthropologists and missiologists to combat distasteful ethnocentrism. The unity of humankind just as effectively removes any ground for ethnocentrism by relativizing all cultures. The Bible, whether dealing with humankind as God's creatures or with Christians as the redeemed humanity, consistently sets aside prideful distinctions of culture, race, and nation. God's providential care extends to each individual (Acts 14:16–17). In redemption there is a new self. "Here there is no Greek or Jew, circumcised or uncircumcised, barbarian, Scythian, slave or free, but Christ is all, and is in all" (Col. 3:11).

The commonality of humankind further implies commonality in our relationship to God regardless of culture. All human beings are accountable in the same way to the one true God, and all can and should relate in the same way to him. Paul, the Jewish apostle to the Gentiles, could make his gospel intelligible to the Stoic and Epicurean Athenians on this basis (Acts 17:26–31).

---

13. Kraft, *Christianity in Culture,* 332.

Sources of Culture

Anthropologists see as the source of culture humankind's transmittal of acquired knowledge from generation to generation. The Bible identifies three sources: (1) God, (2) man, and (3) Satan.[14]

(1) Paul's speeches at Lystra (Acts 14:15–17) and Athens (17:22–31) and Genesis 1–11 provide the basic biblical teaching on those aspects of human culture of which God is the source. Paul is speaking to predominantly, if not totally, pagan audiences. His purpose is preevangelistic, and his approach is to call into question the Lystran, Epicurean, and Stoic cultural center and world-view and to declare the truth about the one true God, the Creator of humankind, who ordained human cultural structures and tasks. In that way, Paul purposes to establish his audience's accountability to God and, consequently, their need for repentance and conversion. In the process, Paul reveals some important facts about God's relationship to humankind and to culture.

The Genesis narration of God's creation and ordering of human existence as well as the description of the first cultural initiatives provides a rich source for the Bible's perspective on human culture. From the beginning, God established social structures, tasks, ideology, and behavior patterns in three areas, placing human beings within a natural, a societal, and a spiritual system.[15]

In the natural system two types of tasks, geopolitical and econo-technological, were assigned. The command to "fill the earth and subdue it" has geopolitical implications (Gen. 1:26, 28; see also 9:1). People were to fully occupy the planet; the expression is the same one used to describe Israel's conquest of Canaan (*kābaš*, "subdue"; cf. Num. 32:22, 29; Josh. 18:1). In the process of filling and subduing, men and women were to exercise dominion over the physical creation (Gen. 1:28; Ps. 8:6). Though the Genesis account gives no explicit indication of the pattern, evidence in later passages indicates that the ordained plan was to fill the earth with a diversity of cultures. Moses' song celebrating God's providential care for Israel is set in such a context. The nations of the world are given their inheritance, dividing humankind and setting ethnic boundaries (Deut. 32:8). Paul on Mars Hill refers more explicitly to this context: "From one man he made every nation of men, that they should inhabit the whole earth; and he determined the times set for them and the exact places where they should live" (Acts 17:26).

---

14. Bruce J. Nicholls, *Contextualization: A Theology of Gospel and Culture* (Downers Grove, Ill.: Inter-Varsity, 1979), 13–19.

15. Stephen A. Grunlan and Marvin K. Mayers, *Cultural Anthropology: A Christian Perspective* (Grand Rapids: Zondervan, 1979), 41.

Many critics hold that God's judgment at Babel, when he confused the language and scattered the people, is the origin of linguistic, ethnic, and political diversity (Gen. 9:19; 11:4, 8–9).[16] Yet it is interesting to note that two different words are used in Genesis 10–11 to describe human movement to fill the earth. When related to divine judgment as at Babel, it is called a "scattering" *(pûṣ)*. When related to God's providence, it becomes a "spreading out" *(pārad;* see 10:5, 32). At Babel, God instantaneously did what he had purposed to accomplish more gradually and naturally as the families of humankind filled the earth. Each grouping would experience its own history and, in response to its physical environment, would develop its own culture. The variety of experience and environments would create a diversity of cultures. Very early evidence occurs for this cultural diversification in terms of econotechnological and artistic cultural tasks. Abel keeps flocks; Cain works the soil (4:2). Jabal is a nomadic herder; Jubal is a musician; Tubal-Cain is a metalworker (vv. 20–22).

After the flood, God again explicitly commands the human families to fill the earth (Gen. 9:1). Noah's sons are enumerated according to "their clans and languages, in their territories and nations" (10:20, 31; see also v. 5)—a description suggesting an orderly pattern of diverse cultures across the face of all the earth. Viewing Genesis 10–11 as an etiology explaining the origin of the diversity of languages, Claus Westermann makes a similar point: "The human race exists in a plurality of peoples over the earth with an abundance of potential for development in individual peoples, cf. 10:5, 20, 31. This is what humanity is and this is what preserves it in being."[17]

There are also econotechnological tasks in the natural system. The Genesis account stresses that God has given human beings resources to sustain physical life, namely, plants and animals for food (1:29; 2:9, 16; 9:1–3). We are placed in a position of rulership over the rest of creation (1:26–28; Ps. 8:6–8; 115:16). These resources and position entail the responsibility of being a steward of creation, especially by working or tending the ground and in keeping its plants so that they will bear fruit (Gen. 2:15; see also 2:5; 4:2). The Book of Proverbs places working the ground within God's moral order and promises abundance to those who fulfil this responsibility (12:11; 28:19; cf. Eccles. 5:12). One aspect of the future ideal for a restored Israel is a well-tilled land (Ezek. 36:9, 36).

While Paul does not identify God as the source of the social system and its structures, roles, and tasks, he does affirm God's interest in and involvement with humankind at the societal level when he reviews God's dealing with nations (Acts 14:16; 17:26). From the creation account forward, God is shown to be the source of the human social system in a number of areas.

---

16. Engle, "Contextualization in Missions," 91–92.

17. Claus Westermann, *Genesis 1–11: A Commentary* (Minneapolis: Augsburg, 1974), 556.

The sexual identity of human beings is integrally related to our being made in the image of God (Gen. 1:26–27). That social structure is not to be violated in aberrant behavior—transvestite, homosexual, or lesbian (Deut. 22:5; Rom. 1:24–27). Men and women are to use their sexuality in the heterosexual structure of monogamous marriage. This social framework for the family, given by God from the beginning, is confirmed by Jesus in his remarks on divorce (Gen. 2:23–24; Matt. 19:4–5). God further specifies authority and role relationships within the family. The creation account supplies scant information, referring only to the wife as helper (Gen. 2:18), but the New Testament treatment of the roles of husband and wife amplifies the creation account to demonstrate that these are structures and roles God has ordained from the beginning. The husband has responsibility of leadership, being head of the household (Eph. 5:23; 1 Cor. 11:8–10).[18] He is to love his wife and provide for her. He and his wife are to be fruitful and multiply (Gen. 1:28). In raising his children, the father is to transmit the God-ordained cultural beliefs, values, tasks, and behavior patterns (Eph. 5:28–29; 6:4; Deut. 6:6–9). The wife's role is that of helper to her husband (Gen. 2:18), a role she exercises in voluntary subordination within the authority structure of marriage (Eph. 5:22; 1 Cor. 11:8–10).[19] The child's role is obedience to parents (Eph. 6:1–3; Col. 3:20).

Political and economic aspects of social structures and roles are dealt with in Scripture. It is consistently affirmed that political authority is ordained by God, though no specific political system is singled out for approval. Scripture further details the proper attitudes and behavior of good citizens (Rom. 13:1–7; 1 Peter 2:13–17) and describes fitting relationships between economic superiors and subordinates (Eph. 6:5–9; Col. 3:22–4:1; Titus 2:9–10). A number of scholars contend that God is the source of culture only on the level of world-view and values. However, the evidence indicates that God has prescribed not only meaning but also form in the human system of social structures.

---

18. At the 1986 annual meeting of the Evangelical Theological Society there was a debate concerning the meaning of headship as "source" or "boss" ("The Battle of the Lexicons," *CT* 31, no. 1 [16 January 1987]: 44).

19. Some argue that "helper" does not indicate a subordinate position (Phyllis Trible, "Depatriarchalizing Biblical Interpretation," *Journal of the American Academy of Religion* 41 [1973]: 36; R. David Freedman, "Woman, a Power Equal to Man: Translation of Woman as a 'Fit Helpmate' for Man Is Questioned," *Biblical Archaeology Review* 9 [1983]: 56–58). But Westermann convincingly points out that while the mutuality of the relationship is presented in the passage, this complementarity of companionship does not exclude a relationship of subordination. In the context the term *helper* could not be used equally to describe the man (*Genesis 1–11*, 262).

The structure of female subordination is often identified as part of the curse (Phyllis A. Bird, "'Male and Female He Created Them': Gen. 1:27b in the Context of the Priestly Account of Creation," *Harvard Theological Review* 74 [1981]: 158). But cf. George W. Knight III, *The New Testament Teaching on the Role Relationship of Men and Women* (Grand Rapids: Baker, 1977), 25.

system #3

The most important system in which human beings are placed is a spiritual system. As Paul tells the Athenians, humankind is created to dwell on the earth and to seek after God (Acts 17:27). In another place he demonstrates that seeking after God involves worship and thanksgiving (Rom. 1:21). At Lystra the apostle indicates the natural context in which such thanksgiving should take place. Our existence is so structured that the knowledge of God as Creator and Sustainer, derived from a spiritual relationship, should lead to thankfulness in our environmental relationships as we complete our God-given economic and technological tasks. It is God who gives "rain from heaven and crops in their seasons; he provides you with plenty of food and fills your hearts with joy" (Acts 14:17).

Two other dimensions in this spiritual system are human creativity and morality. Creativity begins with a rational mind which has the capacity for verbal communication. Just as God named things he had made (Gen. 1:5), so man creatively assigned names to the animals (2:19–20). We also use this creativity to subdue the earth, to have dominion over the creatures, and to invent ingenious objects and systems for enrichment of life (Amos 6:5; Exod. 31:3–4).

At creation, man, the moral being, is presented in explicit relationship to God. The moral imperative involves obedience to God (Gen. 2:17). Paul provides clear indications that the moral part of the divinely ordained spiritual system included from the beginning precepts regarding one's fellows (Rom. 1:29–32; 2:14–15). This means that the spiritual system has implications for the social system. The structures and tasks ordained for interpersonal relationships are the ethical norm for human beings created in the image of, and accountable to, God. Monogamous marriage, for example, is not only a cultural structure but also an ethical matter. The basic duties in the spiritual system are to seek God through worship and fellowship and in thankfulness as one pursues one's tasks in the natural system. We must also offer moral obedience in fulfilling cultural tasks within the God-ordained structures of the social and spiritual systems.

The fall radically disrupted human performance within each of the systems. The most severe disruption was in the spiritual system. Since the spiritual system impacts the other systems, the reverberations of the fall must not be underestimated. Adam and Eve's sin in the garden disrupted the spiritual system in two basic ways—by removing from humankind the immediate, intimate knowledge of and fellowship with God, and by leaving men and women in all cultures to grope blindly after the source of their being (Acts 17:27). They still have the structure (i.e., they are still spiritual beings), and they still have the task of seeking after God, but now the raw material from which they can construct concepts about God are objects they empirically perceive, ideas their imaginations create, the reports of other people, and insinuations from the demonic world. The constructions creatively devised from these sources turn out to be myths and fables (1 Tim. 1:4; 4:7; Titus 1:14; 2 Peter 1:16). The prophet Jeremiah graphically portrays the futility of idol worship generated by human artistic imagination (Jer. 10:1–16).

The God-given structures and the tasks remain, as Scripture clearly teaches, but apart from special revelation God no longer provides saving knowledge of himself (Rom. 10:17). For this reason, the source of the myths, world-views, and rituals in a given human culture is either the human race or demons.

Another devastating effect of the fall was the constitution of the human being as a rebel against God. Human moral nature now expresses itself in immoral acts toward God and other people, which doubly darken our blindness. Paul points out that God has not left himself without witness to his divine nature and power. The fruitfulness of the seasons is a token of his faithfulness to the Noahic covenant (Acts 14:17; Gen. 8:22). God is never far away from us; he is our Source, Sustainer, and the Definer of our essence. "In him we live and move and have our being" (Acts 17:28). Why, then, cannot fallen individuals recognize this evidence and worship God as they ought? Because the fall constitutes them rebels against God. When confronted with the proof, even especially when so confronted, human beings choose to suppress that truth (Rom. 1:18) and use a darkened foolish heart to shape gods of their own and devise ways of worshiping them that change worship into idolatry. Such rebellion manifests itself again and again in the humanly concocted religious systems, as Psalms 2; 33:10; and 46:6 attest. The driving force behind them all is a mixture of fear and pride (Gen. 11:4; Ps. 59:8; Rom. 8:15; Heb. 2:14–15). These artificial spiritual systems are a flawed way of coping with the very vulnerable position in which humanity now finds itself. As spiritual beings, we are aware of the transcendent, but we do not know or understand it and cannot control it. In seeking to cope, we are afraid of what is beyond finite existence. These religious systems are also driven by pride, the human attempt to maintain autonomy over against God.

The fall creates a chain of disruption in the other cultural systems. The spiritual system, it should be remembered, is the source of world-view, beliefs, and values. These inevitably guide behavior in the other systems.

The geopolitical duty of existing harmoniously as diverse cultures in lands which are more than able to sustain life is constantly disrupted by wars and hunger and poverty, all resulting from greed and oppression (Mark 13:8; Isa. 3:14–15; James 5:1–6). In the curse on Adam, God points out that economic and technological work now will involve difficulty: "By the sweat of your brow you will eat your food" (Gen. 3:19). Human beings are now blinded to eternal realities, and the economic task involves only meaninglessness. Man works hard all his life only to die and return to the ground he has worked (3:19; Eccles. 1:1–11). These tasks can also become an occasion for false worship. Instead of giving praise and thanks to the one true God, Maker and Sustainer of heaven and earth, fallen men and women serve fertility gods of their own making, which they think they can control to guarantee their survival (see Jesus' censure of the heathen's long prayers in Matt. 6:7). At Lystra and Athens Paul calls his audience to turn away from such practices and points to the living God as the true source of economic fruitfulness (cf. Jer. 14:22).

Prideful rebellion is shown most graphically in the Tower of Babel chronicle (Gen. 11:1–9). In opposition to God's command, the people refused to scatter and fill the earth with a patchwork of diverse cultures. Instead, they planned and executed a city with a tower reaching to the heavens "so that we may make a name for ourselves" (v. 4). Such rebellion is not limited to urban settings. God points out that even agrarian Israel will not praise God for the good land he has given; the people will be tempted to say, "My power and the strength of my hands have produced this wealth for me" (Deut. 8:17).

The fall disrupts totally the social system. In our pride we rebel against the God-ordained structures. Fallen individuals even rebel against their sexual identity; as Paul points out, the greatest rebellion against God is homosexuality (Rom. 1:26–27). Such acts go against nature, against the way God made us. This behavior constitutes rebellion against the basic structures of the social system, whose source is the Creator God. Any attempt to destroy the distinction between male and female contradicts nature and is detestable to God (Deut. 22:5; 1 Cor. 11:14–15). Human culture attempts to develop values and behavior patterns to legitimize such behavior. "But it was not so from the beginning."

Man and wife rebel against the structures and relationships of marriage. The curse on Eve is that though within marriage she is to subordinate herself voluntarily to her husband's leadership, her desire will be to usurp the husband's role (Gen. 3:16). The basic desire described here is for mastery, not for sexual fulfilment (see 4:7 for similar wording).[20] In his rebellion, the husband does not fulfil his role as head, but exercises despotic authority and fails to love his wife (Eph. 5:25). Children disrupt the structure by their disobedience. Sexual activity outside monogamous marriage further disrupts the structure. Those who engage in such behavior dishonor their bodies and show that they do not know God (1 Thess. 4:5; see also Heb. 13:4).

---

20. Westermann, *Genesis 1–11*, 262–63; cf. TWOT, *(tĕšûqâ)* desire, longing (2352a).

Sin has disrupted the social system in the interpersonal, political, and economic areas through alienation and even aggression (see Rom. 1:29–32). Not only do we see the disruption of interpersonal relationships in the first murder, which follows quickly upon the fall (Gen. 4:1–12), but we see the life of nations characterized by military conflict (Matt. 24:7; cf. Isa. 2:4; Mic. 4:3). The internal political order of a nation can be disrupted by rebellious individuals (Rom. 13:2). The relation of economic superiors and inferiors is also strained (Col. 3:22–4:1).

(2) A second source of culture is man as made in God's image, but fallen. At Lystra, Paul describes the history of culture building as the process by which God has permitted each nation to go its own way (Acts 14:16). The ways developed by each nation to pursue its cultural tasks compose its distinctive culture. In the natural system, the first example of human culture building is Adam's exercise of dominion over the lower creation by naming the animals (Gen. 2:19–20). Human cultural innovation and the establishment of distinctive cultural traditions are alluded to in the early origin of various economic vocations: "Adah gave birth to Jabal; he was the father of those who live in tents and raise livestock" (4:20). Scripture is well aware of the ways nations develop in their social systems. Descriptions of the sexual mores set out for Israel consistently make reference to displacement of the customs and practices of the nations (Lev. 18:3, 30). As noted above, since the fall, human beings have become a prime source of world-view and practice in the spiritual system (see Jer. 10:1–16).

The Bible recognizes that culture is transmitted through a learning process in which traditions are handed on from one generation to the next (1 Peter 1:18; Gal. 1:14). There is consistent encouragement to use this process to transmit the special heritage of God's truth and prescribed code of conduct (Exod. 13:9–10, 14–16; Deut. 6:4–8; 1 Cor. 15:1–4). What one receives, one is to pass on to the next spiritual generation through verbal transmission. Thus contemporary anthropology concurs with Scripture in concluding that culture is mediated through language.

(3) The third source of culture is Satan and his demons. Satan is a tempting liar who continues, in the pattern he initiated in the garden, to inspire men and women to express in ideology and behavior their rebellion against God (Gen. 3:1–5; Eph. 2:1–3). Missiologists such as Linwood Barney recognize this fact when they classify sin and evil as part of the supracultural. But the Bible goes further and presents Satan and the demonic powers as the source for the content of the world's cultural outlooks, structures, and customs. The religious centers of human cultures are the special province of Satan and his spiritual hierarchy. Their domination may be expressed as the legalist works-righteousness of Judaism, as the ritualist

polytheism of the Galatians, or in countless other ways. Paul describes them all as bondage to the elemental spirits (Gal. 4:3, 9).[21]

The gods of any human culture, to the degree that they exercise power, are exercising demonic power (1 Cor. 10:20). Scripture teaches that the demonic hierarchy has direct input into the realm of human ideas and theorizing. "Hollow and deceptive philosophy, which depends on human tradition," is controlled by the *stoicheia tou kosmou,* "the basic principles [elemental spirits] of this world" (Col. 2:8). In social structures and behavior patterns, there is also strong influence from satanic forces. Even political structures, which are ordained by God (Rom. 13:1–3), fall under the control of a demonic spiritual hierarchy, as the revelation to Daniel makes plain (Dan. 10:13, 20). Satan boasts of this very fact when tempting Jesus, and his claim is not disputed (Matt. 4:8–9; Luke 4:5–7; see also Eph. 6:12). Patterns of licentious and ascetic behavior can be inspired by the demonic powers. Paul labels as "things taught by demons" prohibition of marriage and abstinence from certain foods (1 Tim. 4:1–3; cf. Col. 2:20). Satan and his minions are the source of much more in human culture than just the supracultural inspiration to sin.

true

Religious Center

religion at a center of culture

One underlying assumption of the Bible is that religion is the integrating center of a culture, a concept that gets its strongest expression in the Old Testament (Jer. 6:16; 18:15). However, the primary purpose of the Bible is to promote the faith of the one true God over the pagan myths of origin, power, and destiny, and so direct reference to the lurid content of such myths is intentionally restricted. Still, we can glean some information from the polemics against pagan religions, especially Baalism, and from certain incidents in Israel's history. The gross apostasy at Mount Sinai provides a clear description of the creation and implementation of a pagan religion. The people, already forgetful of God's deliverance and frightened by the manifestations at the mountain, confront Aaron: "Come, make us gods who will go before us" (Exod. 32:1). Aaron responds to their demand by using their jewelry to fashion the calf, a symbol of fertility and well-being in the herding cultures of the period and region. Aaron's declaration supplies the myth of origin and power: "These are your gods, O Israel, who brought

---

21. F. F. Bruce, *The Epistle to the Galatians: A Commentary on the Greek Text* (Grand Rapids: Eerdmans, 1982), 193–94, 202–5. The *stoicheia* have been variously identified because of the wide range of usage in ancient literature. Are they the rudiments, first principles, of religion? Are they the basic elements of the universe? Are they the elemental spirits of the world? In this passage the type of bondage described (Jewish legalism and Gentile paganism) and the use of the modifier "of the world" point away from basic elements of the physical universe and first principles of religion to the gods and spiritual forces that use the law and ritual to enslave.

you up out of Egypt" (v. 4). Ritual practices for the new religion—singing, dancing, and running wild—erupt spontaneously (vv. 8–9, 25).

Jeremiah's critique of idol worship also assumes myths of origin, power, and destiny (Jer. 2:27; 14:22; cf. Hab. 1:5–11; see also Jer. 10:12–16). The biblical writers understand that the purpose of such myths and the ideas and practices they generate is survival. The gods are worshiped to ensure physical and economic survival amid hostile powers they are thought to control (Jer. 10:1–16; 14:22). Gods are also invoked to protect the political integrity of a nation (2 Kings 18:33; 19:12, 17; Jer. 16:19–21). Personal survival, especially control of present and future circumstances, is sought through divination, sorcery, witchcraft, and the intervention of a medium or spiritist (Deut. 18:9–13; cf. Isa. 43:8–13).

Not only does a culture provide a support system for the survival of those within it, but the culture itself takes on a dynamic aimed at its own survival. It may deal with contradictory elements of thought or behavior either by integrating the foreign element into its social matrix or, if the element is too threatening, by rejecting it and all those who believe or promote it as abnormal (see Deut. 12:30; 29:16, 18; 2 Kings 17:1–23). This dynamic means that the system is always moving toward monolithic dominance. The Scriptures recognize this tendency and foresee its coming to full expression in the end time, when politically, economically, and religiously there will be one system embracing all humankind (Rev. 13, 17–18; cf. Ps. 2; Isa. 23:3). Such cultural structures, including those of the present day, created by fallen human beings and inspired by Satan, do not have the one true God as their religious center. Consequently, the dynamic of cultural survival creates an inevitable conflict between the allegiance demanded by the culture and that demanded by God (Matt. 6:24; 1 John 2:15–17; James 4:4). We cannot serve God and mammon; we cannot love the world and have the love of God in us; we cannot be friends of the world without constituting ourselves enemies of God ("mammon" and "the world" are obvious synonyms for culture).

World-View

The biblical writers recognize the diversity of cultural world-views as part of human experience. When Pilate asks, "What is truth?" (John 18:38), he is acknowledging that we employ ideas or thought-categories for ordering and evaluating what can be known. Information can be questioned and refined within a culture. The Corinthian Christians who reject the idea of resurrection from the dead are still using their Greek belief categories for understanding human destiny, categories that could not accommodate bodily resurrection (1 Cor. 15:12–18; cf. Aeschylus *Eumenides* 648). There are frequent biblical allusions to the values, the desirable behavior, which a culture promotes. Jesus contrasts love for an enemy with the values of tax collectors and pagans, who love those who love them and greet those who greet them (Matt. 5:43–48).

We humans use our world-view to interpret our experience, a fact that Scripture takes into account. Charles Kraft points to several examples that demonstrate how the meaning assigned to an event by a group will be determined largely by its world-view assumptions.[22] The polytheistic residents of Lystra interpret Paul's healing power to mean that "the gods have come down to us in human form!" (Acts 14:11). The Maltese view Paul's snakebite as evidence that the goddess Justice is not permitting a murderer to live (28:4). When he survives, they conclude that he is a god (v. 6).

Human cultures do provide a world-view that influences the way one interprets experience, but this influence does not have to exert total control. Paul can appeal to a self-transcendent, self-critical faculty in human beings that enables them to stand above the prevailing world-view and question its solutions. Paul asks the Lycaonians why they are worshiping him and points out that the true source of his healing power is the living God. Paul and Barnabas are only ordinary men and vehemently reject the notion that they are incarnations of Zeus and Hermes, futile gods who have no power to produce the kind of miracle just witnessed (Acts 14:15). In their constant polemic against idolatry, the Old Testament prophets appeal to the same self-reflective capacity, a human quality that enables one to judge one's culture and to declare its idols worthless. The same quality allows a person freedom to acknowledge the one true and living God as the Creator, economic Sustainer, political and personal Protector, and Controller of the future (Isa. 40; 43:8–13; Jer. 10:1–16; 14:22; 16:19–21).

The consistent biblical calls for repentance and conversion to true worship and away from the religious centers and world-views of the pagan cultures rely on the human capacity to evaluate and reject a culture's world-view in favor of the biblical one. Jacob commands his family at Bethel, "Get rid of the foreign gods you have with you" (Gen. 35:2). Joshua calls on the Israelites at Shechem, "Now fear the LORD and serve him with all faithfulness. Throw away the gods your forefathers worshiped beyond the River and in Egypt" (Josh. 24:14). The persistent proclamation by the prophets and apostles of a salvation for the people of all nations follows the same pattern and assumes that the cultural world-view is not in total control (Isa. 31:6; Jer. 3:11–14; Acts 26:18).[23]

---

22. Kraft, *Christianity in Culture,* 57–58.

23. See John C. Robertson's persuasive argument with reference to the hermeneutical process ("Hermeneutics of Suspicion *versus* Hermeneutics of Goodwill," *Studies in Religion/Sciences religieuses* 8 [1979]: 365–77).

At this point it is appropriate to consider the implications of this type of argumentation for the contentions of relativists, whether radical or moderate, that between one's conceptual scheme and reality there is a dualism which prohibits any unmediated apprehension of objective reality. In this view, every idea or perception is colored by the prevailing world-view, which can be said to monitor the perceiver. The beholder can see no more than what the thought-categories of the culture permit.

The biblical appeal to human beings to make judgments about the reasonableness and truthfulness of their own culture and its idols undermines such dualism. Jeremiah describes how idols come into being as the work of craftsmen using wood, metal, and cloth. He declares what should be evident to all—these idols are lifeless, worthless. "Like a scarecrow in a melon patch, their idols cannot speak; they must be carried because they cannot walk. Do not fear them; they can do no harm nor can they do any good" (Jer. 10:5). Paul at the Areopagus uses a similar argument: "Therefore since we are God's offspring, we should not think that the divine being is like gold or silver or stone—an image made by man's design and skill" (Acts 17:29). In both cases it is assumed that humans can look at reality directly and evaluate their interpretations in the light of it.[24] There is no dualism here; the larger truth context—reality—is always available to us.

First Corinthians 13:12 is often cited as evidence that finite individuals do not have direct perception of reality, only an apprehension that is either totally or partially controlled by a world-view.[25] But such an interpretation of "for now we see in a mirror dimly [lit., in a riddle]" (NASB) misapplies a significant part of the figure of speech. Seeing an image in a mirror is indirect perception, but Paul's emphasis is on the contrast between the way he sees now and the way he will see "then . . . face to face." He goes on to describe the nature of this reflected knowledge. It is characterized by incompleteness ("now I know in part"). But an indirect or mediated image can still be a true, though partial, reflection. This partial knowledge is also characterized by obscurity, as in an enigma or riddle. In the Old Testament such communication from God is set over against direct revelation, as when God spoke to Moses face to face (Num. 12:8). Is such partial, obscure knowledge descriptive of all human perception through the mirror of one's cultural world-view? Though the image may suggest the general and unconscious influence reflected from one's world-view, Paul is not talking about general or unconscious influences; his subject is knowledge of God, of transcendent realities. Mediation and indirectness may be present, but they are the manner of God's revelation to finite, fallen men and women

---

24. See Richard J. Bernstein, *Beyond Objectivism and Relativism: Science, Hermeneutics, and Praxis* (Philadelphia: University of Pennsylvania Press, 1983), 76.

25. Kraft, *Christianity in Culture*, 23, and various other places throughout his work; Eugene A. Nida, letter to the author, January 1987; Hiebert, "Critical Contextualization," 10.

through prophet's word and sage's parable. That knowledge is partial, and even enigmatic, because as finite, fallen creatures we are not yet in a position, the position of glorification, to receive complete and unmediated knowledge of God. Paul Hiebert's trenchant interpretation sums it up best—"We see through a glass darkly, but we do see"—a view that needs to be affirmed and strengthened.[26]

Cultural Structures and Behavior

The perceptive reader of Scripture becomes aware of a variety of cultural structures and behavior invested with a certain meaning as they serve a particular function or purpose in a society. One very simple structure is the protocol for placing dinner guests, each position (or form) indicating a meaning—namely, the relative esteem in which the host held the guest. Jesus grounds a parable on this cultural dynamic of form indicating meaning (Luke 14:7–11). He warns against arriving early and claiming the first places reserved for honored guests, who, in the etiquette of the culture, would exercise the prerogative of arriving late.

Paul describes the cultural behavior of eating meat offered to idols. It had a specific meaning for pagans at Corinth, who believed that meat which had been offered to idols was divine food, beneficial for maintaining or improving one's health (1 Cor. 8:4–8).

The Bible offers very little material with which to evaluate the contention of many anthropologists that for meaning to remain constant from culture to culture, the form in which it is expressed must be adapted to suit the receptor culture. Scripture does demonstrate, however, that the meaning of already prescribed forms can be learned and that it is appropriate to transmit the forms and their meaning from culture to culture. The recommended procedure for such transmission is outlined with regard to the formal Passover celebration in Exodus 13:14–16. Jesus infused new meaning into the cultural form of breaking bread to begin the Passover meal, and he instructed his disciples to transmit this new meaning, which is remembrance of Christ's suffering for us (Luke 22:19–20). The Bible at points indicates when a given behavior or structure is a cultural form by explicitly giving its meaning (e.g., Gen. 38:15; Mark 7:4). Throughout, a difference seems to be understood between simple behavior and cultural behavior.

Change

One of the key factors of a contemporary understanding of culture is the role of change. By definition, cultures are in a constant process of adaptation to relentlessly changing circumstances. Contemporary cultural and

---

26. Hiebert, "Critical Contextualization," 10.

historical analyses, especially those from a relativistic perspective, make change absolute and identify it as the basic characteristic of human experience.

Scripture also recognizes change as a primary aspect of human experience. God's redemptive activity, culminating in the incarnation, death, and resurrection of Jesus, takes place in a history moving toward its climactic conclusion—the return of the Lord Jesus Christ (Rom. 13:11–12; 1 John 2:8). For Christians, there is a certain tension in this matter. On the one hand, they are told not to change but to hold fast to the faith once delivered to the saints (1 Cor. 15:58; Jude 3). On the other hand, they are called to change, to grow in the grace and knowledge of Christ (Eph. 4:15–16; 2 Peter 3:18).

Though Scripture recognizes historical and cultural change as real, it relativizes it in two ways. First, change is not the basic characteristic of human experience. From the biblical perspective, all history is a unit. This perspective includes eternity, the age to come (Matt. 12:32; 13:40; Gal. 1:4; Heb. 6:5). Jesus promised, "Surely I am with you always, to the very end of the age" (Matt. 28:20). Scripture presents the incarnation as the central reference point in history and views all human beings since Christ's resurrection as living in the same time period, the eschatological last days (Acts 2:17; see also 17:30–31), "this present age" (Titus 2:12; cf. 2 Tim. 4:10). When Jesus declared, "The kingdom of God is near" (Mark 1:15), he was saying that the last days have dawned. Paul makes the same point when he describes the Corinthians as those "on whom the fulfillment of the ages has come" (1 Cor. 10:11). A worsening of conditions is anticipated as the last of the final days come (2 Tim. 3:1; 1 John 2:18), but there is no indication that this end time is essentially different from the time period as a whole. Within the redemptive time framework of Scripture, all human beings are in the same time period, and so there can be no radical, or even moderate, historical relativism that puts a "ditch" between the time of the New Testament and contemporary times. This framework of biblical time provides a hermeneutical bridge.

Scripture further relativizes change by emphasizing the impermanence of culture and its driving forces. It does so by declaring that there is something which abides forever and that, when individuals participate in it, that permanent quality will be given to them. John warns against loving the world and the things in it, because "the world and its desires pass away" (1 John 2:17; see also 1 Cor. 7:31).[27] What abides forever is the will of God, and those who do that will also abide forever, by allowing the ideas, beliefs, and values of God's will to interpret their experience and govern their behavior. Their survival is assured, not through adaptation to relentless change, but through faithfulness to God's settled truth. This is not an

---

27. Stephen S. Smalley, 1, 2, 3 John, WBC 51 (Waco, Tex.: Word, 1984), 81ff.

approach that views reality as static, but it does make change and the cultural process so relative that the unchanging truth of an authoritative Scripture can again be in final functional control of the process.

God's Relation to Human Culture

We can expect Scripture to provide information about God's relationship to human culture, information we will need to understand the Bible's authoritative interpretation and application to any given societal group. In addition, there will be implications for Christians in their own relations to and evaluations of culture.

God's predominantly positive relation to human social organization is first expressed in his desire that humankind fill the earth with a diversity of cultures. We have sketched in broad outline the structures, tasks, and behavior patterns which God has ordained for humans in their natural, social, and spiritual systems. God as the sovereign Lord, King of all the earth and of every nation (2 Chron. 20:6; Ps. 47:7–9; 113:4), guarantees a culture's survival (Job 12:23; Ps. 67:6–7). God desires that these cultures relate to him in worship, acknowledging him as Creator (1 Chron. 16:26–29; Ps. 86:9) and sovereign Controller (1 Chron. 16:30–31; Ps. 22:27; 33:11; 46:8–10; 67:1–4).

The object of God's redemption is humankind's living harmoniously in a diversity of cultures. One of the earliest covenant promises is that in Abraham all the nations (cultures) of the earth will be blessed (Gen. 12:3; Acts 3:25; Gal. 3:8). God's mighty acts of deliverance for Israel were intended to let the nations of the earth know that the God of Israel was no run-of-the-mill tribal deity but the one true God (Deut. 4:34; Exod. 34:10; Ps. 126:2; Neh. 6:16; Isa. 52:10), and he provided interpretations of these acts for the nations (Deut. 29:22–28; Jer. 22:8–9). At the same time, he maintains a witness of his existence and eternal power through natural revelation (Rom. 1:20). He shows himself "by giving you rain from heaven and crops in their seasons; he provides you with plenty of food and fills your hearts with joy" (Acts 14:17).

It is significant that Jesus and the New Testament writers direct the universal offer of salvation not to every person, but to every nation. "This gospel of the kingdom will be preached in the whole world as a testimony to all nations" (Matt. 24:14). Jesus commissions his apostles to make disciples of all nations and cultures (28:19). The initial empowerment for witness, Pentecost, is characterized by a miracle of tongues, enabling the listeners to hear the good news in their own native language—the mediator of their culture (Acts 2:5). The fruit of this labor is pictured by John as "a great multitude that no one could count, from every nation, tribe, people and language, standing before the throne" (Rev. 7:9; see also 5:9; Rom. 15:9–12). It may be argued that this is just a way of describing the worldwide scope of

God's saving purposes. The gospel is to be preached to the ends of the earth (Acts 1:8; 10:35), and finite humans have few other ways of representing this scope, since a diversity of cultures is the configuration of their earthly existence. But the evidence for God's original desire being a diversity of cultures living harmoniously together invites the conclusion that cultures can be pleasing to God and will have a place in redemption, a proposition worth analyzing more thoroughly.

Scripture makes it plain again and again that God has used cultures in a positive way to accomplish his redemptive plan. The central event, the incarnation, was not lifted to a mythical plane divorced from ordinary life. God did not come as a generic human being, but as a first-century Palestinian, a Hebrew-speaking Jew, within the Roman Empire. Particular culture apparently mattered a great deal.

The major focus of the Old Testament is the formation and maintenance of Israel as a model culture. Individuals are called to fill strategic roles, but the subject of their efforts is the nation. God's initiative in calling one man, Abraham, out of a culture and constituting from him a new one sets the basic pattern (Gen. 12:1–3).[28] When Israel is liberated from Egypt, Scripture makes plain that God is bringing his chosen nation out of domination by a much more powerful and sophisticated culture.

Something like a process of deculturing occurs from time to time, but it could be more accurately described as purification. The people are commanded to reject the idols and customs carried over from their forebears or borrowed from their neighbors. Obviously God wants a social organism, but not just any customs and religious ideas will do. The goal of his saving action is to preserve the identity of the nation (2 Sam. 7:23–24). Israel's cultural identity is established by God himself, and from that matrix comes their distinctive society (Deut. 4:5–8, 32–40). He communicates directly with the patriarchs and with Moses, revealing the spiritual content for their religious center, the world-view, and appropriate social structures and customs.[29]

---

28. Contrast Nicholls's approach, which, although it takes a similar starting point, describes God's interaction with Israel as "the progressive de-culturalization of elements conflicting with divine self-disclosure" (*Contextualization*, 46).

29. S. Ananda Kumar, in contrast, seems to undertake his investigation of the contribution of the surrounding cultural environment to the inspired record with the assumption that the surrounding culture provided content for each area of culture building. He concludes, "It seems clear enough that God did indeed speak in the context and employed elements of the content of the surrounding cultures in order to convey his message to his ancient people" ("Culture and the Old Testament," in *Gospel and Culture*, 61). When Kumar applies this line of thought to the origin of Genesis 1, he concludes that it is an appropriation and adaptation of the Babylonian creation epic; the adaptation "involved the elimination of polytheistic and idolatrous elements as well as of undignified, absurd and crude mythological factors which were directly contrary to the sovereignty, majesty and dignity of the Creator-God, who revealed himself in the history of Israel" (p. 54). The parallels on which Kumar bases his analysis are not close (see Derek Kidner, *Genesis: An Introduction and Commentary* [London: Tyndale, 1967], 45). Further, Kumar's conclusions fly in the face of the plain reading of the text. God reveals directly his message concerning human origins.

Comparative studies of ancient Near Eastern cultures have revealed many correspondences with Israel's culture. For example, there are similarities between the law collections of the Pentateuch and the Code of Hammurabi. In section 60 of Hammurabi's code, for instance, there are regulations about the seasonal schedule for developing orchards. Four years are required. This is similar to the regulation in Leviticus, "In the fourth year all its fruit will be holy, an offering of praise to the LORD (19:23–25)."[30] Does this similarity indicate that God appropriated ideas from surrounding cultures for his model culture, Israel? If he did so, he would have renovated the elements to bring them into line with his own decrees and his character as a gracious covenant-making and covenant-keeping God. The distinction can be seen in this regulation for developing an orchard. In Israel, any fruit that comes in the fourth year is set aside as a praise offering to God. No such cultic reference is present in Hammurabi's code.[31] Whether God did choose to exercise such appropriation must be finally determined by explicit statements in Scripture.

The political structure of monarchy is a cultural borrowing, one that Scripture admits with embarrassment (Deut. 17:14–20). God had not directed that a king be appointed. Israel's desire was to have a king "like all the nations around us" (v. 14). When Samuel presents the request, God sees it as a rejection of his sovereignty (1 Sam. 8:7). Even so, God lets the nation have its way, but he provides restrictions to ensure that the king rules justly and in the fear of the Lord. God's response to this irreverent request demonstrates that even flawed cultural structures can be properly used, but to conclude that Israel was "guided to incorporate those elements from the surrounding culture which would be beneficial to the nation" is to misunderstand the process by which Israel's model culture was built.[32] Cultural borrowing may occur, but God must ratify its use in his nation, and the nation must receive it as God's revealed will.

The most telling evidence of God's gracious disposal toward human culture is his plan for his church. Intent on creating a model culture to exist within other cultures, sowing her seeds in their fields, God has created a new Israel. The church offers worship due the one true God and exhibits wisdom and love in interpersonal relationships. The world's multiple cultures, permeated by God's culture the church, can achieve his original design.

Any borrowing which New Testament doctrine and ethics has made from first-century philosophical and religious thought took place on the

---

30. James B. Pritchard, ed., *The Ancient Near East: An Anthology of Texts and Pictures* (Princeton, N.J.: Princeton University Press, 1958), 146.

31. Millard C. Lind, "Refocusing Theological Education to Mission: The Old Testament and Contextualization," *Missiology* 10 (1982): 152.

32. Kumar, "Culture and the Old Testament," 58.

same basis as in the Old Testament.[33] Where comparisons are made to first-century practice, as at 1 Corinthians 5:1–8, the biblical writer makes clear that society has not set the standard for the New Testament church.[34]

God's affirmation as well as productive use of human culture is very reassuring. It means a Christian should be able to take advantage of the cultural structures and relationships while living life according to a godly pattern. This does not mean that the Bible views any given human culture as in and of itself neutral. Nor does it mean that God's approach to a given culture was to accept it without preconditions of change before he could work within it. There was a counterbalancing negative evaluation of culture which we need to address. The positive evaluation was the affirmation of those elements in any given culture that are an appropriate expression of the divinely ordained cultural tasks, world-view, structures, and behavior. Jesus and his followers exhibited their enjoyment of human society and friendship, their approval and celebration of marriage, and approval of what is excellent in the world (Luke 10:38–41; 14:1–24; Matt. 19:1–12; Heb. 13:4; Phil. 4:8).[35] Human culture is the context within which Christians must live their lives and carry out their mission. They are, and according to Christ's instruction must be, *in* the world, though they are no longer *of* it (John 17:11, 15). Jesus' prayer is not that they be taken out of the world, but that they be kept from the evil one (v. 15; see also 1 Cor. 5:10). This means that though one's true identity is in Christ, one can maintain one's cultural identity, and even find satisfaction in it. Just how significant the cultural identities are in God's grand design for salvation is proclaimed in the triumphant scene around the throne at the last day. There will be "a great multitude that no one could count, from every nation, tribe, people and language" (Rev. 7:9).

Ethnocentrism

God's regard for human culture provides a basis for and an example of the respect and appreciation Christians should feel for their own culture and also for the cultures of others. Scripture gives evidence that they are to respect the cultural identity of others (Rev. 5:9; 7:9; Acts 15:23; Gal. 2:15).

---

33. Marshall, "Culture and the New Testament," 33–34. An example of possible New Testament borrowing and renovation is the lists of domestic responsibilities, the so-called housetables (Eph. 5:21–6:9; 1 Peter 2:13–3:7); see also David Balch, *Let Wives Be Submissive: The Domestic Code in 1 Peter* (Chico, Calif.: Society of Biblical Literature, 1981), 1–20.

34. Norman R. Ericson, "Implications from the New Testament for Contextualization," in *Theology and Mission*, ed. David J. Hesselgrave (Grand Rapids: Baker, 1978), 71.

35. Marshall, "Culture and the New Testament," 38. E. A. Judge sees the list in Philippians as moral criteria ("Cultural Conformity and Innovation in Paul: Some Clues from Contemporary Documents," *Tyndale Bulletin* 35 [1984]: 14).

This was a lesson early Christians struggled to learn as Jewish and Gentile Christians endeavored to live together. The Jerusalem Council addressed the problem and laid down a pattern of mutual respect. It was not necessary, they concluded, for Gentile Christians to become Jews, accepting circumcision and other requirements of the ritual law. Gentile Christians for their part were instructed to exercise courtesy and respect toward the Jewish observances, particularly when eating with them (Acts 15:6–11, 23–29).

Scripture's overall attitude toward culture is more negative than positive.[36] It judges the prideful and often coercive ethnocentrism with which fallen men and women naturally express their cultural identity. Those who follow God's evaluation must forswear the ethnic pride that labels those of other cultures unclean and treats them as ineligible for God's saving grace (Acts 10:28, 35). No culture—not even Judaism, which had developed from a heritage of divine revelation—can impose its requirements on the new culture, Christianity. The Jerusalem church, as we noted, learned this truth through long and painful experience (10:45; 11:1, 18; 15:1, 3, 7, 12, 14, 17; Gal. 2:11–16). The Scriptures unequivocally affirm that God, who knows all hearts, saves by grace through faith apart from the adoption of customs of any human culture, even one whose core God has provided (Acts 15:6–11).

Two basic scriptural truths that refute ethnocentrism are the unity of humankind and the higher common identity of all those who are in Christ. As Paul says, Christians have "put on the new self, which is being renewed in knowledge in the image of its Creator. Here there is no Greek or Jew, circumcised or uncircumcised, barbarian, Scythian, slave or free, but Christ is all, and is in all" (Col. 3:10–11; see also Gal. 3:28; Eph. 2:13–22; 3:6; Rom. 9:24, 30). No human culture is absolute. All are relative to the common humanity in Adam and the new common identity in Christ. In this area, anthropology has done a service to missiology and more recently to biblical scholarship by highlighting this factor in hermeneutical endeavors and cross-cultural communication efforts. The behavior sciences concur in rejecting ethnocentrism.

There are certainly implications here for cultural flexibility. Christians, because they desire to evangelize all people and because their basic identity now is in Christ, can encounter almost any culture, participate in it, and seek to identify with persons in it (1 Cor. 9:19–22). Such identification, though genuine, must also be limited for those two reasons. Their purpose is the same as Paul's, who says he can identify with all sorts of people for the purpose of rescuing them out of the kingdom of darkness and winning them as subjects for Jesus Christ in the kingdom of light (Acts 26:18; 1 Cor. 9:22; Col. 1:13). Also like Paul, Christians today will be at pains to be sure

---

36. See H. Richard Niebuhr, *Christ and Culture* (New York: Harper & Row, 1951), 45–49.

that their identity in Christ is in authoritative control of their cultural relationships. They may seek to identify, for instance, with those outside the
law, but in such a way that they will always show themselves to be "under
Christ's law" (1 Cor. 9:21).

The Christian actually has a remarkable freedom in cultural encounters,
even in the midst of a pagan society. Thus the early Christians were free to
purchase meat in the market without raising questions about its origin and
to eat it, though it had been offered to idols, unless by eating they offended
someone of sensitive conscience (1 Cor. 8:4–8; 10:25–26). They could not,
however, go to a feast honoring a pagan god and there eat the idol's meat
(1 Cor. 10:14–22, 27–30). Such a cultural form takes its entire meaning and
function from the pagan religious center and its world-view, so that par-
ticipating becomes an action against God. Still, the action of eating such
meat, when separated from the cultural meaning, was harmless.

It seems that many actions can be performed apart from cultural meanings. The cultural forms themselves, however, are not so neutral. For a
cultural form is by definition a behavior pattern invested by a given culture
with a given meaning and function.

In his analysis, Charles Kraft makes no distinction between simple actions related to the physical environment and actions as cultural forms. This
has led him to apply to cultural forms the biblical teaching about the neutrality, even the essential goodness, of objects in the physical environment—"Nothing is unclean in itself" (Rom. 14:14 NASB).[37] But there is a
distinction, as Paul clearly shows, and to see it one must evaluate one's
cultural context in relation to the larger truth context of reality. Within that
context one can test to find which cultural forms are aligned with God-
ordained structures and tasks and thus are appropriate for Christians to
use.

It is characteristic of Paul to qualify his directions for various authority
relationships—between husband and wife, master and servant, parents
and children—with the phrase "in the Lord." This can mean only that God
calls Christians in every cultural setting to express obedience, responsibility,
and love in these relationships by renewing, redeeming, and redirecting the
practices of their particular culture (Eph. 6:1; Col. 3:18). God's instructions
concerning the monarchy (Deut. 17:14–20) show how a cultural structure
can be adapted by God's people. It must be redirected toward a new religious center. The king must revere the Lord his God and must be so
disciplined that his actions reflect God's law—in this case, social righteousness and justice.

Despite God's merciful disposition toward and beneficent use of many
cultural elements, there is a darker side to the picture. Human cultures are

---

37. Kraft, *Christianity in Culture*, 106, 113.

planted and bear their fruits in soil ruined by the fall. Fallen men and women captivated by Satan and the demonic world generate cultures that express and try to maintain a rebellious autonomy. God holds cultures accountable and will judge them in the end (Ps. 9:17, 19; Joel 3; Obad. 15; Jer. 46–51; Acts 17:30–31). God's exercise of sovereign control and discipline over cultures is a severe mercy that preserves them from wanton destruction of themselves and others. He thwarts the cultures that exalt themselves against God (Ps. 9:5; 33:10–11; 59:5); he renders their wisdom foolishness (1 Cor. 1:20–21; 3:18–21).

It is significant that God does not directly reveal to every culture his plan for salvation (Deut. 4:6–8; Ps. 147:19–20; Isa. 2:3; Eph. 2:12). There is, of course, the witness of the creation to God's existence, power, and providence (Rom. 1:20; Acts 14:17); and individuals within diverse cultures may receive preevangelistic communication from God, as Cornelius did (Acts 10:4–6). But as with Cornelius, such communication in and of itself does not provide the saving message. Rather, God sends human messengers who have already believed and received revelation of the biblical gospel (Acts 10:33; 11:14; Rom. 10:14–15).

God has allowed human cultures to go their own way, to grope. They are without the knowledge of God. They have a religion—a power source and ordering principle—but it is not the one true God. The first two of the Ten Commandments are a solemn reminder of the prevailing tendency. Paul provides a graphic description of the spiritual bankruptcy of religion as devised by human culture. It is a "lie," not the "truth of God." It is worship of the "creature," not the "Creator." It is the exchange of "images made to look like mortal man and birds and animals and reptiles" for the "glory of the immortal God" (Rom. 1:23, 25). This anti-God religious center generates the cultures' world-views and behavior, and as a consequence they are not just superficially contaminated; they are evil from the center outward. Old Testament writers knew this well. Ezekiel's description of Israel's rebellion notes how service to other gods led to refusal to keep God's laws and in the end to God's handing the people over to "statutes that were not good and laws they could not live by" (Ezek. 20:25; see also v. 13; Lev. 18:1–3, 24–30; 2 Kings 17:1–23). The warnings in the New Testament against loving or being friends with the world sound a similar note (1 John 2:15–17; James 4:4; Matt. 6:24; 1 Cor. 7:31).

Charles Kraft disputes such a disparaging evaluation of culture, asserting that it takes into account only negative uses of the word *world*.[38] Kraft views culture as basically neutral in its structures and processes and cites Paul's principle "nothing is unclean in itself" (Rom. 14:14 NASB) as applicable to

38. Ibid., 105–6.

culture viewed apart from the evil uses to which it can be put. He recognizes that Satan can use a culture and demand the allegiance of the participants, but in his view this does not make culture itself essentially evil. Kraft's approach coincides with the biblical teaching that God has ordained certain structures and tasks of culture, but it does not sufficiently take into account that since the fall the driving center in the formation of culture has been a religious world-view focused against God. Because of this driving center, all human cultures are unclean in themselves. Kraft misapplies Romans 14:14 when he interprets it to mean that human cultures are neutral; actually, they are basically sinful expressions of fallen humanity in rebellion against God.

This negative evaluation need not constitute an escapist or unconsciously ethnocentric approach to human cultures. It does imply that Christians must consciously claim their basic identity in Christ, their citizenship in heaven (1 Cor. 1:30–31; Col. 3:1–4; Phil. 3:20). One does not deny cultural identity, but it is no longer thought to be the seat of one's basic worth, a thought which is easily converted into ethnic pride. One is now part of that "holy nation" of people of all nations who lift praises to God (1 Peter 2:9). Such a conversion means the replacement of the cultural religious center, whether sacred or secular, with Jesus as Lord (Rom. 10:9–10). As the New Testament consistently points out, true repentance and conversion involve just such a shift (Acts 26:18; Eph. 2:1–10). Converts replace the ideas, beliefs, and values of the prevalent world-view with God's world-view (Rom. 12:1–2). They come to see that "being rich toward God," giving to the poor and supporting God's work, has more value than the consumerism which makes them rich toward themselves (Luke 12:13–21). They reject the culture's sinful customs and practices in favor of God's ways.

Christians are not of this world, which means they are not of their culture (John 15:18; 17:6, 16). They are still in that culture; but their identity, their outlook on the world, and the way they behave in it are not products of that culture. They are set apart and receive a new identity and all that goes with it from the truth, God's Word (John 17:17). Thus Scripture can use Abrahamic imagery (stranger, foreigner, sojourner) to describe the Christian's position in the world (1 Peter 1:17; 2:11; 4:4; Heb. 11:9, 13; cf. Eph. 2:19).[39] Such a stance often places Christians at a distance from, and even in opposition to, their culture (John 15:18–19; Matt. 24:9; 1 John 4:5–6; cf. the world's evaluation of the Christian world-view and practice, 1 Cor. 1:18–25; 4:9,

---

39. See Andrew F. Walls, "The Gospel as the Prisoner and Liberator of Culture," *Missionalia* 10 (1982): 93–105.

13).[40] But even so, they can be of good cheer, for Christ has overcome the culture (John 16:33).

There is, then, sufficient biblical evidence from which to construct a biblical theology of culture the context. Developed within a framework which sees the unity of humankind as more basic than the diversity of cultures, such teaching calls into question both cultural relativism and ethnocentrism. The Bible teaches that God and Satan, as well as human beings, are sources for culture. From creation, God ordained cultural structures and tasks for humankind. In the natural system they were not only to be stewards of the earth, but to fill and subdue it in a harmonious pattern of diverse cultures. In the social system they were to live a responsible family life of lifelong monogamous marriage, with each member of the family properly fulfilling his or her role. In the spiritual system God alone was to be worshiped and his law obeyed. The fall severely disrupted each of these systems, so that in succeeding generations man the rebel, encouraged by Satan, constructed cultures with religious centers other than the one true God. Human cultures now stand not only as expressions of humankind's efforts to fulfil God-ordained cultural tasks, but as the embodiment of their sinful attempts to maintain autonomy.

God in creation and salvation relates positively to cultures. He can include renovated cultural borrowing as part of his revelation. He calls men and women to live out their new life in Christ in their given culture, though they are no longer of it. God relates negatively to human cultures by judging both the ethnocentrism they foster and the religious power center which energizes them. He calls his people to replace the false religious center with Jesus as Lord and to live as God's model culture, the church, in the midst of their culture.

---

40. See E. A. Judge's analysis of Paul's approach to Greek culture ("Cultural Conformity," 3–24; "The Reaction Against Classical Education in the New Testament," ERT 9 [1985]: 166–74).

14

Revelation and Truth

The second large area of a biblical theology of hermeneutics and culture can be encompassed under the heading "God the Communicator." Here we will examine the basic characteristics of God's revelation. What does the Bible teach about revelation, truth, and meaning? What does it teach about its own nature and authority? What is the role of the Holy Spirit in communicating revelation? Biblical answers to these questions should provide key content for the metacultural and metahistorical framework within which we can interpret, apply, and communicate Scripture's message across time and culture. They should also furnish guidelines for critiquing contemporary hermeneutics.

chapter thesis

Revelation

Verbal and Propositional Revelation

What is the biblical perspective of revelation? How does God communicate with human beings? How does he disclose himself and his will? The most obvious and incontrovertible characteristic of God's revelation is that it is verbal and propositional. God uses human language to tell us things.[1]

God uses what we understand

---

1. James I. Packer, "The Adequacy of Human Language," in *Inerrancy*, ed. Norman L. Geisler (Grand Rapids: Zondervan, 1979), 206.

From the very beginning God the Creator uses language, and he creates human beings in his image as language users. God's first act after creating man and woman is to bless them and direct them: "Be fruitful and increase in number; fill the earth and subdue it." He also communicates information about the provision of sustenance (Gen. 1:28–30). Even after the fall God continues to use human language to communicate. It is God's vehicle to declare his will, to bless, and to curse. But he also uses it as an appropriate medium for self-disclosure. To Noah he declares that he is a God who must punish sin but who also desires to establish a covenant with those who are righteous, who find favor in his sight (Gen. 6:13, 18).

The Bible portrays God directly addressing the patriarchs in language they can understand. He does so as a covenant-making God who uses words to make promises and establish covenant obligations that will span generations. Abraham undertakes his covenant journey on the basis of what God has said to him (Gen. 12:1–3). "I will make you into a great nation" not only spans time, it spans culture—"all peoples on earth will be blessed through you." The everlasting sign of the covenant is revealed to Abraham through words. At the opening of the episode we read, "The Lord appeared to him and said. . . ." The mode of the revelation is also emphasized as the account closes: "When he had finished speaking with Abraham, God went up from him" (17:1, 22). As each new element of the covenant is introduced, God speaks it (vv. 3, 9, 15, 19).

The pattern continues with succeeding patriarchs. God reconfirms the covenant promises with Isaac (Gen. 26:1–5). He appears in a dream to Jacob at Bethel, and here again the main component is verbal communication confirming the covenant and promising to be present with Jacob in his travels (28:12–15). Later when Jacob commemorates the revelation at Bethel, a ceremony God instructs him to perform (35:1–7), he describes the experience as a direct answer in his distress, a spoken promise that has proved true, for God "has been with me wherever I have gone" (v. 3).

With Moses the direct verbal communication from God intensifies. God's covenant with Israel is renewed through Moses, and at Sinai he enunciates in more detail the obligations of covenant obedience, giving the moral, ceremonial, and civil law. From this point on, God's verbal communication involves two new aspects. Whereas in the past a single man was the recipient of God's revelation and served as a messenger to his family, God now institutes the office of prophet and apostle. The people are to receive the words of the prophet as the words of God. The pattern is illustrated by Moses' hearing God's words on Sinai and then speaking them to the people. Moses goes up the mountain, and the Lord calls to him, makes a declaration of his saving activity in rescuing the people from Egypt, and gives his covenant promise that if they will obey him, they will be a treasured possession to him. In concluding he says, "These are the words you are to speak to the Israelites." Moses goes down from the mountain, calls the elders of the people, and sets "before them all the words the LORD had commanded him to speak." The people respond, "We will do everything the LORD has said" (Exod. 19:6–8). Moses takes their answer back to the Lord. This method of revelation that uses the prophet as the courier of God extends the communication link somewhat, but the medium remains the same—human language. The prophetic pattern has been set: "The word of the LORD came to [the prophet]," and when the prophet relays the word to the people, he says, "This is what the LORD says." This pattern remains the hallmark of true prophecy throughout the Bible (e.g., Jer. 2:1, 5; Ezek. 1:3; 2:4; Mic. 1:1; 3:5).

The other new aspect of God's communication with Moses is that for the first time verbal revelation is given in written form. "When the LORD finished speaking to Moses on Mount Sinai, he gave him the two tablets of the Testimony, the tablets of stone inscribed by the finger of God" (Exod. 31:18). Written revelation is obviously appropriate for making and keeping a covenant. At the heart of a covenant relationship is the promise of both parties to do certain things in the future. An authoritative written record of these stipulations—the duties of the people, the blessings and curses of God for performance and nonperformance—and of ratification by the parties is essential. It provides motivation and guidance from generation to generation in what the Lord requires (24:3–4, 7–8).

Some seven hundred years later, during the kingdom period, the Book of the Law compiled at Sinai and during the wilderness wanderings has been lost and forgotten. It is uncovered in the temple during Josiah's reign, and the written record fulfils its function to instruct and inspire the people. The king hears the book read with its regulations and curses for noncompliance and concludes, "Great is the LORD's anger that burns against us because our fathers have not obeyed the words of this book; they have not acted in accordance with all that is written there concerning us" (2 Kings 22:13). Josiah takes action and leads his people in renewing the covenant by listening to the regulations and promising to keep them (23:2–3). The Passover is celebrated, "as it is written in this Book of the Covenant" (v. 21). The written covenant also serves in this and other instances as a necessary witness against the people and their rebellious noncompliance (Deut. 31:19, 26; Isa. 30:8).

During the period of the kings, God continued to speak through his messengers, the prophets. God's covenant promise of the Messiah comes to David through the word of the Lord to the prophet Nathan (2 Sam. 7:4–17). Phrases are sprinkled throughout this passage that reiterate the prophetic pattern. The revelation is heard in human language from God, and the prophet speaks the same message to David, who receives it as the very words of God. "Go and tell my servant David, 'This is what the LORD says. . . .' Now then, tell my servant David, 'This is what the LORD Almighty says. . . . The LORD declares to you'" (vv. 5, 8, 11). More than 130 times, the prophet's message is introduced by "The word of the LORD came to . . ." (e.g., Isa. 38:4; Hos. 1:1; Jonah 1:1). Over 360 times—from Isaiah to Malachi—the prophetic message is punctuated with the phrase "This is what the LORD says" (NIV) or "Thus says the LORD" (NASB). These communications could be preserved in writing (see Jer. 36).

The united witness of the Old Testament is that God communicates in human language. James Barr concurs: "Direct verbal communication between God and particular men on particular occasions . . . is, I believe, an inescapable fact of the Bible and of the O.T. in particular."[2]

also in NT The New Testament also bears witness to the fact that God's revelation is verbal, propositional, in human words, and usually through a messenger. At points during Jesus' ministry—at his baptism, at the transfiguration, and before the crucifixion—God speaks directly from heaven, testifying to Jesus' true nature ("This is my Son"), to human accountability to him ("Listen to him!"), and to God's intention to glorify his own name in the Son's mission (Matt. 3:17; 17:5; John 12:28).

God speaks in the New Testament through this appointed messenger, the incarnate Son. John consistently points out that what Jesus heard in the Father's presence he now speaks in the world. Jesus emphasizes that he is not the source of his own teaching, but is faithfully transmitting what God the Father has taught him (John 3:34; 7:16; 8:26–27, 38; 12:49–50; 14:24; 17:8). *same pattern* The prophetic pattern is the same: Jesus hears and tells, but with greater certainty that he is speaking God's words. He has been in the Father's very presence in heaven, "so whatever I say is just what the Father has told me to say" (12:50); and the whole process involves language. There is no hint that *hmm* there is a qualitative difference between the verbal communication in heaven and Jesus' communication in human language on earth. The incarnation demonstrates that it is possible for God to use human language to tell us things in a way that ensures that the message we hear is precisely what God intends to say on the matter. Jesus identifies the one difficulty in the *the problem in comm.* communication link. The sinful heart will believe a lie rather than the truth. "Why is my language not clear to you? Because you are unable to hear what I say. You belong to your father, the devil. . . . He is a liar and the father of lies. Yet because I tell the truth, you do not believe me! . . . He who belongs to God hears what God says. The reason you do not hear me is that you do not belong to God" (8:43–47). The problem is not with human language as a vehicle of revelation, nor even the gulf between infinite God and finite

---

2. James Barr, "The Interpretation of Scripture II: Revelation Through History in the Old Testament and in Modern Theology," *Interpretation* 17 (1963): 201.

human beings, but rather the distance between a holy and truthful God and rebellious sinners.

The early church experiences verbal revelation both by direct speech from God and by messages through his apostles. God addresses Paul and Peter directly (Acts 9:4; 10:13; 18:9–10). The gospel they hand on to others as the Word of God is, according to the same prophetic pattern, what they have heard from the ascended Lord (1 Cor. 2:13; Gal. 1:8–12). Paul's remarks to the Thessalonians serve as verification: "When you received the word of God, which you heard from us, you accepted it not as the word of men, but as it actually is, the word of God, which is at work in you who believe" (1 Thess. 2:13). The New Testament writers view not only the oral but also the written form of the apostles' message as God's revealed Word. Peter acknowledges Paul's writings as Scripture (2 Peter 3:16). God presents himself as a language user, from the first chapter of Genesis to the Book of Revelation, whose author "testifies to everything he saw—that is, the word of God" (Rev. 1:2). In the simplest terms, God uses human language to tell us things.[3]

Objections to the Doctrine of Verbal Revelation

There are challenges to the adequacy of human language as a vehicle of divine revelation.[4] James Barr and Dennis Nineham, for example, together with certain adherents of the biblical theology movement, contend that human language is historically conditioned and therefore restricted. They contend that any revelation in human language will suffer from these limitations. Many missiologists also view language as the medium of a particular culture and therefore as limited and culturally conditioned. As a consequence, any revelation in human language will lose something in the translation from culture to culture. Both these analyses seem to interpret the verbal component in revelation as "the Word behind the words of Scripture" or as supracultural truth that can be expressed only in the Bible's culturally conditioned language. There is also the objection that human speech cannot carry content outside of sensory experience, which would mean that it cannot convey God's self-disclosure of his nature and will.[5]

---

3. Packer, "Adequacy of Human Language," 206; see also Wayne A. Grudem, "Scripture's Self-Attestation and the Problem of Formulating a Doctrine of Scripture," in *Scripture and Truth*, ed. D. A. Carson and John D. Woodbridge (Grand Rapids: Zondervan, 1983), 19–59.

4. Paul R. Wells, "Covenant, Humanity, and Scripture: Some Theological Reflections," *WTJ* 48 (1986): 20.

5. Donald Bloesch asserts that human language concerning God is either metaphorical or at the most analogical. Such language points beyond itself to a supernatural reality that transcends the compass of human cognitive faculties (*Essentials of Evangelical Theology*, vol. 1, *God, Authority, and Salvation* [New York: Harper & Row, 1978], 75).

None of these factors figures in the biblical view of human language. The Bible ratifies it over and over as the medium to convey divine revelation. As the sovereign Lord of history, God declares in one time period what will happen in a later period and brings it to pass. He uses human language to make promises, give commands, and disclose future events. Human language is not assumed to be historically conditioned, but is unhesitatingly enlisted to communicate meaning over time. In a psalm celebrating the God of Israel, David explicitly states that God's covenant promise is forever, "commanded, for a thousand generations" (1 Chron. 16:15). The Sabbath ritual in Israel is "for the generations to come as a lasting covenant" (Exod. 31:16). The prophets declare that God's decrees span time. "I foretold the former things long ago, my mouth announced them and I made them known; then suddenly I acted, and they came to pass" (Isa. 48:3; see also 37:26; 65:24). When the New Testament apostles recognize fulfilment of a prophecy, they point to the transhistorical revelation by introducing the Old Testament quotation with phrases such as "it stands written" or "it was fulfilled what was spoken" (e.g., Mark 1:2; Matt. 2:15; 12:17).

Jesus declares himself to be the only way to the Father, and his apostles assert that there is salvation in no one else (John 14:6; Acts 4:12). Jesus commands that this single message be taken to all nations (Matt. 28:18–20). It cannot be disputed that God intends the same message given by verbal revelation to be taken to persons of all cultures, and it follows logically that human language must be adequate for the task. Culturally conditioned limits would render the assignment impossible. As the apostles set out to fulfil their mission, they understand that God intends, according to the Old Testament promise, to gather into one people believers from many nations (Acts 15:16–18/Amos 9:11–12). If the one message is applicable to all cultures, the language in which it was revealed must not have cultural conditionedness as its basic characteristic. Paul's cross-cultural witness is conclusive proof (Rom. 10:11–15). He presents his message, the word of Christ, as the means by which faith is awakened in all who believe. "For there is no difference between Jew and Gentile—the same Lord is Lord of all and richly blesses all who call on him, for, 'Everyone who calls on the name of the Lord will be saved'" (vv. 12–13).

That words are well fitted for communication between God and human beings is confirmed by their being the medium whenever God offers self-disclosure. In the encounter at the burning bush when God makes himself known to Moses, he speaks, cautioning Moses to respect his holiness and declaring his identity and his name: "I am the God of your father, the God of Abraham, the God of Isaac and the God of Jacob. . . . I AM WHO I AM" (Exod. 3:6, 14). Language is the designated carrier for this awesome revelation. At Mount Sinai when Moses asks that he may see God's glory, the divine essence (33:18), God responds by coming down in a cloud; thus obscured, he stands with Moses and passes in front of him. Visible disclosure is too risky, so God resorts to words to proclaim his name as the Lord and his nature as "the compassionate and gracious God, slow to anger, abounding in love and faithfulness" (34:6).

God's holiness burns in such brilliant purity that sinners dare not look, lest they be consumed. Moses hides his face at the burning bush after God's holiness has been declared (Exod. 3:5–6). Limits are set about Mount Sinai to protect the people, and they are warned not to break through, for fear they might see God and perish (19:20–21). Moses himself, who communicates with God "face to face," must be hidden in the cleft of the rock while God causes all his glory to pass by (33:21–23). Since such extreme precautions are not called for in verbal communication, one can hardly avoid the conclusion that language is the proper vehicle for revelation. Moses has to hide his face, but he does not stop his ears. In the New Testament, the divine disclosure follows the same pattern. In the incarnate Son of God the glory is veiled in flesh, but his words declare who God is by making him known (John 1:17–18; 14:6–11).

It is true that at times God chooses to make his verbal communication unintelligible to some, who hear it as thunder, a trumpet blast, or a strange sound (Exod. 19:9, 16–19; John 12:28–29; Acts 9:7; 22:9). In each such instance the extraordinary sign authenticates the divine source of the verbal communication, which comes simultaneously. While the air fills with reverberations, the one for whom the message is intended hears and understands words. Even Jesus, who needs no intermediary, receives messages which use words.

When the people hear thunder and trumpet at Sinai, they tremble and ask Moses to beg God not to speak with them, lest they die. Moses tells them not to fear and explains that the purpose of God's thundering is to test them, "so that the fear of God will be with you to keep you from sinning" (Exod. 20:20). The affirmation of verbal propositional revelation as the means of divine self-disclosure cannot be idolatry, since language is the essential ingredient in God's telling us things about himself.

Those who do not hold that divine revelation is in its very nature verbal often understand it as dynamic activity in which God reveals himself in mighty acts in history. Any words involved are, they say, either human interpretation of the historical acts or information communicated in culturally controlled conditions. James Barr points to the flaws in such an approach: "If we persist in saying that this direct, specific communication must be subsumed under revelation through events in history and taken as subsidiary interpretation of the latter, I shall say that we are abandoning the Bible's own representation of the matter for another which is apologetically more comfortable."[6]

---

6. Barr, "Interpretation," 201–2.

Speech first,
act second

God communicates his information by means of direct, specific speech. Any visible actions are subsidiary. While God's acts seem necessary to the validation of his word of prophecy, the word is still primary. It is the basis for the fulfilment and the source of the prophecy's meaning and significance. Without verbal explanation, the significance of the Spirit's outpouring at Pentecost would be just as obscure to us as it was to the first onlookers. "Amazed and perplexed, they asked one another, 'What does

no more
visions?

this mean?'" (Acts 2:12). But through Joel the prophet, God had revealed that such an event would happen in the last days (Joel 2:28–32). Peter the apostle now declares that this event fulfils Joel's prediction and that it means that salvation is for everyone who calls on the name of the Lord (Acts 2:16, 21). Merrill Tenney provides a precise summary of the relationship: "God has spoken, and His utterance has eventuated in corresponding action. This action appears in His providential guidance of the trends of history as they contributed to the fulfillment of His purpose and to the coming of the Messiah, the Servant who would speak His Word."[7]

Eugene Nida and Charles Kraft maintain that revelation consists in God's dynamic acts and not in language. Nida contends that the Hebrew *dbr* word group points to event as the medium for biblical revelation.[8] An assessment of the evidence does not support this conclusion. According to Earl S. Kalland, "as 'word' *dābār* basically means what God said or says. . . . The *dābār* is sometimes what is done and sometimes a report of what is done."[9] When used to refer to a thing or event connected with God, *dābār* usually appears in a context of promise and fulfilment. The *dābār* is the event that fulfils God's previously given word. For example, the Lord predicts Isaac's birth (Gen. 18:10). Sarah laughs, and the Lord remonstrates with her, "Is anything [*dābār*] too hard for the Lord?" (v. 14; see also Ps. 105:27; 145:5; Isa. 38:4, 7).

Kraft similarly argues for a dynamic understanding of revelation, appealing to John 14:6; 18:31–38; and 15:10–11, where he claims that truth is presented as personal, active, and dynamic rather than simply as true information.[10] He also argues that Paul's discussion of revelation in 1 Corinthians 2:9–11 deals with the act of revelation, not the content. Analysis of the passage shows, however, that Paul is indeed concerned with wisdom, the content that God has revealed.[11] It is called a message of wisdom, God's

---

7. Merrill C. Tenney, "The Meaning of the Word," in *The Bible: The Living Word of Revelation*, ed. Merrill C. Tenney (Grand Rapids: Zondervan, 1968), 21.

8. Eugene A. Nida, *Message and Mission* (New York: Harper, 1960), 224.

9. *TWOT*, s.v. (*dābār*) word, speaking, speech, thing, anything (399a).

10. Charles H. Kraft, *Christianity in Culture* (Maryknoll, N.Y.: Orbis, 1979), 179.

11. Note Walter C. Kaiser's comment, "To conclude that God's revelation is merely the revelation of a person, or solely revelation of God's great acts in history, is to fail to hear the claims of vss. 6–9. Revelation is that, but it is also propositional: it is 'wisdom'" ("A Neglected Text in Bibliology Discussions: I Corinthians 2:6–16," *WTJ* 43 [1981]: 313).

secret wisdom, spiritual truths, things that come from the Spirit of God
(vv. 6–7, 13–14). Paul says that God has revealed this secret wisdom to us.
The rulers of this age and the natural man cannot understand this wisdom
(vv. 8, 14). But those who have received the Spirit from God can "understand what God has freely given us" (v. 12). It is impossible to avoid the
conclusion that the Bible understands revelation as verbal and propositional.

Truth

Any contemporary discussion of the biblical view of truth must address
the following concerns: How does the Bible identify the quality of truth? Is
truth transmitted only in propositions, the message of verbal revelation? Or
is truth characterized by personal or basically dynamic action? What is the
nature of truth? Is there one underlying theory of truth in the Bible? Or does
the Bible manifest a polymorphous understanding in which no single theory is adequate to explain the full range of the concept's meaning? Does
truth possess objectivity, absoluteness, and, at the same time, the possibility of being directly comprehended through inscripturated human language?

The Biblical Concept of Truth

Any study of the biblical concept of truth must take into account both the
'āman root in the Old Testament, particularly its cognates 'ĕmûnâ (firmness,
fidelity) and 'ĕmet (firmness, truth), and alētheia (truth) and its cognates in
the New Testament.[12]

Truth is a quality or state attributed to persons, things, and actions.[13]
God is by definition truth, the one true God, the source of truth. The Old
and New Testaments consistently identify him as the true God vis-à-vis
idols and the false gods of the nations. Jeremiah's polemic against idolatry
stresses the element of truth: "What the craftsman and goldsmith have
made is then dressed in blue and purple. . . . But the LORD is the true God;
he is the living God, the eternal King" (Jer. 10:9–10; see also 2 Chron. 15:3).
We meet the same perspective in Paul's words to the Thessalonians: "You
turned to God from idols to serve the living and true God" (1 Thess. 1:9; see
also John 17:3). God is also portrayed as faithful (Deut. 7:9; Rev. 6:10). Truth
is ascribed to all three persons of the Trinity. God the Father is the "God of

12. *TWOT*, s.v. ('āman) to confirm, support (116); Michael Darton, ed., *Modern Concordance to the New Testament* (Garden City, N.Y.: Doubleday, 1976), s.v. "True-Amen."
13. John V. Dahms, "The Nature of Truth," *JETS* 28 (1985): 455–66.

truth" (Isa. 65:16). The Son declares himself to be "the truth" (John 14:6; see also Rev. 19:11). The Holy Spirit is called the "Spirit of truth" (John 14:17; 16:13). Humans may also be true, faithful, and trustworthy, usually in contrast to being false and deceitful. "The LORD detests lying lips, but he delights in men who are truthful" (Prov. 12:22).

Truth also resides in God's words. Both Old and New Testament assert that God's verbal communication is true. "All your words are true" (Ps. 119:160); "your word is truth" (John 17:17). Truth is so integral a part of God's verbal communication that it is often termed "the word of truth" or simply "the truth" (Ps. 26:3; Col. 1:5–6; 1 Tim. 2:4), particularly in New Testament references to the gospel message (see Eph. 1:13). Human words can also be true. In the context of the law court Moses directs that a report or verbal testimony be investigated to see whether it is true (Deut. 13:14; 17:4). Paul commands the Ephesians to "put off falsehood and speak truthfully" to their neighbors (Eph. 4:25).

God's acts are also called true and faithful. "All the ways of the LORD are loving and faithful" (Ps. 25:10); "Just and true are your ways, King of the ages" (Rev. 15:3). Certain aspects of creation are called true or faithful. For example, the psalmist declares that God's covenant with David "will be established forever like the moon, the faithful witness in the sky" (Ps. 89:37). In addition, the Bible calls for true and faithful conduct. Such conduct can turn God's wrath to forgiveness. God commands Jeremiah to "go up and down the streets of Jerusalem, look around and consider. . . . If you can find but one person who deals honestly and seeks the truth, I will forgive this city" (Jer. 5:1). God desires us to live by the truth (John 3:20–21; 1 John 1:6).

Since truth can reside in persons, words, and actions, any analysis of the Bible's understanding of truth must take all three into account. Liberation theology views truth as a dynamic act that supersedes the need to locate the quality in words, even God's Word. At the same time, these theologians emphasize that the biblical understanding of truth includes the dynamic for life transformation. Charles Kraft also espouses this view.[14] But in salvation God chooses "to give us birth through the word of truth" (James 1:18). Jesus prays, "Sanctify them by the truth; your word is truth" (John 17:17). These instances and many others explicitly identify God's Word, his message, as truth. Defining truth as dynamic act confuses the effect with the cause and also cuts one off from the true cause, the gospel—the verbal message that is to be believed and obeyed (Col. 1:5; 2 Thess. 2:12; 1 Peter 1:22).

Many hold that the Bible's view of truth is essentially personal, citing as their authority John 14:6, in which Jesus declares himself to be the truth,

---

14. Kraft, *Christianity in Culture*, 179.

and John 1:14, which describes him as "full of grace and truth."[15] Such a proposition misunderstands the Scripture's view of the relationship between truth and persons. Another logical misstep occurs when it is argued that because the term *truth* is predicated of persons, its essence is basically personal in a way that cannot be accounted for if it is understood only as a quality of propositions, as true information. The Bible, however, offers no support for pitting one part of the data against the other. Truth can be present in a person or a proposition. The immediate context of these passages in John also carries implicit or explicit reference to words of truth. In expounding for the disciples what it means for him to be the way and the truth and the life, Jesus tells them that these words are not his own, but come from the Father, who lives in him, and that by believing these words one sees the Father. And in its context John's proclamation that Jesus is full of grace and truth stands as a contrast to the law of Moses, a contrast that is effective because truth involves verbal content as the law did. A comprehensive definition of truth must extend its existence to persons, words, and actions.

The traditional correspondence concept of truth, that whatever is true corresponds to reality, provides the most suitable framework for the biblical understanding of truth. Roger Nicole defines the biblical understanding of truth as "that firm conformity to reality that proves to be wholly reliable, so that those who accept a statement may depend on it that it will not turn out to be false or deceitful."[16] When applying the concept of truth to persons, words, and actions, we can readily see that correspondence to experience, facts, and events—in short, to reality—is the measure of truth. Though the correspondence theory has been under attack in recent years, it is the biblical view of truth.[17]

The declaration that the God of Israel is the true God means that his nature and actions correspond to what deity should be and do (Jer. 10:10). False gods and idols are a "fraud; they have no breath in them" (v. 14). "Man-made gods are no gods at all" (Acts 19:26). The God revealed in the Bible is the one true God (1 Thess. 1:9). He declares his nature in his name "I am who I am"—the unconditioned, ever-existent, living God. He is not worthless, futile, or unable to accomplish and sustain his works. Paul urges the Lystrans to "turn from these worthless things to the living God, who made heaven and earth and sea and everything in them. . . . He has shown kindness by giving you rain from heaven and crops in their seasons; he provides you with plenty of food and fills your hearts with joy" (Acts

---

15. Ibid.

16. Roger Nicole, "The Biblical Concept of Truth," in *Scripture and Truth*, 288. See also Norman L. Geisler, "The Concept of Truth in the Inerrancy Debate," *BS* 137 (1980): 327–39.

17. *NIDNTT*, s.v. "Truth," especially pp. 894–901.

14:15, 17; see also Ps. 104:13–15; Jer. 14:22). The Scriptures refer to the Father as the God of truth and to the Son and the Spirit as truth itself (Ps. 31:5; John 14:6; 1 John 5:7), thus affirming that God is ultimate reality.[18] God himself guarantees the objective reality of the world and everything in it. He makes it possible for truth to exist. When considering the quality of truth in any object other than God in his essence, one must use the principle of correspondence. When God's words—his revelation in its variety of forms—are affirmed as true, in each case truthfulness signifies that the words correspond to existing states of reality.

Both David and Solomon pray that God's promises to establish David's house forever may come true (1 Chron. 17:23–24; 1 Kings 8:26). True promises are those that are fulfilled in such a way that the results match the words. Laws are true when they correspond to justice and right. God's laws are true because their content corresponds to his own righteous character (Ps. 33:4; 119:150–52; Rom. 2:20). His righteousness is contrasted to wickedness, deceit, and falsehood. The psalmist proclaims, "I walk continually in your truth. I do not sit with deceitful men, nor do I consort with hypocrites; I abhor the assembly of evildoers and refuse to sit with the wicked" (Ps. 26:3–5). In contrast to "godless myths and old wives' tales," the gospel is declared to be the truth (1 Tim. 4:7; 2 Peter 1:16–18). Again the distinction is based on correspondence to reality. The gospel represents itself as divine revelation because it is the Word of God (1 Thess. 2:13). If God has actually revealed it, the gospel may be considered the word of truth, as it is consistently presented in the New Testament (e.g., Eph. 1:13; Col. 1:5; 2 Thess. 2:12). This revelation occurs in space and time, and those who bear witness to it are reporting what they have seen and heard (Luke 24:48; 1 John 1:1–3).

In just such a context the early Christians viewed themselves as witnesses and invited investigation of the content of their message, especially the resurrection, to see if it was true, if it fit the facts. Peter's witness to Cornelius carefully details the eyewitness support for the gospel message (Acts 10:39–42). Paul witnesses to Agrippa, "What I am saying is true and reasonable. The king is familiar with these things, and I can speak freely to him. I am convinced that none of this has escaped his notice, because it was not done in a corner" (26:25–26). Such detailed witness is required to establish the grand claim of the gospel message to be of divine origin, the good news from God himself. The gospel message is established as true because its witness to God's saving acts corresponds to what actually did occur. The New Testament message shows God's revelation to be true because it declares the fulfilment of Old Testament prophecy; what God said he would do he has done, and what the prophet's words predicted has happened.

---

18. Dahms, "Nature of Truth," 458ff.

Fulfilment demonstrates that the prophecies are true; they correspond to reality as it exists in the observable fulfilment.

The Bible never shrinks from this criterion as the test for distinguishing between true and false prophecy. Very early in their national life the Israelites asked, "How can we know when a message has not been spoken by the LORD?" Moses relays God's answer, "If what a prophet proclaims in the name of the LORD does not take place or come true, that is a message the LORD has not spoken" (Deut. 18:21–22; see also Jer. 23:25–29). According to Isaiah, fulfilled prophecy is one of the chief evidences that God is the only true God. God calls forth witnesses to testify to what he has done (Isa. 43:8–11; see also Dan. 8:26; 10:1). The New Testament consistently emphasizes that Jesus' saving death and resurrection have fulfilled the Old Testament prophecy (e.g., Luke 24:46–48; Acts 2:31–32; 13:27; 1 Cor. 15:3–4). Peter declares, "But this is how God fulfilled what he had foretold through all the prophets" (Acts 3:18). Whether as promise, law, gospel, or prophecy, God's words are true because they correspond to reality.[19]

One approach to biblical truth emphasizes faithfulness as its foundation rather than truthfulness or correspondence of words to facts. Faithfulness is certainly a divine characteristic, one that Scripture emphasizes (Deut. 7:9; 32:4; Isa. 25:1). God is faithful in carrying out his covenant promises and his sovereign plan of salvation for human history. This faithfulness, however, is essentially different from truth and actually fills a subsidiary role, providing the sweep and setting in which God's words show themselves to be true. Faithfulness occurs over a period of time; God consistently commits himself to fulfilling his promises. The Bible frequently says that God's words are faithful and trustworthy (2 Sam. 7:28; Ps. 119:86; 1 Tim. 3:1; 4:9). But the two concepts are not synonymous, and faithfulness is not the primary idea. God's words are faithful and can be depended on because they are true, not the other way around. His words are true because they correspond to the way things are, just as the God of truth purposed them to be.

Two illustrations from contexts other than God's covenant dealings may help to bring the concept of correspondence to reality into focus. The first is a court setting where a report of idol worship is being investigated and

---

19. Kevin J. Vanhoozer basically agrees, but would reframe the affirmation to account for the various literary genres by which the truth is expressed. "While Truth may be 'about' Reality (what *is*), we only receive the full picture *of* Reality (*what* is) by contemplating 'true' history, 'true' parable, 'true' song, 'true' poetry" ("The Semantics of Biblical Literature: Truth and Scripture's Diverse Literary Forms," in *Hermeneutics, Authority, and Canon*, ed. D. A. Carson and John D. Woodbridge [Grand Rapids: Zondervan, 1986], 85). Vanhoozer's qualification can be helpful as long as false implications are not accepted. No matter the genre, a single, definite, fixed meaning is the goal of interpretation and is achievable to a greater or lesser degree. And as he himself points out, the various ways in which reality may be talked about do not create competing kinds of truth, but various kinds of *fact*, whether historical, metaphysical, or moral.

judgment must be handed down. "If it is true and it has been proved that this detestable thing has been done in Israel," the guilty party will be punished (Deut. 17:4–5). True words, true testimonies, are words that have stood the test of thorough investigation, have been confirmed by witness, and have been proved to correspond to the facts. Peter's understanding of his nighttime release from prison also illustrates what is meant by correspondence to reality. While the angel was conducting him out of the prison, Peter did not think that what was happening to him could be "real" (*alēthes*, Acts 12:9). But once outside the prison and awake, he knew "truly" (*alēthōs*, v. 11) that God had sent his angel to release him; the words and the facts corresponded.

Anthony Thiselton and Alan Johnson contend that the biblical concept of truth must be expanded beyond the correspondence theory.[20] To establish the correspondence theory as comprehensive, it will be necessary to show that correspondence to reality is the unifying concept which provides foundation for, and binds all facets of, the range of meaning of "truth." Thiselton argues that to cover the full range of meaning, truth must involve several concepts, not just one: (1) faithfulness; (2) the gospel of Christ; (3) what is real, or correspondence; (4) that which exposes; (5) and valid witness. We have already seen how truth as correspondence includes both facts and faithfulness. Correspondence is related to both; God and individuals who are faithful produce deeds that correspond with their words, and show that they have integrity and deal honestly (2 Kings 22:7; Ps. 25:10). The quality of faithfulness is a guarantee of truth, but is not truth itself. To understand what it means to be faithful, one must first know what truth is as it corresponds to reality.

The gospel of Christ is assuredly true and truth. But this proposition can be subsumed into the correspondence theory of truth. The gospel claims to be a message from the God of truth, not myth; since it is the only true way to know God and salvation, it can be called truth. In opposition to the lies of the devil, the gospel provides the knowledge of true facts, spiritual facts, that liberate when they are believed (John 8:31–34, 44–47). These spiritual facts represent spiritual realities, namely, the incarnate Son of God speaking a message from the Father and dying for the sins of the world, actual events of which the gospel speaks the truth.

To identify something as real—Thiselton's third category—one must rely on correspondence. The language of John, both figurative and literal, makes this clear. Jesus states that he is "the true bread from heaven . . .

---

20. Anthony C. Thiselton, *The Two Horizons: New Testament Hermeneutics and Philosophical Description, with Special Reference to Heidegger, Bultmann, Gadamer, and Wittgenstein* (Grand Rapids: Eerdmans, 1980), 411–15; Alan F. Johnson, "A Response to Problems of Normativeness in Scripture: Cultural Versus Permanent," in *Hermeneutics, Inerrancy, and the Bible*, ed. Earl D. Radmacher and Robert D. Preus (Grand Rapids: Zondervan, 1984), 260.

[who] gives life to the world" (John 6:32–33). There is inherent in this figure a correspondence of contrast with the manna of the wilderness experience. That divinely given bread provided physical sustenance, but is only a shadow of the bread that sustains unto eternal life. Jesus is the true bread because he gives eternal life—true life, participation in the life of God, who is ultimate reality. Thus in Scripture, when the term *true* in the sense of "real" is applied to something or someone, it means that the person or thing corresponds fully to the reality being depicted and asserted (e.g., John 1:9; 6:55; 15:1; Heb. 8:2; 9:24).

Thiselton's fourth category, truth as that which exposes, does not require a separate examination. Here, too, the pattern is one of correspondence to facts, especially spiritual facts, as opposed to deception (John 8:44–45). Thiselton's references for this category speak of either the Spirit as the Spirit of truth or the Spirit's testimony as the truth (14:17; 15:26; 16:13; 1 John 4:6; 5:6).

The final category, truth as validity of witness or testimony, again assumes the correspondence of verbal statements with events and situations. Truth is what distinguishes what is valid from what is not. Validity of testimony is determined by the agreement of multiple eyewitnesses to the same event (John 8:17). The assumptions here are that something happened and that a valid account consists of reports from witnesses that agree about the nature of the event. A particular testimony is established as valid by its agreement with that of other witnesses. In the final analysis, a valid witness or testimony is one in which the facts as stated correspond to the way the facts really are. In his continuing controversy with the Jewish leaders, Jesus followed the Mosaic rules for validating the testimony about himself; he cited another witness, John the Baptist (5:31–32; 8:13–14). Clearly we are not dealing with another category of the biblical concept of truth. Here as in the other examples, what is true is what corresponds to the facts. We have come full circle and in so doing have identified correspondence as the underlying concept which unifies all parts of the range of meaning.

The Objectivity and Absoluteness of Truth

Having formulated a biblical concept of truth, it is time to ask whether truth is objective and absolute. Radical cultural relativists will immediately answer no. Moderate epistemological cultural relativists assert that, at the very least, there is always a historical or cultural element embedded in the thought-categories of sender or receiver, probably both, that colors and distorts the formulation and comprehension of messages about reality. One can never be totally objective, a qualification that applies also to the truth being addressed.

To claim that there is absolute truth agitates the cultural and historical

relativists, but that is a challenge we must face, concentrating on the historical. Is it possible for a statement to be so absolutely true that the erosion of
time does not invalidate it? There is also a subsidiary question. If objective
and absolute truth exists, can human beings know it directly?

But first matters first: Does the Bible claim that the Scriptures as truth are
objective, absolute, and knowable? The psalmist answers affirmatively: "All
your words are true; all your righteous laws are eternal" (Ps. 119:160). Paul's
description in the New Testament is no less inclusive: "All Scripture is God-
breathed" (2 Tim. 3:16). If the Bible contains God's message, a message
framed so as to make a person wise for salvation and so as to teach, rebuke,
correct, and train, that message must have an objectivity that permits any
individual, no matter the culture, to apply it personally. If this truth is
intended to make a person wise to salvation and so thoroughly equip one
for every good work that no other instruction is needed, then its content
must of necessity be absolute. That its objective content is knowable is
presupposed by the purposes for which it was given and has been transmitted. Paul's remarks to Timothy give an indication of its power and importance: "From infancy you have known the holy Scriptures, which are able to
make you wise for salvation through faith in Christ Jesus" (v. 15). The
inference that the truth of Scripture is objective, absolute, and knowable is
unmistakable. It will be beneficial to gather evidence for each attribute from
the rest of Scripture to buttress this conclusion.

Scripture establishes the objectivity of God's truth in three ways. First, in
the biblical perspective true statements are those that correspond to facts
and events as they exist. Such statements are by definition objective, which
means that their truth is independent of the maker or hearer of the statements. In the final analysis, without objectivity there is no way to establish
the truth or falsehood of any statement. The angel in Revelation says,
"These words are trustworthy and true. The Lord, the God of the spirits of
the prophets, sent his angel to show his servants the things that must soon
take place" (22:6). The angel establishes the objectivity of God's true *words*
by linking them to events that must take place soon.

A second way that the Bible establishes God's truth as objective is by
emphasizing the source. The message comes from God, not from humans
in their cultural context. As we have noted, the gospel is consistently referred to as "the truth" or "the word of truth" (e.g., Col. 1:5–6; 2 Tim. 2:18).
Throughout his writings Paul consistently distinguishes the truth of God
from human content by using modifiers like *kata anthrōpon*, "according to
man," and *anthrōpinos*, "human" (Rom. 3:5; 6:19). To the Galatians Paul
declares, "I want you to know, brothers, that the gospel I preached is not
something that man made up. I did not receive it from any man, nor was I
taught it; rather, I received it by revelation from Jesus Christ" (1:11–12).

When such an understanding of the origin and character of divinely revealed truth is combined with the affirmation of human language as an adequate vehicle for such revelation, then its full objectivity can be confidently asserted.

However, affirming the full objectivity of divine revelation, we must still ask whether Scripture takes into account the role of the world-views of the sender and receptor in the communication of truth. The Bible does recognize this factor, but does not see it as capable of interfering with the objectivity of its truth. In fact, the role of the speaker and hearer can be acknowledged and corrected so that the truth will be heard. Agrippa interrupts Paul, "You are out of your mind, Paul! Your great learning is driving you insane." Paul replies, "What I am saying is true and reasonable" (Acts 26:24–25). Paul is recognizing his role as speaker and correcting Agrippa's estimate of it by affirming, in effect, "I am not insane." Paul's role does not diminish the objective truth of what he is saying. His report is true, and Agrippa can check it out, for what has been reported was not done in a corner. The receptor's mindset also plays a role, one acknowledged by Paul when he writes to the Thessalonians, "When you received the word of God, which you heard from us, you accepted it not as the word of men, but as it actually is, the word of God, which is at work in you who believe" (1 Thess. 2:13). That receptors have a certain presuppositional grid and therefore can place a wrong evaluation on the truth they hear does not mean the truth is any less objective. Rather, because the truth is objective, it is possible to hear the message as it *truly* is so that the true meaning of the gospel will be maintained. Paul makes it clear that he had to deal with some interference in transmitting the gospel to the Galatians (2:5, 14). But his goal was achievable because the truth of the gospel is by nature objective.

The absoluteness of divinely revealed truth, as opposed to historical relativism, is consistently asserted throughout Scripture. Aware of time and its normal effects on creation, the Bible points to God's continuity, referring to his decrees as "ancient laws" (Ps. 119:52) and to the sweep of redemption history—"In the past God spoke to our forefathers through the prophets . . . but in these last days he has spoken to us by his Son" (Heb. 1:1–2). The Scriptures dare to take the most enduring aspects of creation and declare that God's Word, the Law and the Prophets, is more permanent: "It is easier for heaven and earth to disappear than for the least stroke of a pen to drop out of the law" (Luke 16:17; see also Ps. 119:89–91; Matt. 5:17–19). In other words, the least change that would alter the meaning of a word (be it merely the change of one letter) and in turn invalidate its authority will not happen to God's law. Its truth is absolute and never to be invalidated by any historical factor.

The absoluteness belonging to divinely revealed truth over time is explicitly claimed for God's promises, prophecies, and law. For example, we read in Isaiah 55:3, "Give ear and come to me . . . I will make an everlasting covenant with you, my faithful love promised to David." God made the Davidic covenant, knowing that fulfilment of his promise to David would span the generations. Paul notes how God's promises bridge time: "Christ has become a servant of the Jews on behalf of God's truth, to confirm the promises made to the patriarchs" (Rom. 15:8). There are two thousand years between the promises to the patriarchs and Christ's ministry in confirming them, yet they remain absolutely true throughout.

no △ time

The absolute truth of prophecy likewise maintains itself in the interim between the prediction and the time of its fulfilment. Daniel receives due instruction, "The vision of the evenings and mornings that has been given you is true, but seal up the vision, for it concerns the distant future" (Dan. 8:26; see also 10:1). The New Testament testifies to this absoluteness by pointing to the many fulfilled prophecies. Peter's proclamation at Pentecost includes a description of the prophetic process that spans history. A thousand years before Christ, David spoke of Christ's resurrection, and now God has raised Jesus, a fact of which the apostles are witnesses (Acts 2:30–32).

The absolute authority of God's moral law is also emphasized in Scripture: "Long ago I learned from your statutes that you established them to last forever" (Ps. 119:152). The law is seen to be as firm as the heavens and the earth: "Your word, O LORD, is eternal. . . . Your laws endure to this day" (vv. 89–91; see also v. 160). Those who declare God's law to be obsolete, relative in its authority, normative for a bygone age but not for another, are not telling the truth about God's law, for "until heaven and earth disappear, not the smallest letter, not the least stroke of a pen, will by any means disappear . . . until everything is accomplished" (Matt. 5:18). Breaking God's law as well as teaching others to do so does not affect the absolute truth of the law; it simply makes the perpetrators least in the kingdom of heaven, if they enter at all (vv. 19–20).

There are some moderate epistemological relativists who would affirm the existence of absolute truth, but deny that one can know absolute truth directly. Truth comes only in a culturally conditioned form, which is the mode of expression of a given culture. This issue was dealt with in our discussion of the adequacy of human language for divine revelation, but there are some words of Jesus in the Gospel of John that effectively encapsulate the factors in the knowability of divinely revealed truth. Jesus is well aware of the gulf between God and human beings. "You are from below; I am from above. You are of this world; I am not of this world" (John 8:23). Jesus' line of argument suggests that because of their sins the crowd cannot understand and know that he is telling them absolute truth. They will die in their sins; they are enslaved to sin; they have no room for Christ's word;

they are of the devil, the liar; they do not belong to God (vv. 24, 34, 37, 44). *[handwritten marginal note: Sin, Not our finite mind, prevents us from knowing]* Our finite mind does not prevent our knowing absolute truth, but our sin and spiritual deadness do. Those who belong to God hear what he says. "The reason you do not hear is that you do not belong to God" (v. 47).

Jesus repeatedly stresses that his incarnation has bridged the gap between above and below, between earth and heaven. He was present with the Father and is also now in this world. He has spoken absolute truth to humankind. "He who sent me is reliable, and what I have heard from him I tell [lit., speak into] the world. . . . [I] speak just what the Father has taught me. . . . I am telling you what I have seen in the Father's presence. . . . [I have] told you the truth that I heard from God" (John 8:26, 28, 38, 40). The incarnation has decisively broken down any barrier between the noumenal and the phenomenal, the above and below.

What kind of response does Jesus expect from one who has heard his absolute truth? First there must be faith in him and in his message, which is *[handwritten marginal note: our response]* indeed absolute truth. Faith must be followed by holding to his teaching, remaining in his Word. As a result, one knows the truth. Truth sets us free from the power of sin and at the same time gives us a new birth that certifies our being numbered among those who belong to God (John 8:30–32, 36, 47).

Our apprehension or expression of absolute truth is of course incomplete and partial, but that does not make such apprehension or expression relative. Sin is the main barrier to knowing God's absolute truth. When that impediment is decisively broken by regeneration, we may confidently affirm that though our knowledge is not absolute, we do know God's absolute and divinely revealed truth, a truth that liberates.

The Bible presents divine revelation as God's using human language to tell us things. Revelation is in its very nature verbal and propositional. God used human language in oral or written form to communicate with and through the patriarchs, Moses, and the prophets in the Old Testament, and Jesus and the apostles in the New Testament. God's saving acts can be revelatory only if they are accompanied by his revealed interpretation.

The Bible teaches that truth may be descriptive of persons, words, things, or actions. Therefore truth as personal should not be pitted against truth as information. Since divine revelation is verbal and propositional, it is true information. The correspondence theory of truth—true words fit the facts of reality—is the biblical view. It serves as a basic framework for all other meanings of the biblical concept of truth. The Bible sees truth as objective, absolute, and capable of being known directly, as well as expressed in inscripturated form.

15

Language and Meaning

Since God communicates his revealed truth in human language, it would be well to examine the biblical view of the nature of language. Where does the Bible locate the origin of meaning in verbal communication? Does the Bible see meaning, and especially its own meaning, as definite and literal as opposed to metaphorical, as single rather than multiple or many-layered, as fixed and stable instead of indeterminate and amorphous? Is meaning a matter of the author's intent, or is it textually or contextually generated? What role does context play in the determination of meaning? What is the impact of the text's literary-grammatical structure, of the ancient historical-cultural context, and the contemporary cultural context?

Sign Theory of Meaning

Current semantic discussion of the nature of meaning has produced a multiplicity of theories, each of which seems incomplete and inconclusive and therefore unable to account for all the factors involved in communicating meaning. For our purposes we must look for the theory that expresses most fully the biblical understanding of meaning and provides the best starting point from which to account for the factors that constitute meaningful communication of divinely revealed truth. The traditional sign theory of meaning, which is conceptualism, fills this prescription best. According to conceptualist theory, the locus of meaning in verbal communication is in *def* the author's intended sense in regard to an extralinguistic referent, a sense conveyed by linguistic signs (i.e., words). Certain missiologists prefer a functionalist approach to meaning, which sees the locus of meaning as the linguistic-cultural context.[1] In this view, language functions as a system of verbal symbols originating in human convention and is used to describe objects and behavior, not eternal essences. The Genesis account of Adam's naming the animals (2:19–20) is often cited as substantiation for this view. Yet when we look at all the elements in the Genesis passage and set it in the larger context of the creation accounts, it seems to presuppose an approach to language that accords better with the traditional sign theory of meaning.

The Genesis Account

The Genesis creation account describes the origin and use of language.[2] God speaks, and elements of the physical universe come into being. "God said, 'Let there be light,' and there was light" (1:3). The creative power of God's words calls worlds into being. Human language also has creative *creative* power. Certain language forms create realities by declaring them to be, as in *power* the case of the covenant between man and wife in a marriage ceremony or of any other contract or compact. There is also artistic linguistic creation; words have the power to disclose a world, an imaginative universe. This function, however, is not the basic purpose of language or the primary mode for creating meaning.[3]

From the creation account forward, the Bible follows an instrumental approach to language and its purpose. Language functions as a tool to communicate information. Thus, immediately after using language as a means of creation, God names what is created: "God called the light 'day,' and the darkness he called 'night.' . . . God called the expanse 'sky' [*šāmayim*] . . . the dry ground 'land' ['*ereṣ*], and the gathered waters he called 'seas' [*yamîm*]" (Gen. 1:5, 8, 10). He then uses these designations in communicating the cultural ordinances for man, the creature in his own image. "Fill the earth ['*ereṣ*]. . . . Rule over the fish of the sea [*yām*] and the birds of the air [*šāmayim*]" (v. 28). The assignment of names to various components of the created order from the very beginning suggests that the

---

1. Eugene A. Nida, *Message and Mission* (New York: Harper, 1960), 224.
2. Carl F. H. Henry, *God, Revelation, and Authority*, 6 vols. (Waco, Tex.: Word, 1976–1979), 3:390ff.; see also Gordon H. Clark, "Special Divine Revelation as Rational," in *Revelation and the Bible: Contemporary Evangelical Thought*, ed. Carl F. H. Henry (Grand Rapids: Baker, 1959), 41; idem, *Religion, Reason, and Revelation* (Nutley, N.J.: Craig, 1961), 134–35.
3. James I. Packer, "The Adequacy of Human Language," in *Inerrancy*, ed. Norman L. Geisler (Grand Rapids: Zondervan, 1979), 209.

Bible views reality as essentially segmented.[4] Humankind is created in God's image with the power of speech, the potential for using signs and symbols, a capacity indicated by God's addressing Adam in language. Not only is he commanded to reproduce and fill the earth, instructions the fish and birds also receive (v. 22), but he is commanded to undertake activities that require cognitive understanding and rationality. He is to rule over the rest of creation; he is told that plants are to be his food; he is to cultivate them; he is given the prohibition not to eat of the tree of knowledge of good and evil; and his sovereignty over the animal kingdom includes naming the animals (vv. 28–29; 2:16–17, 19–20).

The naming of the animals juxtaposes the segmented reality of the divinely created universe and the human symbolizing potential, the ability to create words and to use them to stand for aspects of reality. Genesis 2:19 indicates the permanence of the relationship between word, meaning, and reality: "Whatever the man called each living creature, that was its name."

Humankind is seen using its power to create language and meaning before there is any societal context to provide a locus of meaning. The world is inhabited by one man with the power to create meanings. The woman is not yet created, and the narrative explicitly states that God has assigned the task of naming the animals to Adam in a situation that has no shared meanings. In such a setting the man creates and uses meaningful language. The evidence of the text offers no support for a functionalist theory of meaning that places the locus in sociolinguistic context. A theory that locates meaning in conventional use is also out of place here, for Adam assigns meanings to words as he applies them to referents in reality. There is no socially supplied vocabulary stock from which to extract conventional meaning. The creation of words having assigned meanings that refer to identifiable objects in segmented reality fits very neatly into the traditional sign theory of meaning.[5]

The functional approach to language, which locates meaning in sociocultural context, can deal only empirically with the diversity of discrete languages as they currently exist. It has no implements for dealing

---

4. Robert E. Longacre argues against radical epistemological relativism in linguistics by pointing out that languages segment certain aspects of reality in a rather consistent manner and that "this points to a 'natural' segmentation of reality perhaps inescapable for us as human beings" ("Review of *Language and Reality* by Wilbur M. Urban, and Four Articles on Metalinguistics by Benjamin Lee Whorf," *Language* 32 [1956]: 304).

5. See H. C. Leupold's comment that the process indicates a high level of intelligence and that to name is to give "a designation expressive of the nature or character of the one named" (*Exposition of Genesis*, 2 vols. [London: Evangelical Press, 1942; reprint 1972], 1:131). Cf. Gerhard von Rad's approach, which sees language as a means of giving form to the confusion of the world. Naming is an act of appropriate ordering "by which man intellectually objectifies the creatures for himself" (*Genesis: A Commentary* [Philadelphia: Westminster, 1961], 81).

with language as a generic phenomenon or for accounting for the commonalities of structure and dynamics that exist among languages.[6] The Genesis account provides the historical basis for the existence and priority of language vis-à-vis specific languages when it depicts one language serving for the whole world from creation to its confusion at the Tower of Babel (Gen. 1:1–11:6). The priority of language (vs. languages) comes from the origin of language as an aspect of humankind created in the image of God with innate cognitive thought-structures (1:26–27),[7] another attribute that is compatible with the traditional sign theory of meaning.

The Bible presents a continuity in language from Adam to Babel, and there is no basis for concluding that the way of assigning meaning has changed. The divine intervention at Babel brought about instantaneously the process that would have unfolded naturally over a longer period of time. Changes in meaning and ways of expressing meaning occur in a language in response to changing circumstances and experiences of its culture. Differences in physical environment will obviously have an impact on vocabulary. An Eskimo language will have numerous terms for designating snow and related phenomena, while the language of a people in a temperate climate might have only one. Differences in world-view and history also affect the language system. God's original plan for a diversity of cultures living in harmony across the face of the earth would have led in time to a diversity of languages.[8] Diversity of language, like diversity of culture, is secondary to the unity of humankind; but though secondary, it is an integral part of God's design. Still the diversity must be understood within the framework of elements common to all human beings as language producers and users, a principle inherent in the traditional sign theory of meaning.

The Biblical Perspective on Translation

The biblical perspective on translation is also in accord with the traditional sign theory. This becomes readily apparent at those points where the New Testament reproduces a Hebrew or Aramaic word or phrase in transliterated form and then translates it by giving the corresponding Greek word(s). This is the procedure followed in the announcement of Christ's birth: *Emmanouēl,* meaning, "God with us" (Matt. 1:23); in a narrative of healing: *Talitha koum!* meaning, "Little girl, I say to you, get up!" (Mark

---

6. Longacre, "Review," 300.

7. Henry, *God, Revelation, and Authority,* 3:389ff.

8. Claus Westermann asserts that the positive purpose of a plurality of peoples and languages is to provide "an abundance of potential for development in individual peoples" (*Genesis 1–11: A Commentary* [Minneapolis: Augsburg, 1974], 556.

5:41); and in an account of the passion: *Elōi, Elōi, lema sabachthani?* meaning, "My God, my God, why have you forsaken me?" (15:34). In each case the locus of meaning is assumed to be in an extralinguistic referent and sense indicated by the speaker when using the other language, which has now been transliterated. The Gospel writers communicate the same message by pointing to this extralinguistic referent and saying the same things about it, using appropriate terms in their own language. Such equivalence is indicated by the term *methermēneuō,* "translate." So *Emmanouēl* is rendered in Greek as *Meth' hēmōn ho theos; Talitha koum* as *To korasion,* [*soi legō,*] *egeire;* and *Elōi, Elōi, lema sabachthani* as *ho theos mou, ho theos mou, eis ti enkatelipes me?* As can readily be seen from this transliteration of both elements of the Greek text, the concern for a common meaning does not mean formal equivalence in the sense that each transliterated Hebrew or Aramaic form is represented by only one Greek word. In each of these cases more Greek forms are required to communicate the same meaning for a smaller number of transliterated forms. This of course results from the differences in structure between the languages. One can say "my God" with one word in Aramaic by taking the noun and adding a first-person possessive suffix. In Greek, as in English, two forms are required *(theos mou,* "my God").

By setting these equivalent forms side by side, translating one by the other, the New Testament asserts that translation is not only possible but can be complete from language to language. Though one language may require more forms to express the same thing, the assumption is that languages are flexible enough that each can fully communicate authorially intended linguistic meaning. The Bible gives no hint that translations are only approximate, as those who see the locus of meaning in sociocultural context contend.

Interpretation of Verbal Communication Within the Bible

Interpretation of verbal communication within the biblical text seems to operate within the framework of a sign theory of meaning. In the New Testament, interpretation or explanation is required for parables and for citations of Old Testament Scripture. The interpretation process in both cases is basically concerned with the referents and senses to which the words point. When the disciples ask Jesus to "explain to us the parable of the weeds in the field," he elucidates the spiritual reality or referent to which each physical detail points. "The one who sowed the good seed is the Son of Man. The field is the world" (Matt. 13:36–38). Philip, engaging the Ethiopian eunuch in conversation about the meaning of Isaiah 53:7–8, is asked, "Who is the prophet talking about, himself or someone else?" (Acts

8:34). Philip begins from that passage to preach Jesus. Interpretation involves identification of the extralinguistic referents and the meanings conveyed by specific messages. Only such an approach will permit an objective validation of interpretation. If the locus of meaning is the extralinguistic referent and sense to which the words point, then there is an objective context in which to judge the soundness of any given interpretation of the text.[9]

The biblical view of truth is that true statements correspond to reality, the way things are (see chap. 14). According to this standard, only statements whose meaning is rooted in extralinguistic referents and sense can be judged true or false. When meaning is found in social context, there is no essential connection with a referent in reality, and consequently the meaning cannot be judged objectively. In a decisive way the traditional sign theory is foundational to the biblical understanding of truth.

Objections to the Sign Theory

One of the major objections to the traditional sign theory of meaning in understanding language is that insistence on a stable relation between words and meaning does not take into account the fact that words change meaning from cultural context to cultural context and even, over a period of time, within the same context. Clark Pinnock points out that the Bible recognizes such semantic change over time.[10] An example is found in 1 Samuel 9:9: "Formerly in Israel, if a man went to inquire of God, he would say, 'Come, let us go to the seer,' because the prophet of today used to be called a seer." The word *prophet* has taken a new component into its semantic range, displacing a comparable part in the range of meaning for "seer." Alan Johnson cites "Man shall not live by bread alone" (Deut. 8:3) as an example of the need today to employ a word other than "man," because in late twentieth-century American English, "man" is used less and less as a generic designation for human beings.

Instead of undermining the stable relationship between word and meaning and the extralinguistic referent as the locus of meaning, the examples indicate that without such a relationship there would be no way of telling that change in meaning has occurred. To understand that "prophet" and

---

9. There is support in the philosophy of language and linguistics for such an approach to language and interpretation. See William P. Alston's *Philosophy of Language* (Englewood Cliffs, N.J.: Prentice-Hall, 1964), 12. He describes a sophisticated referential theory that avoids the problems of the referential fallacy. A number of scholars see an extralinguistic locus of meaning as necessary for a message to be actually communicated, accurately translated, and validly interpreted (Alan Gardiner, *The Theory of Speech and Language*, 2d ed. [Oxford: Clarendon, 1951], 7–8; Gustaf Stern, *Meaning and Change of Meaning, with Special Reference to the English Language* [Göteborg, 1931], 30ff.; Stephen Ullmann, *The Principles of Semantics*, 2d ed. [Oxford: Blackwell, 1957], 85).

10. Clark H. Pinnock, *The Scripture Principle* (San Francisco: Harper & Row, 1984), 108.

"seer" have the same meaning, a common extralinguistic referent must be assumed, the prescient man of God, to which both terms point. The obsolescence of "man" as a translation for *hā'ādām* can be properly understood only when we note that the generic component of the range of meaning for the Hebrew word is what the author pointed to and that a faithful translation into another language at a given point in time will use a form that points to the same generic meaning. So today one should probably use the gender-neutral term *person* to translate *hā'ādām*. A problem arises only when one identifies the permanence of the form-meaning relationship in terms of the core meaning of a word, in this case, "man, male." However, core meanings are abstractions, and only that part of the range of meaning that the author shows through placement of the term in a literary-grammatical context communicates what the term meant then and how it should be translated now.

A stable relation between word and meaning in a given utterance at a given time does not imply that the range of meaning for words does not change over time. The range does change. Nor does a stable relation imply that exact formal equivalence can be found between words of different language systems, that terms in one language system have coterminous ranges of meaning with terms in another. The existence of a stable meaning for any given word, as used in a specific sense by an author in reference to an extralinguistic correlative, means that the same locus of meaning can be realized in another language system through its creative capacity to describe ever-changing reality. Herein lies the possibility for translation, for saying the same thing, though one is removed in time and place and culture from the original context of the utterance.

Literal or Figurative Meaning?

In our discussion of human language as adequate to express divinely revealed truth and the human ability to know absolute truth directly, we touched on the problem of whether such divinely revealed truth is communicated by means of definite and explicit or metaphorical and figurative language. The issue needs to be dealt with more fully. It is true that the Bible communicates divine truth in both figurative and literal expression. We need look only at God's encounter with Adam and Eve immediately after the fall to see this. God's questions are literal: "Where are you? . . . Have you eaten from the tree that I commanded you not to eat from?" (Gen. 3:9, 11). He uses figurative language, however, when issuing the curse: "By the sweat of your brow/you will eat your food/until you return to the ground,/since from it you were taken;/for dust you are/ and to dust you will return" (v. 19).

Since both modes of expression, the literal and the figurative, are present, is there any indication in the way they are presented that the Bible views one type as more basic and more appropriate for its message? Plain and literal meaning can be shown to be more basic, for even when Scripture presents God's message in figurative language, a literal interpretation with a plain and definite meaning is usually provided. This is certainly the case with Old Testament interpretation of visions and acted parables of the prophets (e.g., Dan. 7:1–14, 15–28; Ezek. 37:15–17, 18–27). It also occurs when the prophet receives a figurative message identified as a parable (*māšāl*). Twice Ezekiel is given a parable to utter, one a story about two eagles and a vine and the other about an encrusted cooking pot (17:1–10; 24:3–5). In each case a literal interpretation follows, identifying the elements in the story with current aspects of Israel's rebellious history (17:11–24; 24:6–14). The first eagle is the king of Babylon; the crust in the pot is Jerusalem's lewdness. Though the interpretation skilfully interweaves literal and figurative language, the purpose of providing a definite meaning is apparent, and the definite meaning can be applied and interpreted in terms of God's coming judgment.[11]

The metaphorical approach to meaning developed for literary criticism asserts that words in a written piece have a metaphorical meaning that is self-contained and self-regulated within a self-generated system of referents. While such a paradigm may be useful for determining meaning in a piece of literature which by its nature is intended as an imitation of reality, it is inappropriate as a construct for interpreting Scripture. Scripture is intended not simply to imitate reality, but to make true statements about it. Even when an imaginative genre such as parable is used, the larger aim is still operative. For this reason one looks in the parable's interpretation for definite meaning that can be formulated as truth statements and applied to reality.

Some biblical interpreters insist that religious language must be metaphorical. They point to the New Testament parables, particularly those that occur without interpretations, to substantiate their claims. Even when interpretations are present, they are dismissed as secondary additions.[12] The basic pattern and purpose we observed in the Old Testament is present in the New. There is, however, a major difference that needs to be examined.

---

11. See A. S. Herbert's characterization of the purpose of the *māšāl*. In the Old Testament it had "a clearly recognisable purpose: that of quickening an apprehension of the real as distinct from the wished for . . . of compelling the hearer or reader to form a judgment on himself, his situation or his conduct" ("The 'Parable' [MĀŠĀL] in the Old Testament," *SJT* 7 [1954]: 196).

12. It is a commonplace of parable study to conclude that the interpretations are secondary, not the authentic words of Jesus (Joachim Jeremias, *The Parables of Jesus*, 2d ed. [London: SCM, 1963], 77–79). The continuity of pattern and purpose between Old and New Testament parables indicates the opposite, however (see I. H. Marshall, *The Gospel of Luke: A Commentary on the Greek Text* [Grand Rapids: Eerdmans, 1978], 323–24).

hey...

...and why

Jesus does not give an interpretation for his parables unless an explanation is requested. I suggest that this selective approach is not intended to show preference for metaphorical over definite, plain speaking. Rather, Jesus is providing an unsurpassed opportunity for the exercise of the one thing needed for understanding—faith. Those who ask for an explanation are depending on Jesus alone as the source of God's message. He says to his disciples, "The knowledge of the secrets of the kingdom of God has been given to you, but to others I speak in parables, so that, 'though seeing, they may not see; though hearing, they may not understand'" (Luke 8:10).

When Jesus uses figurative language in a parable without interpretation, the metaphors communicate no meaning at all.[13] They function to raise questions in the hearer's mind with regard to preconceived notions and judgments about spiritual matters. It is the first step in what A. S. Herbert described as "quickening an apprehension of the real as distinct from the wished for."[14] Only to those who ask for an interpretation, a literal explanation with definite meaning, will understanding come. The Gospels depict Jesus explaining his parables to his disciples and answering their questions (Matt. 13:36; 15:15; 16:5–12; Mark 4:33–34; Luke 8:9–10). The fact that only a few of the parabolic sayings have extensive explicit interpretation does not indicate that metaphoric language is best suited to communicate divine truth. Jesus frequently told his parables in such a way that the definite meaning was immediately apparent. "When the chief priests and the Pharisees heard Jesus' parables [e.g., the parable of the wicked husbandmen], they knew he was talking about them" (Matt. 21:45). Sometimes the Gospel writer points in the direction of the interpretation as he introduces a parable. This assistance combined with Jesus' own application makes the parable's interpretation, its definite meaning, clear. For example, Luke introduces the parable of the persistent widow with the comment, "Then Jesus told his disciples a parable to show them that they should always pray and not give up" (18:1). Jesus' application is a question, "However, when the Son of Man comes, will he find faith on the earth?" (v. 8). Jesus used parables to elicit a faith response from his disciples, so it seems reasonable to conclude that, in the case of the parables that occur without interpretation, Jesus expected the disciples to perceive the interpretation directly as they grew in faith. Following his lead, the early church handed on the parable tradition and the

two indirect methods of explanation

---

13. See I. H. Marshall's discussion of whether the *hina* that introduces the quotation of Isaiah 6:9 in Luke 8:10 indicates purpose, result, cause, or simply scriptural fulfilment (*Luke*, 323). The most natural rendering is purpose; though it is seen as harsh by many, it fits well with the context. One sees it as a harsh understanding of Jesus' ministry only if one does not take into account that it is God's prerogative to reveal. It is the role and responsibility of the audience to depend on nothing in themselves, not even their intellect, but in faith to depend on the Lord to provide the understanding. An uninterpreted parable offers the opportunity for such to happen.

14. Herbert, "'Parable,'" 196.

Gospel writers recorded it, assuming that their faithful readers could also exercise such direct spiritual insight.

Jesus speaks figuratively in warning his disciples to watch out for "the yeast of the Pharisees and Sadducees" (Matt. 16:6). When they interpret "yeast" literally, Jesus remonstrates with them for not understanding that it meant the teaching of the Pharisees and Sadducees. There was a definite spiritual reality to which the physical object as figuratively used was intended to point. The disciples' earlier observation of Jesus' miraculous provision of literal bread should have enabled them to perceive the definite spiritual meaning of the metaphor.

This brief consideration of figurative language as it occurs in parables shows that the language used to communicate divinely revealed truth conveys definite, not metaphorical meaning, even when framed in figurative terms. With a greater or lesser degree of certainty, we can express all of Scripture's truth in propositions of definite meaning, no matter in which form it was originally given.[15]

Stability of Meaning

We must now ask whether the meaning of language is stable. Is meaning, especially in the language of Scripture, single, fixed, and according to the author's intent? Or does meaning go beyond what the original writer intended because language is polyvalent and ever open to new understandings?

The Challenge of Process Hermeneutics

Process hermeneutics adopts the latter view. From this perspective words must be polyvalent in order to cope with ever-changing reality and because the words of an ancient text constitute a complex phenomenon which shows itself always open to yield new understandings for existential questions. This approach rejects any contention that a text, especially one which claims to communicate meaning in all historical periods, can have a single meaning that remains fixed and as the author intended.

The Bible disagrees. Scripture sees no contradiction in a message that is alive with meaning for every age, meaning that remains single and fixed

---

15. Clark, "Special Divine Revelation," 39; see also Ramesh P. Richard, "Methodological Proposals for Scripture Relevance. Part 1: Selected Issues in Theoretical Hermeneutics," *BS* 143 (1986): 17. Richard contends that it is possible for a literal interpretation to arrive at definite meaning and gives guidelines for the process.

according to God's intention as he first gave it. Peter picks up Isaiah's affirmation and sees it as applicable to the gospel: "For you have been born again, not of perishable seed, but of imperishable, through the living and enduring word of God. For, 'All men are like grass,/and all their glory is like the flowers of the field;/the grass withers and the flowers fall,/but the word of the Lord stands forever.' And this is the word that was preached to you" (1 Peter 1:24–25). Though the Bible recognizes the reality of change, it affirms a larger reality, the eternal immutability of God. This immutable God communicates, and his messages have the same quality. "Your word, O LORD, is eternal; it stands firm in the heavens" (Ps. 119:89). God himself is the guarantee that meaning can be single, fixed, and according to the writer's intent. Human beings made in his image are capable of receiving and communicating such messages. Scripture's enduring quality does not contradict its ability to be alive in each future generation. Rather, since its single meaning—truth—gives life, that meaning must remain the same in order to continue its life-changing work. If its meaning were indeterminate, constantly changing with the context, its source would be corruptible human beings, but its eternally constant meaning signifies eternal life for those who believe it. When Jesus asks whether his disciples will also defect in the face of hard teaching, "Simon Peter answered him, 'Lord, to whom shall we go? You have the words of eternal life'" (John 6:68).

a single fixed meaning

The Challenge of Literary Criticism and Sociology of Knowledge

Hermeneutical discussion from the perspectives of literary criticism and the sociology of knowledge also challenges the idea that meaning can be fixed and stable. In the view of literary critics the words of Scripture operate with semantic autonomy, creating a self-contained universe of meanings. As religious language, the words have many potential meanings, and it is this characteristic that permits the text to have meaning in a variety of historical and cultural contexts. The sociology-of-knowledge approach and Gadamer's philosophical hermeneutics contend that a text's meaning is constantly changing, since the locus of meaning or a component of it is the interpreter in his or her constantly changing sociocultural context. E. D. Hirsch, Jr., who is a literary critic, finds the indeterminacy-of-meaning approach flawed: "Quite clearly, to view the text as an autonomous piece of language and interpretation as an infinite process is really to deny that the text has *any* determinate meaning, for a determinate entity is what it is and not another thing, but an inexhaustible array of possibilities is an hypostatization that is nothing in particular."[16]

---

16. E. D. Hirsch, Jr., *Validity in Interpretation* (New Haven, Conn.: Yale University Press, 1967), 249.

The New Testament uses the Old Testament and applies its meaning in a way that refutes the concept of indeterminate meaning. The New Testament makes frequent use of the prophetic promises from the Old Testament that are now or will be fulfilled. Old Testament standards for truth and conduct are cited to validate New Testament teaching. Both of these practices require that Scripture have a single, fixed, authorially intended meaning.

Unless a prophetic prediction has a single and fixed meaning intended by the prophet-author that can maintain itself in spite of time and the historical process, its validity as true prophecy, substantiated by fulfilment at a later time, can never be established. Not only does the New Testament exhibit this understanding when it declares that a given prophecy has been fulfilled (e.g., Matt. 1:22–23; Rom. 11:26–27; 1 Peter 2:6), but the descriptions of the process of prophetic utterance explicitly indicate that such is the case.[17] Peter at Pentecost claims that Psalm 16:8–11 is fulfilled in Christ's resurrection because David "was a prophet. . . . Seeing what was ahead, he spoke of the resurrection of the Christ" (Acts 2:30–31). After quoting the prophecy and interpreting it, Peter goes on to say, "God has raised this Jesus to life, and we are all witnesses of the fact" (v. 32). That the meaning of the psalm is single, fixed, and authorially intended is essential if the argument is to carry any force.

Admittedly, Peter's interpretation of this passage as a messianic prophecy has been the subject of much discussion, since at first reading the psalm does not seem to refer to the Messiah but to David. Among some evangelicals this is taken as evidence that the dual authorship of Scripture, divine and human, produced a dual referent flowing from a single intended sense.[18] Other evangelicals view Peter's interpretation as a problem that cannot be satisfactorily resolved by comparing an exegesis of the psalm with Peter's explanation.[19] Still, as Walter Kaiser points out, the passage does give the New Testament view of what David intended to say, and in that sense it has great value for showing the biblical concept of the relationship between the meaning of a prophetic text and its fulfilment.[20]

---

17. Douglas J. Moo proposes that a broader understanding of fulfilment language (a New Testament event "fills up" an Old Testament motif) may be found at points where the *plēroō* words are used in introductory formulas stating that a particular historical detail is the fulfilment of a particular prophecy. Greek uses *plēroō* with words like "prophecy," "promise," "law," "obligation," "request" (Bauer, s.v. πληρόω; see LXX 1 Kings 2:27; 2 Chron. 36:21; Josephus *Antiquitates* 5.145). The idea normally is that words of promise or obligation have the possibility of being put into action by deeds and in that way showing their validity or authority or accomplishing their purpose. They are fulfilled. In the example Moo cites, this seems to be the meaning still called for (Matt. 2:15/Hos. 11:1). An event, Jesus' sojourn in Egypt, fulfils what the Lord spoke through the prophet ("The Problem of *Sensus Plenior*," in *Hermeneutics, Authority, and Canon*, ed. D. A. Carson and John D. Woodbridge [Grand Rapids: Zondervan, 1986], 191).

18. Elliott E. Johnson, "Author's Intention and Biblical Interpretation," in *Hermeneutics, Inerrancy, and the Bible*, ed. Earl D. Radmacher and Robert D. Preus (Grand Rapids: Zondervan, 1984), 417; see also Darrell L. Bock, "Evangelicals and the Use of the Old Testament in the New," part 2, *BS* 142 (1985): 309.

19. Moo, "Problem of *Sensus Plenior*," 211.

20. Walter C. Kaiser, Jr., *The Uses of the Old Testament in the New* (Chicago: Moody, 1985), 37–38.

It is interesting to note that Peter in his first epistle again reflects on the prophet's intended meaning and its fulfilment (1:10–12; see also 2 Peter 1:21). Peter says that the Spirit of Christ in the prophets was predicting the sufferings of Christ and the glory that was to follow. When they inquired about "the time and the circumstances" of fulfilment, it was revealed that they were serving not themselves but those of the last days to whom the gospel would be preached. There is also debate over this passage as to whether it describes a process involving *sensus plenior* and double fulfilment, meaning that the Old Testament authors wrote better than they knew, the divine author intending some meaning of which the human author was not conscious.[21] The prophets were careful to distinguish what they did know from what they did not; this would indicate that they were asking for additional information. Peter says as much, letting us know that their inquiry had to do with timing. "It was revealed to them that they were not serving themselves but you." In this passage the meaning at the time of promise is explicitly separated from its fulfilment in the future, and yet the fulfilment is recognized when it comes. For this to happen the Old Testament prophet had to deliver a message that meant what he intended to say and that would hold its meaning across the centuries.

Similarly, Scripture could not be used as a standard for truth and conduct unless its meaning is single and unchanging. The hortatory passages are often introduced by the formula "it is written"—*gegraptai*, the perfect tense of *graphō*. Use of the perfect tense indicates that what was written in the past has continuing validity into the present, an impossibility unless the meaning also continues single and true to its original intent. The New Testament appeals to older Scripture as a proof and authority for its truth statements, but these frequent appeals would have no force if the meaning of the Old Testament texts were not stable. Jesus quotes Deuteronomy 8:3 as a standard of truth in refusing Satan's invitation to turn stones to bread. "It is written: 'Man does not live on bread alone, but on every word that comes from the mouth of God'" (Matt. 4:4). In another context Paul declares, "For in the gospel a righteousness from God is revealed, a righteousness that is by faith from first to last, just as it is written: 'The righteous will live by faith'" (Rom. 1:17/Hab. 2:4). When Peter calls for holiness of life, he backs up his exhortation by saying, "For it is written: 'Be holy, because I am holy'" (1 Peter 1:16/Lev. 11:44).

---

21. Philip B. Payne says yes ("The Fallacy of Equating Meaning with the Human Author's Intention," *JETS* 20 [1977]: 249). Walter C. Kaiser, Jr., says no ("The Eschatological Hermeneutics of 'Epangelicalism': Promise Theology," *JETS* 13 [1970]: 93–96). See Raju D. Kunjummen's recent case for *sensus plenior* within an evangelical framework ("The Single Intent of Scripture—Critical Examination of a Theological Construct," *GTJ* 7 [1986]: 81–110).

We have stressed throughout this discussion of the scriptural view of meaning that the author's intention is a determining factor.[22] Formulas used in the New Testament to introduce quotations from the Old are again the main substantiating evidence. The New Testament consistently highlights the role of the human writer. This practice is not simply for the sake of identifying the source. John explains the unbelieving response of the Jews to Jesus' teaching by citing Isaiah: "This was to fulfill the word of Isaiah the prophet . . . as Isaiah says elsewhere" (John 12:38–39). Peter presents David as a prophet and introduces his words that speak of the resurrection of the Christ (Acts 2:25, 31). Paul introduces Old Testament substantiation of the "remnant" concept by saying, "Isaiah cries out concerning Israel" (Rom. 9:27).

The divine author is also highlighted. This occurs most naturally when the Old Testament quotation contains the reported speech of God. So Paul presents the divine oracle of Isaiah 42 by saying, "For this is what the Lord has commanded us" (Acts 13:47). Often the introductory formula is in the passive, with no expressed agent of action (what has been called the divine passive), though there is explicit reference to the human agent and implied reference to God as the ultimate source. For example, "This is he who was spoken of through the prophet Isaiah" (Matt. 3:3); "this was to fulfill what was spoken through the prophet Isaiah" (8:17). It is also interesting to note that an Old Testament quotation is sometimes introduced as God's words even though the passage was not originally recorded as divine speech. Jesus identifies Moses' editorial comment about marriage as God's words: "Haven't you read . . . that at the beginning the Creator 'made them male and female,' and said, 'For this reason a man will leave his father and mother . . .'?" (Matt. 19:4–5/Gen. 1:27; 2:24).

A number of times the New Testament introduces an Old Testament quotation with a concurrent reference to the role of both the divine and human authors. Sometimes it is the human author aided by God: "How is it then that David, speaking by the Spirit, calls him 'Lord'?" (Matt. 22:43). Sometimes it is God speaking through the human writer: "The Holy Spirit spoke the truth to your forefathers when he said through Isaiah the prophet . . ." (Acts 28:25). Many quotations are introduced by the simple phrase "it is written." But the fact that so many identify and point to the

---

22. New Testament scholars using literary criticism charge that to make such a claim is to participate in the "intentional fallacy." But as E. D. Hirsch, Jr., has ably pointed out, such a judgment is based on a misunderstanding of the intentional fallacy as originally conceived and applied. It had to do with the success of the author, the misconception that writers always convey what they intend. In fact, it is necessary to identify the intended meaning of the author with the meaning of the text if one is to make a judgment that the author has been successful (*Validity in Interpretation*, 12).

author as the source leads to the conclusion that the writer's intended meaning and the text's meaning are the same.

Two passages where the interpretation of an Old Testament passage is the issue also bear this out. Peter's argument concerning the messianic interpretation of Psalm 16 turns on what David intended to say about the resurrection of the Messiah (Acts 2:25–31). The Ethiopian eunuch's questions about Isaiah 53 center on the prophet's intention: "Tell me, please, who is the prophet talking about, himself or someone else?" (8:34). It should also be noted that New Testament writers consistently make conscious reference to their own intentions (Luke 1:1–4; John 20:31; Phil. 4:10–17; 1 Peter 5:12; 1 John 5:13).

Many evangelicals who agree that the text's meaning reflects the writer's intent disagree about whether the human and divine writer always intend the same meaning. Walter C. Kaiser, Jr., has championed what Darrell Bock has labeled the "full human intent" approach.[23] According to this view, the Old Testament prophets had a fairly comprehensive understanding of what they were declaring as the ultimate consummation of God's promises. The divine intent and the human intent were the same. There is no *sensus plenior* in which God's intended meaning supersedes the human author's understanding. Raju Kunjummen develops the opposite case and seeks to establish on biblical evidence that the human and divine author's intents are distinguished in Scripture and that human instrumentality in the production of inspired Scripture "does not demand the full participation of the speaker's will and judgment."[24] He points to the facts that a human author often simply reports the speech of God (Gen. 3:15), that inspired seers may hear but not understand revelation (Dan. 12:8–9), and that, according to 2 Peter 1:21, "men spoke from God as they were carried along by the Holy Spirit." He also argues from the phenomena of Scripture—the nature of messianic prophecy, prediction and fulfilment, and biblical types—that God's intended meaning for Old Testament passages may not always be what the human writer intended or understood.

Kunjummen convincingly establishes the distinction between divine author and human author in Scripture, a distinction borne out by the character of introductory formulas. The distinction, however, is one of source, not intention. God speaks, and the prophet reports his words. The fact that Daniel does not understand what he hears and yet reports it does not indicate that his intended meaning and God's are distinguishable, but that he has subordinated his own intention to the divine intention. Likewise,

---

23. Kaiser, "The Current Crisis in Exegesis and the Apostolic Use of Deuteronomy 25:4 in 1 Corinthians 9:8–10," *JETS* 21 (1978): 3–18; idem, "Legitimate Hermeneutics," in *Inerrancy*, 117–47; idem, *Uses of the Old Testament*. See also Darrell L. Bock, "Evangelicals and the Use of the Old Testament in the New," part 1, *BS* 142 (1985): 210–12.

24. Kunjummen, "Single Intent," 99.

Peter's reference to prophets' speaking from God makes no distinction in intent. Lack of understanding is presented as something of which the prophet or seer is aware and tries to correct, an indication that normally the prophet expected to understand what God said and to hand it on. Daniel asks, "My lord, what will the outcome of all this be?" (12:8). Peter notes that prophets to whom the suffering of Christ is revealed ask the time and circumstances in which it will occur. The prophet so weds his purpose with God's that when he does not understand or has not been informed about some aspect of the message, he inquires. The Scriptures, though they may distinguish between the human and divine source of prophecy, do not drive a wedge between human intention and divine intention. God speaks through the prophet; the prophet speaks by the Holy Spirit. The important point to bear in mind is that the single, fixed, and author-intended meaning of the text must be recovered by a grammatical-historical-literary study of the text in context.[25]

Kunjummen and others have pointed out that many uses of Old Testament material in the New seem unrelated to the meaning intended by the original writer. Many prophetic appropriations of the text (e.g., Matt. 2:15/Hos. 11:1; Matt. 27:9–10/Zech. 11:12–13 and Jer. 32:6–9; Acts 15:16–17/Amos 9:11–12) and appeals to the Old Testament for proof (Rom. 10:6–8/Deut. 9:4 and 30:12–14; 1 Cor. 2:9/Isa. 64:4; 1 Cor. 9:9/Deut. 25:4; Heb. 3:7–11/Ps. 95:7–11) "give the impression that unwarranted liberties were taken with the Old Testament text in the light of its context."[26] Some scholars espouse this argument and conclude that it is impossible to reproduce the New Testament's exegesis of the Old without violating the Old Testament context. Other exegetes see different factors in the New Testament's approach to the Old. Some contend that the early church used Jewish exegetical methods that were little concerned with respecting the original Old Testament context. Others insist, as we have noted, that as a result of the inspiration of Scripture there is a divine intent issuing in a *sensus plenior* that supersedes the original human author's intent. Still others see the evidence as mixed: "Can we reproduce the exegesis of the New Testament? . . . We must answer both 'No' and 'Yes.' Where that exegesis is based upon a revelatory stance, where it evidences itself to be merely cultural, or . . . circumstantial or *ad hominem* in nature, 'No.' Where, however, it treats the Old Testament in more literal fashion, following the course of what we speak of today as historico-grammatical exegesis, 'Yes.'"[27]

---

25. Norman L. Geisler, "The Relation of Purpose and Meaning in Interpreting Scripture," *GTJ* 5 (1984): 229–45.

26. Gleason L. Archer and Gregory C. Chirichigno, *Old Testament Quotations in the New Testament* (Chicago: Moody, 1983), xxviii.

27. Richard N. Longenecker, *Biblical Exegesis in the Apostolic Period* (Grand Rapids: Eerdmans, 1975), 219. See his discussion of approaches (pp. 214ff.); see also Moo, "Problem of *Sensus Plenior*," 184–204; Bock, "Evangelicals," part 1, 209–23.

But there is another option. We can conclude with Gleason Archer that "when due consideration is given to the basic message of the Hebrew passage and the particular purpose that the New Testament author had in mind (under the guidance of God's Spirit), in each case it will be seen that, far from wresting or perverting the original verse, the inspired servant of Jesus brings out in a profound and meaningful way its implications and connotations."[28] Thus we can affirm that the New Testament's authority extends to its interpretation of the Old, and that such interpretation does not violate the single, fixed, and definite meaning of the Old Testament text.

Even after establishing this point and clarifying the nature of meaning, there are still difficult texts to be dealt with, a task made easier when two distinctions are made. In dealing with fulfilment of Old Testament prophecy, it is helpful to distinguish between predictive prophecy and prophetic typology. For example, Matthew's use of Hosea 11:1 ("Out of Egypt I called my son") to describe Jesus' sojourn there does not violate the original context when the event is understood as the fulfilment of prophetic typology. Matthew presents the exodus deliverance of national Israel as "a prophetic event for which the coming of the Messiah as personal Israel was the antitypical fulfillment."[29] Paul also presents fulfilled prophetic typology in the phrase "Christ, our Passover lamb, has been sacrificed" (1 Cor. 5:7). The writer to the Hebrews deals heavily in biblical types, presenting the pattern of the tabernacle and its inner veil which God the Holy Spirit intended as a parable to teach about the spiritual realities of heaven and the approach to God (Heb. 8:5; 9:8–9). Moses furthered this typological intent by obediently making everything according to the pattern disclosed on the mountain.[30]

In the case of appropriation of Old Testament texts in nonprophetic contexts, a distinction needs to be made between interpretation and application, between the meaning of a passage and the significance. Whether the New Testament is interpreting or applying the Old Testament text can be determined by examining the introductory formula and the way it functions in the New Testament context. Thus Romans 10:6–8 does not, even with its *pesher* ("interpretation") form, give the meaning of Deuteronomy 9:4 and 30:12–14. It does not indicate that the writer of Deuteronomy inquires who would go up into heaven to bring the Messiah down. Rather, it gives the significance for the Christian of the dynamics of righteousness by faith as described in the Deuteronomy passage. In this example, the firmly

---

28. Archer and Chirichigno, *Old Testament Quotations*, xxviii; cf. Bruce Waltke's canonical approach (Bock, "Evangelicals," part 1, 219).

29. Archer and Chirichigno, *Old Testament Quotations*, 147.

30. These passages from Hebrews cannot properly be used as evidence that God's intent and Moses' were not the same. Cf. Kunjummen, "Single Intent," 106–9.

established meaning of the Old Testament text is the basis for its appropriation by the New.

Role of Context

If, then, the Bible rejects context as the locus of meaning, is there a positive role for context? At least three contexts impact the meaning of an ancient literary document: the grammatical-literary, the historical-sociocultural, and the reality contexts.[31]

The Grammatical-Literary Context

The grammatical-literary context involves both the immediate and larger literary context and also the vocabulary stock. The Scriptures, while not evidencing either a structuralist or functionalist approach to meaning, do see the immediate grammatical-literary context as essential for identifying within a range of meaning the particular meaning of a word the author employs in that context. Jesus' interpretational question about Psalm 110 is raised on the basis of context (Luke 20:41–44). David calls his son "my Lord." In context, the referent of "Lord" is qualified in such a way that he is shown to be greater than David. How can that be true of David's son the Messiah? The problem arises because meaning is identified by context. Other words in the context, namely, "Sit at my right hand," solve the puzzle. David calls the Messiah his Lord because he is the divine Son who would be exalted to the Father's right hand at the resurrection (Luke 22:69; Acts 2:32–34).

The Historical-Sociological Context

Language with its stock of vocabulary is also a part of the historical-sociocultural context. Since Scripture uses the human language, which entails words with wide ranges of potential meaning, to communicate its message, it is appropriate to investigate extrabiblical sources to discover how Greek and Semitic words were being used at the time of the Bible's writing. This does not imply, however, that revelation is culture-bound. The range of potential meanings found in extrabiblical literature does not determine the meaning of particular linguistic expressions in the biblical text. The total range of potential meanings is merely the raw material from which the

---

31. Charles R. Taber specifies the grammatical-literary and sociocultural contexts more precisely, dividing them into a total of seven ("Translation as Interpretation," *Interpretation* 32 [1978]: 136.

message is fashioned. The immediate grammatical and literary context indicates the meaning the biblical writer intends.

The term *exousia*, for example, has the following range of meaning in ancient Greek:

I. Power, authority to do a thing
  A. Ability to perform an act provided there is no hindrance
  B. Possibility granted by a higher authority, in terms of position or mandate, to do something (freedom, permission, authority); authority or power in legal, political, social, and moral areas
    1. Authority
      a. Right of position (king, property owner, parent)
      b. Right of authorization
      c. Right of moral freedom
    2. Power
      a. Official
      b. Delegated
      c. Moral
  C. Abuse of authority: license, arrogance
  D. Poetic license
II. Office
  A. Office, magistracy
  B. Body of magistrates
    1. Honorary title
    2. Spiritual authorities
III. Abundance of means, resources; excessive wealth
IV. Pomp
V. Crowd[32]

When Jesus declares in Mark 2:10, "The Son of Man has *exousian* on earth to forgive sins," the immediate grammatical-literary context, with "Son of Man" as subject and the infinitive "to forgive" modifying *exousian*, indicates that the writer intends authority as a right of position (meaning I.B.l.a.). Extrabiblical evidence provides the range of possible meanings, but the immediate context and the larger context of divine revelation, specifically the Old Testament Hebrew references to the authority of the Son of man in Daniel 7:13–14, identify the intended meaning. This is a distinctly biblical use since the authority referred to is spiritual, not simply moral. Divine revelation in the language of the time, then, means that the sociocultural context has a contribution to make through information about vocabulary

---

32. S.v. ἐξουσία in Henry G. Liddell and Robert Scott, *A Greek-English Lexicon*, rev. and aug. Henry Stuart Jones (Oxford: Clarendon, 1968); Bauer; and *TDNT*.

stock, but such a contribution serves rather than controls the divinely intended meaning.

The historical-sociocultural context of an ancient work includes the world-view, structures, and behavior patterns in which the original writer and audience participate. These factors provide an implicit background, some points of which the writer will make explicit. For example, Joseph's not eating with his brothers in Egypt is explained, "They served him by himself, the brothers by themselves, and the Egyptians who ate with him by themselves, because Egyptians could not eat with Hebrews, for that is detestable to Egyptians" (Gen. 43:32). John explains the Samaritan woman's surprise when Jesus asks her for a drink, "For Jews do not associate with Samaritans" (John 4:9). Sometimes implicit information is referred to without explanation. Luke uses a cultural term for the distance between the Mount of Olives and Jerusalem, "a Sabbath day's walk" (Acts 1:12), the distance which the rabbis had determined could be traveled on the Sabbath without violating the fourth commandment.

The use of background information from ancient thought and life is certainly valuable in illumining the text's meaning. Paul's words "For in Christ all the fullness of the Deity lives in bodily form" (Col. 2:9) are intelligible without reference to background information, but the deeper significance of this radical claim comes to light when we understand that "fullness" was a technical term for the divine in the Gnostic thought Paul was combating and that such thought, with its spirit-body dualism, could never affirm the incarnation the way Paul did.[33]

Scripture sometimes uses extrabiblical cultural information in expressing its own truth. On Mars Hill, Paul substantiates his point about the Creator's relationship to his creatures, human beings, by appealing to such a source: "He is not far from each one of us. 'For in him we live and move and have our being.' As some of your own poets have said, 'We are his offspring'" (Acts 17:27–28; Aratus *Phaenomena* 5).

Though extrabiblical cultural information may be used to illumine meaning, it must never be employed to limit or undercut the authoritative claims of Scripture. It is interesting that New Testament writers never use such information to interpret the Old Testament Scriptures they quote. Jesus condemned the Pharisees for using human traditions to overturn Scripture's authority in the matter of the fifth commandment. The rabbinic casuistry had developed a device for avoiding material aid to parents. One could declare to a parent, "Whatever help you might otherwise have received from me is a gift devoted to God." Jesus condemned the result: "You nullify the word of God for the sake of your tradition" (Matt. 15:5–6).

---

33. I. Howard Marshall, "Culture and the New Testament," in *Gospel and Culture*, ed. John R. W. Stott and Robert T. Coote (Pasadena, Calif.: William Carey Library, 1979), 32–33.

The Reality Context

The context of reality is essential in the setting forth of Scripture's true message, which corresponds to the way things are, the real world. The Scriptures generally distinguish between the definite meaning and the broader significance of a verbal message, a distinction denied by many in current hermeneutical discussion who so load the role of the interpreter with preunderstanding, existential concerns, and the need for application that significance and meaning run together. The Scriptures, however, preserve the distinction. When focusing on significance, the biblical writer will state explicitly why a particular event or object has spiritual import. The Hebrew elders are to explain the significance of the Passover to the younger generation when they are asked, "What does this ceremony mean to you?" (Exod. 12:26). The stone memorial at the Jordan is "to serve as a sign among you. In the future, when your children ask you, 'What do these stones mean [lit., mean to you]?' tell them . . ." (Josh. 4:6).

When the emphasis is on meaning in terms of content and intention, constructions normally translated into English by the verb "to mean" are employed. Aside from literal translation in the text (e.g., "Immanuel— which means . . ." [Matt. 1:23]), the Bible presents the meaning of phrases by identifying sense and referent. Mark reports that the disciples were "discussing what 'rising from the dead' meant" after Jesus foretold his passion (Mark 9:10). The intention of a speaker or a divine act is often emphasized. Ezekiel relays God's query, "What do you people mean by quoting this proverb?" (Ezek. 18:2). Even when dealing with an aspect of meaning that could also involve the significance of an event or message for the audience, Luke always emphasizes what God or his apostle intends to mean. The perplexed Pentecost crowd blurts out, literally, "What does this desire to be?" (Acts 2:12; see also 17:20). Peter is at a loss to understand what the vision of the sheet and unclean animals "might mean" (lit., "might intend to be," an optative form of the verb "to be" [10:17]). Jesus comes the closest to wedding meaning and significance when he challenges to proper interpretation and action the Pharisees who are objecting to his violation of their regulations: "But go and learn what this means: 'I desire mercy, not sacrifice'" (Matt. 9:13/Hos. 6:6; see also Matt. 12:7). But even here the distinction between meaning and significance remains clear. The Pharisees are to learn the meaning, and having understood it, they must then apply its significance to their circumstances.

From the creation account and the use of language in the rest of Scripture, it may be concluded that the Bible assumes a traditional sign or conceptualist theory of meaning. The locus of meaning is the author's intended sense about extralinguistic referents. That meaning, which is conveyed by words, is definite, single, and fixed. The presence of a divine author as well as human authors for Scripture does not undercut this definition. Understanding that at points the New Testament's use of the Old is a matter of drawing out its significance and applying its meaning helps us to explain why at first sight some New Testament usage does not seem to square with the original writer's intent. The Bible recognizes the value of the grammatical-literary context for identifying meaning. It is aware of the range of possible meanings in the extrabiblical historical-sociocultural context. It is always cognizant of the reality context in which it proclaims its true message. The Bible recognizes the difference between the meaning of a verbal message and its significance. It does not collapse one into the other.

16

Scripture and Spirit

The foregoing considerations of Scripture's teaching on the God who communicates have been laying the foundation for the questions we must now address. Does the Bible view itself as inspired revelation of God? Does it speak God's truth inerrantly? Is its authority unique, full, and final? How does it function authoritatively? Does the Bible view the canon as closed? Is there biblical support for the unity of Scripture? What is the Holy Spirit's role in communicating God's truth? The answers to these questions in conjunction with our understanding of revelation, truth, and meaning will determine in large measure our method of interpretation and application.

Scripture

Inspiration and Inerrancy

BIBLICAL EVIDENCE FOR THE INSPIRATION OF SCRIPTURE

Evangelicals have consistently marshaled biblical evidence to support the conclusion that the sixty-six books of the Old and New Testaments are by their own testimony the inspired Word of God.[1] The evidence may be

---

1. Alan M. Stibbs, "The Witness of Scripture to Its Inspiration," in *Revelation and the Bible: Contemporary Evangelical Thought*, ed. Carl F. H. Henry (Grand Rapids: Baker, 1959), 105–18; John W.

grouped in two categories: what the New Testament says about the Old, and what it says about itself. The New Testament expressly describes Old Testament Scriptures as "God-breathed" and states that they came into being when "men spoke from God as they were carried along by the Holy Spirit" (2 Tim. 3:16; 2 Peter 1:21). The formulas used by the New Testament writers to introduce Old Testament quotations often identify God as the source. This is the case not only when the quotation contains words spoken by God himself, but also when the words are those of the Old Testament writer. For example, God's words to Moses concerning the reward for obedience are introduced by Paul in 2 Corinthians 6:16 with the formula "as God has said." Jesus quotes the editorial comment of Moses on marriage ("for this reason a man will leave his father and mother . . .") as what the Creator said (Matt. 19:5/Gen. 2:24). Peter, quoting David's statement, "The kings of the earth take their stand . . . against the LORD" (Ps. 2:2), describes it as what God "spoke by the Holy Spirit through the mouth of your servant, our father David" (Acts 4:25). So closely do the New Testament writers identify what Scripture says with what God says that Paul, quoting God's words to Moses that make up the message to Pharaoh (Rom. 9:17/Exod. 9:16), says, "The Scripture says to Pharaoh."

How does the New Testament view itself? Here the evidence is not as plentiful, but it is just as strong. Peter refers to Paul's letters as containing some parts which are hard to understand and "which ignorant and unstable people distort, as they do the other Scriptures, to their own destruction" (2 Peter 3:16). Peter uses *graphas*, the technical term for the Scriptures, with the adjective *loipas*, meaning "the rest of" or "the other." Peter considers Paul's writings as Scripture, because they are in the same category as the Old Testament. New Testament writers indicate the parity between Old and New Testament writings in several ways. Peter does so in terms of authorship: "I want you to recall the words spoken in the past by the holy prophets and the command given by our Lord and Savior through your apostles" (v. 2). After using the introductory formula "for the Scripture says," Paul quotes the Old and New Testaments side by side: "'Do not muzzle the ox while it is treading out the grain' and 'The worker deserves his wages'" (1 Tim. 5:18/Deut. 25:4; Luke 10:7). Paul says that the apostles participate in the same process as did the Old Testament inspired writers, with the same result: "We speak . . . in words taught by the Spirit, expressing spiritual truths in spiritual words" (1 Cor. 2:13).[2] John holds the same

---

Wenham, "Christ's View of Scripture," in *Inerrancy*, ed. Norman L. Geisler (Grand Rapids: Zondervan, 1979), 3–38; Edwin A. Blum, "The Apostles' View of Scripture," ibid., 39–53; Wayne A. Grudem, "Scripture's Self-Attestation and the Problem of Formulating a Doctrine of Scripture," in *Scripture and Truth*, ed. D. A. Carson and John D. Woodbridge (Grand Rapids: Zondervan, 1983), 19–59.

2. The last phrase can be variously translated as "interpreting spiritual things in spiritual words," or "interpreting spiritual things to spiritual men," or "combining spiritual things with spiritual words." As Wayne Grudem points out, all are "translations compatible with this interpretation" ("Scripture's Self-Attestation," 365 n. 61).

view: "Then the angel said to me, 'Write.'" And he adds, "These are the true words of God" (Rev. 19:9).

Even this brief review of the major evidence for biblical inspiration reveals that the biblical understanding is a concursive view rather than a dictation theory on the one hand, or a vaguely defined divine-influence theory on the other. "God in his sovereignty so supervised and controlled the human writers of Scripture that although what they wrote was genuinely their own, and in their own idiom, it was nevertheless the very word of God, right down to the individual words."[3] The matter of biblical evidence was dealt with in our discussion of the intent of divine and human authors. That evidence supports a concursive view of inspiration (e.g., Matt. 22:42; Acts 4:25; 2 Peter 1:21).

OBJECTIONS TO THE DOCTRINE OF INSPIRATION

Biblical interpreters who do not affirm Scripture's divine inspiration sometimes take the position that as a human book, a product in history, Scripture cannot be inspired by God and speak transhistorical truth. Gotthold Lessing and Immanuel Kant both took this position. The contemporary form of this argument, grounded in a radical relativist epistemology, denies that biblical revelation received in an ancient culture can speak transcultural divine truth. Other critics deny inspiration on the grounds that Scripture has a theological diversity characterized by internal contradictions. The historical-critical method has led many to the position that the Bible contains historical errors that discredit divine inspiration.

Those who continue to affirm that the Bible is inspired often follow an approach that redefines inspiration. Peter Stuhlmacher and the WCC documents understand inspiration to be the effect the Scriptures create, their ability to inspire readers, to speak to them afresh in every age. Charles Kraft considers the Bible an inspired casebook, an expression of God's truth in terms of particular cultures. Its inspiration is attested by the fact that God has led the church to preserve and use it in a unique way to discern and follow God's leading. In James Dunn's opinion, the historical errors in Scripture and its cultural conditioning can be squared with inspiration, since Scripture's own teaching about its inspiration does not entail inerrancy.[4]

Some of the objections to the inspiration of Scripture and the defects in the redefinitions of inspiration have already been addressed in considering the epistemological framework of the Bible. It has also been determined that the Bible sees no impediment in human language to the communication of

---

3. D. A. Carson, "Recent Developments in the Doctrine of Scripture," in *Hermeneutics, Authority, and Canon*, ed. D. A. Carson and John D. Woodbridge (Grand Rapids: Zondervan, 1986), 29.

4. Cf. Clark H. Pinnock, *The Scripture Principle* (San Francisco: Harper & Row, 1984), 92, 98.

universal and eternal divine truth. The same is true for the cultural factors. Objections based on historical-critical assessment of Scripture require a response that goes beyond the scope of this work, which is concentrating on Scripture's teaching about itself. But a reply is possible, and D. A. Carson and James I. Packer have ably defended the internal unity of Scripture and the lack of contradiction even in its diversity.[5] Alleged historical errors have been consistently addressed by evangelicals. Gleason Archer's work is a helpful compendium.[6]

The Bible undeniably considers God's Word as alive, powerful, and inspiring (e.g., Heb. 4:12; 1 Peter 1:23), but the adjective *theopneustos*, "God-breathed-out," used of the Scriptures in 2 Timothy 3:16–17, goes far beyond these other descriptions. The declaration here is that the source and character of the Scriptures are divine. Just as breath passing over the vocal cords produces words from a human being (that person's "breathed-out" words), so God's breath, his Spirit, produced the words of the Bible. It is this inspired character that enables them to inspire. Charles Kraft, as we have seen, cannot admit such unqualified inspiration and dilutes the possibility with ethnocultural factors. James Dunn, as we shall see, desires to affirm both inspiration and errancy.

THE BIBLE AND INERRANCY

Does the Bible itself claim to be inerrant? Yes; its own witness is that it teaches truth, and it affirms again and again that God's Word is true (John 17:17). It grounds its claim to unlimited truthfulness in its author—God, who never lies (Titus 1:2). According to the psalmist, God's commands are perfect in the absolute sense (119:96).[7] Two statements by Jesus focus the issue precisely. The first—"I tell you the truth, until heaven and earth disappear, not the smallest letter, not the least stroke of a pen, will by any means disappear from the Law until everything is accomplished" (Matt. 5:18)—is straightforward. A passage in John is a bit more complex: "If he called them 'gods,' to whom the word of God came—and the Scripture cannot be broken . . ." (John 10:35). Scripture's message is so certain that the most enduring aspects of the natural world will pass away before the smallest letter or part of a letter can be removed. Why? Because even a small alteration could change the meaning. The bold conclusion is that nothing in this world is able to set aside Scripture's authority. This puts such conclusions as the one that there are errors in the biblical text on very shaky ground, for Jesus himself says that the Scripture cannot be broken, asserting

---

5. D. A. Carson, "Unity and Diversity in the New Testament: The Possibility of Systematic Theology," in *Scripture and Truth*, 65–100; James I. Packer, "Upholding the Unity of Scripture Today," *JETS* 25 (1982): 409–14.

6. Gleason L. Archer, *Encyclopedia of Bible Difficulties* (Grand Rapids: Zondervan, 1982).

7. See Grudem, "Scripture's Self-Attestation," 27–36, 58.

thereby that its authority cannot be overturned even by such tactics as trying to find errors and calling it wrong.

James Dunn, while affirming the inspiration and authority of Scripture, is not convinced that the Bible teaches its own inerrancy.[8] In his view, the two passages that teach biblical inspiration (2 Tim. 3:16–17; 2 Peter 1:20–21) do not indicate that the Bible is inerrant. It is true that neither passage specifically states that the Bible is true and without error. However, that attribute is inextricably entailed in the contrast each author is drawing. Paul warns Timothy that "evil men and impostors will go from bad to worse, deceiving and being deceived" (2 Tim. 3:13), and so Timothy is to remain steadfast in what he has been taught. Those teachings came from human agents and have been beneficial, but their ultimate source is God (vv. 14–15). Paul emphasizes this last point: "All Scripture is God-breathed" (v. 16). Scripture is a completely sufficient source for teaching faith and life, "so that the man of God may be thoroughly equipped for every good work" (v. 17). Paul contrasts the salvation that has come to Timothy through scriptural teaching and training with the deception that comes to evil men. Paul's exposition necessarily assumes that the Scriptures are completely true. Otherwise, his rationale would collapse.

In his evaluation of Scripture Peter contrasts "cleverly invented stories" (2 Peter 1:16) with the eyewitness accounts of Jesus' transfiguration. These accounts substantiate the word of the prophets about the Messiah's glorious return. Indeed, those prophecies did not originate by human interpretation, but "men spoke from God as they were carried along by the Holy Spirit" (v. 21).[9] Peter's argument brings the contrast full circle. Cleverly devised myths claiming to be true prophecy are in the end only human interpretations posing as divine oracles and cannot stand against the prophecy of Scripture, which comes not from the prophet but from God. Origin is an issue, but the issue is also truth. Which prophecy is really what it claims to be? Which prophecy is certain; which tells the truth so that what it says actually comes to pass? Peter asserts that the prophecy of Scripture, spoken by Spirit-inspired men, does tell the truth about what will happen. Peter characterizes biblical prophecy as truthful.

The most explicit claim to scriptural inerrancy is Jesus' statement "the Scripture cannot be broken" (John 10:35). Dunn partially accepts Leon Morris's paraphrase "Scripture cannot be emptied of its force by being shown to

---

8. James D. G. Dunn, "The Authority of Scripture According to Scripture," *Churchman* 96 (1982): 107–10. See Roger Nicole's critique, "The Inspiration and Authority of Scripture: J. D. G. Dunn Versus B. B. Warfield," *Churchman* 97 (1983): 198–215; 98 (1984): 7–27, 198–208).

9. An alternate understanding is that Peter is saying that prophecy should not be interpreted privately. But such a thought is irrelevant to Peter's line of argument here. See Michael Green, *The Second Epistle General of Peter and the General Epistle of Jude: An Introduction and Commentary* (Grand Rapids: Eerdmans, 1968), 89–90.

be erroneous," but claims that the point is not whether the psalmist was in error, but whether his words had significance.[10] Dunn would interpret "the Scripture cannot be broken" as, if we may paraphrase, "the Scripture cannot be emptied of its force by being shown to be without significance." Dunn correctly analyzes the form of the argument as a fortiori, but he misunderstands the function of the quotation in the passage.

The controversy is over the Jews' evaluation of Jesus' claim to be the Son of God. They call it blasphemy and have challenged the truthfulness of Jesus' words. Jesus counters with an Old Testament quotation introduced by "Is it not written?" This is a perfect periphrastic emphasizing continuing validity. The quotation is a divine declaration that those who receive God's Word for use in making judgments are "gods." Jesus argues that if those to whom God's Word comes are called gods by God, and if the Scriptures containing that statement cannot be emptied of their force by being shown to be untruthful, then the one whom the Father sanctified and sent into the world has much more right to say that he is the Son of God. The accusation of blasphemy is false because Jesus is truthful. His words correspond to his Father's. The point of the argument, then, is Jesus' truthfulness when he declares himself to be divine. He establishes his veracity through argument from the lesser (those who receive God's Word) to the greater (the one who comes from God). If the truth of the declaration concerning the lesser is to be accepted—"and the Scripture cannot be broken"—the second claim must be accepted. Thus, when all elements of the controversy are taken into account, the issue is truth and error, not significance and insignificance. Jesus' comment that the Scripture cannot be broken must refer to inerrancy if it is to function properly in the argument.

Dunn contends that the boundaries set by Jesus for the stability of God's law, the passing away of heaven and earth (Matt. 5:18), render this text ambiguous for those who appeal to it to substantiate inerrancy. Dunn does not take into account that the Old Testament references to the stability of the heavens and the earth are a positive comparative image for the continuing validity of God's covenant (Ps. 89:35–37; see also Gen. 8:21–22; Ps. 119:89–91). In this light, Jesus' assertion that the least part of a letter would not pass away from the Law until heaven and earth pass away is the strongest claim one could make for the continuing validity of the Law. Further, "until everything is accomplished" should be understood as a reference to the Law's achieving its intended goal either in the actions of those who obey it and so fulfil it, or in the actions of God who brings promised salvation or judgment to pass and so fulfils prophecy. In either case, Jesus claims an absolute authority for Scripture. He says that the meaning of God's Word will remain inviolate until its purposes are achieved. One of the ways that

---

10. Dunn, "Authority of Scripture," 109.

Scripture's meaning and authority could be undercut is for error to be found in it. Jesus' claims for Scripture in this passage, then, necessarily entail inerrancy.

Biblical Authority

As we saw earlier (pp. 45–47), James Barr has enunciated five key questions which the relativistic approach raises against biblical authority. These must now be addressed in an order that fits the case we are building. We will also consider an additional question about the extent of biblical authority.

THE UNIQUE AUTHORITY OF THE BIBLE

Barr's fourth question is, Is the Bible a *unique* authority, or is it simply one authority among many that may be appealed to for principles of theology and ethics? The Bible claims to be a unique authority, basing this claim on its source, on its edifying nature, and on the inviolability of its content. The Bible as divine revelation comes from the one true God. Paul describes such revelation as a mystery, a message that one can understand only when it is revealed by God. Paul's gospel is "the proclamation of Jesus Christ, according to the revelation of the mystery hidden for long ages past, but now revealed and made known through the prophetic writings by the command of the eternal God" (Rom. 16:25–26). Such an origin gives Scripture a unique authority; no other authority can rival it. Its message is from above; all other messages are from below, either from demons (1 Tim. 4:1) or from human beings, whose authority can never be placed on an equal footing with that of divine revelation. Paul captures the difference as he contends that he does not speak the wisdom of this age, but "God's secret wisdom, a wisdom that has been hidden and that God destined for our glory before time began. None of the rulers of this age understood it, for if they had, they would not have crucified the Lord of glory" (1 Cor. 2:7–8).[11]

The benefit of Scripture is fully sufficient and provides another evidence of its unique authority. Paul insists that the benefit of inspired Scripture for faith and life is fully adequate and that those who receive its teaching are "thoroughly equipped for every good work" (2 Tim. 3:17). No supplement is needed to prepare them for action in good works.

Both the Old and New Testaments contain strong warnings against adding to or taking away from Scripture. The old covenant is given with the stipulation, "See that you do all I command you; do not add to it or take away from it" (Deut. 12:32). The only holy and true God is speaking, whose

---

11. See Walter Kaiser, "A Neglected Text in Bibliology Discussions: 1 Corinthians 2:6–16," *WTJ* 43 (1981): 301–19.

word is inviolable, which necessarily means it must have unique authority.[12] At the very end of the Bible, the Book of Revelation sounds the same note: "I warn everyone who hears the words of the prophecy of this book: If anyone adds anything to them, God will add to him the plagues described in this book" (22:18). Treating the Bible as one authority among many amounts to adding other words to those of Scripture and is a violation of this command.

The use of Scripture by Jesus and the early church both for witness and for edification demonstrates its unique authority. Jesus places his own mission under scriptural authority when he declares that he has not come to destroy the Law and the Prophets but to fulfil them. And we see him living out this proclamation by consistently appealing to the Old Testament text when confronting theological and ethical issues raised by his adversaries. A question about the reality of personal resurrection is answered by appeal to the scriptural record of God's statement to Moses at the burning bush (Matt. 22:31–32/Exod. 3:6). The question of divorce is handled by pointing the inquirers to Genesis (Matt. 19:4–6/Gen. 1:27; 2:24). Jesus places his saving work—his death and resurrection—under the authority of the whole Old Testament: "Everything must be fulfilled that is written about me in the Law of Moses, the Prophets and the Psalms. . . . The Christ will suffer and rise from the dead on the third day" (Luke 24:44, 46 [see also 22:37]/Isa. 53:12). In matters of salvation, faith, and life, Jesus cites—and he himself follows—Scripture as the unique authority.

The early church adopts the same pattern. Its saving witness is grounded in the unique authority of God's Word. Defending himself before Agrippa, Paul contends, "I am saying nothing beyond what the prophets and Moses said would happen—that the Christ would suffer and, as the first to rise from the dead, would proclaim light to his own people and to the Gentiles" (Acts 26:22–23). Paul follows the same principle in his evangelistic preaching as he consistently appeals to Scripture (e.g., Acts 13:32–37/Ps. 2:7; Isa. 55:3; Ps. 16:10). Before a Gentile audience, the well-read Paul in proclaiming his gospel occasionally refers to such secular authorities as the Stoic poets (Acts 17:28), but only as a confirming illustration. His primary proclamation is based on God's revealed will; all else is secondary.

Paul consistently affirms Scripture's benefit as a guide for faith and life (e.g., 2 Tim. 3:16–17; Rom. 15:4) and just as consistently appeals to Scripture in doctrinal and ethical matters. When arguing for the certainty of the resurrection, he quotes Isaiah (1 Cor. 15:54/Isa. 25:8). When giving ethical guidance, he refers to the Old Testament moral law (Rom. 13:8–10/Exod. 20:13–15; Lev. 19:18).

---

12. Grudem, "Scripture's Self-Attestation," 29.

The pattern is the same in the early church. Instruction and edification are grounded on the authority of the Old Testament. Since the New Testament also views itself as God's Word, this unique authority attaches to it as well.

THE FINAL AUTHORITY OF THE BIBLE

The Bible's unique authority logically implies that it must be the highest and the final authority as well. When Enlightenment thought submitted everything, including the Bible and its teaching, to the test of reason, it challenged this unique authority and actively sought to undermine it. Such disruptive ideas should be rejected. Any proposal that affirms the Bible as one authority among many equal authorities or places tradition on an equal footing also violates the biblical teaching.

Even the assertion of multiple authorities, with Scripture as the final one, as suggested by Alan Johnson and Harvie Conn, must be carefully handled to ensure that the Bible does in fact continue to exercise final authority.[13] The danger arises when a scriptural view is contradicted by a view on the same subject generated by a recognized human authority such as the behavioral sciences. In such cases the Scripture's interpretation, evaluation, and provisions are authoritative. The Scripture presents situations calling for such choices. For example, in arguing for chastity Paul cites slogans of the day popular with the Corinthians: "Everything is permissible for me" and "Food for the stomach and the stomach for food" (1 Cor. 6:12–13).[14] To demonstrate the faultiness of the view that sex is simply another physical appetite to be gratified at will, just as one eats when one gets hungry, Paul appeals to Genesis—"The two will become one flesh" (2:24). He is showing that something happens in the physical union that makes this attribute of human nature much more than just another physical appetite, indeed, so much more that sexual relations outside of marriage constitute a sin against one's own body (1 Cor. 6:16, 18). In this argument, Paul uses Scripture as the unique and final authority, maintaining its understanding of the proper use of human sexuality in the face of ancient society's decadence.

Another approach to the matter of Scripture as the final authority is indicated by Barr's third question: Is biblical authority final in the sense that the divine revelation has ceased and the canon is closed? Both the World Council of Churches and Charles Kraft dispute the idea that revelation, or at least inspiration, has ceased. The WCC documents argue from the perspective of inspiration, citing the arresting effect of Scripture as subsequently

Bible is the final authority

---

13. Donald W. Dayton discusses John Wesley's quadrilateral—Scripture, reason, tradition, and experience, with Scripture as final authority ("The Use of Scripture in the Wesleyan Tradition," in *The Use of the Bible in Theology/Evangelical Options,* ed. Robert K. Johnston [Atlanta: John Knox, 1985], 135.

14. Jerome Murphy-O'Connor, "Corinthian Slogans in 1 Cor. 6:12–20," *CBQ* 40 (1978): 394.

interpreted and applied by theologians and preachers, writers and thinkers, in different historical periods. Their efforts are viewed as the means for continuing revelation, that is, for God's message to come alive for individuals in every age. For Kraft, the dynamic quality of God's revelatory process in the divine-human encounter in Old and New Testament times makes it unreasonable "to believe that as soon as the last New Testament document was committed to writing, [God] totally changed his method of operation to such an extent that he now limits himself to the written record."[15]

What is the scriptural evidence that God intended the New Testament canon to be closed? David Dunbar develops such an argument, one worth following. Recognizing that the New Testament does not delineate the canon, he argues that biblical evidence still points to the New Testament canon as the "logical and organic development of certain principles resident in the New Testament documents and in redemptive-historical events that brought the church into existence."[16]

The New Testament specifically acknowledges the existence of the canon of the Old Testament by referring to its established divisions, either as the Law and the Prophets, or as the Law, the Prophets, and the Psalms (Matt. 5:17–20; Luke 24:44; Acts 24:14; 28:23). Just as often, Jesus and the New Testament writers appeal to the canon for authority by saying that all the Scriptures prophesied of Christ or that it is our duty to be instructed by all of Scripture (Acts 10:43; Rom. 15:4). Such appeals would be meaningless without a definable body of literature, an acknowledged canon, to indicate what the Scriptures are. New Testament writers often cite several texts, gathering them from each Old Testament division, to give their argument the added force of completeness. For example, to show that the mystifying Jewish rejection and Gentile reception of the gospel message were foreseen long before, first by Moses and then by Isaiah, Paul quotes the Law and the Prophets (Rom. 10:19–21).

The authoritative Old Testament canon played an influential role in shaping New Testament preaching and teaching. But another, even greater dynamic was at work. Jesus' own authority paved the way for a New Testament canon. God's Son, Jesus, was not only the final apostle and prophet; he was the embodiment of divine revelation, the Word incarnate. The writer to the Hebrews is very much aware of the process. In the past God had spoken to his people many times and in various ways, and now in these last days he "has spoken to us by his Son" (Heb. 1:2). The author of Hebrews musters all the linguistic power at his command to convey the fulness and finality of such a revelation: "The Son is the radiance of God's

---

15. Charles H. Kraft, *Christianity in Culture* (Maryknoll, N.Y.: Orbis, 1979), 212.
16. David G. Dunbar, "The Biblical Canon," in *Hermeneutics, Authority, and Canon*, 318.

glory and the exact representation of his being. . . . After he had provided
purification for sins, he sat down at the right hand of the Majesty in heaven"
(v. 3). John makes the same point more simply: in Jesus we see the Father
(John 14:9). God's eternally planned redemptive work has been accomplished once and for all in Jesus, who can now sit down at the Father's right
hand to signal its completion.[17] Jesus' incarnation, death, and resurrection
as the center of history have made a radical difference in the way God
relates to and communicates with the world. What was shadowy promise is
now an open secret, a mystery to be proclaimed as good news to the ends
of the earth (Rom. 16:25–27). To the Athenians, Gentiles afar off, Paul declares, "In the past God overlooked such ignorance, but now he commands
all people everywhere to repent. For he has set a day when he will judge
the world with justice by the man he has appointed. He has given proof of
this to all men by raising him from the dead" (Acts 17:30–31).

The finality of God's revelation at a particular point in time in the incarnate Christ shatters the logic of Kraft's expectation of continuing revelation.
It would be superfluous; there is nothing more to be said. This final revelation, the fulfilment of the old covenant and the inauguration of the new,
must of necessity be preserved in written form so that all persons of all
cultures in all succeeding generations can trust and obey the one true
gospel of grace and the rule of love. The role and authority that Jesus gave
the apostles indicate that he intended and provided for such a development.

The authority of the apostles is of primary importance in the argument
for a closed New Testament canon. In the enterprise of communicating
divine revelation, did the apostles have a function that was unique and
therefore restricted to the first apostolic generation? Or to put it another
way, did the process of revelation cease after that apostolic generation so
that the divine communication could be gathered into a fixed collection of
books, as the Old Testament writings had been? Is there biblical evidence to
indicate that the apostolic function was limited to so brief a period? The
apostles are presented as having been chosen individually by Jesus (Mark
3:14) and as having such close association with the earthly Jesus that they
knew his teaching and were eyewitnesses of the mighty acts of his ministry
and particularly of the resurrection. The risen Lord's Great Commission to
the apostles specifies teaching new Christians "to obey everything I have
commanded you" (Matt. 28:20). Many times Jesus instructs them in the
content of the gospel, as well as in authoritative interpretation of the Old
Testament (Luke 24:44–48; cf. 1 Cor. 15:1–4). When it becomes necessary to
select a replacement for Judas, Peter sets out the qualifications: "Therefore it

---

17. Philip Edgcumbe Hughes, *A Commentary on the Epistle to the Hebrews* (Grand Rapids: Eerdmans,
1977), 43, 47.

is necessary to choose one of the men who have been with us the whole time the Lord Jesus went in and out among us, beginning from John's baptism to the time when Jesus was taken up from us. For one of these must become a witness with us of his resurrection" (Acts 1:21–22).

Some might be inclined to view Paul's apostleship as evidence that divine revelation can continue beyond the first apostolic generation, the eyewitnesses. It must be noted, however, that Paul, though asserting his legitimate apostleship, acknowledges its extraordinary character and lays great stress on the time element: "And last of all he appeared to me also, as to one abnormally born" (1 Cor. 15:8). The word translated "abnormally born" points to abnormality in timing—"an untimely birth, miscarriage."[18] Paul became an apostle out of the proper sequence, being chosen by the risen Lord, who appeared from heaven after his ascension. Paul's selection was extraordinary in every way; he had no part in Jesus' earthly ministry. The norm is the experience of the Twelve and Matthias.

The authority accorded the apostles and their teaching in the early church is positively attested by the New Testament and further confirms the New Testament canon as the natural culmination of their work. The apostles are given the singular place as pillars and foundation stones in the body of Christ (Matt. 16:19; Gal. 2:9). It is "built on the foundation of the apostles and prophets, with Christ Jesus himself as the chief cornerstone" (Eph. 2:20; see also Rev. 21:14). The church devoted itself to their teaching (Acts 2:42). Though the New Testament warns against adhering to human traditions (Matt. 15:6; 1 Peter 1:18), it does not hesitate to command obedience to the tradition handed on by the apostles in doctrine (1 Cor. 15:3), in ethics (Rom. 6:17), and in ecclesiastical practice (1 Cor. 11:2). Writing at the end of the first apostolic generation, Peter ranks the apostles' teaching with that of the Old Testament prophets, indeed with the Scriptures (2 Peter 3:2, 16).

The apostles could hardly have exercised such a unique function unless it was Jesus' express intention. Speaking to them in the upper room, he promises to send his Spirit, who "will teach you all things and will remind you of everything I have said to you" (John 14:26). That Spirit "will testify about me. And you also must testify, for you have been with me from the

---

18. Bauer, s.v. ἔκτρωμα. George Nickelsburg identifies three other possible understandings of the figure's significance (in addition to temporal): (1) monstrous birth—Paul the persecutor in an abnormal manner becomes an apostle; (2) stillborn child, most wretched of men (see Job 3:16; Eccles. 6:3); (3) miscarriage, embryonic stillbirth, or incompleteness failing to reach potential. Nickelsburg opts for the third meaning and concentrates on how Paul's life as a persecutor seemed to cut off prematurely his appointment from his mother's womb (Gal. 1:15)—but God in grace saved him ("An *EKTPΩMA*, Though Appointed from the Womb: Paul's Apostolic Self-Description in 1 Corinthians 15 and Galatians 1," *Harvard Theological Review* 79 [1986]: 198–205). Nickelsburg, while relating the image to Paul's self-description, does not relate it to the heavy interest in the time sequence and eyewitnesses in the preceding context, elements which necessitate bringing into consideration the abnormal time factor concerning the last and least apostle.

beginning" (15:26–27). The Spirit will guide the apostles into all truth; he will take what is Christ's and speak it to them; he will show them things to come (16:13). Two of these passages emphasize that the Spirit is being sent to those who have been with Jesus from the beginning and have heard his teaching. Stressing that the Spirit's presence will fill Jesus' absence, the third passage lays great emphasis on this continuity between Christ and the Spirit. The Spirit will speak only what he hears from Jesus. To interpret these passages as evidence that the Spirit continues his revelation in the life of every Christian disregards the primary referent in each passage—the apostles.[19] Rather, the passages actually provide the foundation for understanding not only the unique, but also the final revelation which that first apostolic generation received.

why the
canon was
the logical
end-result
#1
The New Testament canon was the natural and logical end-product for such a revelatory process, a conclusion supported by two further practical considerations: (1) Since the apostles spoke God's universal truth, their message was for all, and the best way to disseminate and preserve that message was in a written form. The circular letters of the New Testament were the beginning of that process. Paul instructed the Colossians, "After this letter has been read to you, see that it is also read in the church of the Laodiceans" (4:16). Peter and John also sent circular letters (1 Peter 1:1; Rev. 1:11). (2) It was also essential to preserve in writing the oral witness of the
#2
first apostolic generation. They alone received the final revelation, and access to the authentic apostolic tradition can be had only through written documents. The New Testament canon, then, was not only the logical development of God's revelatory process, it was a practical necessity if the intended benefits of that revelation were to be received by people in all generations.[20]

One other factor in the environment of the early centuries made the New Testament canon a practical necessity. The presence of false teachers and doctrines made it necessary to distinguish the true gospel and the moral directives of God from false ones. Paul distinguishes between the true and false gospel (Gal. 1:6–9) and between healthy and false doctrine (1 Tim. 6:3, 20). John distinguishes between teaching flowing from true and from false anointing (1 John 2:26–27). Jude writes of the true faith once delivered to the saints and warns of the presence of godless people who try to alter that faith (vv. 3–4). Each writer is encouraging the Christian to hold fast to a defined body of divine truth in contrast to error. A closed canon defines the limits of truth.

19. Carl F. H. Henry, *God, Revelation, and Authority*, 6 vols. (Waco, Tex.: Word, 1976–1979), 4:276.
20. Dunbar, "Biblical Canon," 321.

The full authority of the Bible

Those who accept the Bible's unique and final authority still disagree on one question: In what sense can the Scriptures be said to have full authority? The approach articulated by Robertson McQuilkin asserts that a person should assume every teaching in Scripture to be universal and fully authoritative unless the Bible itself treats it as limited. Alan Johnson, Gordon Fee, and a number of other scholars operate on the assumption that the cultural factor in Scripture and the fact that much of Scripture is occasional literature, written to specific audiences, require treating each teaching as a specific word of God limited to its historical-cultural context unless Scripture indicates otherwise by expressly designating it as universal. These scholars hold that teaching that is specific to a given situation can also be binding, but only on the level of meaning or principle.

Scripture supports the concept of full authority in a number of ways.[21] As has been shown in other contexts, the Bible consistently asserts that the full range of its content bears witness to the gospel of truth. All the prophets testify of Christ's saving death and resurrection (Luke 24:44; Acts 10:43; see also Ps. 119:160). All Scripture is profitable for teaching, reproof, correction, and instruction in righteousness (2 Tim. 3:16). It was written, even the self-reflective psalms picturing Christ's suffering, for our instruction. All Scripture is universally applicable, either directly or indirectly. Scripture does not limit direct applicability because of cultural specifics in the text, as can be seen from the way the tenth commandment of the eternal covenant is framed with a mixture of general and culture-specific stipulations: "You shall not covet your neighbor's house. You shall not covet your neighbor's wife, or his manservant or maidservant, his ox or donkey, or anything that belongs to your neighbor" (Exod. 20:17).

If this is the perspective of Scripture, there should be instances in which the New Testament treats cultural factors in Old Testament passages as fully authoritative. There are indeed such examples in the citations about the social structure of marriage and parent-child relations (Matt. 19:4–6/Gen. 1:27; 2:24; Eph. 6:1–3/Deut. 5:16). The New Testament mentions several times the number of eyewitnesses necessary to establish the truth of testimony—"every matter may be established by the testimony of two or three witnesses" (Matt. 18:16; 2 Cor. 13:1; 1 Tim. 5:19/Deut. 19:15). Jesus appropriates this practice into the ecclesiastical disciplinary process. If a man is unsuccessful in a sincere attempt to be reconciled to a brother who has sinned against him, he is to take one or two others as witnesses and make another attempt. If this effort also fails, he is to report the matter to the

---

21. See George W. Knight III, "From Hermeneutics to Practice: Scriptural Normativity and Culture, Revisited," *Presbyterion* 12 (1986): 94–99.

church. The truth of the report will be established by means of the witnesses, in accordance with the Old Testament practice.[22]

While Scripture is fully authoritative for direct application of certain divinely mandated cultural factors, it should be pointed out that biblical writers are also very much aware of the historical and cultural differences between time periods and peoples. These are taken into account in several ways when Old Testament materials are appropriated. Often the appeal is to Old Testament moral directives or principles expressed in general terms. Paul says, "The entire law is summed up in a single command: 'Love your neighbor as yourself'" (Gal. 5:14/Lev. 19:18). Sometimes quotations are abbreviated to remove historical or culture-specific material. To encourage mutual giving, Paul cites the divine principle of equality that operated in the collection of manna in the wilderness: "He who gathered much did not have too much, and he who gathered little did not have too little" (2 Cor. 8:15/Exod. 16:18). From the original context Paul has omitted the words "and when they measured it out by the omer." When repeating the promise for honoring father and mother—"that you may enjoy long life on the earth"—Paul lifts it out of the Old Testament historical context by deleting the closing words "[the land] the LORD your God is giving you" (Eph. 6:3/Deut. 5:16). As A. Skevington Wood points out, "What was originally a specific assurance to the Jews becomes a generalization for Christians."[23] Specific Old Testament regulations are sometimes elevated to more general principles. Thus Paul quotes Deuteronomy 25:4, "Do not muzzle an ox while it is treading out the grain," in support of pay for Christian workers, and then he adds, "Is it about oxen that God is concerned? Surely he says this for us, doesn't he?" (1 Cor. 9:9–10).[24]

The occasional nature of the New Testament Epistles does not restrict the principle of full authority. Richard Longenecker makes a helpful distinction between tractate-type and pastoral letters, describing the former as general letters containing the characteristic teaching of the apostles targeted for wide dissemination and intended to convey apostolic presence and authority. Such letters did not have a specific situation in mind and consequently make few specific references. He classes Romans, Ephesians, Hebrews, James, 1 John, and 1 Peter as tractate-type letters. The rest are pastoral letters, which were also meant to convey apostolic presence, teaching, and authority. Since apostolic authority extended to the whole church,

22. D. A. Carson, *Matthew*, in *Matthew, Mark, Luke*, EBC 8 (Grand Rapids: Zondervan, 1984), 402.

23. A. Skevington Wood, *Ephesians*, in *Ephesians–Philemon*, EBC 11 (Grand Rapids: Zondervan, 1978), 81.

24. Walter C. Kaiser, Jr., *The Uses of the Old Testament in the New* (Chicago: Moody, 1985), 203–20.

these pastoral letters, though addressed to a particular community situation, were intended to be read widely, as Paul explicitly points out (Col. 4:16; 1 Thess. 5:27).[25]

Longenecker asserts that the tradition of the apostolic letters allows one to assume that the teaching written to deal pastorally with then-current issues is universal unless the letters themselves indicate that it is situation-specific. But how can this be determined? Again there is a division of opinion. Some insist that the overall situation-specific purpose of a letter be assumed and used to explain the extent of the application of its directives. Gordon Fee focuses the issue as he deals with the purpose and application of 1 Timothy: "Do imperatives directed toward the church in Ephesus in A.D. 62, to correct abuses of wayward elders, function as eternal norms, obligatory in every culture in every age in an absolute way?" He answers that since the teaching was not specifically intended to teach universally normative church order, one is responsible only for obeying the central point of the text, "its 'spirit' if you will, even if at times the specifics are not followed to the 'letter.'"[26] Using such an approach, one can see the principles, not the specifics, of instruction on women's role in ministry and on the qualifications for an elder (1 Tim. 2:11–12; 3:2) as normative.

Fee is correct in calling for consistency of application on the part of evangelicals who would treat 1 Timothy as an authoritative manual of church order. We cannot pick and choose what we will view as normative *true* according to our own predilections. Having said this, Fee then makes a serious hermeneutical misstep in letting his own reconstruction of the Ephesians' circumstances determine what he will view as normative in the text. Obviously, Paul is setting out instructions on church order in a situation beset by false teachers, but he does not indicate how the positive instructions as expressed in this immediate context are explicitly limited by the particular false teaching. In fact, Paul appeals to the creation order and the events of the fall as his rationale for limiting the role of women in ministry (1 Tim. 2:13–15). He indicates that Eve was deceived. This could be linked with a deceptive false teaching in Ephesus, but Paul does not make the point that women are particularly deceived by it. His list of qualifications for church office focuses on character traits that accord with other tables of Christian virtues (Rom. 12:9–21; Gal. 5:22–23; Col. 3:12–17; James 3:13–18). Unless references to the false teaching are given in such a way as to indicate

---

25. Richard N. Longenecker, "On the Form, Function, and Authority of New Testament Letters," in *Scripture and Truth*, 104–5. John L. White has a similar assessment: Paul writes with universal apostolic authority, as one who must prepare "pure and blameless Gentile congregations for the day of the Lord" ("Saint Paul and the Apostolic Letter Tradition," *CBQ* 45 [1983]: 439).

26. Gordon D. Fee, "Reflections on Church Order in the Pastoral Epistles, with Further Reflection on the Hermeneutics of *Ad Hoc* Documents," *JETS* 28 (1985): 150.

that the positive instructions are intended as correctives only for persons immediately affected by such false teaching, those instructions have full apostolic authority for all Christians in all times and places. Only in this way can the Scriptures be applied with the full authority that is their author's intention.

THE QUESTION OF INTELLIGIBILITY

Though Scripture may claim unique, final, and full authority, the relativist perspective has three more questions which could undercut it. Barr's second question concerns the matter of intelligibility: How can we expect the same meaning to be communicated to us in a different time and culture as was communicated between the writers and audiences of biblical times? This question has received attention in the discussions of God's relation to culture, the adequacy of human language to convey divine revelation, and the nature of truth and meaning. Suffice it to say that the New Testament's use of the Old does not anticipate, encounter, or project an intelligibility problem. Paul can appeal to centuries-old statements from Isaiah and the Psalms to substantiate his contention that all are under sin (Rom. 3:9–18/Ps. 5:9; 10:7; 14:1–3; 36:1; 140:3; Isa. 59:7–8). He can apply Scripture across cultures as he takes lessons from Israel's history and its covenant regulations to convince the Gentile Christians in Galatia that they should resist the Judaizers (Gal. 3:7–9/Gen. 12:3; Gal. 3:10–14/Deut. 27:26; Hab. 2:4; Lev. 18:5; Deut. 21:23). He is confident that the promise to Abraham, the curse of the law on those who lack perfect obedience, and the cursedness of Jesus' death by crucifixion are intelligible to animistic pagans who have only recently come to faith in Christ.

THE COMPELLING AUTHORITY OF THE BIBLE

Another hard question from the relativist camp concerns relevance. It is Barr's first question: "How can material from that very different biblical situation be decisive for our problems?" A book which is relevant to and decisive for contemporary individuals will speak with *compelling* authority. Once hearing it, a person can do nothing but submit to it.

Enlightenment thinkers asked whether the Bible, a product of history, could have such compelling authority that its truths could stand the test of autonomous reason. Their answer was no, and radical relativists continue to echo these sentiments. In their view, the Bible, written so long ago, can have no decisive claim on, or compelling influence over, the modern mind. A moderate relativist would affirm the Bible's compelling authority, but would then neutralize that authority by reducing it to the Scriptures' ability to speak to new issues through reasoned elaboration or through extending the interpretive discourse, a structuralist idea. The WCC documents locate biblical authority in its ability to arrest our attention as we hear God speaking to us. Process thought would say that the Bible's authority rests in its "experienced importance," its ability to generate motivating visions that help us live productively. Jack B. Rogers articulates the direction of these approaches:

> The Bible's claim to authority rests not on some doctrine of Scripture or theory of inspiration or anxious insistence that the Bible contains objective, propositional truth about God that forecloses all questions and doubts. Biblical authority is established as, from its pages read, studied, and preached the God who has sought us and found us addresses us, engages us, illumines our thoughts, clarifies human experience, and reads right to the depth of the human condition, offering more answers and raising more questions than ever we imagined possible.[27]

Does the Bible teach that Scripture has compelling authority? The answer is yes, but under certain conditions. There are an attraction and a spiritual generative power in God's Word that draw people to it. Psalm 119 consistently exalts the value of God's Word and its attractiveness: "I rejoice in following your statutes as one rejoices in great riches" (v. 14); "Open my eyes that I may see wonderful things in your law" (v. 18); "I love your commands more than gold, more than pure gold" (v. 127). The experience of the Emmaus disciples is a case study of Scripture's power seen in their response to the christocentric interpretation of the Old Testament: "Were not our hearts burning within us while he talked with us on the road and opened the Scriptures to us?" (Luke 24:32). Peter and James affirm the spiritual productiveness of God's Word: "For you have been born again, not of perishable seed, but of imperishable, through the living and enduring word of God" (1 Peter 1:23); "He chose to give us birth through the word of truth" (James 1:18).

The Scripture's compelling authority presents itself on its own terms, in marked contrast to the Enlightenment and contemporary approaches that place the final authority with human beings. Humans judge Scripture's content and find it compelling if it passes the test of their reason or their existential concerns, or if they find it relevant. The Bible consistently prescribes faith as the precondition for experiencing Scripture's authority. Jesus chastises the Emmaus disciples for not meeting that condition: "How foolish you are, and how slow of heart to believe all that the prophets have spoken!" (Luke 24:25). He goes on to declare the truth; they believe him and urge him to stay (v. 29). It was their believing hearing that caused their

---

27. Jack B. Rogers, Jr., "The Book That Reads Us," *Interpretation* 39 (1985): 399.

hearts to burn within them, an experience of Scripture's compelling authority. Similarly, in his earthly ministry Jesus points to belief in the Old Testament Scriptures as the key to receiving the benefits of their spiritual power—namely, eternal life (John 5:39–40, 46–47).

The Scripture's compelling authority is not subordinate to human understanding and desires, and it is not automatic. The benefits of the Word are shown to operate within a context of imperatives that require one to abide in its truth. Paul tells Timothy to continue in what he has learned from the Scriptures, which are God-breathed (2 Tim. 3:14–16). Peter urges believers, "Like newborn babies, crave pure spiritual milk, so that by it you may grow up in your salvation, now that you have tasted that the Lord is good" (1 Peter 2:2–3). Jesus compares those who hear the Word and retain it to good soil which can by persevering effort produce a crop (Luke 8:15). In each case, a conscious effort must be exerted to remain under the Word's authority. If the Word's authority were compelling in the sense of being irresistible, such commands and encouragements would be unnecessary. The Word of God has compelling authority, but its force lies in our confrontation with truth: either we yield to truth now and know salvation, or we resist now and face judgment later. The writer to the Hebrews, when encouraging Christians in the life of faith to make every effort to enter God's rest, warns them that if they fall by following Israel's example of disobedience, they will face judgment through the Word of God. Indeed, the scrutiny is already occurring. "For the word of God is living and active . . . it penetrates even to dividing soul and spirit . . . it judges the thoughts and attitudes of the heart" (Heb. 4:12). One may resist the compelling authority now; later, one will not be able to.

THE USE OF SCRIPTURE AS AN AUTHORITY

The final problem addressed by the relativist is how to use Scripture as an authority. "Do we not evade our responsibility or distort the biblical message if we take as our responsibility simply the restating or reinterpreting of the Bible?" asks Barr in his fifth question. In doing so, he challenges the standard referential approach for using Scripture as an authority. Other options are introduced, including the casebook or model approach, the use of the Bible as a platform from which to project further thought, and interaction with the Bible in the dynamic process of journeying toward truth. Are these options biblical?

The Bible viewed as the referential standard harmonizes best with its unique, final, and full authority. Since the Bible is the only source for the content of the Christian faith, one must appeal to it as wellspring and standard for establishing true doctrine and ethics. Clark Pinnock points out that "the Bible is the one and only normative pole of theological information and that the claims of tradition or modernity possess no inner-theological relevance."[28] The other approaches set themselves up to a greater or lesser extent against the referential. Carl Henry recognizes the problem: "Every effort to maintain scriptural authority on any other basis issues in the demolition of the authority of the Bible by expanding that concept into divergent and contradictory notions, none of which can be taken as objectively definitive, and each of which becomes more confusing than illuminating on a merely functional base."[29]

The referential approach, which has been consistently practiced by Protestant orthodoxy, and in which both the structural exegesis of sacred texts and Harvie Conn's covenant conscientization participate, is supported by the Bible in teaching and in practice. As Paul points out, the Scriptures can make a person "wise for salvation through faith in Christ Jesus" (2 Tim. 3:15). The Bible is clearly presented as the source of knowledge that makes the difference between salvation and condemnation. In the areas of truth and life, Scripture is profitable for "teaching, rebuking, correcting and training in righteousness" (v. 16). This means it is not only the source, but also the standard by which to measure and judge one's thoughts and actions. Psalm 119 is the epic presentation of Scripture as the source and standard for the righteous and blessed life.

The New Testament regularly uses the Old as a referential standard, frequently introducing the reference with the formula *hōs gegraptai*. This phrase, which combines the comparative conjunction "as" and the perfect passive of the verb "to write," means "as it stands written." It signals an appeal to the Old Testament Scriptures for confirmation of a point. The New Testament writer wants to demonstrate the truth of what he is saying by showing that it corresponds with what the Old Testament says. Indeed, the Old Testament text is acknowledged to have binding authority; what was spoken through it once has continuing power. Old Testament passages often provide the foundation for New Testament thought.

Examples abound that show how Old Testament material is used in the New as a referential standard. Paul substantiates his assertion that the righteousness of God is received through faith by appealing to Habakkuk 2:4: "A righteousness that is by faith from first to last, just as it is written: 'The righteous will live by faith'" (Rom. 1:17). Paul says, in effect, "You can see that what I am saying is true when you compare it with the words of the Old Testament prophet." Prophetic promises and salvation promises can be corroborated by appeal to the Old Testament. At the Last Supper Jesus says, "It is written: 'And he was numbered with the transgressors'; and I tell you that this must be fulfilled in me. Yes, what is written about me is reaching its fulfillment" (Luke 22:37). Isaiah 53:12 is the source of this

Bible is source of knowledge

---

28. Clark H. Pinnock, "How I Use the Bible in Doing Theology," in *Use of the Bible*, 18.
29. Henry, *God, Revelation, and Authority*, 4:474.

prophetic word and provides the criterion for judging whether the prophecy is coming to fulfilment in specific events. These events will make up the dangerous time for which the disciples must prepare themselves. The Old Testament prophecy will provide the perspective in which to understand why Jesus will be treated and evaluated as one numbered among transgressors. Its authority will give meaning to events that otherwise would make no sense at all.

Reference is also made to the Old Testament to find guidance for action. The writer to the Hebrews exhorts the readers to avoid covetousness "because God has said, 'Never will I leave you; never will I forsake you'" (Heb. 13:5/Deut. 31:6). This appeal to God's ancient promise of providential care is offered to New Testament Christians as an antidote for discontent with their circumstances.

James declares, "If you really keep the royal law found in Scripture, 'Love your neighbor as yourself,' you are doing right" (James 2:8/Lev. 19:18). Scripture provides the standard for judging whether one's conduct is right. So whether the New Testament is dealing with truth, prophetic and personal promises, or with ethics and conduct, the writers refer to the Scriptures as their authoritative standard.

It is possible for the Scriptures to serve also as a casebook, a platform for further elaboration, or as an occasion for the ongoing dynamic of truth seeking. There is a place for such interpretive options as long as they remain subsidiary to the primary function of Scripture as the standard of reference.

It is interesting to note that the Bible occasionally treats itself as a casebook. Paul views the wilderness experiences of the Hebrews as types or examples, historical case studies intended to keep those who follow after from falling into the same sins. They "were written down as warnings for us, on whom the fulfillment of the ages has come" (1 Cor. 10:11). However, Paul views these scriptural narratives as more than case studies. They are reports of God's dealings with his people, designed not just as a model but as the authoritative paradigm for the dynamics of divine-human interaction. God as sovereign arranged them to serve as an authoritative model.[30] Indeed, they were written down in a form that could serve through the ages as guidance and warning. This casebook has none of the latitude that char-

---

30. C. K. Barrett is more cautious, saying that this passage does not legitimize a typological method for deducing Christian doctrine from the Old Testament. Paul's doctrinal use of the Old Testament "is as a rule direct" (*A Commentary on the First Epistle to the Corinthians* [New York: Harper & Row, 1968], 227). We note, however, that Paul's typological approach is reserved for dealing with Old Testament narrative. It extends and does not contradict his direct approach. Thus all the Old Testament may be appropriated for New Testament instruction.

acterizes Kraft's yardstick analogy, which classifies behavior as ideal, sub-ideal but acceptable, and unacceptable. Only one way is taught here—faith and obedience to the living God. Those dynamics are so consistent throughout Israel's history that Paul with a simple statement can line up Ishmael's opposition to Isaac with that of legalistic Jews to Christians and say, "It is the same now" (Gal. 4:29). He can relate the concept of the remnant presented in Elijah's day with the meager Jewish response to the gospel in his own: "So too, at the present time there is a remnant chosen by grace" (Rom. 11:5). Is the Bible an inspired casebook? Yes, but one that is much more, for in addition to the truths, promises, and commands that provide the referential standard, it supplies the one authoritative pattern for divine-human interaction.

Scripture can function as the platform for reasonable elaboration, provided the process is confined to application, which means dealing with the text's significance rather than its meaning. The Bible does anticipate that its message will be useful to audiences other than the original one. People of God in every generation find that the Scriptures thoroughly equip them for every good work (2 Tim. 3:17). Paul commends this principle to Timothy generations after the first giving of the Law and the Prophets. He relates the faithful suffering of the psalmist to that of Jesus and then applies the example to his readers, saying that whatsoever was written beforehand was written for our instruction (Rom. 15:3–4).

Paul's use of Isaiah 52:7 is an example of applying the significance of Scripture's message. "How beautiful on the mountains are the feet of those who bring good news" originally referred to the welcome sight of messengers who proclaim the liberation of the Jews and their return from captivity.[31] Paul draws a comparison between the messengers who bring glad tidings and missionaries who will take the good news of salvation to the ends of the earth. He applies the Isaiah text to demonstrate that the activity of preaching will be a part of God's plan. The preacher is one who is sent: "And how can they preach unless they are sent?" (Rom. 10:15). The meaning of the Old Testament passage with its good news about God's saving acts in the past has been taken up and applied so as to provide a basic principle of the Christian missionary movement.[32] Paul sees the significance of Isaiah's words for this new situation, the challenge of proclaiming good news to all peoples, and so he appropriates those words without violating the original meaning. Paul was no doubt well aware that Gentile

---

31. Franz Delitzsch, *Biblical Commentary on the Prophecies of Isaiah*, 2 vols. (Grand Rapids: Eerdmans, 1949), 2:298.
32. Paul D. Hanson, "Isaiah 52:7–10: Expository Article," *Interpretation* 33 (1979): 389.

inclusion in God's saving acts forms part of the context in Isaiah—"and all the ends of the earth will see the salvation of our God" (52:10).[33]

The Unity of Scripture

One final characteristic of Scripture concerns an essential presupposition for the process of interpretation and application. Scripture presents itself as a unity ultimately from one author, God.[34] Scripture's evidence for its inspiration should be employed at this point to affirm its unity as well. Besides having only one author, Scripture has but one central message to which all portions point—salvation through faith in Jesus Christ (Luke 24:25, 44–48). Jesus himself interprets in all the Scriptures the things concerning himself. The practice of various New Testament writers of combining quotations from various parts of the Old Testament to establish their points also assumes Scripture's unity (e.g., Matt. 27:9–10/Zech. 11:12–13 and Jer. 32:6–9; Acts 13:33–35/Ps. 2:7; Isa. 55:3; and Ps. 16:10; Heb. 1:5–14/Ps. 2:7; Deut. 32:43; Ps. 104:4; 45:6–7; 102:25–27; 110:1).

The unity of Scripture entails certain implications for interpretation and application. Negatively, the process of exegesis and interpretation will not find internal contradictions, so that one Scripture portion is set over against another. Scripture's inerrancy assures this. Positively, it is permissible—indeed, desirable—to use the principle of the analogy of faith in interpretation. The best interpreter of Scripture is Scripture; therefore, one passage should be used to clarify the meaning of another.[35]

There are many examples of the analogy-of-faith principle at work in the New Testament use of the Old. For instance, Paul's sermon at Pisidian Antioch argues that Jesus the Messiah fulfilled prophecy when he died and rose again. The necessity of the resurrection is predicated on the eternally sure covenant promises made to David (Acts 13:30, 34/Isa. 55:3).[36] The precise nature of the connection is not immediately clear, however. Paul solves the problem by setting two Old Testament texts next to each other in such a way that one interprets the other: "The fact that God raised him from the dead, never to decay, is stated in these words: 'I will give you the holy and sure blessings promised to David [Isa. 55:3].' So it is stated elsewhere: 'You will not let your Holy One see decay [Ps. 16:10].'" In the light of the resurrection there is no longer a puzzle.

---

33. John Murray sees the prophecy as having a broader reference, but does not go into detail (*The Epistle to the Romans*, 2 vols. [Grand Rapids: Eerdmans, 1965], 2:59).

34. Packer, "Upholding the Unity," 409–14; Carson, "Unity and Diversity," 65–100.

35. Robert L. Thomas, "A Hermeneutical Ambiguity of Eschatology: The Analogy of Faith," *JETS* 23 (1980): 45–53.

36. See Walter C. Kaiser, Jr., "The Promise to David in Psalm 16 and Its Application in Acts 2:25–33 and 13:32–37," *JETS* 23 (1980): 224–26.

The Bible and the Holy Spirit

Inspiration

The Holy Spirit plays an essential role in the giving of divine revelation, the activity called inspiration. It should be noted again that the Bible presents God the Holy Spirit as the inspirer of its writers: "All Scripture is God-breathed" (2 Tim. 3:16); "Men spoke from God as they were carried along by the Holy Spirit" (2 Peter 1:21; see also 1 Peter 1:10; Eph. 3:5; 1 Cor. 2:13). The New Testament writers introduce Old Testament material in phrases that acknowledge and emphasize its inspired nature. The work of the Holy Spirit in Scripture involves his speaking through the human writer (Acts 28:25), the writer's speaking by the Holy Spirit (Matt. 22:43), or the Spirit's speaking the Word directly (Heb. 3:7; 10:15). The Holy Spirit has accomplished in the apostles the work Jesus promised. He did teach them all things, bring to their remembrance what Jesus had said, guide them into all truth, and show them things to come (John 14:26; 16:13). The result is the New Testament, which, together with the writings of the inspired prophets, makes up our Bible.

Holy Spirit inspired

Illumination

The Holy Spirit also has a continuing role in the interpretation and application of the Scriptures in multiple historical and cultural contexts; this is the process of illumination. On the basis of New Testament references John Frame asserts that "by the internal testimony of the Spirit, He enables the 'hearers' of the Word of God to savingly appropriate it."[37] R. C. Sproul and others have also supplied classic texts on the internal witness of the Spirit, though only a few texts explicitly relate Spirit and Scripture.[38] Using texts that relate Spirit and revelation (1 Cor. 2:11–14), Spirit and the gospel (1 Thess. 1:5), Spirit and the truth (1 John 2:26–27), and Spirit and wisdom and knowledge (Eph. 1:17–19), it is possible to profile the nature of the Spirit's illumination in the life of the Christian, illumination that may be appropriated for handling Scripture.

H.S. illuminates the Bible

At conversion, when one turns to the Lord, who is the Spirit, a veil is removed, and the believer beholds directly the Lord's glory and is transformed into his likeness with ever-increasing glory (2 Cor. 3:18). This veil, a

---

37. John M. Frame, "The Spirit and the Scriptures," in *Hermeneutics, Authority, and Canon*, 217.

38. Of Frame's six passages, only one brings together Spirit and Scripture, and the latter is referred to there in terms of revelation (1 Cor. 2:10–16; cf. the other texts: Rom. 8:14–17; 1 Thess. 1:5; 2:13; 1 John 2:27; 5:9). Of the ten classic texts R. C. Sproul cites as support for the truth of "the work of the Spirit in securing our confidence in the Word" ("The Internal Testimony of the Holy Spirit," in *Inerrancy*, 353), again only 1 Corinthians 2 explicitly relates Spirit and Scripture (cf. the other texts: 2 Cor. 4:3–6; 1 John 1:10; 2:14; 5:20; Col. 2:2; 1 Thess. 1:5; Gal. 4:6; Rom. 8:15–16; 2 Cor. 3:1–11).

barrier to receiving and appropriating the gospel, Paul uses as a figure to describe the condition of unconverted Jews, whose thoughts have become dull and hardened. Whenever the Old Testament Scriptures are read in their hearing, the veil remains on. There is also a veil over their heart (vv. 14–15). But when one turns to the Lord, the Spirit, the veil is removed.

Paul describes the removing of the veil as he writes to the Thessalonians about their conversion: "Our gospel came to you not simply with words, but also with power, with the Holy Spirit and with deep conviction. . . . You welcomed the message with the joy given by the Holy Spirit" (1 Thess. 1:5–6). God the Holy Spirit works the deep conviction or full assurance in the hearer that the gospel message is the true Word of God which must be believed and obeyed (see 2:13). The hearer then receives (dechomai) it, welcoming and accepting it with pleasure, willingness, and eagerness.[39] Paul says that joy from the Holy Spirit accompanies such a reception.

Does the Holy Spirit's work at conversion include making the Word of God intelligible? This question is raised by the veil imagery in 2 Corinthians 3 and the blindness imagery that follows: "The god of this age has blinded the minds of unbelievers, so that they cannot see the light of the gospel" (2 Cor. 4:4). It is brought to sharp focus by Paul's contention that "the man without the Spirit does not accept the things that come from the Spirit of God, for they are foolishness to him, and he cannot understand them, because they are spiritually discerned" (1 Cor. 2:14).

Does the Spirit's illumination operate for cognition or for evaluation of the revelation of God, or both? The answer has implications for one's approach to evangelism and to interpretation and application of Scripture and for understanding the Spirit's role in the process. Does the individual need to have the Holy Spirit's illumination for the Scripture to be intelligible? Or is it possible to understand but still be unable to evaluate the Scriptures correctly so that one can judge them to be wisdom to be welcomed rather than foolishness to be rejected?

In the context of hearing the gospel, Paul supplies two parallel statements that deal not with intelligibility per se, but with evaluating truthfulness.[40] According to 1 Corinthians 2:14, the natural man makes a judgment that the things of God are foolishness, and on that basis he does not accept or welcome them (cf. 1 Thess. 1:6). The things of God cannot be accepted because the proper appraisal or evaluation of them must be spiritual. The verb "to accept" has as its basic meaning, "embracing things as they really are." A literal translation of 1 Corinthians 2:14 would be, "The

---

39. Daniel P. Fuller, "The Holy Spirit's Role in Biblical Interpretation," in *Scripture, Tradition, and Interpretation*, ed. W. Ward Gasque and William Sanford LaSor (Grand Rapids: Eerdmans, 1978), 191.

40. Gordon H. Clark, *First Corinthians: A Contemporary Commentary* (Nutley, N.J.: Presbyterian & Reformed, 1975), 57.

natural man does not embrace the realities represented by the Bible's teachings."[41]

Paul uses the verb "to know" in the sense of "understanding" in Romans 10:19–21, where he is explaining the fact that unregenerate people continue to disbelieve the gospel and reject it. In answer to the question "Did Israel not understand [egnō]?" Paul supplies Old Testament evidence that God's plan was to provoke them to jealousy by the Gentiles' acceptance of the gospel, while Israel would remain disobedient and obstinate. Paul implies that Israel did comprehend the message intellectually; their jealousy proves it. Yet they continued to reject the message because they lacked true understanding. Paul distinguishes between mental intelligibility and true understanding.

By equating hardened thoughts with the veil, stating that the veil is over the heart, and attributing blindness to unbelievers, Paul locates the barrier in the area of evaluation rather than cognition. "Because the Bible's view of reality clashes with the way people, apart from the work of the Holy Spirit, want to see things, its message will therefore be regarded as foolishness." The Holy Spirit illumines the mind by removing the barrier to a positive judgment and welcoming of the truth of God's Word. The same type of illumination operates in the process of interpretation and application. As Daniel Fuller describes it, "the Holy Spirit's role is to change the heart of the interpreter, so that he loves the message that is conveyed by nothing more than the historical-grammatical data," a text intelligible through normal exegetical study.[42]

One benefit of the Holy Spirit's illumination is knowledge of the spiritual resources that are available now and in the future. Paul prays that the Ephesians may have the Spirit of wisdom and revelation, an enlightening of the eyes of their hearts, so that they may know what is the hope of their calling, the riches of the glorious inheritance that is theirs in the future, and the greatness of the resurrection power that is theirs now (1:17–19; see also 1 Cor. 2:9–10). Later he prays that they may be strengthened by the Spirit in the inner person so they can comprehend the extent of God's love, which surpasses knowledge (Eph. 3:16–19). Admittedly, neither of these passages explicitly relates the Spirit's work to the Scriptures, but since the content and purpose of Scripture make one "wise unto salvation," it seems reasonable to conclude that the Spirit's illumination applies to Christians as they study the one source that can tell them about the saving benefits in Christ.

The Spirit's illumination also guides the believer in applying Scripture. Paul asks God to fill the Colossians "with the knowledge of his will through

---

41. Fuller, "Holy Spirit's Role," 190–91.
42. Ibid., 192.

all spiritual wisdom and understanding. And we pray this in order that you may live a life worthy of the Lord and may please him in every way: bearing fruit in every good work, growing in the knowledge of God" (Col. 1:9–10). Again Scripture is not specifically mentioned here, but given Scripture's purpose ("that the man of God may be thoroughly equipped for every good work") and the purpose of spiritual wisdom (a life that "bears fruit in every good work"), there is a positive link indicating that the Holy Spirit will illumine application. He will give wisdom and insight for implementing the Bible's mandates and principles in a person's own context. The Holy Spirit can be seen at work in the early church in the Jerusalem Council deliberations. The church was so confidently aware of the Spirit's illumination as it applied Leviticus 17–18 to the current situation that it prefaced its findings with, "It seemed good to the Holy Spirit and to us not to burden you with anything beyond the following requirements . . ." (Acts 15:28).

The illumination of the Spirit also aids in distinguishing between truth and error and in the ability to hold fast to the truth, a quality not unlike the gift for evaluation that comes initially at conversion. At that time, a person is enabled to see the truth of God as wisdom rather than foolishness, as truth from God rather than cleverly devised human myths. Later, when confronted with false teaching, the Christian will be able to evaluate correctly all things. Not being subject to the judgment of others, the Christian does not need to adjust the truth to meet current cultural criteria. For the believer has the mind of Christ (1 Cor. 2:15–16). John uses the term *anointing* when describing this particular operation of the Spirit. He encourages believers in an environment of false teaching by reminding them that they have an anointing: "The anointing you received from him remains in you, and you do not need anyone to teach you. But as his anointing teaches you about all things and as that anointing is real [true], not counterfeit [false]—just as it has taught you, remain in him" (1 John 2:27). John assures them that the anointing is fully sufficient (i.e., teaches all things) and that its teaching is true. The correspondence here with what the Scriptures teach about themselves as the product of the Spirit who would guide the apostles into all truth is unmistakable (John 16:13; see also 17:17). Paul instructs Timothy to "guard the good deposit that was entrusted to you—guard it with the help of the Holy Spirit who lives in us" (2 Tim. 1:14). The Holy Spirit's illumination aids the Christian in keeping sound teaching, God's truth, from being adulterated.

John's statement could possibly be taken to mean that the Spirit's illumination is inspiration, a point used to argue that revelation continues. A number of exegetes take this position, though without reference to this passage in 1 John. However, the indicators here point to illumination. In the same context, John speaks of the objective inspired truth as "that [which] you have heard from the beginning," and urges his flock to let that remain in them (1 John 2:24; see also 1:1). One question is whether the "anointing," because it teaches "concerning all things," involves new revelatory content or instruction by the "Word of life" which was from the beginning. Note that John argues for truth against falsehood by opposing the truth which was from the beginning to the many antichrists that have kept cropping up to trouble the new Christians (2:18). If the Spirit's anointing resulted in new revelation, there would be no way to distinguish the truth they had from the beginning from the assortment of new ideas. The teaching concerning all things, then, indicates the full sufficiency of content rather than ongoing inspiration.[43]

In his instruction to Timothy, Paul clearly identifies this work of the Spirit as illumination. With economic imagery, he exhorts the younger man to guard the deposit of sound teaching that has been given to him in the expectation that he will return it to his master, the Lord Jesus, without any change or any additions. The Spirit will help him do that.

In a passage that speaks of both inspiration and illumination, Paul clearly distinguishes between the two. He uses the first-person plural when speaking of the Spirit's imparting the wisdom of God (1 Cor. 2:6–13), a definite reference to the inspiration process. He switches to the third-person singular to describe illumination (vv. 14–16). These grammatical changes signal a shift in topic from Paul's "speaking" the message taught by the Spirit through inspiration, to "accepting" the things of the Spirit of God as a consequence of his illuminating work. To make the distinction more sure—since he has used the word *receive (lambanō)* in describing the process of inspiration (v. 12)—Paul uses a different word for "receive" *(dechomai)*, which means "welcoming, positively evaluating," when he speaks of illumination. This work of the Spirit is subsequent to and not the same as inspiration. The Spirit illumines, but he illumines the believer's mind and heart to believe, love, and guard an already existent inspired Word.

The Bible teaches that it is a divinely inspired Word, the verbal, propositional revelation from God. It records affirmations of its own inerrancy. Scripture's instruction concerning its authority decisively answers the relativist's challenge. It views its authority as intelligible and compelling, but the kind of compulsion that confronts us with the truth and invites a faith response. The Bible's authority is unique and final. It is also a full authority extending to divinely mandated cultural forms. Christians are to use the Bible as a referential standard, bringing their thoughts and actions into line with it. But they may also use it as a casebook of examples to follow and a

---

43. According to Stephen Smalley, "'about everything' is best understood as meaning 'all that you need to know at any one time,' rather than permanently valid omniscience" (*1, 2, 3 John*, WBC 51 [Waco, Tex.: Word, 1984], 126).

platform from which to undertake reasoned elaboration of its meaning. Scripture is a unity and should be interpreted by the principle of the analogy of faith.

key

  The Holy Spirit illumines the mind at conversion not by making God's Word intelligible, but by convincing sinners that it is true. Throughout their life, Christians have the Spirit's presence to help them realize their spiritual resources, to aid them in application, and to assist them in distinguishing between truth and error.

17

Sin, Preunderstanding, and the Hermeneutical Bridge

In the end, the communication process must focus on man the interpreter. Human beings stand in their cultural context, receiving God's message by means of a book from an ancient and different cultural context. They are responsible for interpreting, applying, and then communicating the Bible's meaning to their context and even cross-culturally through contextualization. Having considered the biblical teaching with regard to culture the context and to the God who communicates, we must now analyze man the interpreter, the knowing subject. What does the Bible teach about the human person and the process of interpretation, application, and contextualization? Just as sin radically affects us as culture builders, so it affects us as interpreters, appliers, and cross-cultural communicators of God's Word. But just what is the nature of that effect? What is the proper role and content for the interpreter's preunderstanding? What are the proper pylons for the hermeneutical bridge?

Effects of Sin

It is rare in hermeneutical discussion to find a description of the effects of sin on attempts at interpretation and application. Liberation theology's "her-

meneutical suspicion" and the evangelical's cautions about antibiblical presuppositions are the exceptions.

sin effects the mind

Scripture describes sin's effects on the mind at the deepest level. Through
Adam all humankind inherited a proud heart in rebellion against God and
his ways. Driven by desires and passions, this heart conjures up wicked
thoughts and plots and plans evil. In Noah's generation God could say that
"every inclination of the thoughts of [man's] heart was only evil all the time"
(Gen. 6:5). Paul offers the same evaluation of all who are outside Christ: "All
of us also lived among them at one time, gratifying the cravings of our sinful
nature and following its desires and thoughts" (Eph. 2:3). It is not just that

thoughts and mind corrupted

human thought-processes are employed for sinful ends; the thoughts themselves, the mind itself, have become corrupted. Paul is saying that everyone
follows the inclinations of a sinful mind, making fulfilment of the desires of
the mind and of the flesh the chief end. We all do this by nature until we
accept life in Christ.

pride

The chief characteristic of this corruption is pride. Paul portrays false
teachers as proud and puffed up in their minds (Col. 2:18; 2 Tim. 3:1–2).
The struggle against false teaching requires divine power to overthrow its
strongholds of thought. "We demolish arguments and every pretension
that sets itself up against the knowledge of God, and we take captive every
thought to make it obedient to Christ" (2 Cor. 10:5). This vaunting of the
sinful human mind is at bottom active rebellion against God and his
thoughts. Paul says that all non-Christians as alienated persons are hostile
in their minds through evil deeds (Col. 1:21). False teachers are men who
"oppose the truth—men of depraved minds" (2 Tim. 3:8). Indeed, the unregenerate mind seeks to establish itself, through reason or existential concern, as autonomous, the final arbiter of what one should know, believe,
and obey.

The proud, rebellious set of the human mind forfeits knowledge of God
and his will for salvation, thought, and conduct. The Bible diagnoses the

mentally blind

human mental condition as blind and futile. The hardness of mind that is
unbelief, whether among Jew or Gentile, places a veil of blindness on the
mind, so that one cannot understand and receive the gospel (2 Cor. 3:14;
4:4; see also Eph. 4:18). Having refused to worship the one true God,
humankind uses all the faculties and resources of the mind to live out the
cultural task in an atmosphere of futile rebellion. Human cultures never

spiritual goals never achieved

accomplish the goals they set in the spiritual system, for they aim at the
wrong objective. The irrationality of idolatry is patent evidence that sinful
human beings have indeed become futile in their thoughts and their foolish
heart is darkened (Rom. 1:21–23). This futility affects more than the religious or spiritual areas of life. It poisons every sphere of human activity—
domestic, economic, and political. So Paul can describe the Gentiles who

follow the futility of their own thinking as those who "have given them-selves over to sensuality so as to indulge in every kind of impurity" (Eph. 4:19).

It should be noted that the degree of corruption of the fallen mind is. directly related to the nature of the subject matter under consideration. Jesus acknowledges that the children of this age can sometimes think and act more effectively in worldly affairs than do the children of the kingdom (Luke 16:8). The same is not true in spiritual matters, for as Kenneth Kant-zer observes, "The nearer a man gets to the vital core of his obedience to God, the greater is the corruption of his thinking due to sin."[1]

Doubt

The unregenerate mind applies reason to the Scriptures and arrives at interpretations characterized by doubt, fragmentation, and distortion. It is therefore never able by itself to come to a saving and sanctifying knowledge of God's truth. Just as faith is the condition for knowledge (2 Cor. 4:13), so doubt or skepticism is the condition for remaining in ignorance of the truth. When speaking of his former persecution of the church, Paul says he was acting "in ignorance and unbelief" (1 Tim. 1:13).

Note the disciples' reaction to the risen Lord when he appeared to them in Galilee: "When they saw him, they worshiped him; but some doubted" (Matt. 28:17).[2] The senses and rational faculties of a skeptical, doubting mind are too handicapped to understand the truth presented to it, and such a mind cannot even assure itself that it is witnessing truth. This con-dition renders skeptics incapable of saying with certainty that they have seen the truth. Their uncertainty only deepens when they are faced with verbal or written testimony of truth, for such a declaration demands the transfer of authority from one's own reason as final arbiter to the witness declared to be true. Jesus knew how difficult, indeed impossible, such a transfer of trust is. He said to the Jews who did not receive his testimony, "If you believed Moses, you would believe me, for he wrote about me. But since you do not believe what he wrote, how are you going to believe what I say?" (John 5:46–47).

Jesus' parable of the rich man and Lazarus (Luke 16:19–31) points out the pervasive blindness of such skepticism. The rich man asks that Lazarus be

---

1. Kenneth S. Kantzer, "The Communication of Revelation," in *The Bible: The Living Word of Revelation*, ed. Merrill C. Tenney (Grand Rapids: Zondervan, 1968), 67.

2. See E. Margaret Howe's study of the combination of sense perception with other factors in collectively establishing the resurrection. But the other factors (e.g., the Great Commission and christocentric Old Testament interpretation) are grounded in the sense perception of seeing and hearing the risen Lord ("'. . . But Some Doubted' [Matt. 28:17]: A Re-Appraisal of Factors Influencing the Easter Faith of the Early Christian Community," *JETS* 18 [1975]: 180).

sent back from the dead so that the empirical evidence of the miracle will give authority to the warning that a life of unrighteousness leads to eternal judgment. The rich man is confident that such evidence will convince his brothers. Abraham replies that the brothers already have a witness of sufficient authority to be believed, the written testimony of Moses and the Prophets. The rich man insists that a miracle is what his brothers need. Abraham answers, "If they do not listen to Moses and the Prophets, they will not be convinced even if someone rises from the dead" (v. 31). Because their doubt flows from a rebellious heart claiming autonomous reason, no external evidence involving surrender of that autonomy will compel them to believe. Abraham's answer solves the problem of Lessing's ugly ditch by identifying the true source of the problem. The source lies not in the kind of evidence presented to reason, but in autonomous reason's skeptical stance in the face of all evidence. When one starts with doubt, evaluation of the text will never lead to certainty.

skepticism

Doubt may manifest itself not only as skepticism but as mockery of God's work and message, attributing God's work either to the devil or to natural causes. The Pharisees evaluate Jesus' miracles in this way: "It is only by Beelzebub, the prince of demons, that this fellow drives out demons" (Matt. 12:24). Some in the crowd at Pentecost mock, viewing the miracle of speaking in tongues as the effects of alcohol (Acts 2:13). Paul understood this mockery on the part of the skeptic, and it led him to conclude that "the message of the cross is foolishness to those who are perishing" (1 Cor. 1:18). At Athens, the Epicureans, who are atomistic materialists, jeer at Paul and his message of Jesus and the resurrection: "What is this babbler trying to say?" (Acts 17:18). "Babbler" (or "seed picker") is a term of contempt for a teacher who presents secondhand instruction he or she has scavenged from others, like the bird who picks through garbage.[3] Doubt is so much a part of unregenerate life that unbelievers are listed among those who will not inherit the kingdom of heaven (Rev. 21:8).

mockery

Fragmentation

Fragmentation is the second characteristic of fallen reason. It studies Scripture to find contradictions. By reasserting the noncontradictory nature of Scripture, Jesus dealt with the Sadducees, who set one part of Scripture against another. They did not believe in a resurrection of the dead and claimed that such an idea rendered absurd one of Moses' laws, levirate marriage (Matt. 22:23–33/Deut. 25:5–6). Jesus responded, "You are in error because you do not know the Scriptures or the power of God" (Matt. 22:29).

def.

---

3. See Maurice A. Robinson, "SPERMOLOGOS: Did Paul Preach from Jesus' Parables?" *Biblica* 56 (1975): 231–40.

If the Sadducees really knew the Scriptures, they would know that resurrection is just as well attested as the levirate law (Matt. 22:31–32/Exod. 3:6). Knowledge of the power of God would have shown them that there is no contradiction between the passages because there is no marriage in the resurrected, glorified state (Matt. 22:30).

One wonders whether in a contemporary context the continuous uncovering of more and more supposed contradictions in Scripture is not a manifestation of the same fallen reason in rebellion against the claims of biblical revelation. Apparent contradictions stimulate autonomous reason to divide and conquer by choosing authoritatively among the diversity it has discovered. Yet in the end this is also an exercise in futility. One cannot arrive at the finally authoritative truth of Scripture by this method.

Fragmentation is the fruit of controversies created by introducing contrived distinctions into Scripture. These distinctions involve adding extrabiblical content to doctrine. Paul warns Timothy of false teachers who have "an unhealthy interest in controversies and quarrels about words that result in envy, strife, malicious talk, evil suspicions" (1 Tim. 6:4). Such divisive persons have introduced an extrabiblical doctrine of asceticism: "They forbid people to marry and order them to abstain from certain foods" (4:3). To maintain their teaching, they have to segment Scripture and ignore much of its teaching. Paul alludes to the goodness of all creation as he corrects their teaching: "For everything God created is good, and nothing is to be rejected if it is received with thanksgiving" (v. 4).

Such fragmentation is robust in contemporary interpretation. Samuel Escobar evaluates the polarities in current theological discussion: Old Testament/New Testament; Gospel/Epistle; Jesus/Paul; prophets of the left/kings of the right. "The polarities usually come from ideologies or philosophic systems foreign to the text, to the world of the Bible, world views that are opposed in content and intention to the saving purpose of God."[4] Mark Branson agrees and says that it is convenient to ignore Scripture that challenges any power base or particular status quo of a church-based, theologically defined, or politically oriented system one is trying to defend.[5] Metaphysical and epistemological distinctions unsubstantiated by revelation so compartmentalize Scripture that cultural material cannot be viewed as normative. This mental process may also be an expression of the futility of fallen reason.

Distortion

The futility of fallen reason also causes distortion, the reinterpretation of Scripture to fit human doctrines (2 Peter 3:16). Sometimes distortion takes

---

4. Samuel Escobar, "Our Hermeneutical Task Today," in *Conflict and Context: Hermeneutics in the Americas,* ed. Mark Lau Branson and C. René Padilla (Grand Rapids: Eerdmans, 1986), 5.

5. Mark Lau Branson, "Response to Escobar," in *Conflict and Context,* 10.

place when a person adds a man-made concept to the Word of God, as the Judaizers did in adding circumcision to the gospel of grace received by faith alone (Gal. 1:6–9).One sometimes chooses the human word over the Word of God, like the false teachers Peter confronted who denied the promise of Christ's return in favor of their own logic (2 Peter 3:4).[6] False teachers turn aside from God's truth to myths (2 Tim. 4:3–4), being deluded by plausible but false arguments (Col. 2:4). Proud reason is pleased to find a way to *pride* rebel, to accept a human word against God's Word. Such exercise in blindness and futility distorts or rejects God's truth and prevents any true knowledge.

Do the effects of sin on the mind extend to the preunderstanding? The Scriptures definitely understand that culture is under the control of a demonic hierarchy (the *stoicheia*) and is transmitted by tradition from generation to generation. This produces a world-view that is the essential ingredient in human preunderstanding. This mindset so harmonizes with human sinful nature that only a conscious effort can override it. Paul, using the astronomical jargon of planet convergence, instructs the Romans to stop aligning themselves with the values of the surrounding culture (Rom. 12:2). Their preunderstanding is a mindset that does not evaluate things as God does (Matt. 16:23) and does not see God's will as good, perfect, and acceptable. Only a transformed mind can do that (Rom. 12:2), while natural preunderstanding is hostile to God (Rom. 8:7). When autonomous reason applies the hostile preunderstanding to Scripture, the result is doubt, fragmentation, and distortion.

The Epicureans had a materialist metaphysics: atoms are in ceaseless motion, fusing and dissolving. The concept of supernatural resurrection did not exist for them, and they were skeptical of a message in which the risen Christ is central. Timothy confronted false teachers who believed the physical world is essentially evil. They called for abstinence, and in that way denied that God made creation good. The Judaizers distorted the gospel of grace with the view that outward ritual is the means for gaining God's favor. In our own day, the historical-critical method makes a virtue of skepticism. Fragmentation of the Scripture occurs when contemporary social egalitarianism sets Paul the subjugator of women over against Paul the feminist. *absolute truth is key* The contention that one cannot know absolute truth leads to distortion, for the truth of Scripture will be interpreted as personal rather than as factual information that corresponds to reality. Preunderstanding also involves the current concerns of the interpreter.[7] When these concerns do not correspond with the concerns of the text, the interpreter will ask questions the

6. Michael Green, *The Second Epistle General of Peter and the General Epistle of Jude: An Introduction and Commentary* (Grand Rapids: Eerdmans, 1968), 38.

7. Walter M. Dunnett, *The Interpretation of Holy Scripture* (Nashville: Nelson, 1984), 88.

text cannot answer, and the interpreter will not be able to hear the answers the text is giving. These difficulties are expressions of the fragmenting effect of sin.

Mind and Preunderstanding

Another aspect of the interpreter's mind and preunderstanding figures into the process of interpretation and application. The mind of the interpreter, whether regenerate or unregenerate, evidences the fact that humans are made in God's image (Gen. 1:26). One reflection of this image is the ability to engage in rational thought-processes, analyzing and synthesizing to organize one's perception of reality in categories that correspond to the segmentation of the divinely created universe. Though Scripture does not give an epistemological statement on the nature of these innate thought-categories, the Bible's view of truth, meaning, and language does give us some indication. Adam's first rational act, naming the animals, seems to depend on rational thought-processes operating in a correspondence between segmented reality and its innate categories and using his creative language-making ability (Gen. 2:19–20) quite independently of any world-view information supplied by cultural preunderstanding. The consistent practice of Christian witnesses among unbelievers relies on such processes. At Thessalonica, Paul "reasoned with them from the Scriptures, explaining and proving that the Christ had to suffer and rise from the dead. 'This Jesus I am proclaiming to you is the Christ'" (Acts 17:2–3). Reason can and should be used to explain the truth of Scripture to unbelievers, as well as believers, since the rational thought-categories and processes are the shared birthright of those made in God's image. However, sin has corrupted the human mind and preunderstanding to such an extent that not all who hear and understand the reasoning will welcome the message as true.

The other reflection of God's image in the human mind is the ability to transcend preunderstanding, evaluate it, and change it. The witness of Jesus and the apostles proceeds on this assumption. Jesus challenges the Jewish expectation of the Messiah as a human descendant of David by asking how the Scripture can report that David calls him Lord (Luke 20:41–44). Jesus' question would have had no purpose if it were impossible for the Jews to transcend their preunderstanding and ask whether the Messiah would be more than a man. In a dramatic scene at Lystra, Paul assumes that those pagans can transcend their animistic understandings of deity when he shouts among those who are worshiping him, "Men, why are you doing this? We too are only men, human like you. We are bringing you good news, telling you to turn from these worthless things to the living God" (Acts 14:15). The Bible consistently demonstrates that people are not so captive to their preunderstanding that they cannot transcend it. Admittedly, the effects of sin on the mind are such that a use of reason alone cannot bring a person to a saving knowledge of God's Word, but this fact must be held in tension with the Bible's teaching about the role of reason in the process of interpretation and application. Human reason can fulfil its proper role by submitting to the authority of Scripture. In this way one can strive toward Paul's goal to "take captive every thought to make it obedient to Christ" (2 Cor. 10:5).

Renewed Mind and Proper Preunderstanding

Paul speaks of the renewed mind (Rom. 12:2; Col. 3:2). Such a state of mind renews the preunderstanding, enabling one to interpret and apply Scripture correctly. The renewed mind replaces doubt with faith, fragmentation with a commitment to the whole counsel of God in Scripture, distortion with a commitment to "rightly divide the word of truth" and discard the extrabiblical concepts that are not consistent with that truth. In practice, faith amounts to trust in the truthfulness of the Bible, confidence that it is God's Word and is communicating a message from him and that faith is the only starting point from which to interpret and apply it correctly. The Bible's claims to be God's unique, final, and fully authoritative revelation elicit a humble, believing stance. If the Bible can make one wise unto salvation, if the God-breathed Scriptures are so beneficial that one needs no other instruction in truth and conduct, then trust must be our first step (2 Tim. 3:14–17). Faith is the act of loving God with the mind (Matt. 22:37).

Commitment to the whole counsel of God is the antidote to fragmentation, the remedy Jesus applied to the Emmaus disciples whose foolish hearts were slow to believe all that the prophets had spoken about the Messiah: "And beginning with Moses and all the Prophets, he explained to them what was said in all the Scriptures concerning himself" (Luke 24:27). This approach assumes the unity of Scripture, uses the analogy of faith to bring out its meaning, and treats all its content as authoritative. Concentration on the text, its concerns, and intended meaning ensures that personal and cultural concerns do not block out or impede what God is saying in that text.

Distortion can be overcome by a commitment to seek out the definite and fixed meaning intended by the author of the text and to use Scripture as the final critical authority for judging extrabiblical thought-patterns. Paul referred to the plain meaning, the definite sense, of Old Testament texts to overcome the Judaizers' distorted understanding of God's way of salvation. They used Abraham as their model for salvation through obedience,[8] but Paul, by quoting the plain sense of Genesis 15:6 and 12:3 ("he believed God and it was credited to him as righteousness" and "all nations will be blessed through you"), showed that Abraham modeled the way of faith, the way in which the Gentiles are to be justified (Gal. 3:6, 8).

One's cultural preunderstanding can often control one's exegesis so that what is perceived as the meaning of a text is really foisted on it by the contemporary context. However, interpreters who consciously set aside their cultural preunderstanding can be confident that the grammatical-historical-literary context will enable them to find the plain and definite meaning of the text.

Ideas, beliefs, and values taught by Scripture itself provide the content for a preunderstanding suitable for interpreting and applying Scripture. God's covenant promise is, "I will put my law in their minds and write it on their hearts" (Jer. 31:33). Jesus pointed out that those who have God's Word dwelling in them will believe the testimony of the Scripture about him (John 5:38). Paul says that the spiritual person has the mind of Christ and is able to appraise spiritual things, approving the truth of what comes from God (1 Cor. 2:15–16). John speaks of an anointing and a word dwelling in believers that teaches them all things (1 John 2:14, 24, 27). The consistent challenge is to cultivate a mind filled with the ideas, beliefs, and values of God's revealed will. Paul puts it in plain words: "Set your minds on things above" (Col. 3:2); "put on the new self, which is being renewed in knowledge in the image of its Creator" (v. 10).

A biblical hermeneutic embraces the concept that true ideas, beliefs, and values are those given by God, and that human language is adequate for the communication of divine revelation. In the area of ideas, the common experience of the prophets was that God had put his words in their mouths (see Jer. 1:9). In the area of metaphysics (beliefs), God, the Creator of the universe and of humans, provides the framework of reality (Acts 17:24–28). In the area of values, there is the God-given code of conduct that people are to internalize as they test and approve what his good, pleasing, and perfect will is (Rom. 12:2).

But does not this view of the Bible as the source of its own preunderstanding for interpretation constitute a spiritual version of the hermeneutical circle? Has the whole process been set within a closed system of biblical thought? Can such a statement as "one is to read the Scriptures with

---

8. See C. E. B. Cranfield, *A Critical and Exegetical Commentary on the Epistle to the Romans*, vol. 1, *Introduction and Commentary on Romans i–viii* (Edinburgh: T. & T. Clark, 1975), 229, for examples.

the spectacles of the Scripture" function as an affirmation that a finally authoritative Scripture is absolutely self-sufficient?

The answer is yes. For the kind of truth being sought is truth that corresponds to reality. This immediately introduces an outside reference point against which alien influences of preunderstanding can be tested. The early Christian witnesses invited such examination. Luke describes the Bereans: "They received the message with great eagerness and examined the Scriptures every day to see if what Paul said was true" (Acts 17:11). If the biblical preunderstanding involves true content, then its use in interpretation and application will produce nothing false. Preunderstanding developed from extrabiblical content will be false to a greater or lesser degree and therefore unserviceable in the interpretation process. A text best communicates its intended message when it can do so on its own terms. The late Abraham Heschel once remarked to a gathering of theologians, "It has seemed puzzling to me how greatly attached to the Bible you seem to be and yet how much like pagans you handle it. The great challenge to those of us who wish to take the Bible seriously is to let it teach us its own essential categories; and then for us to think *with* them, instead of just *about* them." Albert Outler, who provides this reminiscence, says that these words have become for him "a sort of charter for a hermeneutical approach that would be more and more relevant in a postliberal age."9

The hermeneutical circle is actually, as René Padilla suggests, a hermeneutical spiral in which interpreters through successive exposure to God's Word are able to bring their preunderstanding and, as a result, their interpretation and application closer and closer to alignment with Scripture's truth. The same process brings progress in the Christian life. One is able more and more to say no to sinful cultural preunderstanding and yes to a growing biblical preunderstanding. Paul describes the sanctification process in terms that suggest this hermeneutical spiral (Rom. 12:1–2; Eph. 4:22–24; Col. 3:8–10). He presents four elements: the rejection of sinful attitudes and behavior, the reception of righteous ones, the renewing of the mind as the basis for accomplishing the transition, and the presence of a standard of truth and right to govern the new life. These passages use present-tense verb forms to indicate that this is a continuing process and not a one-time transaction; it is a spiral, not a circle. At the very heart of the hermeneutical process correctly undertaken is a sanctification process. The Word of God challenges, corrects, and informs the interpreter's preunderstanding, and renews the mind, so that one can understand and apply the Word to the details of living the new lifestyle. So, at the very heart of the sanctification process, there is a hermeneutical process.

---

9. Albert C. Outler, "Toward a Postliberal Hermeneutic," *TT* 42 (1985): 290.

The Hermeneutical Bridge

Five elements of biblical teaching that have been surveyed in chapters 13–16 supply building blocks with which to construct the hermeneutical bridge. A brief review will line them up under the headings of language, God, Scripture, humankind, and history.

For obvious reasons, the Scriptures do not presuppose or acknowledge the need for a hermeneutical bridge. The meaning of Scripture written in human language is the same for all time; it does not change across time periods and cultures. Since its meaning is located in the author's intended sense about an extralinguistic referent, that meaning remains constant and can be recovered at any time. The basis for this continuing stability of meaning rests on its nature as conceived in the traditional sign theory— meaning that is single, definite, and fixed, and thus can bridge time and culture.

God has from the beginning used human language to reveal his will to humankind in communication that is verbal and propositional. His words and propositions carry a message that is true and corresponds to reality. God's eternal and universal truth is objective and absolute as it impacts time and culture. This truth in God's words has been inscripturated and so is accessible and knowable. In such a situation biblical interpreters can reasonably expect to be able to understand and apply biblical content, even though the original text was presented in a time and cultural context distant from their own.

God's action in inspiring those writers who inscripturated the revelation of his absolute truth continues in the third person of the Trinity, the Holy Spirit, who illumines the minds of interpreters so that they can understand and apply the message for salvation. It is possible for Scripture's message to be intellectually understood apart from the Holy Spirit, but the illuminating Spirit must be present for the message to be perceived as true. His illumination also guides the interpreter in correctly distinguishing between truth and error and in avoiding the damaging cultural influences that distort and fragment the truth. The Spirit also guides in the proper application of the meaning of the text within the interpreter's own social context. The Spirit is an indispensable buttress for the hermeneutical bridge, serving to preserve the truth being transported across it and then serving to show how the message may be put to work in the contemporary cultural context.

The determining characteristics of Scripture provide the basis for confidence that the biblical message can be understood and appropriated for today. In addition to its divine inspiration, the Bible is inerrant. Nothing in reality will ever contradict it or invalidate it by limiting its application to a given culture or period. The Bible's purpose is to give knowledge of God and his will to people of all times and cultures so that they may achieve a right relationship with him and, as a result, know salvation. For those who have this relation, the Bible becomes the guidebook on how to think, what to believe, and how to act in this life. God's Word serves as both a referential standard for direct application and an inspired casebook from which negative and positive examples may be drawn and principles applied in different historical and cultural contexts.

Scripture affirms the unity of the human race in the most fundamental way by locating this unity in the spiritual similarity of all its members. This position makes all cultural differences relative. All humans are created in the image of God and endowed with the same cognitive and linguistic capabilities. They are all rebellious creatures, acting out their revolt in diverse cultural ways, and they are all in need of God's saving grace in Christ. All of us, with the same nature and the same needs over time and across culture, are ourselves a part of the hermeneutical bridge.

The Bible claims to have the one true message from the one true and unchangingly faithful God to meet our constant need. Language used by the truthful God to reveal the universal and eternal truth of his saving will and preserved in an inerrant and finally authoritative Scripture addressed to human beings made in his image, all of them in desperate need of his saving message—these are the pylons of the hermeneutical bridge across which one can pass to the Scriptures. Finally, access to the Scriptures takes place within a historical framework that neutralizes historical distance to such a degree that present-day interpreters are able to identify their time period as one with that of the New Testament writers. Jesus' incarnation is the center of history, the event that inaugurated the last days in which both we and they live.

According to Scripture, the interpreter must deal with the effects of sin on the mind. When handling God's truth, a sinful mind will doubt, interpret in a fragmented or distorted way, and approach the Bible with an unbiblical preunderstanding. But the human mind has been made by God. Part of the image of God in each person is a mind's rational thought-processes and its ability to transcend its own preunderstanding and change it. The renewed mind in Christ replaces doubt with faith, fragmentation with the whole counsel of God, and distortion with right handling of Scripture. In an upward hermeneutical spiral, Scripture continually corrects and informs one's preunderstanding so that the interpreter with renewed mind can ever more fully understand and apply the Word to his or her life.

Scripture's hermeneutical bridge consists of five elements: human language, which can communicate meaning across time and culture; a faithful God, who speaks eternal and universal truth and illumines by his Spirit; an inspired and fully authoritative Scripture, which purposes to instruct humankind in all generations and cultures; humankind, whose unity is more basic than its cultural diversity; and a historical framework, which sees all humankind since Christ living in the same time period, the last days.

18

Interpretation, Application, and Contextualization

The grand overriding intent of Scripture is to recover humankind from its fallen state and to provide instruction and motivation for a God-pleasing life of good works. In tracing the history of biblical criticism and hermeneutics, it has become apparent that many approaches to Scripture view this direct action of Scripture upon human beings and their responsive interaction as no longer possible or at least severely hampered by an accumulation of cultural and historical factors. The thesis of this book, for which the preceding chapters form a preparation, is that the elements for a rigorous interpretation, application, and contextualization of the Bible lie within the Bible itself. Using its teachings and examples as the basic ingredients, it is possible to develop a system of concepts, thought-constructs, and analytical principles recognized and practiced by biblical interpreters and theologians, and also firmly grounded on scriptural content.

Interpretation

The basic conductor for linking the human to the divine in the modern context is the biblico-historical hermeneutical bridge. This construct, which has received so much attention and generated such controversy in theological circles, has always existed, and because it has always been in place, the

305

Bible takes it for granted. The ever-faithful God reveals his absolute truth in understandable human language and preserves it in his inspired and inerrant, unique, fully and finally authoritative Scriptures. His Holy Spirit illumines humans made in the image of God but fallen, all in the same need of salvation, to receive the Scripture's saving message. This hermeneutical bridge, of which humankind is such a part, makes the interpretation of Scripture possible.

The Two Horizons

There are two horizons, two contexts, that must interact for understanding to take place—the horizon of the text and that of the interpreter. An interpreter's horizon of necessity involves one's historical situation and preunderstanding. Scripture in setting forth the good things it offers takes into consideration pressing personal and social concerns. Paul explains to the Roman Christians that the Bible was written for instruction so that through "the encouragement of the Scriptures we might have hope" (15:4).[1] The situation was this: Gentile Christians were being criticized by Jewish Christians for not obeying the full Mosaic law. Their feelings were hurt, but Paul requested them to forgo their full rights and freedom out of respect for the conscience of a weaker brother who might be scandalized (14:3–4, 20–21). To encourage them, Paul reminds them that Jesus did not please himself but took on himself the insults due others, as had been prophesied in Psalm 69. The Scriptures are intended to comfort and encourage, and in doing so they must deal with the concerns of the believer. Personal concerns and one's preunderstanding of necessity play a role in the interpretation process, but they should not play the dominant role.

Scripture has its own purpose; it has answers to questions that have not yet been asked but should be. Scripture's innate preunderstanding stands as judge and corrector of any given cultural preunderstanding. Interpreters may approach Scripture with their own concerns and preunderstanding, but they must let Scripture shed the light of its authority on these elements. Interpreters who come to find answers should not be surprised if very early in the process they are faced with even more radical questions. Did not the writer to the Hebrews describe God's Word as sharper than a double-edged sword which "judges the thoughts and attitudes of the heart" (4:12)?

THE HORIZON OF THE TEXT

The horizon of the text involves its grammatical-historical-literary dimension. This supplies what theologians call distancing, for it allows the interpreter to hear the text on its own terms.

---

1. I concur with C. E. B. Cranfield that the use of *paraklēsis* in the next verse indicates that here the term means "encouragement or comfort," not "exhortation" (*A Critical and Exegetical Commentary on the Epistle to the Romans,* vol. 2 [Edinburgh: T. & T. Clark, 1979], 736).

The New Testament deals primarily with the grammatical-historical-literary method when it interprets and applies texts from the Old. This method is used to find an author's intended meaning with regard to an extralinguistic referent, a meaning that is definite and fixed. Paul provides a striking example in Romans 9. He wants to explain the principle of election and makes use of Exodus 33:19, "I will have mercy on whom I have mercy, and I will have compassion on whom I will have compassion." The concept of God's totally free and unconditioned nature is expressed and emphasized by the grammatical tautology of the text. The relative clauses repeat the subjects and verbs from the main clauses. Each relative pronoun is twice the object of the same subject and verb, creating a repetition, almost a refrain, that communicates the complete freedom of God, without conveying additional information. "I will do what I will do." Knowledge of the historical circumstances further enhances the appropriateness of the quotation. God spoke these words in response to Moses' request to see God's glory, his very nature. The request was granted, and God indicated that he would cause his goodness to pass by Moses, though Moses would not see his face (Exod. 33:19, 23). He would proclaim his name, the Lord, and his very nature as the sovereignly merciful and compassionate God. These words are God's self-declaration concerning his very person. They are the strongest answer to the rhetorical question Paul had posed, "Is God unjust?" (Rom. 9:14). Paul brings the impact of the original historical context to bear on his argument.

Biblical writers consistently alert their readers to literary aspects of the text that affect interpretation.[2] When a particular genre employing figurative, metaphorical, or symbolic language is used, the biblical writer alerts his reader by naming the type. When Samson tells a riddle (Judg. 14:12), Ezekiel utters a parable (Ezek. 17:2), or Habakkuk reports a taunt (Hab. 2:6), the reader knows it and can interpret accordingly. The Gospel writers point out the parables in Jesus' teaching (Matt. 13:24, 31, 33; Mark 12:1; Luke 15:3). New Testament writers also label other genres such as epistle (Rom. 16:22), prophecy (Rev. 1:3), and gospel (Mark 1:1). Such precise designations invite literary analysis. There are general statements about these literary types. Mark says, for example, that Jesus "did not say anything to them without using a parable" (4:34).

Literary analysis of Scripture must always be distinguished by a concern for how the forms are being used to present truth which corresponds to reality. Secular literature, by contrast, is often treated as an imitation of reality. But the Bible, whether speaking through specific literary form or

---

2. See Leland Ryken on the literary element in Scripture (*How to Read the Bible as Literature* [Grand Rapids: Zondervan, 1984], 30).

sustained historical narrative, faithfully represents the real world. One popular literary genre finds no place in the Bible—myth (see 1 Tim. 4:7; 2 Tim. 4:4). A myth is a fictional narrative that exceeds the limits of truth and goes beyond the facts. Such a type is an unfit vehicle for God's revelation, as Peter makes clear: "We did not follow cleverly invented stories [*mythois*] when we told you about the power and coming of our Lord Jesus Christ, but we were eyewitnesses of his majesty" (2 Peter 1:16).[3] Though literary analysis is legitimate and helpful in interpretation, it should always proceed within the bounds congruent with a truthful Scripture.

Another factor in the horizon of the text is the analogy of faith, the use of Scripture to interpret other Scripture. By precept ("comparing spiritual things with spiritual" [1 Cor. 2:13 KJV])[4] and by example (e.g., Luke 24:25–27; 1 Peter 2:6–8), the Scriptures encourage such an approach. In Romans 9:6–18, where Paul is explaining the concept of unconditional election, he uses three Old Testament passages. He begins with God's word to Rebekah about the struggle between Jacob and Esau in the womb: "The older will serve the younger" (v. 12/Gen. 25:23). Does this mean that the reversal of positions is according to choice, God's choice? The Genesis context extends the statement to nations: "One people will be stronger than the other." Is it a matter of human prowess and endeavor after all? Paul appeals to another Scripture to clear away the confusion and point to the source and basis of the role reversals. God himself said, "Jacob I loved, but Esau I hated" (Rom. 9:13/Mal. 1:2–3). God's choice is behind the role reversal. When Paul recognizes the difficulty here—the arbitrariness makes God appear unjust—he appeals for balance to God's self-revelation in Exodus, "I will have mercy on whom I have mercy" (Rom. 9:15/Exod. 33:19). God's unconditioned freedom of choice is part of his very nature. So interpretation employing the grammatical-historical-literary method must also go beyond the immediate context that identifies the author's intended meaning. It must examine the larger context of the rest of Scripture to validate and illumine that meaning. The interpretation must be coherent in terms of the immediate context and the whole of Scripture, bringing information from the larger context into focus with the plain meaning of the specific text.[5]

The final element of the text's horizon is the overall christocentric and soteriological purpose of Scripture. The Scriptures were given to make us "wise for salvation through faith in Christ Jesus" (2 Tim. 3:15). An interpretation of any passage is in part shown to be valid when its contribution to that purpose can be demonstrated.

---

3. See the discussion of "myth" in *NIDNTT*.

4. See C. K. Barrett's discussion of various options for translating this phrase (*A Commentary on the First Epistle to the Corinthians* [New York: Harper & Row, 1968], 76).

5. Robert L. Thomas, "A Hermeneutical Ambiguity of Eschatology: The Analogy of Faith," *JETS* 23 (1980): 53.

In Romans 9, this factor is explicitly brought into play by Paul, for he is using Old Testament texts to establish the principle of election and show its relation to salvation. He patiently makes clear how each text has significance for God's salvation purposes. For example, he shows the significance of Genesis 25:23: "Yet, before the twins were born or had done anything good or bad—in order that God's purpose in election might stand: not by works but by him who calls—she was told, 'The older will serve the younger'" (Rom. 9:11–12). God's declaration, then, not only comforts Rebekah by telling her what the struggle in the womb means for her family, but it gives comfort to future generations, to the Roman Christians and to those of today, that the pattern of God's miraculous oversight of the line of promise that began with his choice of Jacob will continue. The Genesis text does not itself bring out the soteriological implications. However, later accounts report fulfilment of the prediction and indicate that this is according to God's plan, for God confirms the covenant promises to Jacob on his return to Bethel (Gen. 35:11–12). Paul here demonstrates how the meaning of any passage is understood most clearly and fully when seen in relation to Scripture's christocentric and soteriological purpose.

THE HORIZON OF THE INTERPRETER

After interpreters have distanced themselves from their own preunderstanding and concerns and fully entered into the horizon of the text to hear the Bible's message, they must recross the hermeneutical bridge, returning to their own horizon, bringing the meaning of the text with them. Contemporary discussion refers to this process as fusion of horizons. In truly biblical hermeneutics the meaning of the text is fused with the interpreter's horizon, and the result is communication, correction, and significance. Given the nature and locus of meaning, as the first task for fusion interpreters must find words in their vocabulary stock that express the same sense about the same extralinguistic referents as those in the text. These words are then used to express the text's message in the interpreters' own horizon or context. This is not so much a matter of formal equivalence as it is of referential equivalence. The horizon of truth, which is reality, embraces the other horizons, the text's and the interpreter's. In fact, it is the horizon beyond the horizons that makes the process possible.

Although writing about secular texts, Paul Ricoeur is dealing with this horizon of reality when he says that letters, diaries, travel reports, and all other descriptive accounts of reality may provide the reader with the equivalent of ostensive reference (i.e., extralinguistic reference). They assume the referent they point to is a singular identifiable reality that any reader can understand. In such literature, which is intended to be read by the reader "as if he were there," "the heres and theres of the text may be tacitly referred to the absolute here and there of the reader, thanks to the unique spatio-temporal network to which both writer and reader ultimately belong and which they both acknowledge."[6] If the Scripture's truth corresponds to reality, both spatiotemporal and spiritual, then it can be treated as a descriptive account of reality, and its message can be communicated from one context to another by reference to the larger horizon, the spatiotemporal and spiritual network in which both participate.

Gleason Archer and Gregory Chirichigno have made a study demonstrating the remarkable fidelity with which New Testament authors quote the Old.[7] It is interesting to note that when the New Testament quotes from the Old, the wording is never changed to supply a new referent or sense to communicate the same meaning in a different cultural context, and this pattern holds true even for figurative language. Of the thirteen citations in which Archer finds the greatest, though still superficial, variation from Old Testament wording, none of the changes adjust sense and referent in order to preserve meaning in the new context. Figurative language dependent for meaning on ancient Near Eastern practices is brought over without adjustment. For example, Paul quotes Proverbs, "If your enemy is hungry, feed him. . . . In doing this, you will heap burning coals on his head" (Rom. 12:20/Prov. 25:21–22). Do the burning coals stand for future punishment if the enemy remains unrepentant, or for "burning pangs of shame and contrition"?[8] The apostle prefers to risk ambiguity rather than tamper with the sense and referent of the figure as originally given.

Fusion also involves correction. The message must judge the interpreter's preunderstanding and bring it into line with the true world-view delineated by the Bible's ideas and values. Looking at Romans 9 again, notice that Paul quotes "the older will serve the younger" (v. 12/Gen. 25:23) as proof that God's purposes are achieved not by human works, but by the One who calls. In Jewish interpretation, however, the verse was used to prove the opposite. The rabbis said the promise would come true for Jacob if he merited it; this meant keeping God's law. Rabbi Huna commented, "If [Jacob] is deserving, [Esau] shall serve him; if not, [Esau] shall enslave him" (*Midrash Rabbah* 63.7 on Gen. 25:23 [4th cent. A.D.]). Paul uses the text to correct a wrong view of humankind's relation to God, which was part of a

---

6. Paul Ricoeur, *Interpretation Theory: Discourse and the Surplus of Meaning* (Fort Worth: Texas Christian University Press, 1976), 35.

7. Gleason L. Archer and Gregory Chirichigno, *Old Testament Quotations in the New Testament* (Chicago: Moody, 1983), xxv–xxxii. In 301 out of 386 cases, the wording of New Testament citations of the Old Testament accurately renders the Hebrew text, at points agreeing with it over against the Septuagint. The first three quotations in Romans 9:12–16 are accurately rendered by the LXX, but the final quotation is an instance of the New Testament text's agreeing with the Masoretic text over against the LXX.

8. Cranfield, *Romans*, 2:649.

Jewish legalistic preunderstanding. In correcting the wrong view by a right interpretation, the wrong interpretation is also remedied. In correction one dares to ask, How is the gospel "bad news" to the interpreter's cultural preunderstanding?

The final outcome of fusion is significance, which is not the same as meaning, though it does involve the textual meaning. Significance occupies a higher position from which the meaning has an impact on the concerns and needs of the interpreter in the particular historical-cultural situation.[9] The existential concern of the mid-first century for which Paul finds these verses significant is the lack of response of the majority of ethnic Israel to the gospel. If the gospel is true and Jesus is the promised Messiah, why have not the majority of Jews embraced him? To answer this question, Paul establishes the point that God's salvation operates according to his choice and not human works, even the "work" of having been born a Jew. To demonstrate that this has always been God's method of operating, Paul brings into play Old Testament quotations concerning Isaac, Jacob, and Pharaoh. These then are fused with the puzzling historical situation to provide an understanding of the Jews' lack of response. Though the Jews are responsible for their situation, as Paul goes on to point out, God in his larger purpose has chosen only a remnant rather than the many (Rom. 11:1–10). God's purposes have advanced by his choice throughout the promise stage, and it is the same for the fulfilment stage. Not all Israel is true Israel. We could frame the "significance" aspect of fusion as follows:

---

9. Clark Pinnock's discussion of this aspect of interpretation claims that we need to avoid the extremes of rebellious freedom and conservative legalism by the Spirit's dynamically appropriating the text's meaning in a significant way for today (*The Scripture Principle* [San Francisco: Harper & Row, 1984], 201). He points to New Testament examples, claiming that in each of them the New Testament writers are less concerned with what the words meant than with what they can mean now (e.g., Rom. 1:17/Hab. 2:4; Eph. 4:8/Ps. 68:18; Rom. 10:6–8/Deut. 30:12–14). A close study of these quotations will show that their appropriation does not violate their originally intended meaning but is built on it. True, there is an application of the spiritual truth of the passage to the New Testament situation, but that application is always controlled by the originally intended meaning. Pinnock agrees that fidelity to the text must always be a part of the dialectic of Word and Spirit, meaning and significance. Yet his consistent criticism of conservative legalism and his framing the relation of meaning and significance as a dialectic necessitate a clearer description of the way fidelity to the text will enable the original intended meaning to maintain functional control over the significance found. The same remark can be made regarding Anthony Thiselton's formulation of the matter according to an "action model" of discourse analysis. It should be noted that Thiselton builds his case for "significance," or recontextualization of biblical material, on what he concludes is Matthew's new appropriation of the parable of the lost sheep from the gospel tradition (Matt. 18:12–14; cf. Luke 15:1–7). David Lull speaks of James's contemporizing of the Pauline tradition about faith and works. It is better to build one's case on a comparison of texts (e.g., Old Testament quotations in the New) whose relationship is explicitly established. See Roger Lundin, Anthony C. Thiselton, and Clarence Walhout, *The Responsibility of Hermeneutics* (Grand Rapids: Eerdmans, 1985), 110–11; David J. Lull, "What Is 'Process Hermeneutics'?" *Process Studies* 13 (1983): 195.

How is the gospel "good news" to the world-view and concerns of the interpreter's cultural context?

The Church

Another factor in the interpretation process is the church, the context in which and for which interpretation must be performed. God has gifted the church with apostles, prophets, evangelists, pastors, and teachers (Eph. 4:11; 1 Cor. 12:28). They are to minister the Word through preaching and teaching so that the unbelievers will hear and receive the truth of the gospel, and believers will be built up in their faith (Rom. 10:9–17; Eph. 4:12–16). Interpreting and applying the Scriptures are at the heart of this activity (Acts 5:42; 6:4). This is not to say that understanding the Bible's meaning is dependent on the teaching office, which would, in such a case, exercise equal authority with Scripture. Rather, God has chosen to communicate the truth of his Word from one generation to the next and from one culture to another by means of preachers and teachers who faithfully interpret that Word. Each evangelist and teacher is directly accountable to God for the right handling of the Word (2 Tim. 2:15; 1 Thess. 2:4). Paul describes himself as a man entrusted with the gospel by a God who tests hearts. He tells Timothy to give diligence to present himself as approved to God by rightly handling the word of truth.

Preachers and teachers are accountable to others in the sense that each hearer is charged to test their spirits by the Word to make sure that the interpreters are correctly handling Scripture (1 John 4:1–3). By declaring that the Word is beneficial for reproof and correction, Paul indicates that it is the criterion (2 Tim. 3:16). Interpreting the Word in the context of the church allows for mutual correction to take place.[10] Neither interpreter nor hearer should assume that the other will necessarily always have the right interpretation, for as Paul points out, there are interpreters who turn away from the truth and groups of hearers who love to listen to false teaching (1 Tim. 6:5; 2 Tim. 4:3). Interpreting within the church context is essential for countering the effects of sin on the mind. Paul declares that apostles, prophets, evangelists, pastors, and teachers are given to the church so it will not be "blown here and there by every wind of teaching and by the cunning and craftiness of men in their deceitful scheming" (Eph. 4:14). The highest purpose of interpretation of the Word in the church is to enable Christians "in all things [to] grow up into him who is the Head, that is, Christ" (v. 15).

---

10. Mark Branson comments that the church provides accountability, encouragement, resources, and complementary skills so that one's hermeneutic can be accurate (careful and appropriate) and relevant ("Response to Escobar," in *Conflict and Context: Hermeneutics in the Americas*, ed. Mark Lau Branson and C. René Padilla [Grand Rapids: Eerdmans, 1986], 9).

Application

A number of issues remain for investigation as we move to the last important step in the hermeneutical process—application. Are interpretation and application separate steps or one step? How is biblical content to be received as the norm? How is an indicated application implemented? What criteria does the Bible provide for identifying which content is not directly applicable?

The Distinction Between Interpretation and Application

It is important to view interpretation as separate from application. Unlike the approaches of Hans-Georg Gadamer, the advocates of process thought, and René Padilla, which in one way or another maintain that interpreters have not understood the text until they have applied it, the Bible makes a distinction between the meaning and the significance of a text and finds the locus of meaning in the author's intended sense rather than in his context. Such a separation solves a prevailing problem of contemporary hermeneutics, the problem of "evaporating past meaning in the horizons of the present."[11] When meaning and significance retain their distinction, the Bible's authority as a referential standard is maintained; this is essential if Scripture is to fulfil its declared intention to teach, reprove, correct, and instruct in righteousness. In each of these operations the meaning must be ascertained by interpretation and then put to work as a teacher/trainer or reprover/corrector. Such application assumes a definite content that exercises authoritative control over individuals in their context. Only by such authority can Scripture fulfil its purpose to transform life.

Harvie Conn is rightly concerned that evangelicals have too often allowed this distinction between interpretation and application to result in an uncoupling. Earl Radmacher and Robert Preus sounded the same alarm at the conclusion of Summit II of the International Council on Biblical Inerrancy: "Finally, in the process of determining the singular meaning of the text of Scripture, will we be equally aggressive in determining its significance for our own personal lives?"[12] The distinction is essential but delicate to maintain. Interpretation and application should not be so linked that they become identical. Such a process allows the interpreter's context to determine what Scripture means. The appropriate sequence begins with interpretation, understanding the text with the mind. This step should be

---

11. Anthony C. Thiselton, *The Two Horizons: New Testament Hermeneutics and Philosophical Description, with Special Reference to Heidegger, Bultmann, Gadamer, and Wittgenstein* (Grand Rapids: Eerdmans, 1980), 113.

12. Earl D. Radmacher and Robert D. Preus, eds., "Introduction," in *Hermeneutics, Inerrancy, and the Bible* (Grand Rapids: Zondervan, 1984), xiii.

followed by a closely related but still distinct response of the will, obedience which sets in motion application of the text. The link between understanding and obedience is faith. A person who understands is enabled by the Spirit to welcome the message as true and will be impelled by that same Spirit to obey (1 Cor. 2:14–16; Col. 1:9–11).

The Issue of Form and Meaning

The Bible is unequivocal in proclaiming its own full authority. This means that in both form and meaning the teaching of Scripture is the authoritative standard for living, unless Scripture itself indicates otherwise. Ramesh P. Richard states the same principle in different terms: "The fact that a command is cultural does not mean it is nontransferable to this time."[13] However, there are respected modern critics (e.g., Richard Longenecker, Gorden Fee, Alan Johnson, and Charles Kraft) who maintain that the meaning is binding but not the form. Such a position is fraught with difficulty. Since both cultural forms and scriptural instructions deal with human behavior, how can interpreters be sure that in clinically separating the two they are not removing from their purview biblical content intended for application in all times and places? If cultural form and meaning have no essential relationship, where is the authority for such forms as monogamous marriage, the husband-wife relationship, and baptism by water? Proponents of this position insist that this is not the logical implication of their approach. But Robertson McQuilkin observes, "Suddenly I am made aware that every teaching of Scripture is 'cultural' and that the idea of expecting obedience only to the principle [meaning] that can be discerned behind any specific command of Scripture has made possible the rejection of any teaching at all that is not deemed appropriate by any group of people."[14]

The opposite approach treats both form and meaning as normative. Its critics dismiss it as a kind of cultural fundamentalism that raises the cultural factor in Scripture to a normative level. But Scripture itself provides the regulator. As has been stated several times, form and meaning are to be taken as norms unless Scripture itself indicates otherwise. A person is bound by no more cultural fundamentalism than Scripture itself commands. In this regard it is helpful to recall Jesus' discourse with the Pharisees in which he explains that both form and meaning can be normative. Referring to tithing, a form, and to such meanings as justice, mercy, and faithfulness, he says, "You should have practiced the latter, without neglecting the former" (Matt. 23:23).

---

13. Ramesh P. Richard, "Methodological Proposals for Scripture Relevance. Part 3: Application Theory in Relation to the New Testament," *BS* 143 (1986): 212.

14. J. Robertson McQuilkin, "Limits of Cultural Interpretation," *JETS* 23 (1980): 120.

The more one reflects on the debate between these two approaches, as epitomized in the exchange between McQuilkin and Johnson at Summit II, the more one is led to believe that each side may be mishearing the other. There are differences, significant ones, having to do with the nature of Scripture's full authority, but the conclusions about the content of ethical norms in Scripture do not vary greatly. Is this because each approach shares in the same evangelical interpretive tradition? Or is it because both have ways to distinguish between nonnormative and normative teaching in cultural form? McQuilkin argues that cultural form is not a barrier to normativeness, while Johnson maintains that it indicates nonnormativeness. What they fail to see is that these positions are both describing the same application process but with different emphases. Those who emphasize meaning as the determinant consider certain forms framed as universals (such as monogamous marriage) to be norms,[15] while those who emphasize form and meaning consider certain culturally specific teachings to be nonbinding. The obvious reason for adopting the more comprehensive position affirming both form and meaning is that it best upholds the full authority of Scripture and to the same extent that Scripture itself does.

Another approach considers meaning (or principle) and form as normative but often replaces them with a functional equivalent. As the scriptural precedent for this approach, Walter Kaiser cites the replacement of death by stoning with excommunication as the punishment for incest (1 Cor. 5/Lev. 20:11; see also 18:7). This passage fails to provide a precedent, however, because the relationship between the Old Testament situation and the New Testament situation is not paralleled by the relation between the biblical situation and that of the contemporary interpreter. The Bible states explicitly why it is appropriate to replace forms from ancient Israel when applying penalties in the church. The civil law has become redundant with the disappearance of the theocracy. Jesus declares, "My kingdom is not of this world" (John 18:36). God now works through a spiritual kingdom, Christ's body, the church, manifesting itself in a variety of cultures in which its members live under "various civil orders rather than within a specially covenanted theocratic order."[16] There are no such grounds for replacing the apostolically authorized practices of the early church. Only at those points where the text indicates restricted application or a supplanting of the practices is it appropriate to look for a substitute form to implement the meaning.

Criteria for Nonnormativeness

Among evangelicals the usual procedure is to develop criteria for normativeness and to test biblical material by those criteria to determine what is

---

15. See Millard J. Erickson, *Christian Theology* (Grand Rapids: Baker, 1986), 121–22.
16. John Jefferson Davis, *Foundations of Evangelical Theology* (Grand Rapids: Baker, 1984), 258.

binding.[17] However, the premise being put forth here—that all Scripture, including both form and meaning, is binding unless Scripture itself indicates otherwise—requires a different approach; namely, that one develop criteria for nonnormativeness. Nonnormativeness refers only to forms, not to meaning. Where direct application is not warranted by the text, one may look for a principle and a contemporary form compatible with it. Scripture offers examples of such a process. Paul cites a command from Deuteronomy 25:4, "Do not muzzle an ox while it is treading out the grain," and goes on to apply the underlying principle to the question of fair pay for Christian workers. "Surely [Moses] says this for us, doesn't he? Yes, this was written for us, because when the plowman plows and the thresher threshes, they ought to do so in the hope of sharing in the harvest. If we have sown spiritual seed among you, is it too much if we reap a material harvest from you?" (1 Cor. 9:10–11). The writer of Hebrews considers the Old Testament promise "never will I leave you; never will I forsake you." It was originally spoken by Moses to Israel on the verge of their entrance into the Promised Land (Deut. 31:6). The promise was linked to the exhortation not to fear the inhabitants of the land that God would deliver into their hands. In Hebrews 13:5 this exhortation not to fear is replaced by one against covetousness. Thus the promise is reduced to a principle and applied appropriately to a different situation.

Although the Bible has many general commands which may be directly applied—in fact, there are more of them than is usually realized or admitted—there is still the need to identify those culturally specific commands that should be applied only indirectly, that is, by reducing them to a principle. We can identify them by looking for one or more of these characteristics: limited recipient, limited cultural conditions for fulfilment, limited cultural rationale, or a limiting larger context.

There are several examples of these criteria at work in New Testament quotations from the Old. The challenge is to show from concrete evidence in the text that the writer is making indirect application after applying one of the criteria. In Galatians, Paul takes material originally directed to a limited recipient—the promise declared by Sarah with reference to Ishmael, "the slave woman's son will never share in the inheritance with my son Isaac" (Gen. 21:10)—and applies it to the conflict between Judaizers and Gentile Christians in the churches of Galatia. The Gentile Christians who receive the gospel by faith are sons of Abraham through the free woman (Gal. 3:7, 9; 4:31). Paul highlights the characteristics that limit the application by noting that the receivers of the message are different and exist in two distinct (though similar) historical situations. He observes that the Hagar-Sarah

---

17. See Erickson, *Christian Theology*, 121–22; Davis, *Foundations*, 276–79.

account "may be taken figuratively" (4:24).[18] In the first household of Abraham, Ishmael persecuted Isaac—"It is the same now" (4:24, 29). But the principle or meaning behind the form, which was the promise that there is an inheritance exclusively for the children of the free woman, who are born of the power of the Spirit, may now be applied to the Gentile Christians. On the strength of this extended principle, Paul exhorts the new Christians to stand in their freedom in Christ (5:1).

Sometimes cultural conditions so restrict commands or promises in the Old Testament that they inhibit further direct application; the situation regulates the form of the command.[19] God's comforting promise to deliver Israel after the exile is combined with his command to return from Babylon to Jerusalem: "Depart, depart, go out from there! Touch no unclean thing! Come out from it and be pure, you who carry the vessels of the LORD" (Isa. 52:11). The last phrase probably refers to the vessels from the Jerusalem temple, captured by Nebuchadnezzar, which Cyrus did allow the Jews to take back (Ezra 1:7–11). Paul quotes this command to Gentile Christians, urging them to separate themselves from unbelievers engaged in idolatrous practices, but he leaves out the reference to the vessels (2 Cor. 6:17). In that way he extracts and applies the larger principle by removing a historical-cultural factor that would limit the command to persons returning from the exile. Now the underlying meaning comes to the fore and is appropriately applied as a general command to first-century circumstances. C. K. Barrett suggests that the Isaiah passage "has been taken freshly (from memory) from the Old Testament, and given a new, non-cultic interpretation."[20]

The limited cultural rationale of an Old Testament command or promise might go unexpressed and therefore unnoticed in New Testament application. To establish the permanence of marriage when he is asked about proper grounds for divorce, Jesus appeals to the creation order (Matt. 19:4–6/Gen. 1:27; 2:24), pointing out how the limited cultural rationale of the divorce regulations has obscured the nature of marriage. "Moses permitted you to divorce your wives because your hearts were hard. But it was not this way from the beginning" (Matt. 19:8). Thus, the social structure of lifelong monogamous marriage takes precedence over the divorce regulation because it is grounded in God's will at creation.[21] This precedence involves

---

18. F. F. Bruce translates Galatians 4:24 as "this is an allegory" or "these are allegorical entities." This is a better rendering of the Greek than appears in the NIV. Allegory should be understood in the sense of typology: "An aspect of the new covenant is presented in terms of an OT narrative" (*The Epistle to the Galatians: A Commentary on the Greek Text* [Grand Rapids: Eerdmans, 1982], 217).

19. Richard makes these observations of New Testament material, but they are just as true of the Old ("Application Theory," 212–14).

20. C. K. Barrett, *A Commentary on the Second Epistle to the Corinthians* (New York: Harper & Row, 1973), 201. The application is noncultic in that it does not deal with Israelite temple worship, but it still has to do with true and false worship.

21. Davis makes this principle one of two litmus tests for distinguishing between transcultural principles and forms specific to a particular culture: Is the biblical teaching clearly tied to the creation order? (*Foundations*, 276–79).

understanding that divorce, while not intended at creation, is permitted, but only for marital unfaithfulness (vv. 8–9). Cultural rationale cannot overrule the principle grounded in creation-order rationale.

Does the larger biblical context provide grounds for judging whether specific teachings are not binding? Is there evidence in the progress of revelation that later biblical teaching has set aside the direct authority of earlier material? This is certainly the case with Old Testament law. The content of the law may be divided into three areas: moral, ceremonial, and civil. The New Testament explicitly sets aside the last two. Jesus' declarations that his kingdom is not of this world and that there are continuing responsibilities to civil secular powers indicate that the time of theocracy has passed (John 18:36; Luke 20:25; see also Rom. 13:1–7). The regulations for the civil life of Israel are no longer directly applicable. The ceremonial law, in terms of both the sacrificial system and matters of ritual purity, is fulfilled in Christ and done away with. Mark, Luke, and the writer to the Hebrews make this fact explicit (Mark 7:19; Acts 10:15; Heb. 9:27–28; 10:18). But the moral law of God, expressed in the Ten Commandments and summarized in the two great commandments, the foundation and linchpin for all the rest, is declared by the New Testament still to be in force (Matt. 22:37–40).

That this is the case can be seen from the way the New Testament uses material from each of these sections of the old law. The moral law is applied directly, as James does in addressing the problem of prejudice: "If you really keep the royal law found in Scripture, 'Love your neighbor as yourself,' you are doing right. But if you show favoritism, you sin" (2:8–9/Lev. 19:18). The ceremonial law, however, is applied indirectly. The writer to the Hebrews says that the regulations permitting only the high priest to enter the Holy of Holies once a year to make atonement with blood were the Holy Spirit's way of showing that direct access to God had not yet been disclosed. These regulations, repeated over and over, illustrated the truth that while cleansing was needed, gifts and sacrifices could not cleanse the conscience of the worshiper in any lasting way (Heb. 9:7–9). The meaning behind the form can now be seen.

With regard to the civil law, Paul picks up the meaning behind the form of capital punishment for the sin of incest, namely, the removal of unclean persons guilty of unclean practices. He quotes the oft-repeated phrase in Deuteronomy as a prescription for the incest case at Corinth: "Expel the wicked man from among you" (1 Cor. 5:13/Deut. 17:7). But he applies the command indirectly by counseling excommunication instead of execution (1 Cor. 5:5, 13; cf. Lev. 18:7; 20:11). Progressive revelation has limited the type of application.

Contextualization

The biblical teaching on culture and hermeneutics provides the basic elements for an approach to contextualization. Applying biblically mandated behavior in a new context involves interpretation and application that are based on the principles just described. Contextualization of biblical thought involves three major concerns that can be discovered by a study of Paul's preaching to the Stoics and Epicureans in Athens, whose cultural world-view was nonbiblical.

The Epicurean school, founded by Epicurus (342–270 B.C.), held that basic reality consisted of materialistic atoms. Human beings too were only configurations of atoms. They had no immortal soul, and there was no such thing as resurrection. The gods existed, but they did not interact with people and so could not cause harm or be cajoled by prayer (Epicurus "Epistle to Menoeceus" 123–24, 127b–32).

The Stoics, founded by Zeno (336–263 B.C.), were also materialists, but they did believe that a spark of the divine *logos*, or Reason, which was the controlling principle of the universe, resided in every human being. The duty of humans was to obey the reason within and, in that way, to show oneself to be an offspring of the gods, who are Reason (Cleanthes, fragment 537). The Stoics' eschatology was cyclic. Periodically, the universe would burn up and then start again, repeating itself (Chrysippus, fragment 625). There was no concept of resurrection. The Stoics took a positive view of idol worship as a natural means by which individuals could nurture the drive of the divine spark within them to approach God (Dio Chrysostom 12.45–46, 60–61, 80).

Avoidance of Syncretism

Paul was aware of this cultural background, and his preaching to the Athenians (Acts 17:16–32) indicates his contextualizing approach. First, Paul proclaimed his message in a way that maintained its integrity and separated it from Stoic and Epicurean thought. There was no syncretization, as we can tell from the fact that he was accused of "advocating foreign gods" (v. 18). Luke explains that Paul was really preaching Jesus and the resurrection, and here lies the key to his ability to faithfully maintain God's truth in his contextualized proclamation. He focused his message on the objective events of salvation history and their saving significance.

Such presentation did not keep Paul's message from being intelligible. It was understood well enough for the Epicureans, who held there was no resurrection, to mock it. It was understood well enough by the polytheistic Stoics for them to be curious and want to hear more (Acts 17:18, 32). The

integrity

integrity of the message was Paul's primary concern. He was so confident of its truth, its conformity to reality, that he saw its plain proclamation as his first responsibility. Making contact with his audience, showing them the significance or relevance of that message, was also important. But since true significance is based on true meaning, he committed himself to communicating the message in its integrity, even though the unbelieving continued to mock and the curious initially misunderstood because they heard from a distorted perspective. Still, Paul communicated with such clarity and force that the pagan philosophers knew they were hearing something substantial.

Constructive Engagement with the Cultural World-View

constructive Engagement

Paul's second principle is constructive engagement with the cultural world-view. His stance toward the culture is not that of a prophet condemning its religious center out of hand, although his message carries that necessary implication. The Greeks know of the Jews' antagonism toward polytheism, but they do not identify Paul as that kind of apologist. They correctly perceive that Paul is proclaiming a new message. Once positive contact is established, Paul selects illustrations that reinforce this sympathetic stance. He recognizes their religiosity and points out that worship has been the task of the God-ordained spiritual system from the beginning (Acts 17:22–23, 26–27). He quotes approvingly from one of their poets when his assertions line up with the truth (v. 28). Paul's approach is unmistakably constructive engagement. In the situation thus created, he is able to critique their cultural world-view by the truth of God. The Greeks worship, but their idolatrous polytheism demonstrates that they do so ignorantly, aiming their efforts in a direction away from the one true God. Still, they will be held accountable and must repent (v. 30). The Stoic poet sees us as God's offspring because the divine spark is inside us. This flawed notion provides Paul a point from which to proclaim that we can be called God's offspring because, having been created in the image of God, we live, move, and have our being in him (v. 28).

Paul is also able to take the culture's fragmentation of truth and present it whole. The Epicureans say that the gods have no interaction with people. Paul counters that God is not very far away. It is human spiritual blindness, caused by rebellion, that disrupts and even prevents contact. Humans have distorted the truth about God's nature as transcendent and all-powerful Sustainer and express this distortion in their idol worship. Paul proclaims that the one true and living God is the transcendent personal Creator and Sustainer of the universe. The apostle's presentation is based on the truth of biblical revelation in the creation accounts. He carefully avoids any taint of Jewish ethnocentric bias.

Challenge of Personal Change

The final element in Paul's contextualizing the truth is calling for personal
change by altering one's religious power center. Such change would affect
one's world-view and ultimately one's culture. Paul builds his case by stressing the absolute unity of humanity that supersedes the relative diversity of
cultures: "From one man he made every nation [culture] of men" (Acts
17:26). He stresses that our common human nature, as made in the image of
God, has logical implications for worship. It is not proper to think of God as
being like gold or silver or stone (v. 29). One historically particular salvation
event—the death and resurrection of Jesus, the Jews' Messiah (v. 31)—
gives historical objective proof, open to investigation by all, that God will
judge the world in righteousness. Christ's death, resurrection, and return
are inherently relevant to human beings in every culture. By maintaining
the gospel's integrity and by constructive engagement with the cultural
context, Paul is able to appeal effectively for the most important cultural
change any person can undergo: conversion to a new identity (Christian)
and incorporation into a new people (the church).

Biblical teaching and modeling concerning the interpretation process
understand a hermeneutical bridge existing between the horizons of text
and interpreter. Interpreters must study the text on its own terms, using
the grammatical-historical-literary method and the analogy of faith, and
always looking for the author's intended meaning, which fulfils Scripture's
christocentric and soteriological purpose. Interpreters must then bring the
meaning of the text into their own context. They will communicate its
meaning through suitable concepts from their context. They will use the
text's message to correct thought-forms of their context, as well as to bring
"good news" to human needs which the culture is not adequately addressing. They will practice their interpretation within the context of the church.

The Bible exhibits an application process which is distinct from interpretation. The Scripture is to be regarded as normative in form and meaning
unless one of the criteria for nonnormativeness is present: a limited recipient, limited conditions for fulfilment, limited rationale, or limiting larger
context. Then it is to be applied on the level of meaning or principle. Biblical
contextualization will maintain the integrity of the gospel, constructively
engage the culture, and appeal for a personal change of religious power
center. Its foundation will be the proclamation of savingly significant space-
time events: Christ's death and resurrection.

Part 6

Hermeneutical Guidelines

19

Overview and Analysis

I t is now time to put the biblical theology of hermeneutics and culture to work. The following pages present hermeneutical guidelines for understanding and applying the Bible and suggest steps for a Bible-study method. We will illustrate the steps, concentrating particularly on those that involve historical and cultural factors. Since the method is designed for use within one's own culture or in another, illustrations will be taken from both contemporary Western and non-Western contexts to show how authoritative Scripture can faithfully and effectively communicate its message in all contemporary contexts.

This method of interpretation and application moves back and forth between the part and the whole, the text and the various contexts in which it is to be understood. In *overview*, interpreters consciously adopt a biblical preunderstanding in viewing the literary and historical context of the text. They take stock of their own cultural preunderstanding to assess its relation to the message. The next step views the parts through *analysis*, as interpreters study the grammatical, literary, and historical-cultural factors and what they contribute to the meaning. At this point interpreters return to a concern for context, as they engage in *interpretation*. They put together a coherent understanding of the text in its various literary contexts and relate that understanding to their own cultural context, considering how to communicate the message of the text and how to use it to correct and speak

significantly to the contemporary cultural context. The final step is *applica-*
tion, which determines how the message is to be implemented in the immediate context.

application

Overview

Interpreters prepare for analysis, interpretation, and application by
adopting a biblical preunderstanding, surveying the pertinent passage in
literary and historical context, and evaluating the cultural preunderstanding
of their own environment or that of the target audience.

Biblical Preunderstanding

Consciously adopt a biblical preunderstanding by praying for the Holy Spirit's
illumination and by deciding to take the stance of faith toward Scripture, a humbly
repentant stance toward yourself and your historical circumstances, and a receptive
stance toward the truth revealed. A consciously appropriated biblical preunderstanding is the essential starting point. Each time one studies the Bible, one
should begin by thanking God for the spiritual understanding that is a
benefit of the regenerate state. One should also affirm to God implicit trust
in the truth of his Word. This is the stance of faith toward Scripture, without
which its saving and sanctifying truth can never be appropriated and become effective in the interpreter's life.

Continuing in prayerful meditation, the interpreter should identify the
concerns and questions arising from personal historical circumstances and
the broader cultural context with which he or she approaches the text. Since
such circumstances can either blind one to what God has to reveal in the
text or can illumine the text as one searches for answers to pressing concerns, it is essential to make oneself aware of such concerns and their
potential influence. It is a good idea to jot them down. Indeed, one should
declare a sincere desire for the Holy Spirit to lay bare the soul, helping it
recognize and repent of wrong thinking and acting spawned by one's historical and cultural conditions. This is the humbly repentant stance toward
oneself and one's historical circumstances.

humility

Peter K. H. Lee has an existential concern in his interpretive work: preparation of the church in Hong Kong for the return of that territory to the
People's Republic of China in 1997. He seeks to put the message of Luke
11:29–32 in context to provide a Christian sense of guidance: "The Queen of
the South will rise at the judgment with the men of this generation and
condemn them; for she came from the ends of the earth to listen to Solomon's wisdom, and now one greater than Solomon is here" (v. 31). Unfor-
tunately, Lee's critique of the present economic conditions in Hong Kong,

particularly of the skyrocketing land values and neglect of workers' welfare, has blinded him to the proper interpretation of Jesus' comparison of himself with Solomon. Jesus compares the response of a foreign queen with the skeptical response of his generation in their demand for a sign. Even a Gentile queen could appreciate and respond to Solomon's wisdom. Her attitude stands as a judgment on the current lack of response when one greater than Solomon is before them. But Lee reads a reversed significance into the queen's judgmental stance against Jesus' generation: "Could it have been the reverse, i.e., learning from Solomon's limitations? Is it possible that the Queen of Sheba later on was disillusioned by Solomon? Supposing that she was afterwards critical of Solomon's economic policy, among other things, might she not call into question those who followed his policy blindly?"[1] But neither the New Testament nor the Old is concerned to critique Solomon's economic policies. In fact, the queen compliments him on the condition of his servants (see 1 Kings 10:1–13).

In his article on James's condemnation of favoritism (2:1–13), Cain H. Felder, a black New Testament scholar, demonstrates how one's concerns can illumine the study of this text. Most translations developed by committees composed of members from majority cultures use such words as "favoritism," "partiality," and "snobbery," but Felder clearly identifies the sin as prejudice and applies it to the "racial bigotry (blatant and subtle) that so often translates in patterns of severe socioeconomic injustice."[2] His sensitivity to prejudice alerts the church to the relevance of this passage's warning.

Finally, in prayer interpreters should consciously embrace a biblical world-view and its teachings on God-ordained structures and behavior patterns, interpreting all biblical content in the light of it. They must receive God's truth, confident that the Spirit will illumine their minds to perceive the nature and excellence of the teaching. This is a receptive stance toward revealed truth. If interpreters are concerned to understand the nature of humankind and they undertake to study Psalm 8, they will be confronted by the psalm's majestic view of human beings created by a direct act of God in his own image, only slightly lower than the angels, a view they must receive in a culture dominated by evolutionary thought. In addition, a commitment to biblically mandated behavior means that such commands as "each of you must put off falsehood and speak truthfully to his neighbor" (Eph. 4:25) must be followed literally, particularly in a contemporary context where half of all Americans polled by the Internal Revenue Service in 1984

---

1. Peter K. H. Lee, "1997 and the Church in Hong Kong: An Exercise in Contextualization," *Ching Feng* 25 (1982): 240.

2. See *Eight Translation New Testament* (Wheaton, Ill.: Tyndale, 1974); Cain H. Felder, "Partiality and God's Law: An Exegesis of James 2:1–13," *Journal of Religious Thought* 39 (1982): 51. It is interesting to note that the section heading in the TEV is "Warning Against Prejudice."

said that they operate by a "flexible" standard of honesty, that it is acceptable to cheat large stores and insurance companies at least a little.[3]

Preliminary Study of the Text in Context

*Do a preliminary study of the text in its own literary and historical context to
determine the basic message in relationship to its immediate context, to the biblical
book, to Scripture as a whole, and to historical circumstances surrounding the
writing of the book.* Since this interpretation method constantly moves back
and forth between the part (analysis) and the whole (synthesis), it is advisa-
ble to start with the whole, viewing the passage to be studied in its larger
literary and historical context. This can be done by summarizing in a few
sentences the basic message and relating that message to its placement in
the book (its immediate context), as well as trying to see how the passage
functions in the flow of thought of the book as a whole. Since Scripture is a
unity, one must also ask where in the procession of salvation history the
text appears (see fig. 6).

Preliminary study of the text in its historical context should include
introductory questions about authorship, audience, and composition (especially occasion and purpose) to see how these factors illumine the passage.[4] Knowing, for example, that the Thessalonian church was composed
largely of Gentile Christians of Greek extraction helps one understand why
Paul was trying to clear up confusion about the second coming and the role
in it of believers who have already died. For the Greeks, who did not have
resurrection as part of their world-view, it was difficult to comprehend that
believers who have died will really be resurrected.[5] Paul had to address this
confusion and did so with a comforting explanation (1 Thess. 4:13–18).

Cultural Preunderstanding

*Be aware of and evaluate your cultural preunderstanding to discover which ele-
ments in it can transmit the message of the text, what needs to be corrected, and how
the message is significant for your cultural world-view, structures, and behavior
patterns.* Since cultural preunderstanding is mediated through human language and aims at expressing truth to enable those thinking and speaking
with that language to cope with reality, it is not surprising that many linguistic elements are oriented toward truth and are therefore congruent with

---

3. Morton Hunt, "The Truth About Lying," *United Magazine*, April 1986, 61.

4. See Donald Guthrie, "Questions of Introduction," in *New Testament Interpretation: Essays on
Principles and Methods*, ed. I. Howard Marshall (Grand Rapids: Eerdmans, 1977), 105–16.

5. The consistent witness of classical Greek literature is that there is no resurrection (Homer *Iliad*
24.551; Sophocles *Electra* 137ff.; Aeschylus *Eumenides* 648, "Death comes once; there is no resurrection").

Figure 6
Contextual Survey of Philippians 1:3–11

Basic Message   In this passage, Paul gives affectionate thanks to God for the Philippians, especially for their partnership in the gospel. He expresses confidence in their perseverance and prays that God will work out the graces of love, knowledge, blameless life, and the fruit of righteousness in them.

Context	Summary
Immediate	This passage follows the standard beginning of a letter and precedes Paul's statement of his affection for the people. His partnership with them in the gospel motivates him to inform them about his present circumstance in prison and how it has advanced the gospel (vv. 12–14).
The book	Occurring at the beginning of the letter, this passage sets the tone of joyful thanksgiving for the Philippians and also presents prayer concerns for love, holiness, and fruitfulness.
The Bible	In salvation history as a whole, this passage presents a positive model of a life of faith that lives out the promised salvation blessings; Paul describes the qualities that such a life produces.

the biblical world-view. These elements may be used to communicate as well as illustrate the message of a text. The primary relationship of text and interpreter's context is communication. The interpreter's preunderstanding and vocabulary stock, or the preunderstanding and vocabulary stock of the target audience, provide raw material for making the message intelligible. The question to ask at this point is, What in the pertinent cultural world-view and its social apparatus conforms to the message?

The encounter between text and preunderstanding will often involve correction. Every culture has a religious power center that is opposed to God. It is largely from this center that a culture develops its ideas, beliefs, and values to enable rebellious human beings to survive. For this reason many aspects of any cultural preunderstanding will clash with the truths of Scripture and will need to be corrected by them. The question now becomes, For what parts of the world-view, structures, and behavior patterns currently engaged is this message bad news? Further, have I personally accepted the correction? Am I on guard against the doubt, fragmentation, and distortion encouraged by these cultural influences?

Finally, the discovered message may have significance for the particular cultural preunderstanding. The message offers positive consequences for certain concerns or needs that exist in the culture but that cannot be met or met satisfactorily because of the particular makeup of its world outlook. The message is of a true significance, but it is conveyed by thought-forms alien to the cultural thought-pattern. Stated in its simplest form, the significance question is, What in this message is alien to the cultural preunderstanding, though it is significant good news? Again, one must guard against cultural blinders by constantly asking, Am I consciously aware of and open to the truth of the alien thought or behavior, so that my interpretation will not ignore or dismiss it? Some examples here of cultural preunderstandings that are congruent with biblical teaching and can promote communication of its meaning within a culture may be helpful, as will some that exemplify dissonance that needs to be corrected for the form to be used effectively.

Cultural myths must be handled with great care, for they often claim to have a source of revelation quite distinct from scriptural revelation. Ideas and stories drawn from extrabiblical myths cannot add to information in Scripture, though the Bible may serve to indicate whether the myth draws from the ultimate source of all knowledge of God for fallen humans— natural revelation. This source holds in store what we may know of God from observing creation's witness (Acts 14:15; Rom. 1:18–20). Another source is the common historical consciousness that reaches back to what actually happened in the beginning. Genesis 1–11 presents clearly the historical account that myths remember only dimly and in a distorted way.

In Western culture the myth of the big bang has at least one component that is congruent with Genesis 1. The theory concludes that the universe had a beginning at a finite point in time. Western science arrives at this correct conclusion by analyzing the evidence of God's witness to himself in creation.[6] In Africa there are hundreds of myths of creation and of the Supreme Being's "departing" or "going far away" because of human misdeed or misbehavior.[7] This, of course, fits with what actually happened in the beginning according to Genesis 1–3. These myths offer evidence of humankind's historical consciousness, but only what accords with Scripture is true.

The Western Aristotelian view of truth is congruent with the biblical view: "To say of what is that it is not . . . is false, while to say of what is that it is . . . is true."[8] The Muslim view of revelation as inerrant parallels the Bible's view of itself as the inspired, inerrant Word of God (John 10:35; Ps. 119:137, 160).[9]

---

6. Rick Gore, "The Once and Future Universe," *National Geographic* 163 (1983): 710, 741.

7. Charles H. Kraft, *Christianity in Culture* (Maryknoll, N.Y.: Orbis, 1979), 309.

8. *NIDNTT*, s.v. "Truth."

9. Chris Marantika, "Toward an Evangelical Theology in an Islamic Culture," in *The Bible and Theology in Asian Contexts: An Evangelical Perspective on Asian Theology*, ed. Bong R. Ro and Ruth' Eshenaur (Taichung, Taiwan: Asia Theological Association, 1984), 378.

Although Western scientific culture does not allow for the supernatural, it does have the concept of secondary causes and effects in the various laws of physics. This also agrees with scriptural understanding, for some miracles involve God's use of secondary causes. The way through the Red Sea is prepared by God's causing an east wind to blow all night (Exod. 14:21). In the Caribbean, Rastafarianism has concepts that echo Scripture. One is the dignity of human beings.[10]

These are examples of beliefs and ideas. In the area of values there are also many cultural correlations with biblical teaching. Western economic theory retains a strong sense of fair play between employer and employee and between buyer and seller. This value corresponds to biblical teaching (Lev. 25:43, 53; Eph. 6:9; Col. 4:1). In Asian culture, filial piety and obedience are cardinal virtues. Parents are honored and their wishes followed. "In China the elderly are cared for within the family circle instead of being rushed off to a convalescent home at the first sign that they might become a burden."[11] This basic attitude is part of biblical teaching (Exod. 20:12; Matt. 15:4; Eph. 6:2; 1 Tim. 5:8).

Some American legislation prohibits behavior also prohibited by the Bible. In some states new pornography laws ban the display of sexually explicit reading matter in stores.[12] This is congruent with Scripture's condemnation of the actions pornography portrays and the passions it feeds (Mark 7:22; Gal. 5:19; Eph. 4:19; 1 Peter 4:3).

The preunderstanding of Western culture includes the scientific myth of destiny, which asserts that we live in an ever-expanding universe that will eventually collapse into oblivion.[13] This myth needs to be corrected. It contradicts Scripture's eschatological teaching that the Lord Jesus will intervene to end history and that there will be a new heaven and earth (2 Peter 3:1–13).

The cultural preunderstanding of African traditional religions posits a metaphysical chasm between God and human beings. According to the African myth of power, one can communicate with the High God only through a series of intermediaries, never directly.[14] Such notions can be corrected by the biblical teaching of the incarnation and Jesus as the one mediator (Heb. 1:1–6; 1 Tim. 2:5).

In India the prevailing concept of knowing God affirms that the sincere search for God "will ultimately lead . . . to the true God no matter by what

---

10. David H. Sang and Roger Ringenberg, "Towards an Evangelical Caribbean Theology," *ERT* 7 (1983): 145.

11. Morris A. Inch, *Doing Theology Across Cultures* (Grand Rapids: Baker, 1982), 85.

12. "The State of American Values," *U.S. News and World Report* 99, no. 24 (9 December 1985): 58.

13. Gore, "Once and Future Universe," 748.

14. Tokunboh Adeyemo, "Towards an Evangelical African Theology," *ERT* 7 (1983): 148.

name or in what form this God is now worshipped."[15] This idea also needs scriptural correction (John 14:6; Acts 4:12).

The list of such near-truths is endless. Western culture has come to believe that technology has the potential to alter human life fundamentally. The computer chip, with its logic and memory, is considered to have the essence of human intellect.[16] This belief forfeits humankind's dominant position over the physical creation and urgently needs to be remedied (Gen. 1:28; 9:1–3; Ps. 8:6–8).

Traditional religious thought in Africa views the world as "a moving equilibrium that is constantly threatened and sometimes actually disturbed by natural and social calamities."[17] Ritual and magic are used to control cosmic forces and social evils. Such a view needs to be confronted with the scriptural affirmation that a sovereign and merciful Creator controls history for his own glory (Dan. 4:34–35; Job 38–41; Ps. 104:24; 145:7).

Exodus 20:12 teaches that children are to honor parents, and yet polls taken in the 1970s show that a majority of Americans no longer affirm this value. Simultaneous with a lower sense of obligation to children, 67 percent of parents believe that "children do not have an obligation to their parents regardless of what their parents have done for them."[18]

Filipino culture has a value, *hija*, that contradicts Scripture's teaching about one's self-concept. "A sense of shame, embarrassment, inferiority or timidity" is actively encouraged.[19] Scripture undeniably recognizes the value of humility (2 Tim. 1:7; Rom. 8:15), but it also affirms that confidence and boldness are the Christian's hallmark (Acts 4:13, 29; Eph. 6:19; Phil. 1:20).

American behavior patterns in regard to premarital sex contradict biblical teaching (1 Cor. 6:12–20; 1 Thess. 4:1–7). *U.S. News and World Report* documents the trend: "Federal statistics show that about half of the women who married during the early 1960's said they had sex before their weddings. Now, more than four fifths report they had sexual experience."[20] This behavior is promoted by such social structures as value-free sex education in the public schools and by the entertainment media.

In Asian culture, the admirable respect for one's ancestors is tainted by worship of the ancestors and fellowship with the spirits. The suppliant seeks through rituals and sacrifices to be on good terms with *Shen*, the good

---

15. Ken R. Gnanakan, "Biblical Foundations: A South Asian Study," *ERT* 7 (1983): 115.

16. Allen A. Boraiko, "The Chip: Electronic Mini-Marvel," *National Geographic* 162 (1982): 421.

17. Adeyemo, "African Theology," 151.

18. Daniel Yankelovich, *New Rules: Searching for Self-Fulfillment in a World Turned Upside Down* (New York: Bantam, 1982), 103.

19. Rodrigo D. Tano, "Toward an Evangelical Asian Theology," *ERT* 7 (1983): 169.

20. "State of American Values," 55.

spirits, and to be kept safe from *Kivei*, the evil spirits.[21] This aberration can be corrected by acquaintance with the biblical mandates to worship the one true God alone (Exod. 20:2–7; 1 Cor. 8:5–6; 10:20).

Not only can the biblical world-view correct a cultural preunderstanding, it can have significance as it speaks good news into the cultural context. So pervasive is radical or moderate epistemological relativism in Western culture that the very idea of truth seems to be an alien thought-form. In an interview with Katharine Hepburn, Gregory Speck comments on the sad state of affairs in Western culture, of which terrorism is one aspect:

Speck: *We're facing some serious problems, and I see no answers.*

Hepburn: When the truth goes out of style, life becomes extremely difficult. We just don't know what the truth is any longer, and that goes for every-thing. One is simply appalled by it all, by the things people will do to one another. There is simply no way to deal with these terrorists, it seems. When they've got a gun at the head of one of your citizens, your instinct is to try to protect him, but what do you do? They have an entirely different point of view about it all, and actually seem to look forward to death.[22]

Scripture's affirmation that it has the truth can certainly be good news, since it provides answers to the human dilemma.

The concept of verbal and prophetic revelation is alien to Asian thought. "In Hinduism and Buddhism, revelation is a process of interiorization."[23] Through meditation, looking deeply within oneself and ceasing to hear outwardly, one hears inwardly. But what does one hear? Nothing. Christianity offers the good news that God has spoken, in human language by human agents in space and time, a saving message for all to hear.

Some cultures have such distorted values that people are presumed to be dishonest until proven otherwise.[24] Bribery and double contracts (e.g., one for the government and one for the parties involved) are commonplace. Such dishonest dealings are an alien concept in the Bible (Prov. 12:22; Eph. 4:25; James 5:12). What good news this revelation would be for cultures whose social fabric is weakened by such distrust!

In a totalitarian regime, whether left or right, the state is the highest authority. Any structures or behavior patterns that give citizens a real choice

---

21. Inch, *Doing Theology*, 88–89; see also Bong R. Ro, ed., *Christian Alternatives to Ancestor Practices* (Taichung, Taiwan: Asia Theological Association, 1985).

22. Gregory Speck, "Katharine the Great: An Interview," *Eastern Review: The Magazine of Eastern Airlines*, December 1985, 56–57.

23. Sunard Sumithra and Bruce Nicholls, "Towards an Evangelical Theology of the Third World: An Indian Reflection," *ERT* 7 (1983): 182.

24. David J. Hesselgrave, *Communicating Christ Cross-Culturally* (Grand Rapids: Zondervan, 1978), 291.

in political, economic, or religious matters are alien and dangerous. The Bible provides reasonable guidelines to limit political power: "Give to Caesar what is Caesar's, and to God what is God's" (Matt. 22:21). What good news this would be to the countless oppressed people, many of whom are suffering for their faith (see Acts 4:19; 5:29)!

Analysis

A writer communicates meaning by using grammatical, literary, and historical-cultural elements. By analyzing what each of these elements signifies in a text, the interpreter can see what it contributes to the text's meaning.

Grammatical Analysis

Analyze the passage's grammar by a visual representation of its structure and determine what the various grammatical features contribute to the passage's meaning. Every language communicates meaning through a pattern of relationships between three elements: morphemes, function words, and word order. Morphemes are meaningful linguistic units that contain no smaller meaningful parts (e.g., the word *wash* and the suffix *-ed*, which indicates past time in words like "washed," are morphemes). Function words indicate relationship (e.g., conjunctions ["and"], prepositions ["in"], and particles ["indeed"]). They have only a very limited meaning. In uninflected English, word order is especially important for identifying a verb's subject and object. (Did Sam hit Joe or did Joe hit Sam?) A sample analysis of one verse may be helpful (see fig. 7).[25]

Literary Analysis

Analyze the literary conventions, that is, the literary structure, forms, and figures of speech used to communicate the writer's meaning. The writer communicates meaning not only through grammatical patterns but also through recognized literary conventions. These may be classed as literary structure: word play, word order (including chiasm), repetition (parallel or antithetical), and breaks in or needed additions to thought. They include the

---

25. For further help see J. Robertson McQuilkin, *Understanding and Applying the Bible* (Chicago: Moody, 1983), chap. 9; Walter C. Kaiser, Jr., *Toward an Exegetical Theology: Biblical Exegesis for Preaching and Teaching* (Grand Rapids: Baker, 1981), chap. 4; Gordon D. Fee, *New Testament Exegesis: A Handbook for Students and Pastors* (Philadelphia: Westminster, 1983), 60–83.

Figure 7
Mechanical Layout of Romans 1:16

Subject	Verb	Object
I	am not ashamed of	the gospel,

↑ because it is the power of God[a]

↑ for the salvation[b]

↑ of everyone

↑ who believes[c]

= first for the Jew,
then for the Gentile.[d]

Grammatical notes:
a. This clause gives the reason Paul is not ashamed.
b. This phrase shows the purpose of the power.
c. The verb is in the present tense, suggesting a state of belief.
d. These phrases define "everyone" in terms of the order for receiving fulfilment of the promises.

patterns of various literary genres and subgenres: gospel, history, epistle, apocalypse, parable, methods of argument (including use of the Old Testament in the New), worship forms, ethical instruction, and prophetic material (including allegory and typology). They involve figures of speech that communicate by comparison, association, personal dimension, understatement, intensification, or reversal of meaning. In the case of literary structure or form, its function and meaning in ancient culture need to be understood. One must then determine how the writer used it to communicate the intended meaning.

Figures of speech always involve comparing or relating two elements by means of a common quality, expressed or unexpressed, that binds them together. The interpreter should explore the thought and life of the ancient culture to uncover the common quality and to determine how it naturally led to using the figure to powerfully identify the two elements. Details from stories and parables can also be illuminated through such an investigation. To make sure the intended meaning has been identified as precisely as possible, the interpreter should restate the message in definite, literal prose.

In handling cultural literary conventions, two cautions need to be noted if the full authority of Scripture is to be preserved. First, one must be aware that a literary form which by its very nature violates the biblical understanding of truth is never employed in inerrant Scripture. This means such forms as pseudonymous writing or midrashic gospel narrative that claims to be, say, a letter written by Paul or an account of an incident in Jesus' life but is in fact apocryphal. These do not qualify as part of Scripture, which deals only in truth that corresponds with reality. Does this mean that any literary convention that is not literal truth is unfit to be part of Scripture? No, such literary conventions as parables, understatement, hyperbole, and irony appear in the Bible, but the writer specifically indicates that they are not to be interpreted literally. It is this honesty that separates legitimate literary conventions from illegitimate ones. The spurious ones claim to be something they are not. In Scripture a parable is usually introduced as a parable, and irony and hyperbole can be detected by their role in their immediate context.

Second, cultural explanations of a text's literary conventions should not be used to set aside authoritative declarations or commands contained in the passage. Difficulty arises when the text uses understatement, hyperbole, or irony. We do not undercut the Bible's authority by not literally obeying Jesus' word, "If your right eye causes you to sin, gouge it out and throw it away" (Matt. 5:29). Testing the command against the immediate and larger context, it becomes clear that this is a hyperbolic way of showing the seriousness of sinful sexual thought. It is not possible, of course, to prevent such sins by removing the offending physical member, the eye gate, for the adultery is in the heart (v. 28). Moreover, the Lord is the Savior of the body. It is not to be mutilated (1 Cor. 6:13). So our caution stands; any exceptions to biblical declarations are to be identified by interpreting Scripture within its whole context. Scripture, not the literary convention, limits the application.

Literary structure includes certain ancient literary techniques such as chiasmus, which is "the crosswise arrangement of contrasted pairs to give alternate stress."[26] The pattern *abba* can be seen in 1 Timothy 3:16, a Pauline hymn fragment:

> He appeared in a body,
>   was vindicated by the Spirit,
> was seen by angels,
>   was preached among the nations.

The contrast between the earthly and heavenly environments in which Jesus' saving work and the proclamation of it took place comes out clearly in this structural pattern. To do his saving work, Jesus was incarnate on earth

26. Herbert W. Smyth, *Greek Grammar*, rev. Gordon M. Messing (Cambridge, Mass.: Harvard University Press, 1956), 677.

("appeared in a body"); the proclamation of his saving work went to the ends of the earth ("was preached among the nations"). His saving work was vindicated by heaven as the Spirit raised him; heaven rejoiced at the accomplished salvation ("was seen by angels").

The study of the literary form or genre of a given biblical book can be most valuable. Paul has christianized and invested with apostolic authority the ancient letter form by the way in which he describes himself and his readers, and by the way he prays for them and sends greetings (see fig. 8).[27]

The extrabiblical information in literary analysis is sometimes used against the authority of a passage. Eduard Schweizer, for example, classifies certain parts of Paul's letters as "housetables," which were ancient ethical instructions for life in a household. He goes on to draw the conclusion that since the New Testament takes over patterns from ancient culture, such patterns are not fixed forever. Consequently, today's Christians have the responsibility to do the same thing with ethical patterns they find in their contemporary culture. "Jesus' disciples take their ethical obligations seriously, but never possess a rigid and definitely fixed ethical code. On the whole, they share with their world and time the same ethical values and warnings against unethical conduct."[28] Paul's use of the housetables, however, does more than just accept conventional ethics. He christianizes the form by explicit reference to Christ and use of the phrase "in the Lord" (Col. 3:18, 20, 22, 24–25; 4:1). This indicates that Paul intends the housetables to be universally and eternally normative for Christians.

The cultural factor is very evident in the use of figures of speech. The comparisons they engage in are often expressed in such a way that one of the elements of the figure is suppressed, that is, implied and not expressed. For example, a metaphor sometimes suppresses the point of similarity between the topic and the image with which it is being compared. Jesus says of himself: "I am the gate for the sheep" (John 10:7). The point of similarity between Jesus and the shepherd as the gate of the sheepfold is not explicitly given. Yet there is in the immediate context what John Beekman and John Callow call a "pivot word or phrase": "whoever enters through me will be *saved*" (v. 9).[29] Security is what Jesus and the shepherd provide. Extrabiblical cultural information—the fact that the ancient and modern Palestinian shepherds sleep across the entryway of a sheepfold—confirms this interpretation.[30]

---

27. John L. White, "Saint Paul and the Apostolic Letter Tradition," *CBQ* 45 (1983): 433–44.

28. Eduard Schweizer, "Traditional Ethical Patterns in the Pauline and Post-Pauline Letters and Their Development (Lists of Vices and Housetables)," in *Text and Interpretation: Studies in the New Testament Presented to Matthew Black*, ed. Ernest Best and R. McL. Wilson (Cambridge: Cambridge University Press, 1979), 208.

29. John Beekman and John Callow, *Translating the Word of God* (Grand Rapids: Zondervan, 1974), 129.

30. Leon Morris, *The Gospel According to John* (Grand Rapids: Eerdmans, 1971), 507 n. 30.

Figure 8
Comparison of Epistolary Forms

	Ancient Letter	New Testament Letter (Philippians)
Opening		
Sender	Irenaeus	Paul and Timothy, servants of Jesus Christ (1:1)
Addressee	Apollinarius, his dearest brother	All the saints in Christ Jesus at Philippi (v. 1)
Greeting	Many greetings	Grace and peace to you from God our Father and the Lord Jesus Christ (v. 2)
Thanksgiving		I thank my God . . . in all my prayers for you (vv. 3–6)
Wish/prayer	I pray continually for your health; I myself am well	And this is my prayer: that your love may abound (vv. 9–11)
Body		
Introductory formula (disclosure, petition, etc.)	I wish you to know	Now I want you to know, brothers (v. 12)
Ethical section (parenesis)		Rejoice in the Lord. . . . Do not be anxious. . . . Whatever is true . . . noble . . . think about such things (4:4–9)
Closing		
Greetings	Many salutations to your wife and to Serenus	Greet all the saints in Christ Jesus. The brothers who are with me send greetings (vv. 21–22)
Wish/prayer for physical health	Before all else I pray that you may have health and the best success, unharmed by the evil eye	
Farewell	Good-bye	
Benediction		The grace of the Lord Jesus Christ be with your spirit. Amen (4:23)

The ancient letter in this figure is actually a synthesis of two typical letters, one from about A.D. 25 and the other from the second or third century A.D. (C. K. Barrett, ed., *The New Testament Background: Selected Documents* [New York: Macmillan, 1957], 28–29).

Historical-Cultural Analysis

Analyze the word meanings in the light of historical-cultural information and the historical situation described in the passage in order to see what this knowledge contributes to understanding the text. A third way a writer communicates meaning is through cultural understandings shared with the audience, usually by use of the common vocabulary stock. Since the Bible was written in a different historical-cultural context, the modern interpreter must study to uncover the meaning of the term's historical use. Since the Bible is divine revelation in the language of the time, all word study will involve investigation in two contexts—the biblical context and the broader historical-cultural context (see fig. 9).

First, the interpreter must focus a word's meaning in the biblical context. The author's usage, as well as use in the rest of the Bible, provides evidence for aspects of the range of meaning. For example, of the five distinct uses of *exousia* in ancient literature—authority as right or power, office, excessive wealth, pomp, and crowd—only the first two are present in biblical literature.[31]

Because of the impact of God's revelation in word and deed on the language of the Bible, it is best to begin one's search for the background source of New Testament words with Old Testament concepts to see how Old Testament words were shaped by God's communication and dealing with Israel. For example, *diathēkē* means "a last will and testament" in ancient Greek usage; in the New Testament, as already attested in the Septuagint, it means primarily "the divine covenant" (Epictetus *Dissertationes* 2.13.7; Isa. 59:21; Luke 22:20). *Doxa* means "opinion, appearance" in ancient Greek; in the New Testament, as well as the Old Testament, it means "glory" (Plato *Gorgias* 472e; Ps. 29:3 [LXX 28:3]; Rom. 5:2).[32] With the aid of Bible dictionaries and concordances, the interpreter can identify the potential range of meaning for a given word and then decide which particular aspect is being employed in the passage under study. It will be harmonious with the word's use elsewhere in Scripture.

Extrabiblical contexts do sometimes provide evidence for elements in a range of meaning. A Pauline term which appears to have its background context in extrabiblical ancient culture is *stoicheion* (plural, *stoicheia*). There are extrabiblical sources for its entire range of meaning. It can mean "fundamental principles" (Heb. 5:12; Plutarch *De liberis educandis* 16.2), "elemental substances" (2 Peter 3:10, 12; Diogenes Laertius 7.137), "elemental spirits" (Gal. 4:3; Col. 2:8, 20; *Sibylline Oracles* 2.206), or "heavenly

---

31. Compare and contrast the range of meaning for the term in Liddell and Scott, the standard lexicon of ancient Greek, with that in Bauer, the standard lexicon of New Testament Greek.

32. Moisés Silva, *Biblical Words and Their Meaning: An Introduction to Lexical Semantics* (Grand Rapids: Zondervan, 1983), 79.

Figure 9
Language and Thought-Contexts for the Greek New Testament

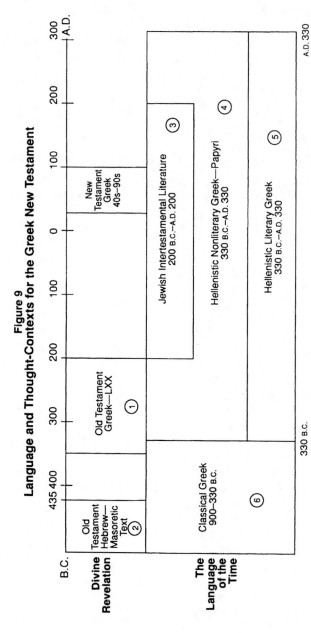

Circled numbers indicate a thought-context's relative nearness to or remoteness from the New Testament. The background and source of thought should be studied beginning with ①. Although LXX translation practice does seem to have influenced New Testament vocabulary, only those portions of the LXX which are directly quoted in the New Testament should be considered divine revelation.

bodies" (possibly Gal. 4:3; Col. 2:8, 20; Diogenes Laertius 6.102).[33] Such extrabiblical cultural information should not be set against the claims regarding the biblical writer's use of the term. It should not be used to challenge Scripture's claims that a given thought or mandate is of divine origin. Paul uses *stoicheia* to describe the bondage in which the "elemental spirits of the world," that is, the spiritual forces of evil, place "religious" non-Christians through the legalistic *elementary principles* of religion. In so doing, he tells us the truth about the *stoicheia*, truth extrabiblical evidence talks about in a fragmentary way. The fact that the covenant between God and Israel follows the same pattern as the ancient suzerainty covenant does not mean that the words of God's covenant are not of divine origin—he could have appropriated this pattern for his own purposes.[34]

The second step is to illumine the word's meaning by viewing its usage in the broader historical-cultural context. How would the word have been understood in the ancient cultural milieu? Such understanding can provide background for biblical vocabulary. New Testament words may be cultural, pointing to particular conditions, physical objects, institutions, or practices in the socioeconomic, political, intellectual, or religious spheres of first-century life. They may be spiritual or figurative terms whose literal or secular usage provides an illuminating background picture. They may be terms which, when compared or contrasted with contemporary usage, will manifest their distinct meaning. The interpreter can investigate evidence from biblical encyclopedias and dictionaries and from such primary sources as Jewish intertestamental literature (e.g., Josephus, Philo, the Apocrypha, and pseudepigrapha) and Hellenistic literary and nonliterary works to get at the meaning.[35]

Two perspectives must be kept in mind as this study is pursued. First, the uncovering of extrabiblical parallels to biblical thought should never be used to supplant the Scripture's claim that its usage is of divine revelatory origin. God can sovereignly choose the human words and meanings he desires to communicate his message. Second, extrabiblical historical-cultural information should not be used to reduce or extend the authority of Scripture in a given passage.

Some parts of Scripture are historical narrative. In those cases, a reconstruction of the historical events can be pursued. This can provide helpful information about cultural details and the meaning of such cultural

---

33. Bauer, s.v. στοιχεῖον; Ernest D. Burton, *A Critical and Exegetical Commentary on the Epistle to the Galatians* (Edinburgh: T. & T. Clark, 1921), 510–18.

34. Meredith G. Kline, *Treaty of the Great King: The Covenant Structure of Deuteronomy, Studies and Commentary* (Grand Rapids: Eerdmans, 1963).

35. John A. Thompson, *Handbook of Life in Bible Times* (Downers Grove, Ill.: Inter-Varsity, 1986); J. Julius Scott, Jr., "On the Value of Intertestamental Jewish Literature for New Testament Theology," *JETS* 23 (1980): 315–24; William Barclay, "The New Testament and the Papyri," in *The New Testament in Historical and Contemporary Perspective: Essays in Memory of G. H. C. MacGregor*, ed. Hugh Anderson and William Barclay (Oxford: Basil Blackwell, 1965), 57–82.

terms as "sixth to ninth hour," "a sabbath day's journey," or "a denarius." Much extrabiblical evidence is included in study Bibles and other reference works.

The ancient context also provides a contemporary background against which one can compare and contrast the biblical use of terms. For example, in a nonbiblical papyrus the term *koinōnia* describes a close relationship in commerce (*Sylloge Inscriptionum Graecarum* 300.54).[36] It is also used in marriage contracts to describe the closest, most intimate of personal relationships: "Lucaina and Hierax have come together for a partnership [*koinōnia*] of life" (*Berliner griechische Urkunden* 4.1051.9). In secular usage the aspect emphasized is closeness, and the focus of the sharing is economic, not just social or psychological.

Paul's use of the term deepens its meaning by transferring it into the spiritual realm. He has a spiritual partnership with the Philippians because of their spiritual relationship with Christ. Yet there is no spiritual-physical dichotomy, for that spiritual partnership has issued in financial support for Paul (Phil. 4:10–19). The Philippians have had "fellowship in the gospel" with Paul. The secular background helps us see this relationship in a fuller way.

Extrabiblical background information should not be used to set aside Scripture's authoritative claims. Bruce N. Kaye describes the political climate at the time Romans was written as a time of good government. On this basis he argues that Paul's pronouncements are a theological projection from a particular situation. The government then was tending toward the good. Kaye concludes, "It is not open to the Christian to hide behind the quite wrong idea that government *per se* and hence all governments are divinely ordained."[37] That "quite wrong idea" is in fact what the Scriptures teach in this passage. It gives a criterion for evaluating whether a government's performance is in line with God's intention (Rom. 13:4). Other Scriptures indicate that when there is an authority conflict, God must be obeyed (Acts 4:19; 5:29). But this passage clearly teaches that God ordains governments and that the Christian is obligated to be a good citizen. That teaching cannot be set aside by extrabiblical evidence about the political conditions under which Paul wrote.

Hermeneutical guidelines based on the biblical teaching involve a process of overview and analysis. By prayerfully deciding to approach Scripture with a biblical preunderstanding, interpreters take a stance of trust and receptivity toward their passage, and they consciously acknowledge their

---

36. James H. Moulton and George Milligan, *The Vocabulary of the Greek Testament, Illustrated from the Papyri and Other Non-Literary Sources* (Grand Rapids: Eerdmans, 1976), 351.

37. Bruce N. Kaye, "Political Obedience in Romans 13:1–7," *Theological Students' Fellowship Bulletin* 63 (1972): 12

own concerns and repent of any wrong thinking. Their overview activity includes a preliminary study of the passage in its literary and historical context. It also entails probing their own cultural preunderstanding to see what in it is serviceable for communicating the message of the text. Interpreters also ask what correction and significant "good news" the Bible will bring to bear on their culture.

Analysis is to be conducted in three areas. The grammatical structure and features of the passage must be studied to see what they tell of the meaning being conveyed. Literary conventions should be scrutinized to see the significance for the message of the writer's use of literary structure, forms, and figures of speech. Historical-cultural features, both word meanings illumined by appropriate background information and historical details from the immediate and larger historical situation, repay close study.

20

Interpretation and Application

Once the interpreter has proceeded through the steps of (1) an overview of his or her own context and of the text in its context and (2) a grammatical-literary-historical analysis of the text, it is necessary to reverse the process and move ahead to a synthesis in which a coherent interpretation emerges from the text viewed in context. That interpretation must then take the message of the text and relate it to the interpreter's context. Having understood the "what" of communication, correction, and significance, it is time to understand the "how." How is the meaning of the text intelligible as bad news or as good news to the interpreter and the target audience? Once this is understood, one can put the text to work in the contemporary context through application.

Interpretation

The Biblical Context

First, state the basic point of the passage concisely and make an exegetical outline which reflects not only content but progression of thought. The passage was taken apart in analysis. Now, using a summary statement of the message and an outline representing the flow of thought indicated by the grammar, put the passage back together. (See figs. 6 and 7 for the raw material for this step.)

#2

Second, relate the message of the text to the immediate context and the purpose of the book in which it is located. How does the immediate context help one better understand the meaning of the text? (See fig. 6.) How does the message of this particular passage promote the book's purposes? The message of Mark 2:1–12, for example, is that the Son of man has authority on earth to forgive sins, an authority demonstrated by his healing the paralytic. Mark's larger purpose is to present the gospel of Jesus Christ, the Son of God (1:1).[1] The healing incident contributes to that purpose by giving evidence that Jesus is the Son of God because healing is supernatural proof of a divine prerogative, the forgiveness of sins. It also presents an important part of the good news: the forgiveness of sins through faith in the Son of man.

Third, trace the congruence of the passage to parallel teaching elsewhere in Scripture. #2 According to the analogy of faith (the principle that Scripture interprets Scripture), a comprehensive interpretation will relate the meaning of this passage to other passages in Scripture in terms of background and parallel or contrasting thought. The term "Son of man" as used in the Gospel of Mark has its proper background in Daniel 7:13, where the heavenly being is described as "one like a son of man," who approaches the Ancient of Days and is given such authority, glory, and sovereign power that all peoples worship him as he reigns in an everlasting kingdom. Other elements in the background include the use of this term in addressing Ezekiel the prophet, its general application to designate a person as a human being (e.g., Ps. 8:4), and its reference to primordial man in the Old Testament or in ancient Near Eastern mythology and to Israel collectively as the heir of Adam.[2] In Aramaic the term is a circumlocution for the pronoun *I.*

In the light of Jesus' explicit reference to its imagery, the Daniel passage is the most probable background, for it contains the elements of authority, suffering, and glory which Jesus spoke of. This background puts in perspective Jesus' claim to divine prerogative when he forgives the sins of the paralytic. The Gospel of Mark offers parallel passages that depict Jesus using the term "Son of man" to refer to his earthly ministry, suffering, resurrection, and glorious return (e.g., 2:28; 8:31; 13:26; 14:41, 62). These other uses establish his soteriological and sovereign authority. The Son of man, who is to die according to God's plan and return to earth as judge, ministers with authority in his first advent.

By reference to similar contexts, comprehensive interpretation undertakes to harmonize any theological difficulties that may arise. For example, when Jesus says to the paralytic, "Son, your sins are forgiven" (Mark 2:5), one could infer that sin is the cause of his sickness. This incident invites

---

1. C. E. B. Cranfield, *The Gospel According to Mark: An Introduction and Commentary* (Cambridge: Cambridge University Press, 1959), 14–15.
2. *NIDNTT*, s.v. "Son of Man."

comparison with Jesus' remarks to his disciples' questions concerning the man born blind: "'Rabbi, who sinned, this man or his parents, that he was born blind?' 'Neither this man nor his parents sinned,' said Jesus, 'but this happened so that the work of God might be displayed in his life'" (John 9:2–3). The apparent contradictions can be harmonized when one recognizes that Mark makes no explicit connection between sin and sickness, though other scriptural passages give multiple reasons or purposes for sickness or suffering. It may be the result of sin. It may be for God's glory (John 9:3; 11:4). It may be for the person's discipline and sanctification (2 Cor. 12:7–10).

The Contemporary Cultural Context

How do interpreters communicate the message through the contemporary world-view and vocabulary stock, their own or that of their audience? Since the locus of meaning is the writer's intent concerning an extralinguistic referent, the interpreter's first responsibility is to identify those words in the vocabulary stock that point to the same referent and communicate the same sense as the text. What words say the same thing that the writer intended to say? Because words constantly change their meanings, adding or dropping referents or senses from their range of meaning, it is a continuing challenge to identify the particular terms in the contemporary linguistic context that best represent what the original writer intended to say.

Even as common a human experience as the nursing infant's desire for milk varies in expression across time periods. Compare the King James (1611) and the New International (1973) translations of 1 Peter 2:2:

KJV: As newborn babes, desire the sincere milk of the word, that ye may grow thereby.

NIV: Like newborn babies, crave pure spiritual milk, so that by it you may grow up in your salvation.

In order to maintain fidelity to the original author's intent expressed by his use of words, the twentieth-century translators had to change words to maintain referential equivalence. The Greek verb *epipotheō*, "long for," was translated "desire" in the King James. However, that English word has been weakened in meaning until in today's American usage it connotes "a feeling that one would get pleasure or satisfaction by obtaining or possessing something." The New International Version maintains the strength of *epipotheō* by translating it "crave." The term *adolos*, "without deceit, unadulterated," describing milk, is translated in the King James by "sincere." In current American usage "sincere" refers mainly to persons who are "free from pretense or deceit in feeling or manner or actions."[3] The New International Version avoids potential misunderstanding by using "pure" to translate *adolos*. Current American usage speaks of "sincere people" but "pure milk." Constant attention to the sense and referent intended by the biblical author, combined with a perceptive handling of word usage, will prepare the way for faithfully and relevantly communicating the message of the text.

What if the thing or event referred to by the biblical words is unknown in the contemporary context? Interpreters can choose a word in their vocabulary stock that is close to the biblical concept and then show by using it in context that they are adding to its range of meaning. The New Testament writers do this with the Hellenistic Greek vocabulary stock. In ancient Greek, *metanoia* meant a sense of regret for a given action, whether good or bad (Plutarch *Timoleon* 6 [I.238d], "for *metanoia* produces shame even for that which has been done well"; *De sollertia animalium* 3 [II.961d], "those who harm dogs and beat horses . . . make for themselves a painful sensation which we call *metanoia*"). When Paul uses the term in Athens, he is calling for conversion, a total change of life. "In the past God overlooked such ignorance, but now he commands all people everywhere to repent" (Acts 17:30; see also 2:38). The range of meaning has definitely been expanded to include repentance as well as regret.[4]

One can also take a generic term from the interpreter's vocabulary stock, modify it by a description of form or function, and make it serviceable to describe a biblical concept. Wycliffe Bible translators in translating Acts 27:40 into Mexican Lalana Chinantec render *pēdalion*, "rudder," as "flat board which steers." The generic term *board* is modified in terms of form and function to communicate the sense and referent of the Greek term. Transliteration with a translation or explanation attached can also be used to bring a word over from the Greek or Hebrew. The New Testament treats Aramaic words in this way. Transliterated *abba* from the Aramaic is accompanied by its translation, *ho patēr*, "father" (Mark 14:36). Wycliffe Bible translation in the Kalinga language of the Philippines renders *hiereus*, "priest," as "priest, the one who deals with that given to God."[5] In these ways the meaning from one context can be communicated into another.[6]

---

3. *Oxford American Dictionary*, s.v. "Desire"; "Sincere." Note the *Oxford English Dictionary's* definitions: *desire*—"to have a strong wish for; to long for, covet, crave"; *sincere*—"pure, unmixed, free from any foreign element." These definitions reflect the history of the usage, including the KJV.

4. *TDNT*, s.v. μετανοέω, μετάνοια.

5. John Beekman and John Callow, *Translating the Word of God* (Grand Rapids: Zondervan, 1974), 197, 200.

6. Beekman and Callow argue for another method of communicating things and events unknown in the interpreter's context: the identification of cultural substitutes. This method, though Beekman and Callow use it with caution, violates the biblical understanding of meaning and truth and should not be pursued (ibid., 201–11).

Ideas, objects, and concepts from a culture's world-view, structures, and behavior patterns may also be of use in communicating Scripture's message. But since human culture is generated by fallen human beings, every aspect of it is tainted by sin. Thus, any appropriation of human culture must involve a correction of what is not true before it can be serviceable for communicating the truth.

The Chagga of Tanzania are among the hundreds of African traditional cultures that believe God created human beings and then separated from them because of human misbehavior. According to their myth, God created humans, placed them in a vessel, and then burst it so they could get out. God commanded the first man "to eat all the fruit of the bananas, also all the potatoes in the banana grove. But the yam which is called *Ula* or *Ukaho*, truly you shall not eat it. Neither you nor your people may eat it, and if any man eats it, his bones shall break and at last he shall die."[7] A stranger visiting the first man deceived him into eating the forbidden yam. At that point, sickness broke out. When the man prayed for deliverance, God told him that if, when he grew old, he shed his skin like a snake, he would be rejuvenated. However, the man was unsuccessful in this, and so death passed on all.

There are enough similarities between the Genesis creation account and the Chagga myth to provide a point of contact for witness. From the perspective of a commonly remembered primeval history, one can point to the prohibition of eating a certain plant and to the deception, disobedience, and fatal consequences. The differences are just as striking and give opportunity for the gospel. God did, indeed, promise deliverance but not through the first man's efforts to achieve rejuvenation by meeting certain conditions which he then failed to fulfil. God himself worked through his incarnate Son, "so that by his death he might destroy him who holds the power of death—that is, the devil—and free those who all their lives were held in slavery by their fear of death" (Heb. 2:14–15). Christ's resurrection, which makes him the second Adam, head of a new race, brings good news to the Chagga, who, after the failure of their first man, had only death to look forward to.

In the Muslim belief in inerrancy as the mark of true divine revelation, there is a point of contact for communicating the truth about Scripture and contending for it as a superior revelation. Chris Marantika presents two suggestions for taking advantage of this belief. Muslims have many questions about the Bible and have accepted the charge of opponents of Christianity that the Bible has errors. The Christian witness should accept responsibility for answering questions about the Bible's accuracy and should explore and explain many seemingly inconsistent passages. The

---

7. John S. Mbiti, *Concepts of God in Africa* (London: S.P.C.K., 1970), 174.

second task is to show that the Koran is not inerrant. This should be done, not by attacking the Koran directly, but by exposing the false teachings of the Talmudic excerpts and apocryphal legends that are in the Koran. In this way "the theologian will present the inerrant Bible as superior to the so-called 'inerrant Koran.'"[8]

The value of *hsiao* (filial piety) in Asian, especially Confucian, culture is congruent with the Bible's commands to "honor your father and your mother" (Exod. 20:12). Jesus stressed the importance of duty to parents when he rebuked the Pharisees for their casuistical rule that allowed children to declare property a gift devoted to God, thus freeing themselves from the obligation to use it to support parents (Matt. 15:3–6). But there is a significant difference between the Confucian and biblical approaches. Chinese culture is ethical in orientation. Viewed religiously, *hsiao* fills all aspects of life. It functions as the Chinese religion, with the parents playing the role of God, and reaches its natural climax in ancestor worship. But the Bible views God as Father and the only person worthy of worship. Wang Chih-hsin puts it succinctly, "the Jews look upon God as Father; the Chinese regard parents as God."[9] This difference presents a challenge to witness and convert alike. How can one continue to practice filial piety as a Christian, obey the fifth commandment, and not break the first—"You shall have no other gods before me" (Exod. 20:3)? The solution will involve the correction of cultural patterns in the matter of Asian ancestor worship.

Now that we have considered the matter of communicating the message, the next issue to be handled is, *How does the interpreter correct those aspects of the culture's world-view, structures, and behavior patterns which Scripture contradicts and thereby judges to be false?* This is the step in which to ask, How is the text's message *bad news* to the culture? Because of a culture's totalitarian drive to give a satisfactory explanation for everything, this bad news often must be spoken before the people are open to receive the good news. They have to realize that something is wrong before they can respond to the call for a radical shift in religious power centers and lifestyle, which conversion to and growth in Christianity represent.

The metaphysical chasm between God and humankind, which all African religions know, leads to the projection of a series of intermediaries through whom the worshiper seeks to approach God. The Shona of Zimbabwe believe that priests, mediums, the living dead (i.e., the recent generation of the deceased, especially of the royal family), and spirits act as

---

8. Chris Marantika, "Toward an Evangelical Theology in an Islamic Culture," in *The Bible and Theology in Asian Contexts: An Evangelical Perspective on Asian Theology*, ed. Bong R. Ro and Ruth Eshenaur (Taichung, Taiwan: Asia Theological Association, 1984), 379.

9. Quoted in Wing Hung-Lam, "Patterns of Chinese Theology," in *Bible and Theology in Asian Contexts*, 334.

intermediaries in taking a person's request to God.[10] The Bible recognizes the need for an intermediary, a mediator in the sense of an arbitrator who must deal with God's wrath against human sin. As Job expresses it, "If only there were someone to arbitrate between us, to lay his hand upon us both, someone to remove God's rod from me" (Job 9:33–34). The good news for the Shona is that God himself provides the mediator in his Son, the Lord Jesus Christ. "For there is one God and one mediator between God and men, the man Christ Jesus, who gave himself as a ransom for all men" (1 Tim. 2:5–6). He opens the most direct access to the Father for those who pray in his name (Heb. 10:19–23; John 15:16). These biblical truths correct the Shona concept of human and spiritual intermediaries by showing that at best they are not needed, and at worst they keep a person from gaining access to God. Because of our sin, an intermediary is necessary, and God has provided one in Christ. The unreliability of a series of intermediaries is replaced by the effectiveness of one man, Christ Jesus, who brings human beings directly into God's presence.

The world-view of India entails an inclusivistic perspective which holds that any sincere search for God, by whatever path, will find him. Ken Gnanakan contends that this perspective must be corrected by the forceful presentation of the uniqueness of Christian revelation and the uncompromising claims of Christ.[11] What Jesus said was unique and original, the truth heard from God and spoken to human beings (John 8:28, 32). The inexorable claims of Jesus as he issues the call to follow him must be heard. Jesus states his exclusive claims (to be the only way to the Father) in terms of the consequences for following or not following him: "For whoever wants to save his life will lose it, but whoever loses his life for me will save it" (Luke 9:24).

Contemporary American values and behavior with regard to premarital sex are summed up by a Northwestern University coed who said, "There has to be concern about birth control and getting an education before people engage in premarital sex, but it's not wrong. It's perfectly natural."[12] Such a view must be corrected by Scripture. Premarital sex is in one sense a natural activity for fallen humans. It is an attempt to satisfy the divinely created sexual appetite (1 Thess. 4:5; 1 Peter 4:3), but in a way outside the bounds decreed by God (1 Thess. 4:3; Heb. 13:4). In a more basic sense, premarital sex is unnatural. For humankind created in the image of God to act naturally is to obey God's laws. Premarital sex is a violation of God's law and is, therefore, unnatural. Paul's argument against it shows in what ways it is unnatural. It is an act in which one is mastered by his or her passions—

---

10. Mbiti, *Concepts*, chap. 19.

11. Ken R. Gnanakan, "Biblical Foundations: A South Asian Study," *ERT* 7 (1983): 115.

12. "The State of American Values," *U.S. News and World Report* 99, no. 24 (9 December 1985): 55.

but we are called to live in self-control (1 Cor. 6:12; 1 Thess. 4:4). It is an act that separates physical appetite from the relationship of lifetime commitment. In so doing, it denies the true unity of our nature as body and spirit and our true purpose. "The body is not meant for sexual immorality but for the Lord" (1 Cor. 6:13). The interpreter has to correct the mistaken view toward sex and present premarital chastity as the truly right and natural practice. Promotion of wholesome social activities such as work projects, spectator sports, group ministry, and artistic endeavors, involving relationships that encompass the whole person, will be a part of the application.

In Asian culture, ancestor worship, a practice which contradicts Scripture, needs scriptural correction through teaching the true nature of the intermediate state after death both for unsaved (Luke 16:23) and saved (Phil. 1:23; 2 Cor. 5:8). An important aspect of such teaching is Scripture's prohibitions against necromancy (Deut. 18:9–13; see also Lev. 19:31; 20:6).[13] The interpreter must instruct the audience so they can understand how worshiping the spirits of the dead is having another god before the one true God (Exod. 20:3–7). Such correction by Scripture's teaching will transform ancestor worship into ancestor respect. The biblical concept of honoring parents (Exod. 20:12; Eph. 6:2) and the lively remembrance of saints who are with the Lord (Heb. 11:1–12:1; Rev. 14:13) are the Christian antidote to ancestor worship. Daniel Hung offers such practical suggestions as replacing the ancestral tablets and idols on the family altar with the Ten Commandments, Bible verses, and a picture of Christ. He also suggests that an annual memorial meeting on a special Ancestor's Day be held in the church at the time of the Chinese Lunar New Year so that a positive commemoration of departed parents may replace the customary sacrifices.[14]

The next step is to determine how the message, including the thought-forms and behavior patterns it introduces, is significant for the contemporary culture. These concepts may be alien to the culture, yet they meet basic human needs in a way that serves God's glory and human good. The message is good news, and the interpreter has the task of showing how it meets needs which the culture experiences but deals with inadequately.

For those seeking to deal with evil in a context where the truth has gone out of style and is no longer known, the Bible has good news. God has spoken his Word, and it is eternally valid (John 17:17; Ps. 119:89–91). That Word gives a true perspective on the human predicament, even in its contemporary form, so that instead of being appalled or even paralyzed by the situation, one can face it with understanding and courage.

---

13. "A Working Document: Towards a Christian Approach to Ancestor Practices," in *Christian Alternatives to Ancestor Practices*, ed. Bong R. Ro (Taichung, Taiwan: Asia Theological Association, 1985), 8–9.

14. Daniel M. Hung, "Mission Blockade: Ancestor Worship," in *Christian Alternatives*, 214–16.

Terrorism is a particularly frightening element in the contemporary scene, but Scripture teaches clearly that the source of terrorism is the human heart: "For out of the heart come evil thoughts, murder, adultery . . ." (Matt. 15:19). Though the forces of terrorism are unmanageable, humanly speaking (and this may be due in no small part to Satan's encouragement), God is sovereign and can change the terrorist's heart by his Spirit through the witness of faithful Christians. Consider Chet Bitterman's faithful witness before he was martyred by Colombian terrorists. Letters to his wife while he was in captivity were filled with Scripture texts that witnessed to God's power and grace. These were printed in full in national newspapers as front-page news.[15] For those willing to accept the idea that truth and faithfulness to it are more important than physical survival, there is no fear of death. They do not fear those who kill the body (Matt. 10:28). Scripture provides comfort as well as courage for the faithful. God practices a heavenly "watchcare" over his children (vv. 29–31).

The Bible has good news for those who have come to view revelation as a process that is essentially internal and private, for Christ as God incarnate in history actively performed his redemptive work in space and time. This active, caring God demonstrates once and for all that the path to knowledge of him is not the way of interior negation by mystic religions that view the external world as illusion (maya). Christ lived in the world that is real, and knowledge of him embraces not only God's Word spoken and written but also the Word personalized, made flesh. Such a Word of God is good news because it brings true wholeness to life. It "maintains the harmony of proclamation, of life style, of action and reflection."[16] The Johannine writings forcefully bring the point home. The disciples ask to have the Father revealed to them. Jesus answers, "Don't you know me, Philip, even after I have been among you such a long time? Anyone who has seen me has seen the Father" (John 14:9). Jesus the truth bears witness to the truth, and this revelation in space and time is proclaimed by his apostles (v. 6; 18:37). "That which was from the beginning, which we have heard, which we have seen with our eyes, which we have looked at and our hands have touched—this we proclaim concerning the Word of life" (1 John 1:1).

Some cultures have so lost touch with the value of truth that a person is presumed to be dishonest unless proven otherwise. In such a context honest dealings are an alien concept and considered very foolish. What good news the standard of honesty would be to such a culture in a number of ways! It would promote trust and a sense of fairness in social dealing. The power of the bribe would be disarmed and would no longer serve as the

---

15. Steve Estes, *Called to Die: The Story of American Linguist Chet Bitterman, Slain by Terrorists* (Grand Rapids: Zondervan, 1986).

16. Sunard Sumithra and Bruce Nicholls, "Towards an Evangelical Theology of the Third World: An Indian Reflection," *ERT* 7 (1983): 181–82.

way to obtain guarantees of general welfare, security, and protection from those in authority. Oppression would be replaced with the justice of a system based on honest dealings, in which each person is as good as his or her word. "Let your 'Yes' be yes, and your 'No,' no" (James 5:12). In the final analysis, truth is the basis for the stability of a just society. "By justice a king gives a country stability, but one who is greedy for bribes tears it down" (Prov. 29:4). It is interesting to note that such a society free from oppression would fulfil the longing of the theology of liberation, particularly the Latin American varieties.[17]

The limits on state power are an alien concept to a totalitarian regime. Jonathan Chao, who has a deep knowledge of the People's Republic of China, describes the totalitarian approach as "the state's overall lordship over its citizens." The end result is a deification of the state and a dehumanization of its citizens, who are deprived of the exercise of their God-given free will and have their human creativity suppressed, so that people become mere tools of the state. How welcome and significant the good news of the biblical teaching about the proper limits of state power could be for those suffering the abuse of power, which is the essence of statism! It would, of course, be bad news and unsettling for those wielding power. The Bible teaches that God, not the state, is the highest authority, that in fact he is the one who grants the state its power. The scriptural message could be presented to the state by those who love their country as a warning of the dangers inherent in deifying the state and its anti-God position (Rom. 13:1–7). The Bible teaches the dignity and worth of all humankind, created in God's image with moral and creative capacities that require the exercise of the will in freedom (Gen. 1:28; 2:17). This truth about human freedom as an inherent human right is the countervailing, liberating concept—good news to those suffering the dehumanizing influences of total state control. It gives the citizen a place to stand. As Chao contends, the Christian has "no obligation to yield unreserved, uncritical, and absolute obedience to the state. . . . Believers should obey the state when obedience is properly due and disobey it when it oversteps its proper boundaries, that is, when it does not uphold justice or when it forces its citizens to act contrary to God's revealed will."[18]

Application

The final step in the hermeneutical process comes in applying the biblical standards and admonitions to the context in which one is working. How

---

17. See Mark Lau Branson and C. René Padilla, eds., *Conflict and Context: Hermeneutics in the Americas* (Grand Rapids: Eerdmans, 1986).

18. Jonathan Chao, "Towards an Evangelical Theology in Totalitarian Cultures, with Special Reference to Socialist China," in *Bible and Theology in Asian Contexts*, 345, 352.

are the commands, promises, and principles to be implemented in ordinary individual lives? The process has three basic steps: (1) locate and analyze normative biblical content that is directly applicable mandate or implemented principle; (2) identify the contemporary situation to which this teaching or principle applies; and (3) develop the appropriate response in terms of the changes required in thought and behavior patterns and the benefits that will ensue from such change. The basic assumption of our approach is that *all biblical teaching—commands, promises, and statements of truth—is normative unless Scripture explicitly indicates otherwise.*

Locating Normative Biblical Content

Test the biblical teaching in the passage to see whether it should be applied directly by using both form and meaning or indirectly by linking meaning with a culturally relevant form. There are definite criteria for determining what calls for indirect application; biblical teaching that does not satisfy one of these criteria should be applied directly:

(1) Indirect application is called for if the direct recipient of the teaching is limited by the immediate context. Such a limitation is often indicated by the way the recipient of a command or promise is named. Jesus uses the indefinite Greek pronoun *tis* when issuing the call for discipleship, "If anyone would come after me" (Luke 9:23). This form indicates the universal extent of his invitation. His final instructions to the disciples to go and teach their converts everything that he had taught them, which presumably includes this invitation, indicates that the form *anyone* is not limited to those present (Matt. 28:18–20). The situation is different when Jesus addresses one individual, the rich young ruler: "If you want to be perfect, go, sell your possessions and give to the poor, and you will have treasure in heaven. Then come, follow me" (Matt. 19:21). The command is limited to a specific recipient and so is not universally binding for all who would follow Christ. However, the meaning or principle that undergirds it is. Riches can be a stumbling block to entrance into the kingdom, which entails a life of radical discipleship. Jesus goes on to say, "It is hard for a rich man to enter the kingdom of heaven" (v. 23); elsewhere he declares that "any of you who does not give up everything he has cannot be my disciple" (Luke 14:33). There is an economic aspect to repentance for the rich, who, under the Spirit's conviction, must apply Jesus' command to themselves if, like the rich young ruler, they have riches as their god. Paul equates covetousness with idolatry and also gives instructions for the rich to practice a generous, humble stewardship of resources (Col. 3:5; 1 Tim. 6:17–19).

(2) Presentation of specific historical or cultural conditions for obedience to the command or reception of a promise indicates that a limited application was intended. Peter assumes a certain political system when he commands Christians to "honor the king" (1 Peter 2:17), and his use of the

terms *king* and *governor* as examples of the human institutions to which we are to be subordinate shows that he was conscious of the assumption. He indicates this further by defining the different types of authority each exercises: "the king, as the supreme authority, or . . . governors, who are sent by him" (vv. 13–14). Ramesh Richard observes that people determine the cultural specificity level of a command almost intuitively: "Somehow people in nonmonarchial political systems know that 1 Peter 2:13 (subjection to the king) stands in a different way to them than it did to those in the first century." However, to depend on intuitive sense alone would land the interpreter in a situation of cultural relativism. If intuitively we ask, "Do the differences between cultural contexts mean that we are to apply the biblical mandate indirectly through a contemporary cultural form that accurately expresses the biblical command's meaning?" the answer must come from the way the writer presents the command in Scripture. Ramesh Richard's contention is true of fully authoritative Scripture: "Specificity and prescriptivity are not mutually exclusive. . . . The fact that a command is cultural does not mean it is nontransferable to this time."[19]

When a prescription with cultural elements, such as baptism, is given in a universal setting, it is a clear indication that the writer intends the command to be followed even when the form and its particular meaning are foreign to the cultural context. It may even be difficult; Christian baptism cannot be easy in frigid or arid areas. But the fact that Christ in his universal authority sent men to disciple all the nations until the end of the age means it must be done.[20]

Phil Parshall contends that Christian baptism communicates the wrong meaning in an Islamic context, and he urges that serious consideration be given to substituting another initiation rite, a form that will be less offensive. When a Muslim is baptized, he "has openly declared himself a traitor to Islamic social structures, political and legal systems, economic patterns; and, worst of all, the religion of his fathers has been profaned and desecrated." This is an unfortunate situation, but another form is not permitted by Scripture. Moreover, a different form would not really solve the problem, because the source of the offense is not the form but the meaning it points to. It is indeed "a 'rite of passage' from Islam and initiation into the community of believers who look to Christ rather than to Mohammed for salvation."[21]

(3) A limited cultural rationale shows that the writer intended to limit the extent of application. One passage in which a limited cultural rationale has been identified is 1 Corinthians 11:2–16: some interpreters see a limited

---

19. Ramesh P. Richard, "Methodological Proposals for Scripture Relevance. Part 3: Application Theory in Relation to the New Testament," *BS* 143 (1986): 209, 212.

20. Millard J. Erickson, *Christian Theology* (Grand Rapids: Baker, 1986), 122.

21. Phil Parshall, *New Paths in Muslim Evangelism* (Grand Rapids: Baker, 1980), 190, 196.

rationale with respect to women's wearing head coverings or long hair and men short hair: "We have no other practice—nor do the churches of God" (v. 16).[22] In this view, Paul is simply appealing to the custom of the churches in general, thus indicating that it is a cultural matter. Others concentrate on the phrase "the churches of God" and construe it as a designation of the whole church and therefore a custom presented as part of the normative apostolic tradition.[23] There are two basic reasons why this passage should not be viewed as containing a limited rationale. It is the climax of Paul's instruction, which began by praising the Corinthians for holding fast to normative apostolic tradition and continued by appealing to the creation order as a rationale for Christian worship practices (vv. 2, 8–9). The conclusion of such a passage should involve the same level of normativeness. Second, a limited rationale would undermine its role in the argument, which is to present the universal practice of the church as a confirmation of the validity of Paul's instructions.

The statement concerning long hair on men may contain a cultural rationale: "Does not the very nature of things teach you that if a man has long hair, it is a disgrace to him?" (1 Cor. 11:14).[24] The assumption is that people understand as natural what their culture has taught them is so. But as George Knight has pointed out, Paul's use of *physis*, "nature," is linked to creation, not to cultural understanding.[25] The arguments for limited rationale in this passage fall short.

(4) The broader context of subsequent revelation can explicitly set aside previous revelation. This is the case when the New Testament explicitly sets aside direct application of the Old Testament's civil and ceremonial law.

Principles should be framed for those commands and promises that call for indirect application of their statements of truth. They should also be framed for positive and negative examples drawn from historical narrative. A principle consists of the underlying meaning in the text that can be stated in universal and absolute terms. The principle should also line up with the writer's intended meaning.

Identifying the Contemporary Situation

Identify the exact contemporary situation to which the commands, promises, statements of truth, or principles from narrative examples can be applied. It is

22. F. F. Bruce, "All Things to All Men: Diversity in Unity and Other Pauline Tensions," in *Unity and Diversity in New Testament Theology: Essays in Honor of George E. Ladd,* ed. Robert A. Guelich (Grand Rapids: Eerdmans, 1978), 95.

23. Bruce K. Waltke, "1 Corinthians 11:2–16: An Interpretation," *BS* 135 (1978): 55–56.

24. J. Robertson McQuilkin, "Problems of Normativeness in Scripture: Cultural Versus Permanent," in *Hermeneutics, Inerrancy, and the Bible,* ed. Earl D. Radmacher and Robert D. Preus (Grand Rapids: Zondervan, 1984), 233.

25. George W. Knight, "A Response to Problems of Normativeness in Scripture: Cultural Versus Permanent," in *Hermeneutics, Inerrancy,* 247–50.

helpful to study the historical context of the ancient text to find similarities to contemporary circumstances, but the identification of such similarities is not a criterion of normativeness. Rather, it is an aid in determining which contemporary circumstances are most appropriate for application. Interpreters must study the cultural context they are addressing, whether it is their own or some other. They must understand the questions being asked, the reasons for and manner of those questions, and the questions the culture should be facing but is not.

Developing the Response

Develop the responses—the changes in thought, attitude, and behavior of Christian and non-Christian—called for as a result of applying these mandates or principles to particular situations. The implementation of such changes must be spelled out in terms of the cultural context. In cases of direct application, the form (the action to be taken) is already determined by the text's normative content. With indirect application, the form to express the principle will be selected from the present-day culture. Application works best when the form already has a meaning that is the same as or congruent with that expressed by the authoritative biblical principle.

The involvement of the application process with the cultural factor is well illustrated by considering how the prohibitions of honorific titles in Matthew 23:7–10 should be obeyed in North American evangelical circles. The application also has implications for non-Western contexts, especially those in which the hierarchical social structure of the culture has affected the church in its worship and its relationships. The comments of Pablo Perez at the Lausanne Congress about Latin America indicate how this is so: "I suggest that besides the multiplicity of inferences which this concept [the hierarchical structure inherent in our society] has and will continue to have as to systems of church government, it also has positive results as to its ethical and liturgical implications."[26]

The passage contains three commands: (1) "But you are not to be called 'Rabbi'" (Matt. 23:8); (2) "Do not call anyone on earth 'father'" (v. 9); (3) "Nor are you to be called 'teacher'" (v. 10). The form of each prohibits designating Christians by these titles. The principle behind the form is the avoidance of feeding one's pride by such constant recognition of one's position. Jesus has just pointed to the Pharisees' sin in this regard: "They love to be greeted in the marketplaces and to have men call them 'Rabbi'" (v. 7).

Examination of the setting in which the command is given shows that the recipient is not limited. These instructions are addressed to the crowds and

---

26. Pablo M. Perez, "Biblical Theology and Cultural Identity in Latin America," in *Let the Earth Hear His Voice*, ed. James D. Douglas (Minneapolis: World Wide, 1975), 1254.

to Jesus' disciples, who are subsequently commanded to teach all future disciples whatever they have been taught. Both form and meaning are normative as far as the criterion of the recipient is concerned.

The passage should be reviewed to see whether there are limiting cultural conditions in the form of the command. The transliterated term *rabbi* does convey a limiting cultural condition (see John 1:38). It points to the intertestamental and first-century Jewish context, and in Jewish Christian circles today it might still have the same meaning. For Gentile Christians in late twentieth-century North America, the functional substitute would be "doctor," possibly "reverend" or "pastor." How is one to understand the type of address being prohibited when "father" and "teacher" are proscribed? "Father" is not to be applied to those other than one's natural father, and "teacher" is not to be used as an honorific title rather than as a descriptive term. Except in the case of "rabbi," the form of the command does not involve limiting cultural conditions and is therefore normative.

The rationale transcends cultural limitations. Christians do not call one another rabbi or teacher, for they have one teacher, Christ. They do not call each other father, for they have one father, God. The rationale is grounded in relationships with God and Christ and is therefore transcultural and transhistorical.

The latter two commands may be directly applied to the contemporary context. Only the first, concerning rabbi, calls for indirect application. The principle involved in all three is that honorific titles which point to one's authoritative teaching or ruling function among the people of God should not be used, because they promote pride and strike at the church's basic spiritual equality—"you are all brothers" (Matt. 23:8).

The contemporary situation to which these commands speak is one of Christian interpersonal relationships, particularly in church and school, whether Bible institute, college, or seminary. Most schools have conformed to the American educational practice of academic ranking and the titles that go with it: assistant professor, associate professor, professor. And it is the common practice of students and colleagues to address persons with doctoral degrees as "doctor." The presence of such titles and initials (e.g., Th.D., Ph.D.) on calling cards and nameplates is also commonplace. The current practice stands in contradiction to the direct and also indirect application of these commands.

What kind of response or behavior pattern is called for in applying the form and meaning of these commands to the contemporary church and academic context? Institutions for Christian education need to foster a heart attitude of humble service to other Christians. The reason for such an attitude is that in a community of faith based on grace there is an essential spiritual equality: "you are all brothers" (Matt. 23:8); "the greatest among you will be your servant" (v. 11). Therefore, it is inappropriate to address anyone (or to insist on being addressed) by an honorific title that grants a higher status to one member of the body over another. As a practical matter, an individual could ask to be addressed simply as "mister" and not "doctor," could refer to colleagues as "brother" or "sister," could remove the degree designation from nameplates and calling cards, and could sign one's name without adding academic rank or degree.

The school, for its part, could eliminate use of the formal titles of academic rank except in official academic publications and in a few other instances, such as when conducting professional business or providing references for students. The Bible does recognize the categories of teachers (Eph. 4:11) and even fathers (1 John 2:13–14), but it never uses these as honorific titles directly linked to a person's name. It does employ and encourage the use of the term *brother*. Ananias addresses the newly converted Paul as "Brother Saul" (Acts 9:17). The word *doctor* may be a dead metaphor that does not carry with it the honorific meaning it once did. The command refers to whatever honorific title is employed to distinguish the authoritative teaching or ruling function today. Any title we love to hear because it feeds the ego is proscribed.

This step-by-step application process is intended to show how it is possible to implement a fully authoritative Scripture in both form and meaning in a present-day context. In the process, the potential for sinful pride in such a small thing as academic titles has surfaced. But confronting it and gaining the victory will promote even greater love among the members of the community of faith based on grace. How refreshing and stimulating to live out one's church and professional life in an essentially status-free environment!

When the Bible is applied fully and finally to the hearts, minds, wills, and actions of regenerate individuals, the surrounding culture will be able to observe how life was meant to be lived, and by the power of the Spirit many will come to the light. "A new command I give you: Love one another. As I have loved you, so you must love one another. By this all men will know that you are my disciples, if you love one another" (John 13:34–35).

Hermeneutical guidelines based on biblical teaching complete the process for understanding and applying the Bible either in one's own or another culture (i.e., contextualizing). The fruit of analysis enables interpreters to synthesize the material of the biblical context to arrive at a coherent interpretation. A concise statement of the passage's message together with an outline is the basis for relating the meaning of the text to the immediate context, to the book as a whole, and to parallel passages in Scripture. Next, interpreters relate the message to their contemporary culture by completing the process begun earlier. They uncover what in their culture will communicate the text's message, as well as what must be corrected by it and in what way. They also probe how the message of the text is significant, that is, how it is good news, for their culture.

When interpreters apply the text, they will do so either directly (following both scriptural form and meaning) or indirectly (implementing the scriptural meaning with a culturally appropriate form). Using the criteria of nonnormativeness will enable interpreters to decide which approach to follow. They must then identify the exact contemporary situation to which the material applies and the response (in terms of attitude and behavior change) it calls for.

Bibliography

Achtemeier, Paul J. *The Inspiration of Scripture: Problems and Proposals.* Philadelphia: Westminster, 1980.

_____ , and Gene M. Tucker. "Biblical Studies: The State of the Discipline." *The Council on the Study of Religion Bulletin* 11 (1980): 72–76.

Adeyemo, Tokunboh. "Towards an Evangelical African Theology." *ERT* 7 (1983): 147–54.

Allmen, Daniel von. "The Birth of Theology: Contextualization as the Dynamic Element in the Formation of New Testament Theology." *International Review of Missions* 64 (1975): 37–52.

Alston, William P. *Philosophy of Language.* Englewood Cliffs, N.J.: Prentice-Hall, 1964.

Anderson, Gerald H., and Thomas F. Stransky, eds. *Mission Trends No. 3: Third World Theologies.* Grand Rapids: Eerdmans, 1976.

Anderson, Neville P. "Biblical Theology and Cultural Identity in the Anglo-Saxon World." In *Let the Earth Hear His Voice,* edited by James D. Douglas, 1278–93. Minneapolis: World Wide, 1975.

Archer, Gleason L. "Contextualization: Some Implications from the Life and Witness of the Old Testament." In *New Horizons in World Mission,* edited by David J. Hesselgrave, 199–216. Grand Rapids: Baker, 1979.

_____ . *Encyclopedia of Bible Difficulties.* Grand Rapids: Zondervan, 1982.

_____ , and Gregory C. Chirichigno. *Old Testament Quotations in the New Testament.* Chicago: Moody, 1983.

Ariarajah, Wesley. "Towards a Theology of Dialogue." *Ecumenical Review* 29 (1977): 3–11.

Assmann, Hugo. "A Statement." In *Theology in the Americas,* edited by Sergio Torres and John Eagleson, 299–303. Maryknoll, N.Y.: Orbis, 1976.

"The Authority of the Bible—Text." *Ecumenical Review* 23 (1971): 419–37.

Baelz, Peter R. "Old Wine in New Bottles." *Theology* 76 (1973): 115–25.

Balch, David. *Let Wives Be Submissive: The Domestic Code in 1 Peter.* Society of Biblical Literature Monograph Series 26. Chico, Calif.: Society of Biblical Literature, 1981.

Barclay, William. "The New Testament and the Papyri." In *The New Testament in Historical and Contemporary Perspective: Essays in Memory of G. H. C. MacGregor,* edited by Hugh Anderson and William Barclay, 57–82. Oxford: Basil Blackwell, 1965.

Barney, G. Linwood. "The Challenge of Anthropology to Current Missiology." *International Bulletin of Missionary Research* 5 (1981): 172–77.

————. "The Supracultural and the Cultural: Implications for Frontier Missions." In *The Gospel and Frontier Peoples: A Report of a Consultation, Dec. 1972,* edited by R. Pierce Beaver, 48–57. Pasadena, Calif.: William Carey Library, 1973.

Barr, James. *The Bible in the Modern World.* New York: Harper & Row, 1973.

————. *Fundamentalism.* Philadelphia: Westminster, 1977.

————. "The Interpretation of Scripture II: Revelation Through History in the Old Testament and in Modern Theology." *Interpretation* 17 (1963): 193–205.

————. "The Old Testament and the New Crisis of Biblical Authority." *Interpretation* 25 (1971): 24–40.

————. *The Scope and the Authority of the Bible.* Philadelphia: Westminster, 1980.

————. *The Semantics of Biblical Language.* New York: Oxford University Press, 1961.

Barrett, Charles Kingsley. *A Commentary on the First Epistle to the Corinthians.* New York: Harper & Row, 1968.

————. *A Commentary on the Second Epistle to the Corinthians.* New York: Harper & Row, 1973.

————, ed. *The New Testament Background: Selected Documents.* New York: Macmillan, 1957.

Bartlett, David L. "Biblical Scholarship Today: A Diversity of New Approaches." *Christian Century* 98 (1981): 1090–94.

"The Battle of the Lexicons." *CT* 31, no. 1 (16 January 1987): 44–45.

Bauer, Walter. *A Greek-English Lexicon of the New Testament and Other Early Christian Literature.* 2d ed. Revised and augmented by Frederick W. Danker and F. Wilbur Gingrich. Chicago: University of Chicago Press, 1979.

Beck, W. David. "A Response to Truth: Relationship of Theories of Truth to Hermeneutics." In *Hermeneutics, Inerrancy, and the Bible,* edited by Earl D. Radmacher and Robert D. Preus, 57–68. Grand Rapids: Zondervan, 1984.

Beekman, John, and John Callow. *Translating the Word of God.* Grand Rapids: Zondervan, 1974.

Belo, Fernando. *A Materialist Reading of the Gospel of Mark.* Translated by Matthew J. O'Connell. Maryknoll, N.Y.: Orbis, 1981.

Berger, Peter L., and Thomas Luckmann. *The Social Construction of Reality: A Treatise in the Sociology of Knowledge.* Garden City, N.Y.: Doubleday, 1967.

Berkouwer, Gerrit Cornelis. *Holy Scripture.* Grand Rapids: Eerdmans, 1975.

Berns, Walter. "The Words According to Brennan." *Wall Street Journal,* 23 October 1985, 32.

Bernstein, Richard J. *Beyond Objectivism and Relativism: Science, Hermeneutics, and Praxis.* Philadelphia: University of Pennsylvania Press, 1983.

Best, Ernest. "The Literal Meaning of Scripture, the Historical-Critical Method, and the Interpretation of Scripture." *Proceedings of the Irish Biblical Association* 5 (1981): 14–35.

Bird, Phyllis A. "'Male and Female He Created Them': Gen. 1:27b in the Context of the Priestly Account of Creation." *Harvard Theological Review* 74 (1981): 129–59.

Bloesch, Donald. "Crisis in Biblical Authority." *TT* 35 (1979): 455–62.

———. *Essentials of Evangelical Theology.* 2 vols. New York: Harper & Row, 1978.

Blum, Edwin. "The Apostles' View of Scripture." In *Inerrancy,* edited by Norman L. Geisler, 39–53. Grand Rapids: Zondervan, 1979.

Bock, Darrell L. "Evangelicals and the Use of the Old Testament in the New," parts 1 and 2. *BS* 142 (1985): 209–23, 306–19.

Bock, Philip K. *Modern Cultural Anthropology: An Introduction.* 2d ed. New York: Knopf, 1969.

Boraiko, Allen A. "The Chip: Electronic Mini-Marvel." *National Geographic* 162 (1982): 420–57.

Botterweck, G. Johannes, and Helmer Ringgren, eds. *Theological Dictionary of the Old Testament.* Translated by John T. Willis. Rev. ed. Grand Rapids: Eerdmans, 1974–.

Bovon, François. "French Structuralism and Biblical Exegesis." In *Structural Analysis and Biblical Exegesis: Interpretational Essays,* by Roland Barthes, François Bovon, Franz J. Leenhardt, Robert Martin-Achard, and Jean Starobinski, 4–20. Translated by Alfred M. Johnson, Jr. Pittsburgh Theological Monograph Series 3. Pittsburgh: Pickwick, 1974.

Branson, Mark Lau. "Response to Escobar." In *Conflict and Context: Hermeneutics in the Americas,* edited by Mark Lau Branson and C. René Padilla, 9–10. Grand Rapids: Eerdmans, 1986.

———, and C. René Padilla, eds. *Conflict and Context: Hermeneutics in the Americas.* Grand Rapids: Eerdmans, 1986.

Bratcher, Robert G. "Toward a Definition of the Authority of the Bible." *Perspectives in Religious Studies* 6 (1979): 109–20.

Brown, Colin, ed. *The New International Dictionary of New Testament Theology.* 3 vols. Grand Rapids: Zondervan, 1978.

Brown, Robert M. "Theology in a New Key: Resolving a Diminished Seventh." *USQR* 33 (1977): 23–34.

———. *Unexpected News: Reading the Bible with Third World Eyes.* Philadelphia: Westminster, 1984.

Bruce, F. F. "All Things to All Men: Diversity in Unity and Other Pauline Tensions." In *Unity and Diversity in New Testament Theology: Essays in Honor of George E. Ladd,* edited by Robert A. Guelich, 82–99. Grand Rapids: Eerdmans, 1978.

———. *The Epistle to the Galatians: A Commentary on the Greek Text.* Grand Rapids: Eerdmans, 1982.

Brueggemann, Walter, and Douglas A. Knight. "Why Study the Bible?" *The Council on the Study of Religion Bulletin* 11 (1980): 76–81.

Bullock, C. Hassell. "Introduction: Interpreting the Bible." In *The Literature and Meaning of Scripture,* edited by Morris A. Inch and C. Hassell Bullock, 11–20. Grand Rapids: Baker, 1981.

Bultmann, Rudolf. "How God Speaks Through the Bible." In *Existence and Faith: Shorter Writings of Rudolf Bultmann,* translated by Schubert M. Ogden, 166–70. Cleveland: World, 1960.

———. "The Problems of Hermeneutics." In *Essays Philosophical and Theological,* translated by J. C. G. Greig, 234–61. London: SCM, 1955.

Burton, Ernest D. *A Critical and Exegetical Commentary on the Epistle to the Galatians.* Edinburgh: T. & T. Clark, 1921.

Buswell, James O., III. "Contextualization: Theory, Tradition, and Method." In *Theology and Mission,* edited by David J. Hesselgrave, 87–111. Grand Rapids: Baker, 1978.

———. "Reply." In *Theology and Mission,* edited by David J. Hesselgrave, 124–27. Grand Rapids: Baker, 1978.

Callaghan, William J. "Charles Sanders Peirce: His General Theory of Signs—Review Article." *Semiotica* 61 (1986): 123–61.

Calvin, John. *Commentaries on the Epistles of Paul to the Galatians and Ephesians.* Translated by William Pringle. Grand Rapids: Eerdmans, 1957.

Carino, Feliciano V. "The Willowbank Report: A Critical Response." *South East Asia Journal of Theology* 19, no. 2 (1978): 38–49.

Carroll, Robert P. "The Sisyphean Task of Biblical Transformation." *SJT* 30 (1977): 501–21.

Carson, D. A. *Matthew.* In *Matthew, Mark, Luke.* EBC 8. Grand Rapids: Zondervan, 1984.

———. "Recent Developments in the Doctrine of Scripture." In *Hermeneutics, Authority, and Canon,* edited by D. A. Carson and John D. Woodbridge, 1–48. Grand Rapids: Zondervan, 1986.

———. "Unity and Diversity in the New Testament: The Possibility of Systematic Theology." In *Scripture and Truth,* edited by D. A. Carson and John D. Woodbridge, 65–100. Grand Rapids: Zondervan, 1983.

———, ed. *Biblical Interpretation and the Church: The Problem of Contextualization.* Nashville: Nelson, 1984.

———, and John D. Woodbridge, eds. *Hermeneutics, Authority, and Canon.* Grand Rapids: Zondervan, 1986.

———. *Scripture and Truth.* Grand Rapids: Zondervan, 1983.

Chao, Jonathan. "Towards an Evangelical Theology in Totalitarian Cultures, with Special Reference to Socialist China." In *The Bible and Theology in Asian Contexts: An Evangelical Perspective on Asian Theology,* edited by Bong R. Ro and Ruth Eshenaur, 343–62. Taichung, Taiwan: Asia Theological Association, 1984.

"The Chicago Statement on Biblical Inerrancy." In *Inerrancy,* edited by Norman L. Geisler, 493–502. Grand Rapids: Zondervan, 1979.

Childs, Brevard S. *Biblical Theology in Crisis.* Philadelphia: Westminster, 1970.

———. *Introduction to the Old Testament as Scripture.* Philadelphia: Fortress, 1979.

———. "The Search for Biblical Authority Today." *Andover Newton Quarterly* 16 (1976): 199–206.

Chomsky, Noam. *Language and Mind.* New York: Harcourt Brace Jovanovich, 1968.

Clark, Gordon H. *First Corinthians: A Contemporary Commentary.* Nutley, N.J.: Presbyterian & Reformed, 1975.

———. *Religion, Reason, and Revelation.* Nutley, N.J.: Craig, 1961.

———. "Special Divine Revelation as Rational." *Revelation and the Bible: Contemporary Evangelical Thought,* edited by Carl F. H. Henry, 25–41. Grand Rapids: Baker, 1959.

Coe, Shoki. "In Search of Renewal in Theological Education." *Theological Education* 9 (1973): 233–43.

"The Concerns and Considerations of Carl F. H. Henry: An Interview." *CT* 25 (1981): 322–27.

Cone, James H. "Biblical Revelation and Social Existence." *Interpretation* 28 (1974): 422–40.

"Conference Findings: Towards a Missiological Christology in the Two-Thirds World." In *Sharing Jesus in the Two-Thirds World: Evangelical Christologies from the Contexts of Poverty, Powerlessness, and Religious Pluralism*, edited by Vinay Samuel and Chris Sugden, 277–79. Grand Rapids: Eerdmans, 1984.

Conn, Harvie M. "Contextualization: A New Dimension for Cross-Cultural Hermeneutic." *Evangelical Missions Quarterly* 14 (1978): 39–48.

_____. "Contextualization: Where Do We Begin?" In *Evangelicals and Liberation*, edited by Carl E. Armerding, 90–119. Nutley, N.J.: Presbyterian & Reformed, 1977.

_____. *Eternal Word and Changing Worlds: Theology, Anthropology, and Mission in Trialogue.* Grand Rapids: Zondervan, 1984.

_____. "Theologies of Liberation: Toward a Common View." In *Tensions in Contemporary Theology*, edited by Stanley N. Gundry and Alan F. Johnson, 395–434. 3d rev. ed. Chicago: Moody, 1979.

_____. "Theology of Liberation." *Presbyterian Journal* 34 (23 July 1975): 7–9.

Corduan, Winfried. "Philosophical Presuppositions Affecting Biblical Hermeneutics." In *Hermeneutics, Inerrancy, and the Bible*, edited by Earl D. Radmacher and Robert D. Preus, 493–514. Grand Rapids: Zondervan, 1984.

Couch, Beatriz M. "Statement." In *Theology in the Americas*, edited by Sergio Torres and John Eagleson, 304–8. Maryknoll, N.Y.: Orbis, 1976.

Cranfield, C. E. B. *A Critical and Exegetical Commentary on the Epistle to the Romans.* 2 vols. Edinburgh: T. & T. Clark, 1975–1979.

_____. *The Gospel According to Mark: An Introduction and Commentary.* Cambridge: Cambridge University Press, 1959.

Croatto, J. Severino. *Exodus: A Hermeneutic of Freedom.* Maryknoll, N.Y.: Orbis, 1981.

Dahl, Nils A. "Nations in the New Testament." In *New Testament Christianity for Africa and the World: Essays in Honour of Harry Sawyerr*, edited by Mark E. Glasswell and Edward W. Fasole-Luke, 54–68. London: S.P.C.K., 1974.

Dahms, John V. "The Nature of Truth." *JETS* 28 (1985): 455–66.

Darton, Michael, ed. *Modern Concordance to the New Testament.* Garden City, N.Y.: Doubleday, 1976.

Davis, John Jefferson. *Foundations of Evangelical Theology.* Grand Rapids: Baker, 1984.

_____. "Some Reflections on Galatians 3:28, Sexual Roles, and Biblical Hermeneutics." *JETS* 19 (1976): 201–8.

Davis, R. J. "Response to Buswell and Ericson." In *Theology and Mission*, edited by David J. Hesselgrave, 115–17. Grand Rapids: Baker, 1978.

Dayton, Donald W. "The Use of Scripture in the Wesleyan Tradition." In *The Use of the Bible in Theology/Evangelical Options*, edited by Robert K. Johnston, 121–37. Atlanta: John Knox, 1985.

Delitzsch, Franz. *Biblical Commentary on the Prophecies of Isaiah.* 2 vols. Grand Rapids: Eerdmans, 1949.

Descartes, René. *Discourse on Method* and *Meditations.* Translated by Laurence J. Lafleur. Indianapolis: Bobbs, 1960.

_____. *Rules for the Direction of the Mind.* Translated by Laurence J. Lafleur. Indianapolis: Bobbs, 1961.

Detweiler, Robert. *Story, Sign, and Self: Phenomenology and Structuralism as Literary Methods.* Philadelphia: Fortress, 1978.

de Waard, Jan, and Eugene A. Nida. *From One Language to Another: Functional Equivalence in Bible Translating*. Nashville: Nelson, 1986.

Dickson, Kwesi A., and Paul Ellingworth, eds. *Biblical Revelation and African Beliefs*. London: Lutterworth, 1969.

Doty, William G. *Contemporary New Testament Interpretation*. Englewood Cliffs, N.J.: Prentice-Hall, 1972.

Douglas, James D., ed. *Let the Earth Hear His Voice*. Minneapolis: World Wide, 1975.

Downing, F. Gerald. "Our Access to Other Cultures, Past and Present (or the Myth of the Culture Gap)." *Modern Churchman* 21 (1977): 28–42.

Dunbar, David G. "The Biblical Canon." In *Hermeneutics, Authority, and Canon*, edited by D. A. Carson and John D. Woodbridge, 295–360. Grand Rapids: Zondervan, 1986.

Dunn, James D. G. "The Authority of Scripture According to Scripture." *Churchman* 96 (1982): 99–122, 201–25.

Dunnett, Walter M. *The Interpretation of Holy Scripture*. Nashville: Nelson, 1984.

Dyson, Anthony O. "Dogmatic or Contextual Theology?" *Study Encounter* 8, no. 3, SE 29 (1972): 1–8.

Eco, Umberto. *A Theory of Semiotics*. Bloomington: Indiana University Press, 1976.

Eight Translation New Testament. Wheaton, Ill.: Tyndale, 1974.

Elwell, Walter A., ed. *Evangelical Dictionary of Theology*. Grand Rapids: Baker, 1984.

Encyclopedia of Philosophy. Edited by Paul Edwards. 8 vols. New York: Macmillan, 1967.

Engle, Richard W. "Contextualization in Missions: A Biblical and Theological Appraisal." *GTJ* 4 (1983): 85–107.

Erickson, Millard J. "Biblical Inerrancy: The Last Twenty-Five Years." *JETS* 25 (1982): 387–94.

———. *Christian Theology*. Grand Rapids: Baker, 1986.

———. "Presuppositions of Non-Evangelical Hermeneutics." In *Hermeneutics, Inerrancy, and the Bible*, edited by Earl D. Radmacher and Robert D. Preus, 591–612. Grand Rapids: Zondervan, 1984.

Ericson, Norman R. "Implications from the New Testament for Contextualization." In *Theology and Mission*, edited by David J. Hesselgrave, 71–85. Grand Rapids: Baker, 1978.

———. "Reply." In *Theology and Mission*, edited by David J. Hesselgrave, 121–23. Grand Rapids: Baker, 1978.

Escobar, Samuel. "Our Hermeneutical Task Today." In *Conflict and Context: Hermeneutics in the Americas*, edited by Mark Lau Branson and C. René Padilla, 3–8. Grand Rapids: Eerdmans, 1986.

Estes, Steve. *Called to Die: The Story of American Linguist Chet Bitterman, Slain by Terrorists*. Grand Rapids: Zondervan, 1986.

Expositor's Bible Commentary. Edited by Frank E. Gaebelein. 12 vols. Grand Rapids: Zondervan, 1976–.

Fasole-Luke, Edward W. "Quest for an African Christian Theology." *Ecumenical Review* 27 (1975): 259–69.

Fee, Gordon D. "The Genre of New Testament Literature and Biblical Hermeneutics." In *Interpreting the Word of God Today*, edited by Samuel J. Schultz and Morris A. Inch, 105–27. Chicago: Moody, 1976.

_____ . "Hermeneutics and Common Sense." In *Inerrancy and Common Sense*, edited by Roger Nicole and J. Ramsey Michaels, 161–86. Grand Rapids: Baker, 1980.

_____ . "Hermeneutics and Historical Precedent—A Major Problem in Pentecostal Hermeneutics." In *Perspectives on the New Pentecostalism*, edited by Russell P. Spittler, 118–33. Grand Rapids: Baker, 1976.

_____ . *New Testament Exegesis: A Handbook for Students and Pastors*. Philadelphia: Westminster, 1983.

_____ . "Reflections on Church Order in the Pastoral Epistles, with Further Reflection on the Hermeneutics of *Ad Hoc* Documents." *JETS* 28 (1985): 141–51.

_____ , and Douglas Stuart. *How to Read the Bible for All Its Worth: A Guide to Understanding the Bible*. Grand Rapids: Zondervan, 1981.

Feinberg, John S. "Truth: Relationship of Theories of Truth to Hermeneutics." In *Hermeneutics, Inerrancy, and the Bible*, edited by Earl D. Radmacher and Robert D. Preus, 1–50. Grand Rapids: Zondervan, 1984.

Feine, Paul, Johannes Behm, and Werner Georg Kummel. *Introduction to the New Testament*. Translated by A. J. Mattill, Jr. 14th rev. ed. Nashville: Abingdon, 1966.

Felder, Cain H. "Partiality and God's Law: An Exegesis of James 2:1–13." *Journal of Religious Thought* 39 (1982): 51–69.

Filson, Floyd V. "How to Interpret the Bible: The Interpreter at Work." *Interpretation* 4 (1950): 178–88.

Fiorenza, Elizabeth S. "Feminist Theology and New Testament Interpretation." *Journal for the Study of the Old Testament* 22 (1982): 32–46.

Fleming, Bruce C. *Contextualization of Theology: An Evangelical Assessment*. Pasadena, Calif.: William Carey Library, 1980.

Flesseman–van Leer, Ellen, ed. *The Bible: Its Authority and Interpretation in the Ecumenical Movement*. Faith and Order Paper 99. Geneva: World Council of Churches, 1980.

Frame, John M. "The Spirit and the Scriptures." In *Hermeneutics, Authority, and Canon*, edited by D. A. Carson and John D. Woodbridge, 213–35. Grand Rapids: Zondervan, 1986.

Franklin, Karl J. "Interpreting Values Cross-Culturally." *Missiology* 7 (1979): 355–64.

Freedman, R. David. "Woman, a Power Equal to Man: Translation of Woman as a 'Fit Helpmate' for Man Is Questioned." *Biblical Archaeology Review* 9 (1983): 56–58.

Frei, Hans W. *The Eclipse of Biblical Narrative: A Study in Eighteenth and Nineteenth Century Hermeneutics*. New Haven, Conn.: Yale University Press, 1974.

Frye, Northrop. *The Great Code: The Bible and Literature*. New York: Harcourt Brace Jovanovich, 1982.

Fuller, Daniel P. "The Holy Spirit's Role in Biblical Interpretation." In *Scripture, Tradition, and Interpretation: Essays Presented to Everett F. Harrison by His Students and Colleagues in Honor of His Seventy-Fifth Birthday*, edited by W. Ward Gasque and William Sanford LaSor, 189–98. Grand Rapids: Eerdmans, 1978.

Gadamer, Hans-Georg. *Truth and Method*. Translated and edited by Garrett Barden and John Cumming. New York: Seabury, 1975.

Gaffin, Richard B. "Comments on: Is There More than One Way to Do Theology?" *Gospel in Context* 1, no. 1 (1978): 22.

Gager, John G. *Kingdom and Community: The Social World of Early Christianity*. Englewood Cliffs, N.J.: Prentice-Hall, 1975.

Gardiner, Alan. *The Theory of Speech and Language.* 2d ed. Oxford: Clarendon, 1951.

Geisler, Norman L. "The Concept of Truth in the Inerrancy Debate." *BS* 137 (1980): 327–39.

————. "Explaining Hermeneutics: A Commentary on the Chicago Statement on Biblical Hermeneutics Articles of Affirmation and Denial." In *Hermeneutics, Inerrancy, and the Bible,* edited by Earl D. Radmacher and Robert D. Preus, 889–904. Grand Rapids: Zondervan, 1984.

————. "Is There Madness in the Method? Rejoinder to Robert H. Gundry." *JETS* 26 (1983): 101–8.

————. "The Relation of Purpose and Meaning in Interpreting Scripture." *GTJ* 5 (1984): 229–45.

————. "A Response to Truth: Relationship of Theories of Truth to Hermeneutics." In *Hermeneutics, Inerrancy, and the Bible,* edited by Earl D. Radmacher and Robert D. Preus, 51–56. Grand Rapids: Zondervan, 1984.

————, ed. *Inerrancy.* Grand Rapids: Zondervan, 1979.

Gibson, Arthur. *Biblical Semantic Logic: A Preliminary Analysis.* New York: St. Martin's, 1981.

Gnanakan, Ken R. "Biblical Foundations: A South Asian Study." *ERT* 7 (1983): 113–22.

Gore, Rick. "The Once and Future Universe." *National Geographic* 163 (1983): 709–49.

"The Gospel, Contextualization, and Syncretism Report." In *Let the Earth Hear His Voice,* edited by James D. Douglas, 1224–28. Minneapolis: World Wide, 1975.

Gottwald, Norman K. *The Tribes of Yahweh: A Sociology of the Religion of Liberated Israel, 1250–1050 B.C.* Maryknoll, N.Y.: Orbis, 1979.

Grech, Prosper. "The 'Testimonia' and Modern Hermeneutics." *New Testament Studies* 19 (1973): 318–24.

Green, Michael. *The Second Epistle General of Peter and the General Epistle of Jude: An Introduction and Commentary.* Grand Rapids: Eerdmans, 1968.

Grudem, Wayne A. "Scripture's Self-Attestation and the Problem of Formulating a Doctrine of Scripture." In *Scripture and Truth,* edited by D. A. Carson and John D. Woodbridge, 19–59. Grand Rapids: Zondervan, 1983.

Gruenler, Royce G. "A Response to the New Hermeneutic." In *Hermeneutics, Inerrancy, and the Bible,* edited by Earl D. Radmacher and Robert D. Preus, 573–90. Grand Rapids: Zondervan, 1984.

Grunlan, Stephen A., and Marvin K. Mayers. *Cultural Anthropology: A Christian Perspective.* Grand Rapids: Zondervan, 1979.

Gundry, Robert H. *Matthew: A Commentary on His Literary and Theological Art.* Grand Rapids: Eerdmans, 1982.

Guthrie, Donald. "Questions of Introduction." In *New Testament Interpretation: Essays on Principles and Methods,* edited by I. Howard Marshall, 105–16. Grand Rapids: Eerdmans, 1977.

Hamilton, Kenneth. *Words and the Word.* Grand Rapids: Eerdmans, 1971.

Hammond, Peter B. *An Introduction to Cultural and Social Anthropology.* 2d ed. New York: Macmillan, 1978.

Hanson, Paul D. "Isaiah 52:7–10: Expository Article." *Interpretation* 33 (1979): 389–94.

Harper Dictionary of Modern Thought. Edited by Alan Bullock and Oliver Stallybrass. New York: Harper & Row, 1977.

Harrington, Daniel J. "Biblical Hermeneutics in Recent Discussion: New Testament." *Religious Studies Review* 10 (1984): 7–9.

_____. "Sociological Concepts and the Early Church: A Decade of Research." *Theological Studies* 41 (1980): 181–90.

_____. "Some New Voices in New Testament Interpretation." *Anglican Theological Review* 64 (1982): 362–70.

Harvey, Van A. *The Historian and the Believer: The Morality of Historical Knowledge and Christian Belief.* Philadelphia: Westminster, 1966.

Haviland, William A. *Cultural Anthropology.* 3d ed. New York: Holt, Rinehart & Winston, 1981.

Henry, Carl F. H. "Comments on: Is There More than One Way to Do Theology?" *Gospel in Context* 1, no. 1 (1978): 22–23.

_____. *God, Revelation, and Authority.* 6 vols. Waco, Tex.: Word, 1976–1979.

_____, ed. *Revelation and the Bible: Contemporary Evangelical Thought.* Grand Rapids: Baker, 1959.

Henry, Patrick. *New Directions in New Testament Study.* Philadelphia: Westminster, 1979.

Herbert, A. S. "The 'Parable' (MĀŠĀL) in the Old Testament." *SJT* 7 (1954): 180–96.

Herskovits, Melville J. *Man and His Works: The Science of Cultural Anthropology.* New York: Knopf, 1956.

Herzog, Frederick. "Liberation Hermeneutic as Ideology Critique?" *Interpretation* 28 (1974): 387–403.

Hesselgrave, David J. *Communicating Christ Cross-Culturally.* Grand Rapids: Zondervan, 1978.

_____. "Contextualization and Revelational Epistemology." In *Hermeneutics, Inerrancy, and the Bible,* edited by Earl D. Radmacher and Robert D. Preus, 691–738. Grand Rapids: Zondervan, 1984.

_____. "The Contextualization Continuum." *Gospel in Context* 2, no. 3 (1979): 4–11.

_____. "Response to Archer and Hiebert." In *New Horizons in World Mission,* edited by David J. Hesselgrave, 233–36. Grand Rapids: Baker, 1979.

_____, ed. *New Horizons in World Mission.* Grand Rapids: Baker, 1979.

_____, ed. *Theology and Mission.* Grand Rapids: Baker, 1978.

Hiebert, Paul G. "Critical Contextualization." Fuller Theological Seminary, Pasadena, Calif., 1986. Photocopy.

_____. *Cultural Anthropology.* Philadelphia: Lippincott, 1976.

_____. "Epistemological Foundations for Science and Theology." *Theological Students' Fellowship Bulletin* 8 (March/April 1985): 5–10.

_____. "The Missiological Implications of an Epistemological Shift." *Theological Students' Fellowship Bulletin* 8 (May/June 1985): 12–18.

_____. "Missions and Anthropology: A Love/Hate Relationship." *Missiology* 6 (1978): 165–80.

Hillmann, Eugene. "Pluriformity in Ethics: A Modern Missionary Problem." *Missiology* 1 (1973): 59–72.

Hirsch, E. D., Jr. *The Aims of Interpretation.* Chicago: University of Chicago Press, 1976.

_____. *Validity in Interpretation.* New Haven, Conn.: Yale University Press, 1967.

Homans, Peter. "Psychology and Hermeneutics: An Exploration of Basic Issues and Resources." *Journal of Religion* 55 (1975): 327–47.

Howard, Roy J. *Three Faces of Hermeneutics: An Introduction to Current Theories of Understanding.* Berkeley: University of California Press, 1982.

Howe, E. Margaret. "'. . . But Some Doubted' (Matt. 28:17): A Re-Appraisal of Factors Influencing the Easter Faith of the Early Christian Community." *JETS* 18 (1975): 173–80.

"How to Evaluate Cultural Practices by Biblical Standards in Maintaining Cultural Identity in Asia Report." In *Let the Earth Hear His Voice*, edited by James D. Douglas, 1249–50. Minneapolis: World Wide, 1975.

Hughes, Philip E. *A Commentary on the Epistle to the Hebrews*. Grand Rapids: Eerdmans, 1977.

Hung, Daniel M. "Mission Blockade: Ancestor Worship." In *Christian Alternatives to Ancestor Practices*, edited by Bong R. Ro, 199–217. Taichung, Taiwan: Asia Theological Association, 1985.

Hunt, Morton. "The Truth About Lying." *United Magazine*, April 1986, 61–68.

Inch, Morris A. *Doing Theology Across Cultures*. Grand Rapids: Baker, 1982.

―――. "A Response to Contextualization and Revelational Epistemology." In *Hermeneutics, Inerrancy, and the Bible*, edited by Earl D. Radmacher and Robert D. Preus, 741–50. Grand Rapids: Zondervan, 1984.

International Encyclopedia of the Social Sciences. Edited by David L. Sills. 17 vols. New York: Macmillan, 1968.

Interpreter's Dictionary of the Bible, Supplementary Volume. Edited by Keith R. Crim. Nashville: Abingdon, 1976.

Jennings, James E. "Interpreting the Historical Books: 2 Samuel 1:17–24; 2:1–4, 12–16." In *The Literature and Meaning of Scripture*, edited by Morris A. Inch and C. Hassell Bullock, 39–62. Grand Rapids: Baker, 1981.

Jenson, Robert W. "On the Problem(s) of Scriptural Authority." *Interpretation* 31 (1977): 237–50.

Jeremias, Joachim. *The Parables of Jesus*. 2d ed. London: SCM, 1963.

Johnson, Alan F. "The Historical-Critical Method: Egyptian Gold or Pagan Precipice?" *JETS* 26 (1983): 3–16.

―――. "History and Culture in New Testament Interpretation." In *Interpreting the Word of God Today*, edited by Samuel J. Schultz and Morris A. Inch, 128–61. Chicago: Moody, 1976.

―――. "A Response to Problems of Normativeness in Scripture: Cultural Versus Permanent." In *Hermeneutics, Inerrancy, and the Bible*, edited by Earl D. Radmacher and Robert D. Preus, 255–82. Grand Rapids: Zondervan, 1984.

Johnson, Alfred M., Jr., ed. and trans. *The New Testament and Structuralism*. Pittsburgh: Pickwick, 1976.

Johnson, Dan R. "Guidelines for the Application of Old Testament Narrative." *Trinity Journal* 7 (1978): 79–84.

Johnson, Elliott E. "Author's Intention and Biblical Interpretation." In *Hermeneutics, Inerrancy, and the Bible*, edited by Earl D. Radmacher and Robert D. Preus, 407–30. Grand Rapids: Zondervan, 1984.

Jones, Peter R. "Biblical Hermeneutics." *Review and Expositor* 22 (1975): 139–47.

Judge, E. A. "Cultural Conformity and Innovation in Paul: Some Clues from Contemporary Documents." *Tyndale Bulletin* 35 (1984): 3–24.

―――. "The Reaction Against Classical Education in the New Testament." *ERT* 9 (1985): 166–74.

Kaiser, Walter C., Jr. "The Current Crisis in Exegesis and the Apostolic Use of Deuteronomy 25:4 in 1 Corinthians 9:8–10." *JETS* 21 (1978): 3–18.

_____ . "The Eschatological Hermeneutics of 'Epangelicalism': Promise Theology." *JETS* 13 (1970): 91–99.

_____ . "Legitimate Hermeneutics." In *Inerrancy,* edited by Norman L. Geisler, 117–47. Grand Rapids: Zondervan, 1979.

_____ . "Meanings from God's Message: Matters for Interpretation." *CT* 22 (1979): 1319–22.

_____ . "A Neglected Text in Bibliology Discussions: 1 Corinthians 2:6–16." *WTJ* 43 (1981): 301–19.

_____ . "The Promise to David in Psalm 16 and Its Application in Acts 2:25–33 and 13:32–37." *JETS* 23 (1980): 219–30.

_____ . *Toward an Exegetical Theology: Biblical Exegesis for Preaching and Teaching.* Grand Rapids: Baker, 1981.

_____ . *The Uses of the Old Testament in the New.* Chicago: Moody, 1985.

Kant, Immanuel. *Critique of Pure Reason.* Translated by J. M. D. Meiklejohn. New York: Dutton, 1934.

_____ . *Religion Within the Limits of Reason Alone.* Translated by Theodore M. Greene and Hoyt H. Hudson. 2d ed. LaSalle, Ill.: Open Court, 1960.

Kantzer, Kenneth S. "The Communication of Revelation." In *The Bible: The Living Word of Revelation,* edited by Merrill C. Tenney, 53–80. Grand Rapids: Zondervan, 1968.

_____ . "Women's Role in Church and Family." *CT* 25 (1981): 254–55.

Kato, Byang H. "Black Theology and African Theology." *ERT* 1 (1977): 35–48.

_____ . "The Gospel, Cultural Contextualization, and Religious Syncretism." In *Let the Earth Hear His Voice,* edited by James D. Douglas, 1216–23. Minneapolis: World Wide, 1975.

Kaufmann, Gordon D. "What Shall We Do with the Bible?" *Interpretation* 25 (1971): 95–112.

Kaye, Bruce N. "Political Obedience in Romans 13:1–7." *Theological Students' Fellowship Bulletin* 63 (1972): 10–12.

Keck, Leander E. "On the Ethos of Early Christians." *Journal of the American Academy of Religion* 42 (1974): 435–52.

Kelly, Louis G. *The True Interpreter: A History of Translation Theory and Practice in the West.* New York: St. Martin's, 1979.

Kelsey, David H. *The Uses of Scripture in Recent Theology.* Philadelphia: Fortress, 1975.

Kidner, Derek. *Genesis: An Introduction and Commentary.* London: Tyndale, 1967.

Kinsler, F. Ross. "Mission and Context: The Current Debate About Contextualization." *Evangelical Missions Quarterly* 14 (1978): 23–30.

Kirk, J. Andrew. "Comments on: Is There More than One Way to Do Theology?" *Gospel in Context* 1, no. 1 (1978): 24–26.

_____ . *Liberation Theology: An Evangelical View from the Third World.* London: Marshall, Morgan & Scott, 1979.

Kistemaker, Simon J. "Current Problems and Projects in New Testament Research." *JETS* 18 (1975): 17–28.

Kline, Meredith G. *Treaty of the Great King: The Covenant Structure of Deuteronomy, Studies and Commentary.* Grand Rapids: Eerdmans, 1963.

Klooster, Fred H. "The Role of the Holy Spirit in the Hermeneutical Process: The Relationship of the Spirit's Illumination to Biblical Interpretation." In *Hermeneutics, Inerrancy, and the Bible,* edited by Earl D. Radmacher and Robert D. Preus, 449–72. Grand Rapids: Zondervan, 1984.

Knapp, Stephen C. "A Preliminary Dialogue with Gutierrez' *A Theology of Liberation*." In *Evangelicals and Liberation*, edited by Carl E. Armerding, 10–42. Nutley, N.J.: Presbyterian & Reformed, 1977.

Knight, George W., III. "From Hermeneutics to Practice: Scriptural Normativity and Culture, Revisited." *Presbyterion* 12 (1986): 93–104.

──────. *The New Testament Teaching on the Role Relationship of Men and Women*. Grand Rapids: Baker, 1977.

──────. "A Response to Problems of Normativeness in Scripture: Cultural Versus Permanent." In *Hermeneutics, Inerrancy, and the Bible*, edited by Earl D. Radmacher and Robert D. Preus, 241–54. Grand Rapids: Zondervan, 1984.

Kovacs, Brian W. "Philosophical Issues in Sociological Structuralism: A Bridge from Social Sciences to Hermeneutics." *USQR* 34 (1979): 149–57.

Kraft, Charles H. "Can Anthropological Insight Assist Evangelical Theology?" *Christian Scholar's Review* 7 (1977): 165–202.

──────. *Christianity in Culture*. Maryknoll, N.Y.: Orbis, 1979.

──────. "Ideological Factors in Intercultural Communication." *Missiology* 2 (1974): 295–312.

──────. "Interpreting in Cultural Context." *JETS* 21 (1978): 357–67.

──────. "Toward a Christian Ethnotheology." In *God, Man, and Church Growth*, edited by Alan R. Tippett, 109–27. Grand Rapids: Eerdmans, 1973.

Krentz, Edgar. *The Historical-Critical Method*. Philadelphia: Fortress, 1975.

Kuhn, Thomas. *The Structure of Scientific Revolutions*. 2d ed. Chicago: University of Chicago Press, 1970.

Kumar, S. Ananda. "Culture and the Old Testament." In *Gospel and Culture*, edited by John R. W. Stott and Robert T. Coote, 33–48. Pasadena, Calif.: William Carey Library, 1979.

Kunjummen, Raju D. "The Single Intent of Scripture—Critical Examination of a Theological Construct." *GTJ* 7 (1986): 81–110.

Kwast, Lloyd. "Christianity and Culture: Biblical Bedrock." In *Crucial Issues in Missions Tomorrow*, edited by Donald A. McGavran, 159–74. Chicago: Moody, 1972.

Ladd, George E. "The Parable of the Sheep and the Goats in Recent Interpretation." In *New Dimensions in New Testament Study*, edited by Richard N. Longenecker and Merrill C. Tenney, 191–99. Grand Rapids: Zondervan, 1974.

Landes, George M. "Biblical Exegesis in Crisis: What Is the Exegetical Task in Theological Context?" *USQR* 26 (1971): 273–98.

"Lausanne Covenant." In *Let the Earth Hear His Voice*, edited by James D. Douglas, 3–9. Minneapolis: World Wide, 1975.

Lee, Peter K. H. "1997 and the Church in Hong Kong: An Exercise in Contextualization." *Ching Feng* 25 (1982): 233–49.

Leith, John H. "The Bible and Theology." *Interpretation* 30 (1976): 227–41.

Lessing, Gotthold E. *Lessing's Theological Writings*. Translated by Henry Chadwick. London: A. & C. Black, 1956.

Leupold, H. C. *Exposition of Genesis*. 2 vols. London: Evangelical Press, 1942, reprint 1972.

Lewis, Gordon R. *Integrative Theology: Historical, Biblical, Systematic, Apologetic, and Practical*. Grand Rapids: Zondervan, 1986.

──────. "A Response to Presuppositions of Non-Evangelical Hermeneutics." In *Hermeneutics, Inerrancy, and the Bible*, edited by Earl D. Radmacher and Robert D. Preus, 613–26. Grand Rapids: Zondervan, 1984.

_____ . *Testing Christianity's Truth Claims.* Chicago: Moody, 1976.

Liddell, Henry G., and Robert Scott. *A Greek-English Lexicon.* Revised and augmented by Henry Stuart Jones. Oxford: Clarendon, 1968.

Lind, Millard C. "Refocusing Theological Education to Mission: The Old Testament and Contextualization." *Missiology* 10 (1982): 141–60.

Lindsell, Harold. "Biblical Infallibility from the Hermeneutical and Cultural Perspectives." *BS* 133 (1976): 312–18.

Lockhead, David. "Hermeneutics and Ideology." *Ecumenist* 15 (1977): 81–84.

Loewen, Jacob. "Evangelism and Culture." In *The New Face of Evangelism: An International Symposium on the Lausanne Covenant,* edited by C. René Padilla, 177–89. London: Hodder & Stoughton, 1976.

Longacre, Robert E. "Review of *Language and Reality* by Wilbur M. Urban, and Four Articles on Metalinguistics by Benjamin Lee Whorf." *Language* 32 (1956): 298–308.

Longenecker, Richard N. *Biblical Exegesis in the Apostolic Period.* Grand Rapids: Eerdmans, 1975.

_____ . "The Hermeneutics of New Testament Social Ethics." Unpublished paper, n.d.

_____ . *New Testament Social Ethics for Today.* Grand Rapids: Eerdmans, 1984.

_____ . "On the Form, Function, and Authority of New Testament Letters." In *Scripture and Truth,* edited by D. A. Carson and John D. Woodbridge, 101–18. Grand Rapids: Zondervan, 1983.

Lull, David J. "What Is 'Process Hermeneutics'?" *Process Studies* 13 (1983): 189–201.

Lundeen, Lyman T. "Authority of the Word in a Process Perspective." *Encounter* 36 (1975): 281–300.

Lundin, Roger, Anthony C. Thiselton, and Clarence Walhout. *The Responsibility of Hermeneutics.* Grand Rapids: Eerdmans, 1985.

Lyons, John. *Semantics.* 2 vols. Cambridge: Cambridge University Press, 1977.

McDonald, H. Dermot. "Theology and Culture: An Evangelical Correlation." In *Toward a Theology for the Future,* edited by Clark H. Pinnock and David F. Wells, 239–74. Carol Stream, Ill.: Creation House, 1971.

McGavran, Donald A. *The Clash Between Christianity and Cultures.* Washington, D.C.: Canon, 1974.

McKnight, Edgar V. *Meaning in Texts: The Historical Shaping of a Narrative Hermeneutics.* Philadelphia: Fortress, 1978.

McQuilkin, J. Robertson. "The Behavioral Sciences Under the Authority of Scripture." *JETS* 20 (1977): 31–43.

_____ . "Biblical Authority Made Functional." Paper presented at the annual meeting of the Evangelical Theological Society, Deerfield, Ill., 27 December 1978.

_____ . "Limits of Cultural Interpretation." *JETS* 23 (1980): 113–24.

_____ . "Problems of Normativeness in Scripture: Cultural Versus Permanent." In *Hermeneutics, Inerrancy, and the Bible,* edited by Earl D. Radmacher and Robert D. Preus, 217–40. Grand Rapids: Zondervan, 1984.

_____ . *Understanding and Applying the Bible.* Chicago: Moody, 1983.

Maier, Gerhard. *The End of the Historical-Critical Method.* Translated by Edwin W. Leverenz and Rudolph F. Norden. St. Louis: Concordia, 1977.

Malina, Bruce J. *The New Testament World: Insights from Cultural Anthropology.* Atlanta: John Knox, 1981.

—————. "The Social Sciences and Biblical Interpretation." *Interpretation* 36 (1982): 229–42.

Marantika, Chris. "Toward an Evangelical Theology in an Islamic Culture." In *The Bible and Theology in Asian Contexts: An Evangelical Perspective on Asian Theology,* edited by Bong R. Ro and Ruth Eshenaur, 365–82. Taichung, Taiwan: Asia Theological Association, 1984.

Mare, W. Harold. "The Meaningful Language of the New Testament." *WTJ* 37 (1974): 95–105.

Marin, Louis. "A Conclusion." In *The New Testament and Structuralism,* edited by Alfred M. Johnson, Jr., 233–49. Pittsburgh: Pickwick, 1976.

Marshall, I. Howard. "Culture and the New Testament." In *Gospel and Culture,* edited by John R. W. Stott and Robert T. Coote, 21–46. Pasadena, Calif.: William Carey Library, 1979.

—————. *The Gospel of Luke: A Commentary on the Greek Text.* Grand Rapids: Eerdmans, 1978.

—————. "How Do We Interpret the Bible Today?" *Themelios* 5, no. 2 (1980): 4–11.

Mbiti, John S. "Christianity and African Culture." *Journal of Theology for Southern Africa* 20 (September 1977): 26–40.

—————. *Concepts of God in Africa.* London: S.P.C.K., 1970.

—————. "New Testament Eschatology in an African Background." In *Readings in Dynamic Indigeneity,* edited by Charles H. Kraft and Tom N. Wisley, 455–64. Pasadena, Calif.: William Carey Library, 1979.

Miguez-Bonino, José. *Doing Theology in a Revolutionary Situation.* Philadelphia: Fortress, 1975.

Miller, G., and P. Johnson-Laird. *Language and Perception.* Cambridge, Mass.: Belknap, 1976.

Miranda, José P. *Communism in the Bible.* Translated by Robert R. Barr. Maryknoll, N.Y.: Orbis, 1982.

Mohr, Martin, and Mary Hull Mohr. "Interpreting the Text and Telling the Story." *Dialog* 21 (1982): 102–6.

Moo, Douglas J. "Matthew and Midrash: An Evaluation of Robert H. Gundry's Approach." *JETS* 26 (1983): 31–40.

—————. "The Problem of *Sensus Plenior.*" In *Hermeneutics, Authority, and Canon,* edited by D. A. Carson and John D. Woodbridge, 175–211. Grand Rapids: Zondervan, 1986.

Morris, Leon. *The Gospel According to John.* Grand Rapids: Eerdmans, 1971.

Moule, Charles F. D. "'Through Jesus Christ Our Lord': Some Questions About the Use of Scripture." *Theology* 80 (1977): 30–36.

Moulton, James H., and George Milligan. *The Vocabulary of the Greek Testament, Illustrated from the Papyri and Other Non-Literary Sources.* Grand Rapids: Eerdmans, 1976.

Mundhenk, Norm. "The Subjectivity of Anachronism." In *On Language, Culture, and Religion: In Honor of Eugene A. Nida,* edited by Matthew Black and William A. Smalley, 259–73. The Hague: Mouton, 1974.

Murphy-O'Connor, Jerome. "Corinthian Slogans in 1 Cor. 6:12–20." *CBQ* 40 (1978): 391–96.

Murray, John. *The Epistle to the Romans.* 2 vols. Grand Rapids: Eerdmans, 1965.

Nacpil, Emerito P. "The Critical Asian Principle." In *What Asian Christians Are Thinking,* edited by Douglas J. Elwood, 3–6. Quezon City, Philippines: New Day, 1976.

Newbigin, Lesslie. "Text and Context: The Bible in the Church." *Near East School of Theology Theological Review* 5 (1982): 5–13.

New International Dictionary of New Testament Theology. Edited by Colin Brown. 3 vols. Grand Rapids: Zondervan, 1978.

Nicholls, Bruce J. *Contextualization: A Theology of Gospel and Culture.* Outreach and Identity: Evangelical Theological Monographs 3. Downers Grove, Ill.: Inter-Varsity, 1979.

———. "Towards a Theology of Gospel and Culture." In *Gospel and Culture,* edited by John R. W. Stott and Robert T. Coote, 69–82. Pasadena, Calif.: William Carey Library, 1979.

Nickelsburg, George W. E. "An *EKTPΩMA,* Though Appointed from the Womb: Paul's Apostolic Self-Description in 1 Corinthians 15 and Galatians 1." *Harvard Theological Review* 79 (1986): 198–205.

Nicole, Roger. "The Biblical Concept of Truth." In *Scripture and Truth,* edited by D. A. Carson and John D. Woodbridge, 287–302. Grand Rapids: Zondervan, 1983.

———. "The Inspiration and Authority of Scripture: J. D. G. Dunn Versus B. B. Warfield." *Churchman* 97 (1983): 198–215; 98 (1984): 7–27, 198–208.

Nida, Eugene A. *Customs and Culture.* New York: Harper, 1954.

———. *Exploring Semantic Structures.* International Library of General Linguistics 11. Munich: W. Fink, 1975.

———. "Implications of Contemporary Linguistics for Biblical Scholarship." *JBL* 91 (1972): 73–89.

———. *Message and Mission.* New York: Harper, 1960.

———, and Charles R. Taber. *The Theory and Practice of Translation.* United Bible Societies' Helps for Translators 8. Leiden: E. J. Brill, 1974.

Niebuhr, H. Richard. *Christ and Culture.* New York: Harper & Row, 1951.

Nineham, Dennis E. "A Partner for Cinderella?" In *What About the New Testament?* edited by Morna Hooker and Colin Hickling, 143–54. London: SCM, 1975.

———. "The Strangeness of the New Testament, I and II." *Theology* 85 (1982): 171–77, 247–55.

———. *The Use and Abuse of the Bible: A Study of the Bible in an Age of Rapid Cultural Change.* New York: Barnes & Noble, 1976.

Nixon, Robin E. "The Authority of the New Testament." In *New Testament Interpretation: Essays on Principles and Methods,* edited by I. Howard Marshall, 334–50. Grand Rapids: Eerdmans, 1977.

Ogden, Schubert M. "The Authority of Scripture for Theology." *Interpretation* 30 (1976): 242–61.

Osborn, Robert T. "The Rise and Fall of the Bible in Recent American Theology." *Duke Divinity School Review* 41 (1976): 57–72.

Osborne, Grant R. "Hermeneutics and Women in the Church." *JETS* 20 (1977): 337–52.

Outler, Albert C. "Toward a Postliberal Hermeneutic." *TT* 42 (1985): 281–91.

Packer, James I. "The Adequacy of Human Language." In *Inerrancy,* edited by Norman L. Geisler, 196–226. Grand Rapids: Zondervan, 1979.

———. "Exposition on Biblical Hermeneutics." In *Hermeneutics, Inerrancy, and the Bible,* edited by Earl D. Radmacher and Robert D. Preus, 905–14. Grand Rapids: Zondervan, 1984.

———. "Hermeneutics and Biblical Authority." *Themelios* 1 (1975): 3–12.

———. "A Response to the New Hermeneutic." In *Hermeneutics, Inerrancy, and the Bible,* edited by Earl D. Radmacher and Robert D. Preus, 561–71. Grand Rapids: Zondervan, 1984.

———. "Upholding the Unity of Scripture Today." *JETS* 25 (1982): 409–14.

Padilla, C. René. "Comments on: Is There More than One Way to Do Theology?" *Gospel in Context* 1, no. 1 (January 1978): 30–31.

————. "Hermeneutics and Culture: A Theological Perspective." In *Gospel and Culture*, edited by John R. W. Stott and Robert T. Coote, 83–108. Pasadena, Calif.: William Carey Library, 1979.

————. "The Interpreted Word: Reflections on Contextual Hermeneutics." *Themelios* 7 (1981): 18–23.

Palmer, Richard E. *Hermeneutics: Interpretation Theory in Schleiermacher, Dilthey, Heidegger, and Gadamer.* Evanston, Ill.: Northwestern University Press, 1969.

Papalia, Dianne E., and Sandy W. Olds. *A Child's World.* 3d ed. New York: McGraw-Hill, 1982.

Parshall, Phil. *New Paths in Muslim Evangelism.* Grand Rapids: Baker, 1980.

Patte, Daniel. *What Is Structural Exegesis?* Philadelphia: Fortress, 1976.

————, and Aline Patte. *Structural Exegesis: From Theory to Practice.* Philadelphia: Fortress, 1978.

Payne, Philip B. "The Fallacy of Equating Meaning with the Human Author's Intention." *JETS* 20 (1977): 243–52.

Perez, Pablo M. "Biblical Theology and Cultural Identity in Latin America." In *Let the Earth Hear His Voice*, edited by James D. Douglas, 1251–62. Minneapolis: World Wide, 1975.

Perrin, Norman. "Eschatology and Hermeneutics: Reflections on Method in the Interpretation of the New Testament." *JBL* 93 (1974): 3–14.

Peters, George W. "Missions in Cultural Perspective." *BS* 136 (1979): 195–205.

Petersen, Norman R. *Literary Criticism for New Testament Critics.* Philadelphia: Fortress, 1978.

Piaget, Jean. *The Origins of Intelligence in Children.* Translated by Margaret Cook. New York: Norton, 1963.

Pike, Kenneth L. "Christianity and Culture I. Conscience and Culture." *Journal of the American Scientific Affiliation* 31 (1979): 8–12.

————. "The Linguist and Axioms Concerning the Language of Scripture." *Journal of the American Scientific Affiliation* 26 (1974): 47–51.

Pinnock, Clark H. "How I Use the Bible in Doing Theology." In *The Use of the Bible in Theology/ Evangelical Options*, edited by Robert K. Johnston, 18–34. Atlanta: John Knox, 1985.

————. *The Scripture Priniciple.* San Francisco: Harper & Row, 1984.

Piper, Otto A. "Principles of New Testament Interpretation." *TT* 3 (1946): 192–204.

Poythress, Vern S. "Adequacy of Language and Accommodation." In *Hermeneutics, Inerrancy, and the Bible*, edited by Earl D. Radmacher and Robert D. Preus, 349–76. Grand Rapids: Zondervan, 1984.

————. "Analyzing a Biblical Text: Some Important Linguistic Distinctions." *SJT* 32 (1979): 113–37.

Pregeant, Russell. *Christology Beyond Dogma.* Philadelphia: Fortress, 1978.

Pritchard, James B., ed. *The Ancient Near East: An Anthology of Texts and Pictures.* Princeton, N.J.: Princeton University Press, 1958.

Radmacher, Earl D., and Robert D. Preus, eds. *Hermeneutics, Inerrancy, and the Bible.* Grand Rapids: Zondervan, 1984.

Richard, Ramesh P. "Methodological Proposals for Scripture Relevance. Part 1: Selected Issues in Theoretical Hermeneutics"; "Part 3: Application Theory in Relation to the New Testament." *BS* 143 (1986): 14–25, 205–17.

Richardson, Peter. "Spirit and Letter: Foundation for Hermeneutics." *Evangelical Quarterly* 45 (1973): 208–18.

Ricoeur, Paul. "Biblical Hermeneutics." *Semeia* 4 (1975): 29–148.

_____ . *Interpretation Theory: Discourse and the Surplus of Meaning.* Fort Worth: Texas Christian University Press, 1976.

_____ . "Toward a Hermeneutic of the Idea of Revelation." In *Essays on Biblical Interpretation*, edited by Lewis S. Mudge. Philadelphia: Fortress, 1980.

_____ . "Two Essays by Paul Ricoeur: The Critique of Religion and the Language of Faith." Translated by R. Bradley DeFord. *USQR* 28 (1973): 203–24.

Ro, Bong R. "Contextualization: Asian Theology." *ERT* 2 (1978): 15–23.

_____ , ed. *Christian Alternatives to Ancestor Practices.* Taichung, Taiwan: Asia Theological Association, 1985.

Ro, Bong R., and Ruth Eshenaur, eds. *The Bible and Theology in Asian Contexts: An Evangelical Perspective on Asian Theology.* Taichung, Taiwan: Asia Theological Association, 1984.

Robertson, David. *The Old Testament and the Literary Critic.* Philadelphia: Fortress, 1977.

Robertson, John C. "Hermeneutics of Suspicion *versus* Hermeneutics of Goodwill." *Studies in Religion/Sciences religieuses* 8 (1979): 365–77.

Robinson, Maurice A. "SPERMOLOGOS: Did Paul Preach from Jesus' Parables?" *Biblica* 56 (1975): 231–40.

Rogers, Jack B. "The Book That Reads Us." *Interpretation* 39 (1985): 388–401.

Rogerson, John W. *Anthropology and the Old Testament.* Atlanta: John Knox, 1979.

Rohrbaugh, Richard L. *The Biblical Interpreter: An Agrarian Bible in an Industrial Age.* Philadelphia: Fortress, 1978.

Rostagno, Sergio. "Is an Interclass Reading of the Bible Legitimate? Notes on the Justice of God." *Communio Viatorum* 17 (1974): 1–14.

Rowen, Samuel. "Response to Buswell and Ericson." In *Theology and Mission*, edited by David J. Hesselgrave, 113–14. Grand Rapids: Baker, 1978.

Runzo, Joseph. "Relativism and Absolutism in Bultmann's Demythologizing Hermeneutic." *SJT* 32 (1979): 401–19.

Ryken, Leland. *How to Read the Bible as Literature.* Grand Rapids: Zondervan, 1984.

_____ . *Reading the Bible as Literature.* Grand Rapids: Zondervan, 1985.

Sanders, James A. "The Bible as Canon." *Christian Century* 98 (1981): 1250–55.

Sanford, A. J., and S. C. Garrod. *Understanding Written Language: Explorations of Comprehension Beyond the Sentence.* New York: Wiley, 1981.

Sang, David H., and Roger Ringenberg. "Towards an Evangelical Caribbean Theology." *ERT* 7 (1983): 132–46.

Saucy, Robert L. "A Response to Presuppositions of Non-Evangelical Hermeneutics." In *Hermeneutics, Inerrancy, and the Bible*, edited by Earl D. Radmacher and Robert D. Preus, 627–38. Grand Rapids: Zondervan, 1984.

Sawyer, John F. A. *Semantics in Biblical Research: New Methods of Defining Hebrew Words for Salvation.* Studies in Biblical Theology, 2d ser., 24. London: SCM, 1972.

Schaeffer, Francis A. *The Great Evangelical Disaster.* Westchester, Ill.: Crossway, 1984.

Schleiermacher, Friedrich. *Hermeneutics: The Handwritten Manuscripts.* Edited by Heinz Kimmerle, translated by James Duke and Jack Frostman. AAR Texts and Translation Series 1. Missoula, Mont.: Scholars Press, 1977.

Schneiders, Sandra M. "Faith, Hermeneutics, and the Literal Sense of Scripture." *Theological Studies* 39 (1978): 719–36.

Schweizer, Eduard. "Traditional Ethical Patterns in the Pauline and Post-Pauline Letters and Their Development (Lists of Vices and Housetables)." In *Text and Interpretation: Studies in the New Testament Presented to Matthew Black*, edited by Ernest Best and R. McL. Wilson, 195–210. Cambridge: Cambridge University Press, 1979.

Scott, J. Julius, Jr. "On the Value of Intertestamental Jewish Literature for New Testament Theology." *JETS* 23 (1980): 315–24.

———. "Some Problems in Hermeneutics for Contemporary Evangelicals." *JETS* 22 (1979): 67–77.

Scroggs, Robin. "The Sociological Interpretation of the New Testament: The Present State of Research." *New Testament Studies* 26 (1980): 164–79.

Scully, Malcolm G. "Faculty Members, Liberal on Politics, Found Conservative on Academic Issues." *Chronicle of Higher Education*, 6 April 1970.

Segundo, Juan L. *Liberation of Theology*. Translated by John Drury. Maryknoll, N.Y.: Orbis, 1976.

"Seoul Declaration." *ERT* 7 (1983): 3–12.

Silva, Moisés. *Biblical Words and Their Meaning*. Grand Rapids: Zondervan, 1983.

Smalley, Stephen S. *1, 2, 3 John*. WBC 51. Waco, Tex.: Word, 1984.

Smalley, William A. "Culture and Superculture." *Practical Anthropology* 2 (1955): 58–71.

———. "Foreword." In *Gospel and Culture*, edited by John R. W. Stott and Robert T. Coote, vii–viii. Pasadena, Calif.: William Carey Library, 1979.

Smyth, Herbert W. *Greek Grammar*. Revised by Gordon M. Messing. Cambridge, Mass.: Harvard University Press, 1956.

Speck, Gregory. "Katharine the Great: An Interview." *Eastern Review: The Magazine of Eastern Airlines*, December 1985, 45–58.

Spradley, James R., and David W. McCurdy. *Anthropology: The Cultural Perspective*. New York: Wiley, 1975.

Sproul, R. C. "The Internal Testimony of the Holy Spirit." In *Inerrancy*, edited by Norman L. Geisler, 337–54. Grand Rapids: Zondervan, 1979.

———. *Knowing Scripture*. Downers Grove, Ill.: Inter-Varsity, 1977.

Stafford, Harry C. *Culture and Cosmology: Essays on the Birth of a World View*. Washington, D.C.: University Press of America, 1981.

Stall, Steven W. "Sociology of Knowledge, Relativism, and Theology." In *Religion and the Sociology of Knowledge: Modernization and Pluralism in Christian Thought and Structure*, edited by Barbara Hargrove, 61–78. New York: Mellen, 1984.

"The State of American Values." *U.S. News and World Report* 99, no. 24 (9 December 1985): 54–58.

Stern, Gustaf. *Meaning and Change of Meaning, with Special Reference to the English Language*. Göteborgs Hogskolas Årsskrift 38. Göteborg, 1931.

Stibbs, Alan M. "The Witness of Scripture to Its Inspiration." In *Revelation and the Bible: Contemporary Evangelical Thought*, edited by Carl F. H. Henry, 105–18. Grand Rapids: Baker, 1959.

Stonehouse, Ned B., and Paul Woolley, eds. *The Infallible Word*. Philadelphia: Presbyterian Guardian, 1946.

Stott, John R. W., and Robert T. Coote, eds. *Gospel and Culture*. Pasadena, Calif.: William Carey Library, 1979.

Stuhlmacher, Peter. *Historical Criticism and Theological Interpretation of Scripture: Towards a Hermeneutic of Consent*. Translated by Roy A. Harrisville. Philadelphia: Fortress, 1977.

Sumithra, Sunard, and Bruce Nicholls. "Towards an Evangelical Theology of the Third World: An Indian Reflection." *ERT* 7 (1983): 172–82.

Taber, Charles R. "Author's Response to Comment on: Is There More than One Way to Do Theology?" *Gospel in Context* 1, no. 1 (1978): 37–39.

_____. "Hermeneutics and Culture: An Anthropological Perspective." In *Gospel and Culture*, edited by John R. W. Stott and Robert T. Coote, 109–34. Pasadena, Calif: William Carey Library, 1979.

_____. "Is There More than One Way to Do Theology?" *Gospel in Context* 1, no. 1 (1978): 4–10.

_____. "The Limits of Indigenization in Theology." *Missiology* 6 (1978): 53–80.

_____. "Translation as Interpretation." *Interpretation* 32 (1978): 130–43.

Tano, Rodrigo D. "Toward an Evangelical Asian Theology." *ERT* 7 (1983): 155–71.

Taylor, Robert B. "Cultural Relativism for the Christian." *Practical Anthropology* 1 (1954): 108–19.

_____. *Cultural Ways: A Compact Introduction to Cultural Anthropology*. Boston: Allyn, 1969.

_____. *Cultural Ways: A Concise Edition of Introduction to Cultural Anthropology*. 2d ed. Boston: Allyn, 1976.

TEF Staff. *Ministry in Context: The Third Mandate Programme of the Theological Education Fund (1970–77)*. Bromley, Kent: Theological Education Fund, 1972.

Tenney, Merrill C. "The Meaning of the Word." In *The Bible: The Living Word of Revelation*, edited by Merrill C. Tenney, 11–27. Grand Rapids: Zondervan, 1968.

_____, ed. *The Bible, the Living Word of Revelation*. Grand Rapids: Zondervan, 1968.

Thalheimer, Fred. "Religiosity and Secularization in the Academic Professions." *Sociology of Education* 46 (1973): 183–202.

Theissen, Gerhard. *Sociology of Early Palestinian Christianity*. Translated by John Bowden. Philadelphia: Fortress, 1978.

Theological Dictionary of the New Testament. Edited by Gerhard Kittel and Gerhard Friedrich. Translated by Geoffrey W. Bromiley. 10 vols. Grand Rapids: Eerdmans, 1964–1976.

Theological Wordbook of the Old Testament. Edited by R. Laird Harris. 2 vols. Chicago: Moody, 1980.

Thielicke, Helmut. *The Evangelical Faith*. 3 vols. Grand Rapids: Eerdmans, 1974–1982.

Thiselton, Anthony C. "Semantics and New Testament Interpretation." In *New Testament Interpretation: Essays on Principles and Methods*, edited by I. Howard Marshall, 75–104. Grand Rapids: Eerdmans, 1977.

_____. *The Two Horizons: New Testament Hermeneutics and Philosophical Description, with Special Reference to Heidegger, Bultmann, Gadamer, and Wittgenstein*. Grand Rapids: Eerdmans, 1980.

Thomas, Robert L. "A Hermeneutical Ambiguity of Eschatology: The Analogy of Faith." *JETS* 23 (1980): 45–53.

Thompson, John A. *Handbook of Life in Bible Times*. Downers Grove, Ill.: Inter-Varsity, 1986.

Tidball, Derek. *The Social Context of the New Testament: A Sociological Analysis*. Grand Rapids: Zondervan, 1984.

Tienou, Tite. *The Theological Task of the Church in Africa*. Achumota, Ghana: Africa Christian Press, 1982.

Torrance, James B. "Interpretation and Understanding in Schleiermacher's Theology: Some Critical Questions." *SJT* 21 (1968): 268–82.

Torres, Sergio, and John Eagleson, eds. *Theology in the Americas*. Maryknoll, N.Y.: Orbis, 1976.

Trible, Phyllis. "Depatriarchalizing Biblical Interpretation." *Journal of the American Academy of Religion* 41 (1973): 30–48.

Troeltsch, Ernst. *The Absoluteness of Christianity and the History of Religions*. Translated by David Reid. Richmond: John Knox, 1971.

Ullmann, Stephen. *The Principles of Semantics*. 2d ed. Oxford: Blackwell, 1957.

Vanhoozer, Kevin J. "The Semantics of Biblical Literature: Truth and Scripture's Diverse Literary Forms." In *Hermeneutics, Authority, and Canon*, edited by D. A. Carson and John D. Woodbridge, 49–104. Grand Rapids: Zondervan, 1986.

Vicencio, Charles V. "The Use of Scripture in Theology." *Journal of Theology for Southern Africa* 37 (December 1981): 3–22.

Virkler, Henry A. *Hermeneutics: Principles and Processes of Biblical Interpretation*. Grand Rapids: Baker, 1981.

Visser't Hooft, Willem A. "Accommodation—True or False." *South East Asia Journal of Theology* 8, no. 3 (1967): 5–18.

Von Rad, Gerhard. *Genesis: A Commentary*. Translated by John H. Marks. Philadelphia: Westminster, 1961.

Walls, Andrew F. "The Gospel as the Prisoner and Liberator of Culture." *Missionalia* 10 (1982): 93–105.

Waltke, Bruce K. "1 Corinthians 11:2–16: An Interpretation." *BS* 135 (1978): 46–57.

Weir, J. Emmette. "The Bible and Marx: A Discussion of the Hermeneutics of Liberation Theology." *SJT* 35 (1982): 337–50.

Wellek, René, and Austin Warren. *Theory of Literature*. Rev. ed. New York: Harcourt, Brace & World, 1956.

Wells, Paul R. "Covenant, Humanity, and Scripture: Some Theological Reflections." *WTJ* 48 (1986): 17–45.

———. *James Barr and the Bible*. Phillipsburg, N.J.: Presbyterian & Reformed, 1980.

Wenham, John W. "Christ's View of Scripture." In *Inerrancy*, edited by Norman L. Geisler, 3–38. Grand Rapids: Zondervan, 1979.

Westermann, Claus. *Genesis 1–11: A Commentary*. Minneapolis: Augsburg, 1974.

White, John L. "Saint Paul and the Apostolic Letter Tradition." *CBQ* 45 (1983): 433–44.

Wilder, Amos N. *Theopoetic: Theology and the Religious Imagination*. Philadelphia: Fortress, 1976.

Williams, Jay G. "Exegesis-Eisegesis: Is There a Difference?" *TT* 30 (1973): 218–27.

"The Willowbank Report." In *Gospel and Culture*, edited by John R. W. Stott and Robert T. Coote, 433–61. Pasadena, Calif.: William Carey Library, 1979.

Wilson, Eugene A. "The Homiletical Application of Old Testament Narrative Passages." *Trinity Journal* 7 (1978): 85–92.

Wilson, Robert R. "Anthropology and the Study of the Old Testament." *USQR* 34 (1979): 175–81.

———. *Genealogy and History in the Biblical World*. New Haven, Conn.: Yale University Press, 1977.

———. *Prophecy and Society in Ancient Israel*. Philadelphia: Fortress, 1980.

Wing Hung-Lam. "Patterns of Chinese Theology." In *The Bible and Theology in Asian Contexts: An Evangelical Perspective on Asian Theology,* edited by Bong R. Ro and Ruth Eshenaur, 327–41. Taichung, Taiwan: Asia Theological Association, 1984.

Wink, Walter. *The Bible in Human Transformation: Toward a New Paradigm for Biblical Study.* Philadelphia: Fortress, 1973.

Wood, A. Skevington. *Ephesians.* In *Ephesians–Philemon.* EBC 11. Grand Rapids: Zondervan, 1978.

Word Biblical Commentary. Edited by David A. Hubbard and Glenn W. Barker. 52 vols. Waco, Tex.: Word, 1982–.

Worgul, George S., Jr. "Anthropological Consciousness and Biblical Theology." *Biblical Theology Bulletin* 9 (1979): 3–12.

"A Working Document: Towards a Christian Approach to Ancestor Practices." In *Christian Alternatives to Ancestor Practices,* edited by Bong R. Ro, 3–11. Taichung, Taiwan: Asia Theological Association, 1985.

Yamauchi, Edwin M. "Christianity and Cultural Differences." *CT* 16 (1971): 901–4.

——— . "Sociology, Scripture, and the Supernatural." *JETS* 27 (1984): 169–92.

Yankelovich, Daniel. *New Rules: Searching for Self-Fulfillment in a World Turned Upside Down.* New York: Bantam, 1982.

Yannoulatos, Anastasios. "Culture and Gospel: Some Observations from the Orthodox Tradition and Experience." *International Review of Missions* 74 (1985): 185–98.

Yego, Josphat K. "Appreciation for and Warnings About Contextualization." *Evangelical Missions Quarterly* 16 (1980): 153–56.

Zuck, Roy B. "Application in Biblical Hermeneutics and Exposition." In *Walvoord: A Tribute,* edited by Donald K. Campbell, 15–38. Chicago: Moody, 1982.

Scripture Index

Subject Index